Information Sciences Series

EDITORS

ROBERT M. HAYES
Director of the Institute of Library Research
University of California at Los Angeles

JOSEPH BECKER
Director of Information Sciences
Interuniversity Communications Council (EDUCOM)

CONSULTANTS

CHARLES P. BOURNE
Director, Advanced Information Systems Division
Programming Services, Inc.

HAROLD BORKO
System Development Corporation

AUTHORS

JOSEPH BECKER
AND ROBERT M. HAYES:
Information Storage and Retrieval

CHARLES P. BOURNE:
Methods of Information Handling

HAROLD BORKO:
Automated Language Processing

RUSSELL D. ARCHIBALD
AND RICHARD VILLORIA:
Network-Based Management Systems (PERT/CPM)

CHARLES T. MEADOW:
The Analysis of Information Systems:
A Programmers Introduction to Information Retrieval

LAUNOR F. CARTER:
National Document-Handling Systems
for Science and Technology

ROBERT M. HAYES:
Mathematics of Information Systems.
In Preparation

National Document-Handling Systems for Science and Technology

LAUNOR F. CARTER

GORDON CANTLEY

JOHN T. ROWELL

LOUISE SCHULTZ

HERBERT R. SEIDEN

EVERETT WALLACE

RICHARD WATSON

RONALD E. WYLLYS

SYSTEM DEVELOPMENT CORPORATION

Santa Monica, California

JOHN WILEY & SONS, INC.   NEW YORK   LONDON   SYDNEY

Information sciences series

Information is the essential ingredient in decision making. The need for improved information systems in recent years has been made critical by the steady growth in size and complexity of organizations and data.

This series is designed to include books that are concerned with various aspects of communicating, utilizing, and storing digital and graphic information. It will embrace a broad spectrum of topics, such as information system theory and design, man-machine relationships, language data processing, artificial intelligence, mechanization of library processes, non-numerical applications of digital computers, storage and retrieval, automatic publishing, command and control, information display, and so on.

Information science may someday be a profession in its own right. The aim of this series is to bring together the interdisciplinary core of knowledge that is apt to form its foundation. Through this consolidation, it is expected that the series will grow to become the focal point for professional education in this field.

Preface

This book has grown out of a study undertaken for the Committee on Scientific and Technical Information (COSATI) Task Group on National System(s) for Scientific and Technical Information in support of their examination of national document and information systems. The emphasis of the study as stated by COSATI is as follows:

"1. Initial and primary priority will be placed on national systems relating to scientific and technical documents, their handling and the management of such documents. Specific matters to be reported on will include, the current organizational and functional situation in the United States; the extent to which known deficiencies are causing a reduction in the potential for technical effectiveness in the United States scientific and technical community; the alternatives which are available and economically feasible for correction of these deficiencies; and one or more action plans which can be followed by governmental (especially including Congress) and non-governmental units.

"2. Secondary attention will be given to development of programs which can be undertaken with Government support for identifying, analyzing, and giving a structure to the total flow of scientific and technical information in the United States."

The System Development Corporation group which participated in the study first assembled in Washington on May 3, 1965, and was faced with the task of completing the first draft of the report by August 1, the final report by September 1, 1965. Because of short schedule, we decided to limit information gathering to analyses of published material and the new understanding that could be gained from short visits to individuals and institutions concerned with the scientific and technical documentation problem.

Although responsibility for writing the first draft of each major portion of the original report was given to individual members of the work group, we all subjected each draft to critical analysis. Thus the contents of this book represent the integrated work of the entire staff.

The ideas in this book are similar to those contained in the report for COSATI, but a number of them have been expanded or clarified. As the report was discussed, it became apparent that we had not always expressed our opinions as clearly as we had hoped and that the emphases given to some of our recommendations needed restatement. In addition, the format and ordering of material has been extensively revised.

Although we are responsible for the content of this book, its tone and emphasis profited greatly from extensive interaction with the COSATI Task Group on National System(s). Several of the sections were reviewed in meetings with the Task Group. This was particularly true with respect to Chapter 6, "Basic Propositions and System Requirements." In addition to the advice we received from the COSATI Task Group, we took advantage of the opportunity to interact freely with Mr. William Knox, Chairman of COSATI, and Colonel Andrew Aines, Secretary of COSATI. Because of their long experience and responsible positions, their assistance was most valuable in guiding our thoughts. Table 2-1 lists the various organizations visited by members of the SDC work group. The individuals interviewed gave major assistance by supplying information and giving insights into the operation of their organizations. Without exception they were cordial and helpful.

In addition to those working directly on this project, a number of others associated with SDC provided aid and guidance. Mr. Joseph J. Maher served as editor for the original report, and Mr. Lauren Doyle was kind enough to prepare the first draft of that part of Appendix 1 in which the most technically advanced current information and document systems are described. We are also indebted to Mr. Christopher Shaw for

undertaking a literature search and supplying documents that formed the basis for the section on equipment and software in Appendix 1. Because SDC is deeply concerned with information systems, an advisory group was formed which consists of Mr. Raymond Barrett, Dr. Harold Borko, Dr. Carlos Cuadra, Mr. Lauren Doyle, Dr. Harold Edmundson, Dr. Robert Katter, Mrs. Frances Neeland, and Dr. Robert Simmons. This group met several times during the course of the project and made many helpful suggestions. Dr. C. West Churchman, Dr. William C. Biel, Dr. Merrill Flood, and General Earl E. Partridge of the SDC Research Advisory Committee met with the work group to review the content of our report. Mr. Lorimer F. McConnell very ably assisted in formatting this book and arranging for its publication. Finally, Dr. Don R. Swanson, Dean of the Graduate Library School at the University of Chicago and consultant to SDC, was good enough to review the first draft. The suggestions of these individuals were most useful and resulted in significant changes in some of the requirement statements as well as in some of the design recommendations. Although all the people listed here gave generously of their time, this book is our responsibility and we offer it as a contribution, and target, to the continuing dialogue on national information systems.

Santa Monica, California
December 1966

LAUNOR F. CARTER
GORDON CANTLEY
JOHN T. ROWELL
LOUISE SCHULTZ[1]
HERBERT R. SEIDEN
EVERETT WALLACE
RICHARD WATSON
RONALD E. WYLLYS[2]

[1] Now at BioSciences Information Service
[2] Now at University of Wisconsin

Contents

National Document-Handling

Systems for

Science and Technology

Chapter One

Introduction

"Information is an agency resource, a federal, national, and international resource.

"Modern information technology has made it possible to place much of the accumulated knowledge of the human race within the reach of a man's fingertips, so to speak. The potentialities of this access to power are awesome, in terms of improving the well-being of our own and other people, as well as in terms of improved education for young and old alike.

"If man's collected knowledge is to become truly accessible, plans and programs must be made, priorities assigned and resources allocated."

> Report of the Committee
> on Goverent Operations,
> United States Senate,
> June 24, 1965

THE NATIONAL PERSPECTIVE

The problem of scientific and technical information is neither a simple one nor a single one. Rather it consists of a multiplicity of problems affecting the users of information, the processors and handlers of information, the federal government, and ultimately the national welfare.

During the past few years many well-informed individuals, committees, and organizations, including those of the executive branch and Congress, have pointed with increasing concern to the deficiencies and limitations of our present de facto national system for handling scientific and technical information. At least fifteen major efforts have been made to develop a rational plan to improve the situation. Although each of these plans stressed somewhat different problems and issues, there can be no doubt that the limitations of our present national information-handling system are numerous and need serious attention.

The growing sense of the urgency of this problem, however, is not created solely by the faults of the present system. Perhaps a more powerful stimulus is in the worldwide awakening to the realization that information is one of the most precious of national resources. The information problem is much more than the sum of local annoyances, inconveniences, and dissatisfactions with document information systems. To ameliorate only current difficulties would be failing to apply the kind of vision required to develop a crucial national resource. It is no longer necessary to argue that the natural resources of the United States represent a national asset, or that the federal government needs to guide the overall development and conservation of such assets. It is recognized that in our increasingly complex society it is necessary for the federal government to take a vigorous lead in such matters.

It is not yet widely recognized, however, that information is one of the most vital of our national resources. To be sure, the recognition is growing both inside and outside the federal government that it is necessary for this resource to be effectively developed, conserved, distributed, and utilized. But the growth of recognition of the importance of information is far outstripping the growth of recognition of the national information problem. For example, there is as yet no consensus on what the minimum acceptable goals of information development and exploitation might be. There is not, in fact, even a consensus on whether it is the responsibility of the federal government to try to set and pursue such goals. In a very real sense it is this lack of consensus that constitutes one of the main national information problems. Until the information problem is widely understood as the national resource exploitation and development problem that it is, we will continue

to take a piecemeal and uncoordinated approach to the problem.

The essence of scientific and technical information transfer is contained in the process of communication. The development of scientific knowledge depends on the communication of new theories and new experimental observations to others. No new idea is afforded acceptance in the scientific community until it has been discussed and evaluated by people knowledgeable in that area, whose knowledge of the idea and background for evaluating it is derived from both formal and informal communications.

The "knowledge explosion" is having a great impact on the organized systems for handling scientific and technical information. The volume of literature is growing so rapidly that no one scientist or engineer can be aware of more than a small portion of it. One result is greater specialization on the part of scientists. A concomitant of this has been strain and specialization of the traditional information services—the journals, abstracting services, and libraries. The handling of knowledge has become more specialized and compartmentalized as the ability of older approaches to serve the new requirements has decreased. No longer can a general library hope to give adequate service in response to highly specialized demands. As a result new forms have evolved—the special science library, the information analysis center, and a host of informal mechanisms.

As knowledge becomes more and more specialized and highly abstruse, we find men, brilliantly competent in their immediate field, who are often less concerned or less able to translate their knowledge to related fields or into practical application. It becomes harder for the engineering innovator to find or understand the applicable ideas that should spring from a highly developed science. Often this is because the communication between the small community of specialized experts and the men of "practical" concern is left to our less than satisfactory scientific and technical information system. If knowledge stays confined to the intimate community in which it originates, it will have little impact on the larger community concerned with the application and exploitation of knowledge. To assure that this does not happen we need an effective scientific and technical information and documentation system. If this system functions well, scientists will be able to communicate easily with one another, and engineers and other practitioners will have the necessary information to translate new knowledge into usable forms. If the system functions poorly, knowledge will remain compartmentalized and undiscovered as a resource for the national welfare.

The study reported here has concentrated on the problem of improving this scientific and technical communication system, with particular emphasis on the formal documentation system. Publications and their effective handling and processing in the libraries and document centers of the country have been our concern. But this is only part of the larger scientific and technical communications problem. The part of the system considered here, the formal document system, is the easiest to distinguish and characterize and hence a good place to begin trying to improve the scientific and technical communication system. Another part of the larger problem, however, is the vast informal system. At the simplest level it is characterized by one scientist visiting with another in his laboratory or study. Ideas and new observations are exchanged. Later, letters or phone calls continue the dialogue with new thoughts or ways of understanding the data. Perhaps this is followed by weekend meetings of the few real experts in the area, or perhaps an informal summer conference is arranged. As the material is developed and elaborated, it is presented as a paper at a national or international meeting, and then finally it may find its way past editorial review boards and into print. Only then does it enter the formal documentation system. But this is late in the life of new knowledge. The real excitement and impact on the specialized area has occurred several years earlier.

The informal communication system is less adequately understood than the formal system. Is it effective? By what standards should it be judged? Is the community of scholars involved in each area so narrow as to inhibit rapid dissemination of new knowledge? Does the informal system promote restrictiveness and proprietariness? What techniques are most effective? How is the informal system supported? It is to be hoped that these and many other questions will be studied, since it seems quite probable that the informal communication system has a larger impact on the advance of science and technology than the formal system.

This book is confined to the scientific and

technical information and documentation system. In some ways the limitation is unfortunate since there is so much other information and so many documents that form a traditional part of the communication and documentation world. The book does not deal with material in the humanities, the law, the arts, or commerce. Traditionally the formal knowledge system, a part of which involves publishers and libraries, has not separated one branch of knowledge from the others as deserving special and preferential treatment. In recent years, however, the federal government has recognized the great importance of science and technology to the general welfare and has given this area unusual and generous support. Scientific and technical information and documentation has played a part in this new emphasis, and because of its central position in transmitting knowledge it has been singled out for special attention. Although this is only natural, it is to be hoped that appropriate attention also will be given to the documentation and library problems in other fields of knowledge and endeavor. It should be mentioned also that this book is concerned largely with journals, monographs, reports, proceedings, books, and so on. Another important part of the formal document system is not included, namely that part dealing with such materials as engineering drawings, specifications, manuals, industrial catalogs, maps, and photographs.

THE APPROACH AND ORGANIZATION OF THIS BOOK

The initial approach in the study of the scientific and technical documetation area* followed three somewhat separate lines of endeavor. In the past there have been a number of ad hoc study groups concerned with this problem. These groups have produced congressional studies, reports by the President's Science Advisory Committee, reports from elsewhere within

---

* Over and over again throughout the book the phrase "scientific and technical information and documentation" appears. It is used to modify such words as "area," "handling," "problem," "processing," etc. We would have liked to use an acronym for the phrase, but could not find one that had a reasonable degree of acceptance. Since none seemed to hit the right chord, we finally settled on "S&T information and documentation." Also, "document" is used here to include books, journal articles, preprints, reprints, reports, pamphlets, and the like.

the government, and studies from private sources. We collected and analyzed these reports to gain an understanding of past proposals. A second area of investigation centered around studies, of which about 450 have been published, regarding user needs for scientific and technical information. We concentrated on 58 studies that seemed to have significant empirical data, in order to gain an understanding of the needs for scientific and technical information as perceived by users. The third and most extensive effort was devoted to understanding the current scientific and technical information system. It is important to recognize that there now exists a large number of institutions in the federal government and in the nonfederal sector, including libraries, universities, professional societies, and private commercial organizations which render scientific and technical information services. We felt it important to understand the role of such organizations, and we visited 47 of them.

As a result of studying these three areas, we were able to formulate a series of basic propositions and system requirements which became the basis for system concepts. As our studies were progressing and the requirements were being defined, we considered and developed ideas regarding several alternative systems which seemed to meet a major portion of the requirements and which had some practical possibility of being implemented. Five different alternative designs were developed and worked out in considerable detail.

Although the approach to the study involved a number of parallel efforts, the organization of this book follows the tradition of describing the present system, stating the problem, formulating basic propositions and requirements, offering possible solutions, and evaluating them.

The chapters that follow this introduction are grouped in four major sections. Part 1 describes the present document-handling system. Chapters 2 and 3 give a comprehensive description of current S&T information and document handling—Chapter 2 from an organizational point of view and Chapter 3 in terms of the production and flow of documents. Chapter 4 summarizes a number of user studies; it considers the extent to which current services satisfy user needs and the extent to which users are aware of the services now available.

Following the presentation of the present system, Part 2 discusses problems associated with

the system and basic propositions and system requirements which must be satisfied by a national S&T document system.

Part 3 consists of four chapters that describe various plans for a national system. Chapter 7 summarizes in textual and tabular form the basic characteristics of fifteen previous proposals in this area and also gives a short description of VINITI, the Russian documentation and abstracting system. Chapter 8 develops the detailed functions and organizations of a proposed capping agency for policy setting and integration, with the companion concept of the delegation of actual operations to designated responsible agents. The next chapter presents three variations on the fundamental idea of consolidating policy formulation, integration, and planning into a highly centralized organization. Chapter 10 discusses various possible ways of strengthening the present system.

Finally, Part 4 gives an evaluation of the suggested systems and a prognosis. Chapter 11 considers all the alternatives from the point of view of the extent to which they meet the requirements stated in Chapter 6 and gives the final argument in favor of the capping agency/responsible agent concept. The book proper concludes with a chapter summarizing some reaction to the proposals and places them within the context of other developments that are now being undertaken.

There are three appendices. The first one presents three relatively advanced information systems that are now operating. To a large extent the detailed solutions to many of the problems facing the S&T documentation field depend on the application of advanced technology and automation. It seems appropriate to see where we now stand and what is possible in the near future. Thus in addition to a description of the three systems there is included material on hardware and software—the current state of the art and probable developments in the next five years. Appendix 2 brings together a compilation of statistical information from many different sources. Appendix 3 is a compilation of the many legislative acts and executive orders that define current federal responsibilities and organizations in this area. Finally, there are a glossary, a bibliography, and an index.

PART ONE

Description of
the Present System

Chapter Two

The Present System:
Document-Handling Institutions

There exists in the United States today a loosely coordinated set of organizations and activities that consitutes a de facto scientific and technical information system. These organizations are in both the federal and nonfederal sectors. This chapter describes the major components of the present system and the relationships between its parts. The system is described in terms of its organizations, operations, and problems.

Data for this chapter were obtained in interviews conducted with key documentation or information system personnel of selected federal and nonfederal organizations or in studies and review of related source materials; for example, Hoshovsky [6] (see references at end of Chapter 3). The operational and organizational aspects of the data were reviewed, and the organizations are grouped according to their principal functions or outstanding roles in the information system. A number of problem areas are identified and described. These problems and other data had implications for a national information system which led to the derivation of a set of system requirements that was integrated with others from parallel efforts of the study. The requirements are presented in Chapter 6.

PRESENT SYSTEM ORGANIZATION

Twenty-four federal and twenty-four nonfederal organizations were visited to obtain the basic data contained in this chapter. These organizations are listed in Table 2-1. Categorization of the individual organizations into functional groups facilitates the examination and description of the present system. This was done, and the organizations in Table 2-1 are grouped in one of five functional categories. These categories, as well as the assignment of an organization to any one category, are somewhat arbitrary. Most of the organizations could easily be identified in more than one category. Assignment, however, is based on the primary role of an organization with respect to document and information activities. In some instances in which a separate entity within the organization clearly fell into a different category it was treated as a separate organization. For example, the National Library of Medicine is grouped among the publication, announcement, and distribution organizations, whereas Health, Education, and Welfare, the parent organization, is grouped among the document generators and users. Table 2-1 indicates the assignment of organizations and summarizes the functions of the five categories into which the organizations were grouped.

The Federal Sector

A proliferation of organizations with significant scientific and technical information activities are contained in the federal sector. The principal elements are identified and the organizational relationship among them are outlined in Figure 2-1. Also included is the line of authority from the President or the Congress, as the case may be. Most of the federal organizations of interest to national system design and planning are within the executive branch. Two notable exceptions report to the Congress: the Government Printing Office and the Library of Congress. The executive branch exercises no direct control over their operations, but both interact extensively with executive departments, and

Table 2-1   Agencies and Organizations Visited

Group*	Functions/Characteristics	Federal	Nonfederal
Libraries	Acquire, catalog, and announce acquisitions with a view toward storing, circulating, and providing selected reference services.	Federal Aviation Agency Department of Interior Library of Congress National Agricultural Library National Library of Medicine Public Health Service Smithsonian Institution	John Crerar Library Harvard University Library Massachusetts Institute of Technology Library New York Public Library University of California at Los Angeles Library University of Maryland Library
Information analysis centers	Acquire, catalog, and index with a view toward reviewing, analyzing, evaluating, synthesizing, integrating, and otherwise reporting on the content or substance of documents. Particular emphasis on use of subject area specialists found here.	Food and Drug Administration National Referral Center Science Information Exchange Coast and Geodetic Survey	Battelle Memorial Institute
Publication, announcement, and distribution	Acquire, abstract, index, copy, publish, announce, and disseminate documents for the purposes of providing documents or secondary representations usually to a wide population of users.	Atomic Energy Commission Clearinghouse for Scientific and Technical Information Defense Documentation Center Government Printing Office National Aeronautics and Space Administration Patent Office	American Chemical Society American Institute of Physics American Petroleum Institute American Society of Metals Association for Computing Machinery Biological Sciences Information Service Chemical Abstract Services, Inc. Engineering Index, Inc. McGraw-Hill Publishing Company Society of Automative Engineers Cambridge Communication Corporation
Document generators/ users	Primarily originate or use documents (although all organizations do this to some degree), tend to be mission oriented and would encompass most industrial organizations (not visited).	Central Intelligence Agency Department of Health, Education, and Welfare National Security Agency	
Administration, policy, and support	Administer, make policy, provide support, or otherwise influence document and information operations but are not in the operational loop with respect to processing or manipulation of documents and information (except for their own use).	National Bureau of Standards National Institutes of Health National Science Foundation Office of Education	American Library Association Association of Research Libraries Council on Library Resources Engineers Joint Council National Federation of Societies of Abstracting and Indexing Services Special Libraries Association

* Functional groupings are in terms of emphasis or prime role of organization in S&T document and information-handling activities.

there are many complex relationships in terms of services supplied to or received from executive agencies.

The Legislature. The library of Congress is the largest and most important library in the United States, both in terms of size and of services. Its services comprehend the entire governmental establishment and the public at large. Its collections contain more than 43 million items (1963 data) of which more than 13 million are books, bound serials, and pamphlets covering all fields of knowledge. In addition to functioning as a resource for the Congress, the Library makes its services generally available to the public. It also performs special services on a contractual basis for several executive agencies.

The Library is supported by appropriations of Congress, income from trust funds and gifts, and funds transferred from executive departments for specific operations and services. Total income exceeded $31 million for fiscal year 1964, when the Library returned over $4.8 million to the U. S. Treasury from copyright fees and from sales of catalog cards and other publications. The Library is organized into an Administrative Department, Copyright Office, Law Library, Legislative Reference Service, Processing Department, and Reference Department. All are under the Librarian of Congress, whose staff totals some 3200 personnel.

The Government Printing Office (GPO), whose activities are under the cognizance of the Joint Congressional Committee on Printing, is considered the book store of the federal government. It makes available, at nominal price, the publications of the federal agencies and the Congress. The Office of Superintendent of Documents, through which distribution is made, was established by the General Printing Act of 1895. Publications are announced in biweekly pricelists and in monthly catalogs. A wide variety of items are published including the *Congressional Record* and *Congressional Committee Prints;* documents issued by the several executive departments and agencies for which widespread public distribution may be expected; and other government documents. Many government reports available elsewhere are duplicated by GPO for wider sales and distribution. The annual payroll for more than 6000 employees during fiscal year 1960 was more than $41.6 million. During that year GPO produced more than 41

million catalog cards for the Library of Congress.

Fifty-three million publications are sold annually for a total of $11 million. Daily orders average 9300. In addition to sales, 96 million items are distributed to libraries and addressees on departmental mailing lists. The sales price for government documents is the cost of producing the copy plus 50 per cent of cost. The GPO is now turning back to the Treasury about $5.5 million per year in excess receipts not required for purchasing additional publications.

The Executive. The executive branch may be divided into two major segments insofar as our review of their organizations and operations is concerned. The first of these are agencies and organizations in the Executive Office of the President; the second are the executive departments and independent agencies. The Executive Office of the President is concerned with administration and policy, whereas the executive departments and independent agencies contain the operating agencies for handling documents and information.

The Executive Office of the President includes the Office of Science and Technology (OST), Bureau of the Budget (BOB), and the National Security Council which includes the Central Intelligence Agency (CIA). There are also two advisory groups: the President's Science Advisory Committee (PSAC) and the Federal Council on Science and Technology (FCST). The CIA does not resemble the typical Executive Office operation in that, with respect to documentation and information handling, it is an operating agency rather than an administrative or policy-setting agency. Data concerning its operations are not available in this book; hence it is not further discussed. With respect to the national information system, extant or planned, the Executive Office formulates policy and provides planning or other support. The BOB has responsibility for reviewing costing of any plans and ascertaining the authority, availability, and source of funds to implement plans. The OST is a policy organization responsive to the advisory organizations, PSAC and FCST. PSAC is composed of eminent nongovernment scientists, whereas FCST consists of government science administrators. PSAC acts directly through special panels, but FCST is supported by the Committee on Scientific and Technical

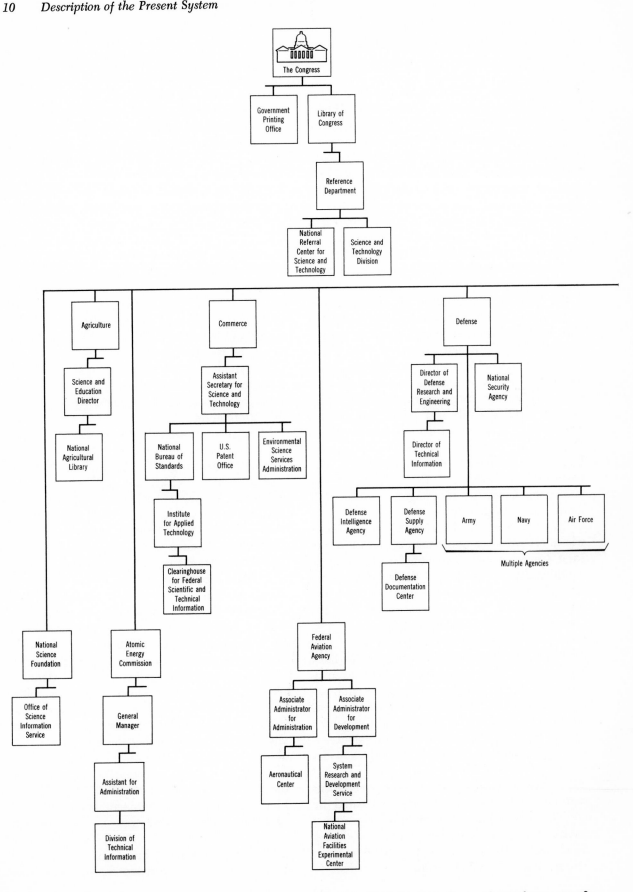

Fig. 2-1   Federal organizations with significant scientific

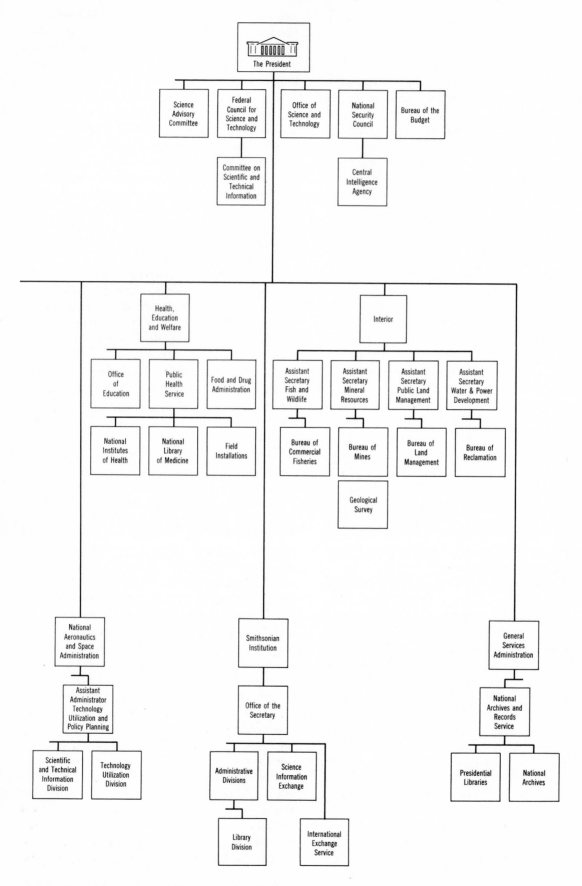

and technical information and documentation activities.

Information (COSATI) in planning and advising with respect to information system requirements and developments. OST provides coordination, personnel, and support as required to COSATI, and maintains cognizance in this area. The plans and requirements specified by PSAC, FCST, or COSATI impinge on the executive departments and independent agencies usually through coordination and committee work. At the pleasure of the President they may be directive upon any or all of the executive departments and independent agencies, but this is not typical. This, of course, is subject to congressional approval when significant funding or changes in the operation of any department or agency are considered. Other organizations such as the recently formed Federal Library Committee also influence policy and effect cooperative arrangements among libraries in the federal sector.

The executive departments and independent agencies with significant S&T information and document activities are depicted in Figure 2-1. They are briefly described here and summarized later in Table 2-3.

The Department of Agriculture has a Director for Science and Education in the Office of the Secretary of Agriculture. Reporting to him is the National Agricultural Library, which is responsible for department-wide coordination of documentation and library activities. It collects all significant material in agriculture and related fields and issues basic bibliographies. (The publication and distribution of bulletins and other department information is in the Office of Information, not in the Library.)

The Atomic Energy Commission (AEC) includes a general manager under whom there is an Assistant for Administration. The Division of Technical Information (DTI) reports to him, and is the major entity in AEC concerned with scientific and technical information. It contains directorates whose services include publishing *Nuclear Science Abstracts* and operating a large extension center at Oak Ridge, Tennessee.

In the Department of Commerce the Assistant Secretary for Science and Technology is responsible for three subordinate activities of interest: The Patent Office, the National Bureau of Standards, and the U. S. Coast and Geodetic Survey. During the course of the study certain organizational changes occurred within the Department of Commerce wherein the U. S. Coast and Geodetic Survey was incorporated into the En-

vironmental Science Service Administration. (Because the data obtained related to the earlier organizations the text continues to use the old names but the new name is incorporated into Figure 2-1.)

The U. S. Patent Office is the repository for all patents granted by the federal government. It announces these patents by means of the weekly *Gazette*. It also sells copies of patents.

In the National Bureau of Standards the Institute for Applied Technology encompasses the Clearinghouse for Federal Scientific and Technical Information (CFSTI), which is responsible for publishing and distributing much of the unclassified or otherwise unrestricted S&T (and other) material produced by the government and its contractors in science and technology. This material is announced through bulletins issued by the Clearinghouse and is available to the public on a fee basis. Certain qualified users may request and obtain documents free of charge.

The U. S. Coast and Geodetic Survey operates basically as an information analysis center, although secondarily it also functions as a library and repository in those areas of interest to the agency.

The Department of Defense contains several organizations of interest to a national information system. The National Security Agency (NSA) and the Defense Intelligence Agency (DIA) are generators and users of documents. They contain their own internal libraries and perform certain analytical services but these are of a special nature and available to limited audiences. Data on the size and cost of NSA and DIA information services were not obtained. The Director of Defense Research and Engineering (DDR&E) is supported by the Office of the Director of Technical Information. This organization is concerned with establishing policy throughout all of DOD for scientific and technical information. The Defense Supply Agency (DSA) is the administrative agency for the Defense Documentation Center (DDC). DDC publishes abstracts and indexes of classified or otherwise restricted DOD (government or contractor) produced documents along with certain other selected documents. These are abstracted and indexed, published in *Technical Abstract Bulletin* (*TAB*), and are widely disseminated to DOD agencies, contractors, and to other qualified organizations which may then request

Table 2-2   *DOD Scientific and Technical Information Facilities*

Name and Address of Facility	Contractor, If Any	Major Subjects Covered by Facility*
Department of Defense:		
Defense Documentation Center, Alexandria, Va.		
Advisory Group on Electron Devices, 346 Broadway, New York, N. Y.	New York University, College of Engineering, Research Division, New York.	c, f, l, i, q
Ballistic Missile Radiation Analysis Center, University of Michigan	Institute of Science and Technology, University of Michigan, Ann Arbor.	
Central Activity for Shock Vibration and Associated Environment, Washington, D. C.		g
Ceramics and Graphite Information Center, AF Materials Laboratory, Wright-Patterson Air Force Base, Ohio.		k
Chemical Propellant Information Agency, Silver Spring, Md. (c/o Applied Physics Laboratory, Johns Hopkins University).	Johns Hopkins University, Baltimore, Md.	d
Constitution of Binary Alloys, Illinois Institute of Technology, Chicago, Ill.	IIT Research Institute, Chicago, Ill.	i
Counterinsurgency Information Analysis Center (COIN), American University, Washington, D. C.	American University, Washington, D. C.	
Defender Information Center, Battelle, Columbus, Ohio.	Battelle Memorial Institute, Columbus, Ohio.	q
Defense Atomic Support Agency Data Center, 735 State St., Santa Barbara, Calif.	General Electric Tempo, Santa Barbara, Calif.	q, c, f, i, l, n
Defense Metals Information Center, Battelle Memorial Institute, Columbus, Ohio.	Battelle Memorial Institute, Columbus, Ohio.	k
Electronic Properties Information Center, Hughes Aircraft Co., Culver City, Calif.	Hughes Aircraft Co., Florence and Centinela, Culver City, Calif.	f
Engineering Design Handbook, U. S. Army Material Command, Washington, D. C.	Engineer Design Handbook Office, Duke University, Durham, N. C.	g, k, p
Evaluation Branch, Coastal Engineering Research Center, Department of the Army, Washington, D. C.		g, k
Hibernation Information Exchange, Office of Naval Research Branch Office, Chicago, Ill.		b
Human Engineering Information and Analysis Services, Project, Medford, Mass. (c/o Tufts University, Institute for Psychological Research).	Tufts University, Medford, Mass.	o
Infrared Information and Analysis Center, Ann Arbor, Mich. (c/o University of Michigan, Institute of Science and Technology).	University of Michigan, Ann Arbor, Mich.	l
Mechanical Properties Data Center, Belfour Engineering Co., Suttons Bay, Mich.	Belfour Engineering Co., Suttons Bay, Mich.	k

* Explanation of code letters:

a. Agriculture	g. Engineering	m. Aerospace physics
b. Biological sciences	h. Health, safety, pollution	n. Nuclear physics
c. Chemistry	i. Mathematics	o. Social sciences and humanities
d. Chemical engineering	j. Medical sciences	p. Transportation
e. Earth sciences	k. Materials	q. Other
f. Electronics	l. Physics	

Table 2-2 (Continued)

Name and Address of Facility	Contractor, If Any	Major Subjects Covered by Facility*
Military Entomology Information Services, Walter Reed Army Medical Center, Washington, D. C.	Biological Sciences Communication Project, George Washington, University, Washington, D. C.	b
National Index of Fungus Cultures, U. S. Army Natick Laboratories, Natick, Mass.		b
National Oceanographic Data Center, Washington, D. C.		e
Nondestructive Testing Information Service, Army Materials Research Agency, Watertown, Mass.		c, f, g, i, j, k, l
Plastics Technical Evaluation Center (PLASTEC), Picatinny Arsenal, Dover, N. J.	Franklin Institute, Philadelphia, Pa.	q
Prevention of Deterioration Center, National Academy of Science, Washington, D. C.	National Academy of Sciences, Washington, D. C.	
Project SETE, New York University, College of Engineering, Research Division, 401 W. 205 St., New York, N. Y.	School of Engineering and Science, New York University, N. Y.	f
Radiation Effects Information Center, Battelle Memorial Institute, 505 King St., Columbus, Ohio.	Battelle Memorial Institute, Columbus, Ohio.	q
Remote Area Conflict Information, Battelle Memorial Institute, Columbus, Ohio.	Battelle Memorial Institute, Columbus, Ohio.	q
Thermophysical Properties Research Center (c/o Purdue University, Department of Mechanical Engineering), Lafayette, Ind.	Department of Mechanical Engineering, Purdue University, Lafayette, Ind.	k
Vela Seismic Information Analysis Center, University of Michigan, Nuclear Detection Office, Advanced Research Projects Agency, Ann Arbor, Mich.	Regents of the University of Michigan, Ann Arbor, Mich.	q
Office of the Secretary of Defense:		
Administrative Services Branch Document Library, Room 1B 687, Pentagon, Washington, D. C.		b, c, e, f, g, i, j, k, l, n, q
Director Administrative Division, Administrative Services Technical Library, 8th Street and Courthouse Rd., Arlington, Va.		f, i, l, m
Department of the Army:		
Army Material Command:		
(*Army Mobility Command*)		
Technical Data Repository and Reference Branch, Army Aviation and Surface Materiel Command, Warren, Mich.		
Technical Information Office, Army Mobility Command, Warren, Mich.		c, f, g, k, p
Army Transportation Research and Engineering Command, Technical Library, Fort Eustis, Va.		c, d, f, g, i, k, l, m, p
Army Tank-Automotive Center, Technical Information, Office, Warren, Mich.		
Army Engineer Research and Development Laboratories, Scientific and Technical Information Branch, Fort Belvoir, Va.		c, d, e, g, i, l, n, k
(*Army Missile Command*)		
Redstone Scientific Information Center, Redstone Arsenal, Ala.		c, d, e, g, k, l, m, n

Table 2-2 (*Continued*)

Name and Address of Facility	Contractor, If Any	Major Subjects Covered by Facility*
(*Army Munitions Command*)		
Technical Information Branch, Picatinny Arsenal, Dover, N. J.		c, d, g, i, k, l, m, q
Technical Information Division, Army Chemical Research and Development Laboratories, Edgewood Arsenal, Md.		h, c, d, e, j, h, i, k, p, l, q
Technical Information Division, Army Biological Laboratories, Fort Detrick, Md.		a, b, c, d, g, h, i, j, l
Library, Frankford Arsenal, Philadelphia, Pa.		b, c, d, g, i, k, l, n
Technical Writing Section, Frankford Arsenal, Pa.		b, c, d, g, i, k, l, n
Foreign Intelligence Section, Frankford Arsenal, Pa.		b, c, d, g, i, k, l, n
Army Test and Evaluation Command:		
Records and Files Section, Yuma Proving Ground, Ariz.		g, h, k
Technical Library, Aberdeen Proving Ground, Md.		g, h, k, c, d, e, i, n
Technical Library, Electronic Proving Ground, Ariz.		c, e, g, i, p q,
Technical Library, Dugway Proving Ground, Utah.		b, c, d, g, h, i, j, k, l, n
Technical Library, White Sands Missile Range, N. Mex.		b, c, d, e, g, h, i, k, l, m, n, p, q
Army Weapons Command:		
Technical Information Services Offices, Benet Research and Engineering Laboratories, Watervliet Arsenal, N. Y.		c, e, i, j, l, q
Technical Information Branch, Rock Island Arsenal, Ill.		c, g, i, k
Technical Information Section, Springfield Armory, Mass.		c, d, j, i, k, l
Army Electronics Command:		
Technical Documents Center, U. S. Army Electronics R & D Laboratories, Ft. Monmouth, N. J.		c, d, i, j, k, n, f c, d, i, j, k, n, f
R & D Directorate:		
Technical Information Office, Harry Diamond Laboratories, Washington, D. C.		c, d, e, g, h, i, j, k, l, m, n
Technical Library, Army Materials Research Agency, Watertown, Mass.		e, i, k, l
Army Cold Regions Research and Engineering Laboratories, Hanover, N. H.		e, g, k
Technical Library, Army Natick Laboratories, Natick, Mass.		c, l, i, m, g, q
Office of the Surgeon General:		
Medical Unit Library, Army Medical Unit, Fort Detrick, Md.		j
Library, Army Medical Research and Nutrition Laboratory, Denver, Colo.		b, c, j
Technical Library, Army Medical Equipment Research and Development Laboratory, Fort Totten, Flushing, N. Y.		q
Army Medical Research Laboratory, Fort Knox, Ky.		b, j, l
Army Aeromedical Research Unit, Fort Rucker, Ala.		j
Army Surgical Research Unit, Publications Branch, Brooks Army Medical Center, Fort Sam Houston, Tex.		j

Table 2-2 (Continued)

Name and Address of Facility	Contractor, If Any	Major Subjects Covered by Facility*
Walter Reed Army Institute of Research, Washington, D. C.	Herner & Co., Washington, D. C.; Colgate-Palmolive Co., New Brunswick, N. J.; Service Bureau Corp., New York	b, c
Library, Walter Reed Army Institute of Research, Washington, D. C.		b, c, j, q
Technical Reference Library, Forest Glen Section, Walter Reed Army Medical Center, Washington, D. C.		j, q
Corps of Engineering:		
Scientific and Technical Information Division, Office of the Chief of Engineers, Washington, D. C.		g
Ohio River Division Engineering Construction Laboratory Library, 5851 Mariemont Ave., Cincinnati, Ohio.		g, k
Research Center Library, Army Engineer Waterways Experiment Station, Vicksburg, Miss.		g, k
Army Combat Development Command:		
Administrative Division, Army Combat Development Command Artillery Agency, Fort Sill, Okla.		
Air Defense Agency, Combined Arms Group, Fort Bliss, Tex.		
Document Control Center, Medical Service Agency, Fort Sam Houston, Tex.		
U. S. Army Combat Development Command, Documentary Library Branch, Fort McClellan, Ala.		
Army Combat Development Command, Nuclear Group, Fort Bliss, Tex.		
Department of the Navy:		
Naval Observatory Library, Washington, D. C.		m
Naval Oceanographic Office Library, Suitland, Md.		e
Technical Library, Special Projects Office, Department of the Navy, Washington, D. C.		g, m, n
Marine Corps Schools, J. C. Breckinridge Library, Quantico, Va.		g
Command Operational Test and Evaluation Force, Information Center, U. S. Naval Station, Norfolk, Va.		
Bureau of Naval Weapons:		
Technical Library, Bureau of Naval Weapons, Department of the Navy, Washington, D. C.		q
Naval Air Development Center Technical Library, Johnsville, Pa.		q
Naval Air Engineering Center Technical Library, Philadelphia, Pa.		g, h, k
Naval Air Test Facility (SI), Library and Technical Files Office, Lakehurst, N. J.		g
Naval Air Turbine Test Station, Technical Library, Trenton, N. J.		g
Naval Avionics Facility Technical Library, Indianapolis, Ind.		f
Technical Library, Naval Missile Test Center, Point Mugu, Calif.		g

Table 2-2 (*Continued*)

Name and Address of Facility	Contractor, If Any	Major Subjects Covered by Facility*
Naval Ordnance Laboratory Library, Corona, Calif.		q
Naval Ordnance Laboratory Technical Library, White Oak, Md.		q
Naval Ordnance Test Station, Technical Information Department, China Lake, Calif.		q
Naval Underwater Ordnance Station, Library and Technical Information Division, Newport, R. I.		g
Naval Weapons Laboratory Technical Library, Dahlgren, Va.		m
Allegany Ballistics Laboratory Technical Library, Hercules Powder Co., Cumberland, Md.	Hercules Powder Co., Cumberland, Md.	c, g
Applied Physics Laboratory Library, Johns Hopkins University, Silver Spring, Md.	Johns Hopkins University, Baltimore, Md.	q
Applied Physics Laboratory Library, University of Washington, Seattle, Wash.	University of Washington, Seattle, Wash.	e, l
Ordnance Aerophysics Laboratory, General Dynamics/Pomona, Daingerfield, Tex.	General Dynamics/Pomona Daingerfield Division, Daingerfield, Tex.	m
Ordnance Research Laboratory, Technical Publications Section, Pennsylvania State University, University Park, Pa.	Pennsylvania State University, University Park, Pa.	g, l
Bureau of Ships:		
Bureau of Ships Technical Library, Department of the Navy, Washington, D. C.		q
David Taylor Model Basin, Technical Information Center, Carderock, Md.		g, i, k, l
Naval Applied Science, Laboratory Technical Library, Brooklyn, N. Y.		g, k
Naval Boiler and Turbine Laboratory Technical Library, Philadelphia, Pa.		g
Navy Electronics Laboratory Technical Library, San Diego, Calif.		e, f
Navy Marine Engineering Laboratory, Annapolis, Md.		g
Navy Mine Defense Laboratory Technical Library, Panama City, Fla.		g, l
Naval Radiological Defense Laboratory Library Branch, San Francisco, Calif.		b, n
Navy Underwater Sound Laboratory Technical Library, New London, Conn.		e, g, l
Office of Naval Research:		
Naval Research Laboratory Technical Information Office, Washington, D. C.		q
Naval Training Device Center Technical Library, Port Washington, N. Y.		g
Navy Underwater Sound Reference Laboratory Library, Orlando, Fla.		l
Naval Biological Laboratory Library, Oakland, Calif.		b
Hudson Laboratories Library, Columbia University, Dobbs Ferry, N. Y.	Columbia University, Dobbs Ferry, N. Y.	e
Bureau of Medicine and Surgery:		
Naval Medical Field Research Laboratory, Camp Lejeune, N. C.		j

Table 2-2 (Continued)

Name and Address of Facility	Contractor, If Any	Major Subjects Covered by Facility*
Navy Medical Neuropsychiatric Research Unit, San Diego, Calif.		j
Naval Medical Research Institute, Technical Reference Library, Bethesda, Md.		j
Naval Medical Research Laboratory, Technical Information Section, Groton, Conn.		j
Naval Medical Research Unit No. 2, Taipei, Taiwan.		j
Naval Medical Research Unit No. 3, FPO, New York, N. Y.		j
Naval School of Aviation Medicine, Pensacola, Fla.		j, m
Bureau of Naval Personnel:		
Personnel Research Activity Technical Library, Washington, D. C.		o
Personnel Research Activity Technical Library, San Diego, Calif.		o
Naval Postgraduate School Library, Monterey, Calif.		q
Bureau of Supplies and Accounts:		
Naval Supply Research and Development Facility Library, Bayonne, N. J.		k, p
Bureau of Yards and Docks:		
Naval Civil Engineering Laboratory Technical Library, Port Hueneme, Calif.		g
Department of the Air Force:		
Air Force Systems Command:		
Headquarters Library, Air Force Systems Command, Andrews Air Force Base, Washington, D. C.		g
Foreign Technology Division:		
Library Division, Foreign Technology Division, Wright-Patterson Air Force Base, Dayton, Ohio.		g
Space Systems Division:		
Technical Library, Los Angeles Air Force Station, Los Angeles, Calif.	Tumpane Co., Inc., Los Angeles, Calif.	g
Research and Technology Division:		
Materials Information Branch, Air Force Materials Laboratory, Wright-Patterson Air Force Base, Dayton, Ohio.	Research Institute, University of Dayton, Dayton, Ohio	k
Rome Air Development Center, Library Services Section, Griffiss Air Force Base, Rome, N. Y.		g
Air Force Weapons Laboratory Technical Information Division, Kirtland Air Force Base, N. Mex.		n
National Ranges Division:		
Air Force Eastern Test Range Technical Library, Patrick Air Force Base, Fla.	Guided Missiles Range Division, Pan American World Airways, Inc., Patrick Air Force Base, Fla.	g
Aerospace Medical Division:		
School of Aviation Medicine, Aeromedical Library, Brooks Air Force Base, Tex.		j
Aeromedical Research Laboratories Library, Wright-Patterson Air Force Base, Ohio.		b, j
6570th Personnel Research Laboratory, Library, Lackland Air Force Base, Tex.		q

Table 2-2 (Continued)

Name and Address of Facility	Contractor, If Any	Major Subjects Covered by Facility*
6571st Aeromedical Research Laboratory Library, Holloman Air Force Base, N. Mex.		j
Arnold Engineering Development Center, Reports Division, Tullahoma, Tenn.		g
Arnold Engineering Development Center, Technical Library, Tullahoma, Tenn.	ARO, Inc., Tullahoma, Tenn.	g
Air Proving Ground Center, Technical Information, Eglin Air Force Base, Fla.		g
Air Force Flight Test Center Technical Library, Edwards Air Force Base, Calif.		g
Air Force Logistics Command:		
2750th Airborne Wing Technical Library, Wright-Patterson Air Force Base, Ohio.		g
Office of Aerospace Research:		
Air Force Office of Scientific Research, Research Library, Washington, D. C.		b, e, g
European Office, Office of Aerospace Research Technical Information Office, APO 667, New York, N. Y.		b, c, e, f, i, k, l, m
Aerospace Research Laboratories, Research Information Office, Wright-Patterson Air Force Base, Ohio.		e, i
Air Force Cambridge Research Laboratories, Technical Services Division, L. G. Hanscom Field, Bedford, Mass.		c, e, g, i, l
Office of Research Analyses Technical Library Holloman Air Force Base, N. Mex.		g

copies of the documents from DDC. Within the three military departments of DOD are a multitude of organizations that share document and information responsibilities. By and large these are document generators or users, but they also contain information analysis centers, libraries, and other organizations that perform all the functions related to information and document services. These are too numerous to describe here; a recent detailed tabulation appears in Elliott [5] and is presented in Table 2-2.

The Federal Aviation Agency has several associate administrators (for Administration, Development, the Aeronautical Center, and the National Aviation Facilities Experimental Center). All of these associate administrators jointly operate the FAA library. For management purposes the library reports to the Associate Administrator for Administration. The FAA collection relates to the duties of FAA as defined in the 1950 act establishing the FAA. The library operates in a traditional fashion, specializing in safety, air traffic control, navigation, and all aspects of commercial and civil aviation, including airports, runways, aircraft facilities, and so on.

The Department of Health, Education, and Welfare has three organizations of interest: the Office of Education, the Public Health Service, and the Food and Drug Administration. With respect to information and communication needs in school systems the Office of Education is concerned primarily with policy and support and in the training or education of information specialists. The Food and Drug Administration generates many documents and operates several information analysis centers. The Public Health Service includes the National Institutes of Health (NIH), the National Library of Medicine (NLM), and other headquarters and field installations. The selected field installations are of interest because of their interaction with the community of users and the fact that they

operate information analysis centers. The National Institutes of Health also contains information analysis centers and is a document generator and user. The National Library of Medicine is a publishing, announcing, and distributing agency. It publishes the *Index Medicus,* a subject index covering most of the medical journals and literature produced in the United States. The *Index* is distributed to libraries or other organizations which further make it available to practitioners. The *Index* is also distributed directly to individuals. The NLM and its system represents one of the more advanced applications of computer technology in the field of subject index distribution to large audiences.

The Department of the Interior has a number of assistant secretaries responsible for activities in various mission or discipline areas—for example, mineral resources and water power and development. Within these secretariats are several bureaus that maintain technical libraries and library services for their own staffs as well as for the general public. Of particular interest are the Bureau of Reclamation, Bureau of Land Management, Geological Survey, Bureau of Mines, and Bureau of Commercial Fisheries.

In the National Aeronautics and Space Administration (NASA), the Office of Technology Utilization has two divisions directly involved in scientific and technical information handling: the Scientific and Technical Information Division (STID) and the Technology Utilization Division (TUD). All American and most foreign aerospace scientific and technical information is covered by these divisions. The STID is concerned with information requirements of NASA, its contractors, and other government agencies. TUD is concerned with informing American industry of technological and scientific research and development results which can be exploited by the American private economy.

STID collects foreign and domestic scientific and technical aerospace report literature which is abstracted, indexed, and announced (by a NASA contractor). In collaboration with NASA, the American Institute of Aeronautics and Astronautics (AIAA) acquires foreign and domestic scientific and technical aerospace published journal literature which it indexes and announces. In addition, STID offers demand bibliographies, specialized research and development reports, listings of NASA translations, and original and reproduced primary and secondary publications. These publications and reports are disseminated by standard distribution, user-initiated computer retrieval procedures, and computer-based selective dissemination procedures.

TUD sponsors meetings involving government and private aerospace, scientific, and technical oranizations. TUD publishes proceedings and records of these and related meetings, and publishes documents available to American industry through the Clearinghouse for Federal Scientific and Technical Information.

The National Science Foundation includes the Office of Science Information Service (OSIS) which supports research and sponsors journals and other ventures in the area of documentation. OSIS operates with a $12 million annual budget (for the fiscal year 1966) which is applied in the following areas: support of research, mostly at universities and nonprofit institutions directly concerned with information sciences and advancing technology in that field; and support and subsidization of new journals and similar ventures which have been judged by OSIS as making a positive contribution to some area of science. A typical example is their subsidy for the initial publication of the journal *American Documentation.*

In the Smithsonian Institution, the Office of the Secretary is the administrative agency within which is a library division operating several libraries within the Washington complex and at Cambridge, Massachusetts, and the Panama Canal Zone. These library operations are primarily for support of Smithsonian personnel, other government agencies, and serious scholars.

The International Exchange Service (IES) within the Smithsonian Institution is the focal point in the federal sector for the exchange of documents with other countries. A significant portion of the documents available for exchange are produced by the Smithsonian, but the majority come from other federal agencies and include many congressional reports and prints. These are sent to the IES offices where they are then forwarded to foreign countries in accordance with agreements. The Exchange Office also receives documents from foreign countries and distributes them to Smithsonian or, when appropriate, to other government agencies.

The Science Information Exchange (SIE), also within the Smithsonian, receives, organizes, and disseminates information about current

scientific research. Its basic mission is to provide information for planning and managing research activities—whether they are government or non-government supported—before such information might otherwise be available. It promotes the exchange of information concerning current research focusing on the prepublication phase to compensate for the information gap between the time a research project is initiated and the time its results become generally available in a publication. SIE functions as an information center. Notices of research projects, each containing a 200-word technical summary, are analyzed, indexed, processed, and stored in computer and manual files so that many items relating to questions about projects can be retrieved quickly. In 1964 more than 100,000 records were established and 34,000 requests processed. Although SIE is operated within the Smithsonian, it is financed by the National Science Foundation.

Table 2-3 summarizes selected organizational characteristics as ascertained by the interview program of the executive departments and agencies.

The Nonfederal Sector

Although the organizations in the nonfederal sector are functionally similar to those in the federal sector, their structure, purposes, and methods of operation differ to considerable degree. They also differ among themselves in the degree to which they interact or depend on the federal sector for support. Nevertheless, a comparable categorization relative to functions can be argued. There is, of course, no central line authority or similar structure as in the federal sector. There sometimes are groupings in terms of functional or work relationships but no legally defined relationships among these clusters. No organization chart or similar device therefore could adequately represent the nonfederal sector. It becomes necessary to discuss clusters or aggregates of organizations which have been similarly categorized. Here, as in the federal sector, there is a diversity of organizational structures and operations.

Libraries. Two groups of nonfederal libraries are of significance with respect to scientific and technical documents and information. These are the university libraries and the larger public libraries. Visits were made to four university li-

braries (Maryland, MIT, Harvard, and UCLA) and to two public libraries (the John Crerar Library* in Chicago, and the New York Public Library). Typically, the university library has a central facility responsible for acquisitions and cataloging plus a number of discipline-oriented branches through the university. Harvard supports some 87 such branches. Although the central facility maintains at least nominal control of the several branches, the branches tend to act autonomously, in acquiring and/or cataloging. The university libraries operate independently of the federal sector except for benefits derived from being part of universities or from their designation as federal depositories.

The public libraries may or may not operate branches (Crerar does not, New York Public does), but the branch libraries are typically not of interest in terms of science and technology. Some public libraries are involved in federal operations. For example, Crerar maintains a repository for GPO, DDC, AEC, and the foreign language translations produced for the Special Libraries Association (SLA) sponsored by NSF.

Nonfederal libraries are a prime source of government-produced or -distributed documentation and information for the many scientists, scholars, and others who do not have access to much of the federal system. They also serve as local distribution points and depositories for federal documentation.

Information Analysis Centers. The information analysis center is very much the same in the private sector as in the federal sector. Only one information center facility was visited in the private sector, the Battelle Memorial Institute, which actually operates about fourteen independent information centers. Several of these are operated for the federal government on contract with DOD. Although these are contractor manned and contractor operated, they are in reality federal information centers. Battelle also operates a number of information centers for commercial or industrial groups.

Partly because the same organization operates the several information centers, the private and federal centers are very much alike in structure and operation. The federally supported centers,

---

* Classified by some authorities as a research or special library, it is here designated as a public library because its charter and *modus operandi* are directed toward public service.

Table 2-3 Summary of Selected Organizational Characteristics of Executive Departments and Agencies Visited

Agency/Organization	Total* Personnel	Annual* Budget (× $1000)	Responsibility/Mission*	Comments
Atomic Energy Commission	225	5,000	Comprehensive technical information program to meet the needs of the AEC, its contractors, other government agencies, industry, and the world-wide scientific community.	Distributes reports, publishes state-of-the-art review journals, publishes *Nuclear Science Abstract* and three other abstract journals, supports data centers, educational projects.
Agriculture Department National Agriculture Library	178	1599	Serves research needs of department and academic community in field of agriculture.	Compiles and publishes bibliography of agriculture.
Commerce Department U. S. Patent Office	60	600	Disseminates information about patents granted by publishing briefs in official *Gazette* (weekly).	Patents available for sale to public. Classification schemes differ from others in information fields. *Gazette* and patent write-up sometimes legalistic rather than technical.
National Bureau of Standards (CFSTI)	300	5,000	Provides unrestricted government technical reports to the public on a fee basis.	Income derived from sales helps offset costs.
Defense Department† DDC	430	11,000	DOD-wide document wholesaler which also performs special services such as preparing request bibliographies.	Serves as major interface with non-DOD agencies, e.g., CFSTI.
Federal Aviation Administration	29	427‡	Provides library services in all branches of civil aviation and all aspects of military aviation related to use of aviation facilities such as navigation aids and airports. Heavy emphasis on flight safety and medical and legal aspects of aviation.	Serves as a basic reference library both for NASA and DOD in areas of concern.
Health, Education, and Welfare Department OE		See comment	Division of library services concerned with improving library facilities including construction of new libraries.	Fiscal year 1964 budget was $55 million but this included library construction funds. Would be involved in implementing S. 600.
PHS-NIH Library	¶70	649	Primarily a scientific and technical library serving NIH.	
PHS-NLM	278	5,000	Primary medical library in United States.	Covers medicine, dentistry, and medical arts, including medical aspects of biochemistry. 100,000 books in library. Starting new automated library system in fiscal year 1966.

Institution			Description	
F&DA	69		Provide data for analysis of drug, food, and cosmetic products.	
Interior Department	150	1,200	Departmental and bureau libraries support Geological Survey, Bureau of Mines, Office of Saline Water and other bureaus in research and information center applications.	
NASA	600‖	20,000	Provision to NASA and NASA contractors of aerospace technical literature to support NASA mission.	Strong program to disseminate NASA research and development results to private nonaerospace firms and societies.
National Science Foundation				
OSIS	43	12,000	Promote new and better techniques for handling and disseminating scientific information and making existing systems more effective. Sponsor research in information sciences. Support journals, translation services, etc., when appropriate.	
Smithsonian Institution				
Libraries	32§	FY '65—300 FY '66—468	Central Library provides technical services. Branch libraries provide reader and information services—tend to be more specialized. International exchange is primary means for federal government exchange programs.	
IES	11	110	Operates foreign exchange program for federal government.	Essentially a mailroom activity.
SIE	75	2,000	Information on research in medicine, biology, physics, etc.	Supported by NSI OSIS. Managed by Smithsonian Institution.

* Refers to document and information services only.
† DDC only, excludes NSA, DIA, and military departments data.
‡ Includes $220,000 for salary and $207,000 for acquisitions in science and technology.
§ Central Library only.
‖ Excludes contractor personnel.
¶ Does not apply.

however, are larger. Permanent staffs are assigned to the particular information centers and these are supplemented by specialists drawn from several possible sources. In the case of Battelle, because the information centers are embedded in a research institute with a major library facility at its disposal, the outside support would come from personnel who are members of the institute.

Publication, Announcement, and Distribution Organizations. Two different groupings of organizations exist in this area. The first are the commercial firms which range from the giant publishers, such as McGraw-Hill, to a host of small abstracting, indexing, or translation services. The second are the professional societies involved in information activities. The publication of *Chemical Abstracts* by the American Chemical Society is an example.

The commercial enterprises in this area are supported only indirectly by the federal government through subscription to their services. The professional societies, on the other hand, are more directly supported in some publications and documentation activities—particularly research. Commercial enterprises object sometimes to such federal support practices of noncommercial entities. Important and innovative services that might not be commercially feasible would not be available, however, without direct support by the federal government.

Document Generators and Users. In the private sector are two major groups that would be so categorized: the industrial organizations and the universities. The industrial organizations are by far the prime producers of report literature, particularly for DOD, NASA, and AEC. This literature is paid for by the government and goes by primary distribution to the government agencies concerned as well as other appropriate organizations. In terms of document generation the interface between the industrial organization and the government would be by means of the contracts officer or the particular operating entity with which the contract has been made.

University sources are contributing more and more to the report literature, but they remain the primary source of serial literature. Insofar as the report literature is based on government-sponsored contracts, their distribution is very similar to that of the industrial groups. The serial literature is input directly to the journals involved with open publication in accordance with the policies and practices of a particular journal.

Both the industrial organizations and universities tend to act in similar ways with respect to the *use* of documents and related services. They typically go through the local library facility for processing requests and performing various reference services such as retroactive search and retrieval. The librarians and their staffs are then responsible for the interaction with the federal sector. The librarians also are responsible for dissemination of materials received other than by requests.

Administration, Policy, and Support. Included in this category are a number of organizations interested or concerned with the operations of document and information services both in the federal and private sectors. They do not become directly involved in such operations, however. Typically these are associations (e.g., the Association of Research Libraries) or professional societies (e.g., the American Library Association) concerned with documentation or information operations. (See Table 2-1 for groupings of organizations visited.)

In some remote sense these organizations can be considered to establish policy for operations within portions of the private sector. This is done by means of standards, agreements, or similar mechanisms which are developed and promulgated by these organizations. Implementation of such policies is possible only on a voluntary basis.

Table 2-4 summarizes selected organizational characteristics as ascertained by the interview program of the private sector organizations.

PRESENT SYSTEM OPERATIONS

In this section the organizations just described will again be reviewed but from an operational point of view. They are grouped here in accordance with the five categories described in Table 2-1, namely: libraries; information centers; publication, announcement, and distribution organizations; document generators/users; and administrative, policy, and support organizations.

In the reviews that follow, organizations are not singled out for individual description. Rather the typical organization's functions and operations (in each category) are discussed and reference is sometimes made to particular organiza-

tions for illustrative purposes. One exception is in the realm of publication, announcement, and distribution organizations where, because of certain unique features in some organizations, each is described individually.

Libraries

The organization and operations of libraries in the United States as they relate to the development of a national system for the efficient handling and use of scientific and technical documentation are here described. Included are descriptions of various categories of libraries, their operations, funding patterns, personnel, and the extent to which they are interdependent, similar, and dissimilar. For perspective it will be useful to cite some overall statistics.

For 1964 it is estimated that there were some 17,000 libraries in the United States and Canada. Total library budget for that year is estimated to be at least $900 million. These libraries were staffed by approximately 70,000 qualified professional librarians of whom some 5 per cent were employed by the federal government. If the American Library Association's standards for public, school, and academic libraries were to be met, twice as many librarians would be required, along with enormously increased support. Yet the total of professionals graduated by the nation's library schools is hardly more than 3000 a year.

The proportion of library budgets and personnel devoted to scientific and technical literature is very difficult to estimate and varies greatly with type of library. For the larger research libraries the proportion of effort devoted to these areas is estimated at 25 to 35 per cent.

Categories of Libraries. For this description the nation's libraries have been categorized as public libraries, academic libraries, special libraries, national libraries, departmental and agency libraries. School libraries are not described. We define public libraries to include those libraries that are funded by private or foundation funds, municipal funds, or other nonfederal monies. Academic libraries are those libraries that are part of colleges and universities. Special libraries include business and industrial libraries not a part of the federal system. National libraries include the Library of Congress, the National Agriculture Library, and the National Library of Medicine. Departmental and agency libraries include all other federally supported libraries.

Any description of libraries in the United States must recognize the importance and pivotal position of the Library of Congress. The public libraries, academic libraries, and a large proportion of the special and departmental libraries look to the Library of Congress for authority in descriptive and subject cataloging. This authority is ensured and perpetuated through the preparation and sale of the Library of Congress cards and various Library of Congress publications, particularly the classification schedules and updates of the list of subject headings used by the Library.

There are many explanations for the preeminence of the Library of Congress as a source of authority and dependence for the libraries of the country. The principal historical reason for the dependence is the development of the card service and the fact that the Library through the copyright laws was able to obtain a comprehensive collection of domestically copyrighted materials.

Second, libraries of all kinds were impelled to reduce the cost of cataloging and other processing. They became increasingly more dependent on the Library of Congress for descriptions and subject categorizations. The Library of Congress became a central collection to which all parts of the country might turn for library materials and reference assistance. Apart from its major mission of serving the Congress, it has given service on a national basis to scholars, scientists, and technologists. This is done through interlibrary loans, photographic reproduction, and direct mail responses. In the course of these activities it built a *National Union Catalog* which records the location of books in research collections throughout the country and is an indispensable feature of the machinery of interlibrary cooperation for American libraries. The *National Union Catalog*, though it has emphasized primarily book materials, has provided a means for making holdings of useful materials known to all libraries and thereby to scholars, scientists, and technologists.

The development of the other two national libraries, which have taken rather different courses in organizing and developing their services to other parts of the research community, particularly with respect to the sciences and the technologies, illustrates both the virtues and the

Table 2-4 Summary of Selected Organizational Characteristics of Nonfederal Sector Organizations Visited

Agency/Organization*	Total† Personnel	Annual Budget† (× $1000)	Responsibility/Mission†	Comment
American Chemical Society (Publications Division)	188	6,100	Publishes 17 chemical journals. Encourages advancement of chemistry.	Conducting research in computer-based photo-composition of chemical structural diagrams.
American Institute of Physics	30	3,500	Publishes 19 primary journals in physics.	Conducts research in documentation techniques.
American Petroleum Institute	36	500	Publishes abstracts and machine-produced indexes to refining literature and patents.	Self-supporting, core literature abstracting function for petroleum companies.
American Society of Metals	32	500	Maintains information storage and retrieval system of the world's literature on metals and metallurgy. Publishes journal.	Includes advanced electronic search capabilities and is an important input to EJC program.
Association for Computing Machinery	7 + 1,400 external	350	Fosters exchange of information about education, research, and applications in data-processing techniques and equipment.	Moving toward machine support in acquisitions and reviewer records management.
Battelle Memorial Institute	190	750	Conducts sponsored research over a broad spectrum of basic and applied sciences. Also operates information centers in conjunction with research laboratories or on a contractual basis.	Probably the largest single collection of information centers including the IRC, Information Research Center on IR.
Biological Sciences Information Service	100	1000	Publishes biological abstracts and machine-produced indexes—keyword coordinate and permuted title.	Developing integrated automated system for acquisitions and abstractors records management. Experiment in direct service to users.
Cambridge Communications Corp.	10 + 100 external	‡	Publishes abstracts for computer, solid-state physics, material, devices literature.	Small, private, self-supporting service; 2000 users.
Chemical Abstracts Service	650 + 3,000 external	7,900	Publishes chemical abstracts and chemical biological activities abstracts journals.	Moving into machine support for producing published journal and machine-searchable tapes.
Engineering Index, Inc.	75	500	Publishes Engineering Index.	Moving into machine support for producing published journal and machine-searchable tapes.
Harvard University Library	510	5400	University library—serves local community primarily, cooperates with industry and other libraries.	Largest academic library in U.S. 25% devoted to science and technology.
John Crerar Library	110	855	Free public library—services many industrial or research groups on a fee basis. Library services in science and technology; emphasis on physics, chemistry, medicine, math,.and engineering.	Major depository for GPO, DDC, AEC, NASA, CFSTI.
MIT Library	145	945	University library serving faculty, students, contract research, industry, and other academic institutions.	Special depository arrangements with AEC, NASA, RAND, DOD. 60% science and technology.

Institution				
McGraw-Hill Publishing Co.			Conducting research in computer-based photo-composition of indexes and directories.	
New York Public Library	2190	16,435	Compiles and publishes *Public Affairs Information Service.* GPO, U.N. depository.	General public and research library covering all fields of knowledge.
Society of Automotive Engineers	23	800	Performs critical review to determine whether to publish. Adopting automated dissemination system based on orders in 1966.	Publishes technical articles in transactions, journals, etc. Emphasis on current awareness.
UCLA Library	425(FTE)	3950	Depository for GPO, AEC, NASA, MEDLARS, and previously CFSTI. Converting MEDLARS tapes for IBM 7094.	University library—services industry, other academic libraries, and the public. Covers all subjects—30–35% science and technology.
University of Maryland Library	143	527	GPO, AEC, NASA depository—30–40% science and technology.	University library serving primarily faculty and students.

* Excludes administration, policy, and support organizations.
† Refers to document and information services only.
‡ Data not available.

inadequacies of the Library of Congress system. The attempt to cover massive collections in very broad subject areas had led to descriptions and services which are inadequate to a highly specialized research, and at the same time rather too ramified for small general libraries. The lesser libraries have made themselves dependent through imitation and, to a degree, unresponsive to the immediate public they serve.

In operation, particularly with respect to scientific and technological literature, the libraries of this country, apart from a few notable exceptions, have operated as "black boxes." They do not in any real sense know what they are receiving with respect to demand and subject matter, nor do they know in detail what is being used, by whom, and for what. Traditional statistical recording has been tied to the internal operations and has been accumulated primarily for budgetary and administrative purposes rather than for knowledge of and adaptation to the needs of users.

The ways in which librarians have chosen to organize their activities, particularly in the larger libraries, from which others take their authority for emulation, has been one of separating the activities into selection, acquisition, cataloging, reference, and circulation. The segregation of materials that are inputted to the libraries are primarily by format in terms of physical forms—books, serials, and manuscripts.

The systems of classifications and subject description in common use derive from traditions of scholarship and the subject distinctions that are made through discipline in the academic area. It should be said that there are two distinct streams of bibliographic and subject descriptions that have come down to us from the pre-World War I era. These are, on the library side, the Dewey Decimal System, the Universal Decimal Classification System, and the Library of Congress Classification System. Other library classification schemes have been invented over the years but have limited influence in the current era. The other stream of bibliographic and subject description is exemplified by the encyclopedic efforts of the early twentieth century represented by the development of *Chemical Abstracts,* the *International Critical Tables,* and the chemical encyclopedias. In most areas of science and technology the perspectives and philosophies of organizing knowledge remain very much as they were in 1910.

The recent emphasis of what we have come to call mission-oriented activities that cut across the so-called disciplinary categorizations of the past, and the emergence of new areas of inquiry and development tend to make past representation systems obsolete and unworkable for the present or future. If progress is to be made, the same kind of effort, imagination, and skill must be brought to bear on the systems of bibliographic and subject description today that was exerted between 1880 and 1910. It will not be sufficient to confine ourselves to the transformation of the manual systems of the present into machine-readable and machine-manipulatable form for computers.

In many ways it can be claimed fairly that the United States has the finest systems of library services in the world. Yet when one considers the enormously variable ways in which libraries are established and maintained, it is clear that apart from the academic community, in which the role of libraries supporting the teaching and research programs of colleges and universities is much more clearly understood, it is truly remarkable that the libraries of the nation satisfy the demands placed on them as well as they do. This is nowhere more clearly illustrated than in the federal system. As has been indicated by Luther Evans [3], the formation and growth of departmental libraries generally has been adventitious:

"In most cases the jurisdiction of a new agency has been defined without reference to the maintenance of a library. Rarely has an agency defined the function of a library and the scope of its acquisition policy in its formative stages, or adequately estimated its future growth and financing. It may seem strange to the student of government agencies or public administration that such a degree of unplanned or unorganized activity has been permitted in Federal libraries. The reason is that seldom have high policy officers in government concerned themselves seriously with library development."

Once the books are on the shelves, the main incentive to review library policy comes from the librarians' demand for more staff and more space rather than from any clear conception of the utility of materials and services to users.

The Library Networks. Figure 2-2 illustrates the contrast for the library users and for the opera-

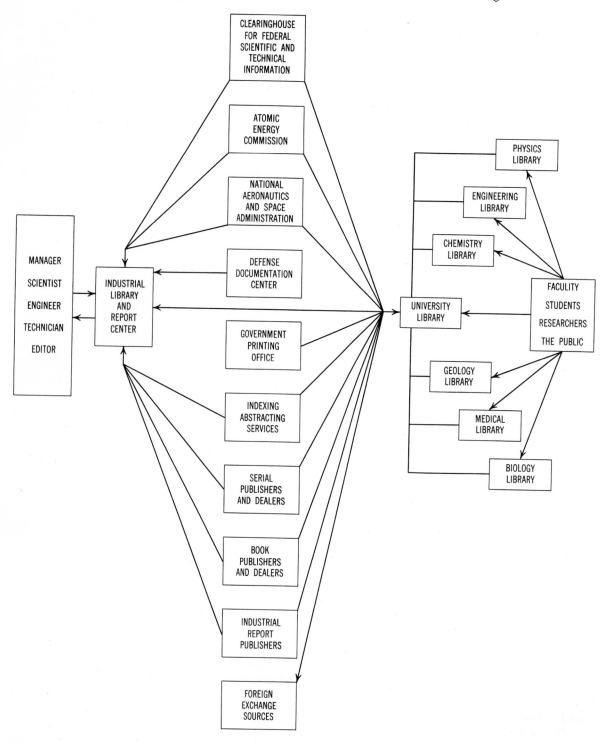

Fig. 2-2 Contrast between university and industrial libraries.

tional situation of a typical special library in industry and a university library. Only major dependencies are shown. The situation illustrated here for the industrial library also is characteristic of many departmental and agency libraries; that is, there is one point to which the user may repair for service in all subject areas. This assumes that the given library will collect in those fields of greatest interest for the firm or agency and will otherwise serve their diverse publics through obtaining materials from other stores on demand.

The situation for the university library is rather different. The user of such a library must know that the specialized subject matters are more likely to be contained within several branch libraries such as a physics library, a chemistry library, a medical library, and so on. He may have to visit several of these to cover his subject requirements as well to draw on a large central collection. With respect to the large public libraries the situation shown for the university libraries is reversed. That is, the specialized collections will most likely be contained within the large central library, with the satellite branches replicating a general collection rather than a specialized one. As with all configurations, ease of access to the content of the library collection is inversely proportional to its size, and depends on the degree to which it is segregated into specialized collections.

The other characteristic which must be recognized is that the typical industrial or small federal agency library depends highly on the existence of the large university or public library collections and, depending on location, upon the national library collections and services. They do not, and probably cannot, collect comprehensively enough to gratify the requirements of their user populations. This dependency is particularly strong in the area of serial literature. Thus the university libraries are a prime library resource for industry in the United States. Relatively few public libraries have collected comprehensively enough in science and technology to be able to serve industry effectively. To cite a single example, in the Los Angeles area, UCLA is a major library resource for industry. It is estimated that about 25 per cent of the total service load experienced by the UCLA Library is attributed to such off-campus users.

The federal department and agency libraries operate in ways very similar to those of the industrial special libraries in that they collect with respect to a specialized public and depend for materials that they do not themselves acquire on the national libraries and other libraries within the federal system. The Washington, D. C., metropolitan area is the focus for federal library activities. The area contains the three national libraries and, with few exceptions, the major department libraries. Apart from the Washington area there are large numbers of branches or independently operated libraries within the departments and agencies. These are relatively small and do not comprise any large proportion of the collections, staff, or effort in the federal system, with the exception of the DOD complex.

As previously indicated in Table 2-2, DOD maintains a large number of relatively small library operations that serve primarily as public libraries for the armed forces and a smaller number of technical libraries, some of which attain considerable size.

The three national libraries are unique institutions that perform functions quite unlike that of most other libraries in the country. They have in common variegated sets of users whose needs and requirements for service are greatly diverse and who are likely to be located in any part of the world. The National Library of Medicine and the National Agriculture Library publish a very comprehensive index of significant documentation within the subject areas for which they are responsible. These are respectively the *Bibliography of Agriculture* and the *Index Medicus*. All three libraries share in acting as an authority through publishing of their practices in cataloging and subject description for other libraries. It is notable, however, that each of these three enterprises has a different system of subject description and bibliographic organization. They differ also in the ways in which they acquire the major proportion of their materials.

With respect to the Library of Congress in the areas of science and technology, the major sources of input are through purchase, copyright deposit, and document or report deposit. This may be contrasted with the Agriculture Department Library whose acquisitions are 70 per cent acquired through exchange. Both the National Agriculture Library and the National Library of Medicine attempt to collect comprehensively in their fields of subject competence, but the Library of Congress does not attempt to collect

comprehensively in the fields of science and technology, nor indeed in any single subject area that is not germane to their major mission of serving the Congress. Although the Library of Congress does not collect comprehensively in all fields, its collections are such that it can be said that after the National Library of Medicine, the Library of Congress contains the most comprehensive medical collection in the United States, and that after the National Agriculture Library the most comprehensive agricultural collection in the United States. All three libraries maintain very extensive exchange arrangements enabling them to obtain all kinds of printed information—books, journals, reports, pamphlets, and public documents—that could be obtained in no other way.

It should also be said here that there is a great deal of duplication in these collections of the national libraries and indeed with other major research libraries in the United States. The national picture is one of great redundancy and duplication of basic journals, books, and other materials, while serious gaps persist in subject and publication coverage.

Internal Library Organization and Operations. Libraries of similar size tend to be organized very similarly whether in the public or private sectors and whether public, academic, or special. For those libraries specializing in the sciences and technology there is a shortage of properly educated and trained personnel on both the professional and nonprofessional levels.

Tables 2-5 and 2-6 show the number of full-time federal library and archives personnel by agency as of October 31, 1962, and the breakdown by Civil Service grade for these personnel as of that date. These data are based on Civil Service Commission unpublished information. The Library of Congress personnel are included in these tables, having been assigned equivalent GS grade ratings. It should be noted that the tables do not include library employees in position classifications other than professional librarians and library assistants.

Federally employed librarians generally receive higher salaries than their colleagues in college and university libraries and more particularly in public libraries. No comprehensive data exist concerning typical wage scales in industrial libraries. The contrast between government salaries and those others cited is particularly

Table 2-5 Federal Government Library and Archives Personnel, All Areas; Number of Full-Time Federal Library Personnel by Civil Service Grade, October 31, 1962

General Schedule Grade	Number* Library Assistant 1950	Librarian (professional) 3311	Salary† Range
1	9	....	$ 3,385– 4,420
2	69	....	3,680– 4,805
3	332	....	4,005– 5,220
4	700	....	4,480– 5,830
5	614	216	5,000– 6,485
6	134	20	5,505– 7,170
7	58	724	6,050– 7,850
8	2	131	6,630– 8,610
9	5	1069	7,220– 9,425
10	2	86	7,900–10,330
11	...	581	8,650–11,305
12	...	215	10,250–13,445
13	...	105	12,075–15,855
14	...	51	14,170–18,580
15	...	19	16,460–21,590
16	...	7	18,935–24,175
17	...	3	21,445–24,445
18	...	....	24,500–

*All data based on Civil Service Commission's unpublished data for "Occupations of Federal White-Collar Workers, October 1962."
† Salary range in effect October 31, 1962.

clear in the executive grades. One might assume from this that the government is able to draw the most able members of the profession into government service at the managerial levels, and in general be in a favorable position with respect to recruitment for all categories.

For the larger libraries, operations may be divided into technical processes and public services. Technical processes include: acquisition, including bibliographic checking on items selected for purchase or received from exchange and gifts to assure a minimum of inadvertent duplication; purchasing books, serials, and other library materials; gift and exchange operations; and serials records operations.

The next functional entity is the cataloging organization which in the larger libraries is divided into descriptive and subject cataloging. This process also requires bibliographic search to establish the entry and assure that needless

Table 2-6   Full-Time Federal Library and Archives Personnel, by Agency, October 31, 1962

Agency	Number Employed				
	Archives Assistant	Archivist (professional)	Library Assistant	Librarian (professional)	Total
Library of Congress	7	8	547	770	1,332
General Services Administration*	350	288	7	10	655
Army	36	9	411	666	1,122
Air Force	17	22	184	415	638
Navy	12	3	233	347	595
Veterans Administration	...	...	36	366	402
Health, Education, and Welfare	...	...	96	146	242
Commerce	35	2	48	95	180
Interior	...	2	57	75	134
Agriculture	1	...	72	62	135
Information Agency	...	...	7	60	67
State	8	...	9	19	36
Atomic Energy Commission	...	...	61	15	76
NASA	...	...	29	42	71
Justice	...	...	14	24	38
Smithsonian Institution	1	1	15	15	32
Government Printing Office	...	...	7	13	20
Labor	...	...	8	16	24
Housing and Home Finance Agency	...	...	6	16	22
Treasury	...	...	3	10	13
Federal Aviation Agency	...	...	8	12	20
Other agencies†	3	2	92	117	214
Total	470	337	1,950	3,311	6,068

* Includes National Archives.
† Excludes Board of Governors, Federal Reserve System, employees of Congress, CIA, and NSA.

duplication is minimized. Depending on the size of the library, there will be centralized or decentralized and specialized reference services that may include bibliographic compilation services. Finally there will be a circulation department which may include responsibility for binding operations.

The division of labor in these cases is mainly a question of size. The chief differences between the public libraries and the university and college libraries is that for the larger operations public libraries typically centralize acquisition and cataloging for all of their departments and branches, whereas in the university setting it is typical to have some parts of these functions decentralized. The trend to creating larger consolidated technical branches enhances this tendency.

The responsibility for selection and the operational procedures for acquisition of library materials varies immensely among the diverse cate-

gories and between sizes of libraries within those categories. It may be said that the library staffs are responsible for the selection of materials, and that this responsibility is shared in the case of college, university, and industrial libraries with the technical staffs who take an interest in seeing to it that the collections reflect their own information needs. Apart from these two categories, the public libraries and the larger libraries within the federal system depend on their staffs for selection. This may involve a rather large continuous effort as in the case of the Library of Congress which has assigned 125 of its personnel as selection officers.

It is fair to say that few libraries have effective means of knowing what they are acquiring in terms of the details of subject matter versus format versus what is already in the collection because much of the materials acquired are from standing exchange arrangements, blanket or serial subscription purchases, and automatic deposit.

In the case of industrial and government laboratory libraries, it is rare for there to be any formal or effective mechanism for the library staffs to be conversant with the research and development programs and to know in detail the resultant document requirements of the technical staffs. In the college and university libraries faculties have a formally recognized role in the selection of library materials. They take a more active interest in what is acquired in support of the teaching and research programs, resulting in better communication and feedback on the adequacy of the current acquisitions. Effectiveness of these mechanisms, however, is also obscured in view of what has been said with respect to automatic acquisition through exchange and deposits and the blanket purchase. For the larger research libraries, and certainly for the national libraries, there is an attitude that one cannot truly foresee with any precision what will be needed in the future, and so an attempt is made to collect as comprehensively as possible in all areas against the day when those materials may be needed.

Items acquired through purchase in libraries are obtained primarily from book and periodical dealers. The larger research libraries and national libraries may maintain several hundred dealers at home and abroad for purchase of back files of serials, out-of-print books, and current imprints.

Evans has reported that in the federal system of libraries an irrational situation exists in numerous agencies regarding library procurement. Special restrictions on the purchase of books and periodicals not required by federal law or regulation, and requirements for bidding procedures and contractual arrangements through competitive bid, have resulted in numerous inadequacies of service. These particularly involve delays in contracting and receiving publications, gaps in collections, and acceptance of contracts with low bidders incapable of providing adequate service. In the survey reported, only a fifth of the reference libraries reported that the library actually places its own orders for publications. These practices lead to delay. "It is evident that a considerable number of agency administrators do not regard rapid procurement of library materials as a matter of much interest" [3]. Nearly all the libraries report difficulties in obtaining proper and reliable acquisitions arrangements for the larger number of countries in the world.

These problems are particularly difficult with respect to the underdeveloped countries and the partly developed countries, as in Latin America, Africa, and the Far East. At the same time there is great redundancy in the use of the same dealers by different institutions. This indicates that some kind of centralized purchasing and acquisitions functions could be made effective at least for the major research libraries. The same may be said for exchange arrangements. There is an immense overlap in the agreements made by the research libraries with scholarly institutions, libraries, and other organizations at home and abroad.

The exchange arrangements within the federal system have been studied by COSATI, which recommended the following:

1. A program to encourage maximum use of information and data received from foreign sources should be started. This would call for better acquisition, translation, and dissemination among users in both public and private sectors.

2. A study should be made of the value of a clearinghouse for foreign scientific and technical information and data.

3. Steps should be taken to bring representatives of the intelligence community specializing in scientific and technical information together with people in other government, scientific, and technical activities with a view to studying relationships, coordinating needs, sharing data, reducing duplication, jointly using products, and planning for the future.

4. There is a need for a clear understanding of the role that the Department of State should play in the field of international data exchange.

5. Special attention should be given to a program of assistance for emerging countries with respect to scientific and technical information and data.

6. The need for a single agency responsible for coordinating international data exchange agreements should be determined. This study should ascertain the mechanisms and programs that have been undertaken to facilitate coordination, and the need for a coordinating group charged with a review of all agency programs involving international exchange.

Although there have been many changes in the details of cataloging practice, the traditions and basic principles in American libraries remain very much what they were in the early

part of the century. In the larger libraries of all types, cataloging operations are divided into descriptive cataloging and subject cataloging. Descriptive cataloging involves the bibliographic description for the physical item according to various standards of description and authorities that have been adopted very widely. Subject cataloging involves the assignment of subject headings for the catalog cards and the assignment of classification categories according to the system in use.

Figure 2-3 illustrates a simplified cataloging flow of a large research library, using the Library of Congress as an authority. Some idea of the complexity of processing operations may be seen in Figure 2-4, which presents a relatively simplified description of major activities related to the flow of materials through the Processing Department of the Library of Congress.

Most libraries in the United States use the Dewey Decimal Classification System. The Library of Congress Classification System is widely used for scholarly and industrial libraries, particularly for science and technology. The Library of Congress cards are commonly used by libraries of all kinds as authorities for descriptive cataloging. The Library of Congress card contains a Dewey as well as a Library of Congress classification number which may be adopted by the user libraries.

There are currently approximately 15,000 active subscribers to the Library of Congress card service or proof sheet service. In addition, the Library of Congress list of subject headings, which is published at broad intervals in book form and updated through a regular serial publication, provides a major authority for the development of subject descriptions for cataloged items in American libraries of all kinds. A similar authority for practice is found in the published schedules of Library of Congress classification and in the frequently revised editions of the decimal classification.

Comparable authorities for the practices within using libraries are provided by the National Library of Agriculture and the National Library of Medicine through their own published lists of subject headings, index vocabularies, and classification schemes. Throughout the country there has been a tendency for the larger research libraries to publish their card catalogs in book form for the benefit of their own scattered operations and cooperative ventures. The major book catalog production, of course, is that of the *National Union Catalog* which is published monthly and accumulated quarterly, annually, and at five-year intervals.

Another important book catalog resource for the nation's libraries is the Library of Congress five-year cumulation of its subject catalog. The *National Union Catalog*, contributed to by 700 to 800 libraries in the United States and Canada, arranges subjects alphabetically by main entry, that is, personal or corporate author. There is no subject catalog for the *National Union Catalog*. The importance of the *National Union Catalog* is primarily that it indicates the location of a book or other catalog bibliographic item in one or more libraries. Ordinarily an attempt is made to record the locations in several libraries located in different parts of the country. Yet some 40 per cent of the entries in the *National Union Catalog* appear attributed to only one library. That is, 40 per cent of book materials obtained throughout the country (in all fields) apparently are obtained only once.

The dependence of American libraries on the Library of Congress as an authority and source of information in cataloging tradition and practice is made less useful than it might otherwise be because the Library is unable to catalog materials and publish cards for the full range of materials now being collected, nor can they publish quickly enough to be of maximum service to libraries. With respect to coverage, we have testimony from our survey and other sources that most research libraries using the Library of Congress cards find that they are having to catalog independently 40 to 60 per cent of their inputs because cards are not available for these items or at least not available when they are needed.

For many libraries that do not use the Library of Congress Classification System and whose practices have grown up independently, the Library of Congress cards are even less useful. For example, Harvard University indicates that it can utilize only about 25 per cent of the Library of Congress cards. The same may be said for the New York Public Library so far as the Reference Department (the research library) is concerned.

The other point concerning cataloging practices is that although there is agreement on basic principles, in actuality there is considerable variation in results. Catalogers have different

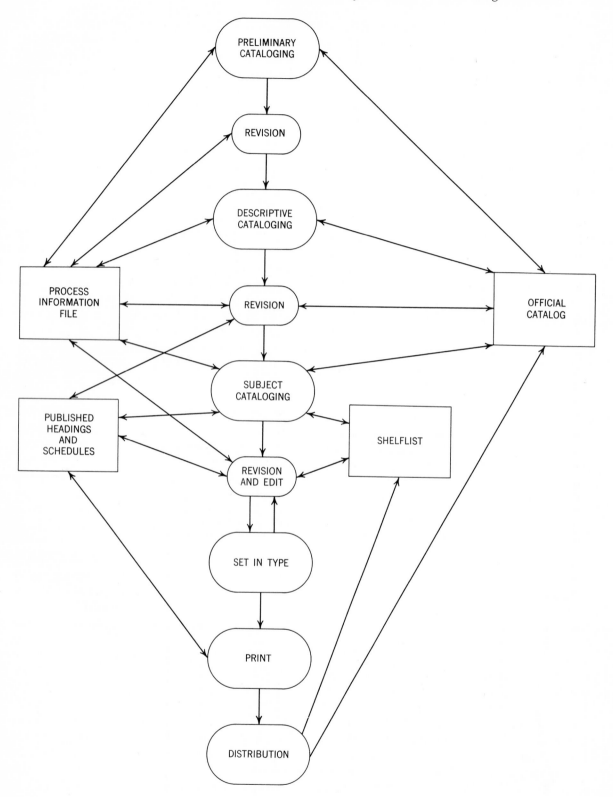

Fig. 2-3 Outline of cataloging process flow.

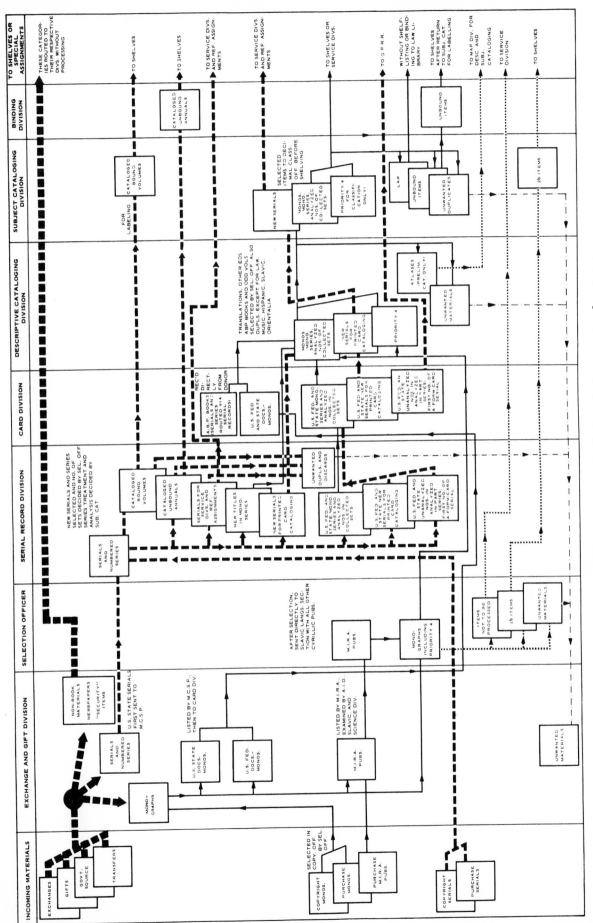

Fig. 2-4 Library of Congress flow of materials through the processing department.

outlooks as to the optimum ways of describing and accessing the library materials in their own collections. The best evidence for this is the *National Union Catalog* which exhibits a broad range of practice in descriptive cataloging. In subject cataloging there is an even wider variety of practices. In general there is no agreement on just what filing conventions are optimum.

Classification schemes tend to reflect the materials held by the library developing them rather than the newest knowledge in the field. For this reason classifications covering new knowledge generally favor highly specialized libraries. These find the general classification like that of the Library of Congress or the Dewey Decimal System inadequate and often expand their own system or invent new systems in their own particular field of knowledge. The difficulties with highly specialized classification schemes for relatively restricted subject matters is that, apart from compatibility problems, those areas dealt with that are marginal to the particular specialization are rarely treated with the same care [3].

The catalogs of a large research collection particularly become rather complicated in terms of filing conventions, and these differ widely from place to place. These factors interfere with the ability of users to use them effectively. There is also an associated problem of the obsolescence of subject descriptions and classification of subject matter. In the sciences this has proven very troublesome, and yet it is difficult to see how many libraries can afford, under the present circumstances, to adapt their files continuously to the changing nomenclature and associated perspectives of the advancing technology.

What has been said in the preceding paragraphs applies primarily to books and other materials traditionally subjected to the cataloging process by libraries. Ordinarily this does not include U. S. Government publications or serials for whose subject access the libraries depend on the GPO, professional societies, commercially published indexes, and abstract services. The same may be said for the report literature where, again, there is heavy dependence on the indexing and abstracting publications of the AEC, NASA, DDC, and CFSTI. The result of these operations is that material becomes segregated by format at the point of the cataloging operation. This means that related materials in the sciences and technologies which happen to be published as public documents, reports, serial articles, or in other specialized formats and microforms become segregated from each other and must be searched and accessed independently. Users must be familiar with an enormous range of index and catalog vocabularies and arrangements in order to make an effective search. Second, from library to library the practices of cataloging description and physical arrangement in catalogs and other special files is very different, creating another kind of obstacle.

This can be illustrated by the practices of various federal libraries. The Geological Survey Library, for example, has elaborated the classification of the Library of Congress for its own purposes. The Food and Drug Administration has developed a rather different system of vocabulary for describing its own area of subject responsibility than that used by the Library of Medicine for similar material. It has been reported that there are some 1800 current indexing and abstracting services offered throughout the world, each of which has a somewhat different practice of nomenclature and searching facilities. This variation of practice makes for relative incompatibility from one function to the next and creates difficulties in effecting any cross-disciplinary search. One reason for the growth of this diversity may lie in the fact that people who are engaged professionally in indexing and in cataloging have little or no contact with those who must use their products. There is relatively ineffective feedback on the utility of their tools from the user standpoint.

Another phenomenon that impedes the utility and convertibility of various systems of description is the growing backlog which forces many libraries to simplify their cataloging practice for many categories of input. This leads to an impaired access for the user. Part of these difficulties are associated with the order of magnitude changes in the workload for these predominantly manual systems. There is a serious question as to whether manual processes can be maintained much longer under the increasing workload and the complexity of organizing manual files for these purposes.

Among the most serious needs that are not being fulfilled within the library community today is that of maintaining a union list of serials. Union lists of serials have previously been supported mainly on a cooperative basis. The size of the tasks involved, however, has

caused most efforts virtually to dwindle away. There is an immense need for locating serial runs in many locations, because few libraries have complete runs of a wide range of serial publications. This is not confined to older materials; the spotty collection of current foreign serial and other publications in the science and technologies is an enduring problem for location and access.

Scientific and technical reference or bibliographic demands on libraries is a function of user population, size, and type of library. Apart from a dozen or so of the largest organizations, public libraries have little specialized reference or bibliographic compilation service in these subject areas. The exceptions, such as the New York Public, John Crerar, and Linda Hall libraries, offer services comparable to those found anywhere. Special libraries maintain effective specialized services but must depend on the larger research libraries for knowledge of and access to a wide range of important literature. The academic research libraries and national libraries provide major reference services for the nation but cannot offer completely effective service to distant users.

Luther Evans reports that the Brookings survey indicated few federal reference libraries have sufficient resources to render the kind of reference services standard in our best libraries. Of 212 responding libraries only 24 per cent prepared abstracts and only 15 per cent compiled legislative histories of statutes of interest to the agencies. Very little professional work, such as preparation of research reports and advice to experts about the state of knowledge in the field, is undertaken in average departmental libraries.

Even in the larger research libraries, providing effective and efficient reference service offers many difficulties. These result in great part from the different treatments accorded books, serials, public documents, reports, etc., already described in the discussion on cataloging. An additional difficulty is that few people outside the library profession know how to make maximum use of the library. They rarely are equipped to use the card catalog or other indexes to the library efficiently, and they do not fully understand how to use or even to locate bibliographies, periodical indexes, abstracts, and many other aids to document research. It is also true that most library users do not fully appreciate that some skill and intellectual labor are required for an effective search of library tools. For illustration, Figure 2-5 presents a simplified overview

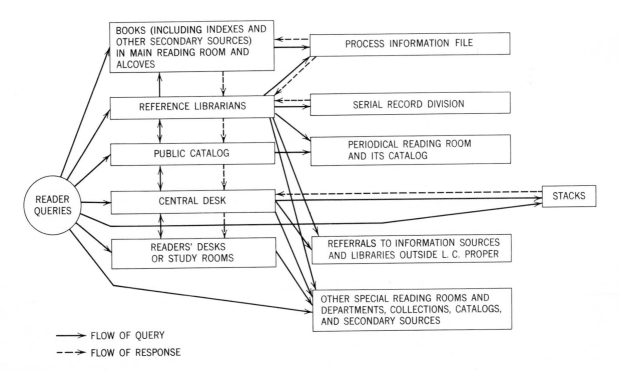

Fig. 2-5   Some steps in typical paths for reader queries.

of typical paths for reader queries in the Library of Congress indicating the major flows and the multiple sources to which a reader may have to go for service. This kind of pattern is replicated in most large research libraries. Figures 2-6 and 2-7 illustrate the logical sequence of decisions that must be made for the simplest kind of search in a catalog—a search for a known author. A complete outline of the variety of decisions that must be made for subject searching would be a much more complex matter because of the net of references and cross references within a large catalog for subject names of related or subordinate subjects. A great deal needs to be done to educate users in the effective use of catalogs and other library reference materials.

In the federal sector, as reported by the Brookings survey [3], only a few federal libraries have sufficiently qualified staffs to provide comprehensive bibliographic services, including literature searches, abstracting, translations, reviews, summaries, and syntheses of special subject literature. The survey attributes this primarily to the inability of librarians to convince budget officers or Congress that such services are a necessity and not a luxury. One of the most common and recurrent problems is that of locating an accessible copy of a known document not in one's own collection. This is due to inadequate or completely lacking tools for referral. The printed *National Union Catalog* covers only material acquired since 1952. The various broad and specialized union lists of serials are grossly inadequate. There is no union list or other comprehensive key to the location of public documents and scientific and technical reports.

It has been said that the size of collections in libraries tends to double every fifteen years. There is some evidence that the doubling time for science and technology is less. The provision of adequate storage facilities is a continuing problem for every category of library. This reflects the planning and funding for appropriate facilities and a very general policy that libraries will maintain indefinitely all literary materials collected. Relatively little attention has been given to weeding and purging collections regularly except under "emergency" conditions of exhausted storage space. The overwhelming preponderance of materials stored and circulated within libraries today is in full-size hard copy

format rather than microforms. The storage, access, and circulation of the materials imposes a heavy material-handling and record-keeping load on all but the smallest of libraries. Under the widespread conditions of inadequate support few libraries afford regular or ongoing inventories for the identification of lost or misplaced items. This leads to impaired accessibility, particularly for those materials most heavily in demand.

The definition of who is a qualified user of libraries, what services are to be offered with respect to circulation, interlibrary loan, and reproduction facilities is extremely variable both in the private and federal sectors. There is very little coordinated policy on these matters in the federal sector; each organization makes its own rules. The same may be said for other libraries. The effectiveness of the cooperative interlibrary loan arrangement has tended to dwindle in recent years, partly because of the advent of the Xerox 914 or similar machines providing inexpensive copies readily, and partly because of the limited ability of libraries everywhere to serve their immediate publics. These factors combine to diminish the ability of a distant user or small library to be served effectively by the large research and federal libraries.

It is rare for any library to keep detailed circulation records that clearly identify the user and what has been used for the guidance of acquisitions and reference functions. Rather, statistics are gathered for operational and budget support purposes and are characteristically recorded by broad category of user and, sporadically, by classification number. Because there is no general requirement for regular purging or relegation to distant stores, there is seldom any mechanism in operation for identification of rarely used materials.

A rather serious paper deterioration problem affects all libraries of large size. It has been estimated that 40 per cent of the books, periodicals, documents, and reports printed before 1939 are likely to deteriorate within another twenty years to the point of being unusable. The libraries of the country generally cannot afford to microfilm or deacidify the collections they hold, and as yet there is no national policy or support for such enterprises.

The application of automation, specialized equipment, and data-processing techniques and equipment to libraries has been limited. Data-processing applications so far have been confined

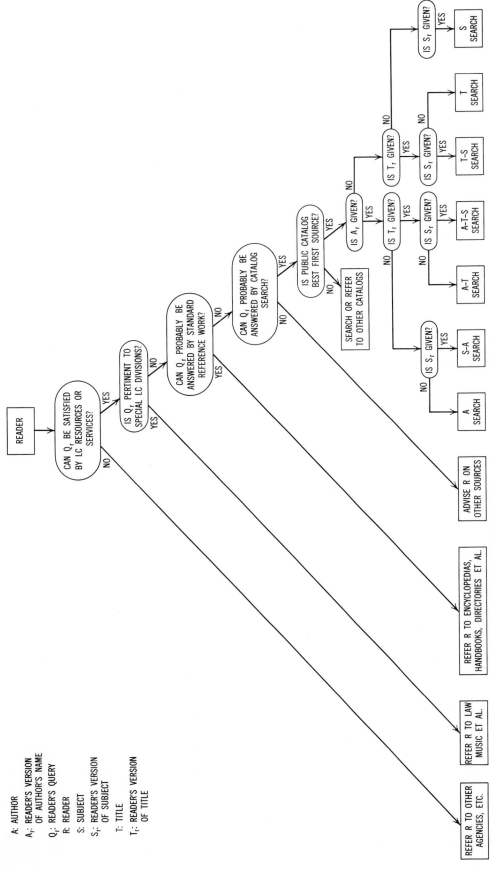

Fig. 2-6 Outline of query analysis and initial catalog search decisions.

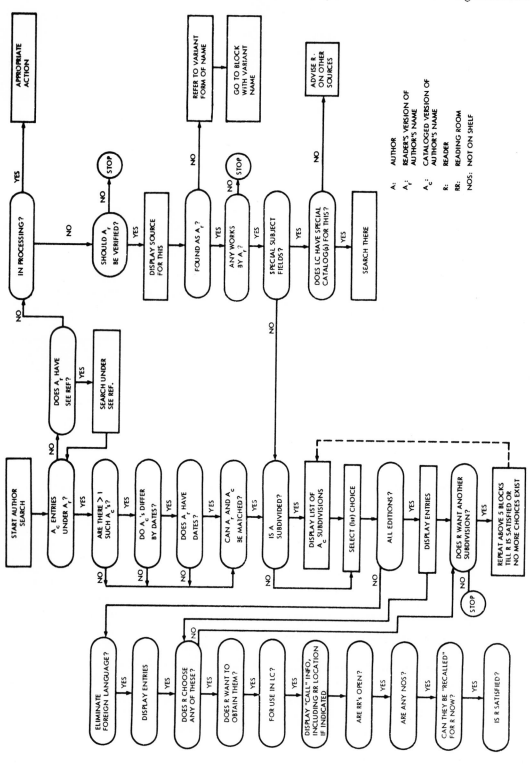

Fig. 2-7 Outline of author search decisions.

primarily to support of technical processes and circulation records. There are exceptions to this, particularly the National Library of Medicine, but in general libraries have just begun to use punched card equipment and only occasionally have been able to make use of computer machinery. Although use of reproduction facilities has increased greatly, microforms still are a very small part of most library operations. There is considerable resistance to the use of microforms by the public primarily because the readers and printers are of relatively low quality. Very little specialized communication equipment is used in libraries. The telephone is still the most useful and prevalent form of electronic communications. Many plans and studies are underway, however, for the application of advanced technology to library processes. The past three years have seen many changes, particularly in the federal system of libraries. The chief obstacle to these applications has been the lack of adequately skilled and trained individuals experienced both in the requirements of library operations and in the computing art. A second, but perhaps equally important, obstacle is that no wholly satisfactory application of data-processing machinery to many library operations has yet been developed.

Information Analysis Centers

There are more than 300 information analysis centers* in the federal sector and as many if not more in the private sector. These organizations perform specific, special-purpose analytical tasks. Typical products of information centers are analytical reports written by subject area specialists in the center's staff and specially manipulated data summary reports prepared through manual or automated procedures by the information center.

The recent growth of information centers has resulted from the apparent inability of conventional library systems to service the needs of the user groups. Information centers differ from libraries in three basic characteristics:

1. Active acquisition of documents judged to be relevant to the mission of the users.

2. Limited subject fields allowing greater depths in the indexing vocabulary for more specialized searches and exploitation.

3. Rapid response to the user needs both in terms of updating the collection being exploited and in terms of providing mission-oriented services.

A number of definitions have been suggested for the information analysis or evaluation center, all sharing the general requirements that the goal of processing in such a center is a synthesis of articles, books, and reports covering a specified fields. In some cases the syntheses include critical or substantive reviews of the literature being compiled and synthesized. Information analysis centers vary in such detail as administration, funding, parent organization structure, and other administrative and financial details. Some of them are supported by more than one federal agency, whereas others are supported by a single federal agency that desires to have a special-purpose analytical function performed by a separate subordinate organization. Other basically private industry information centers subsist mainly on federal government grants that are applied toward government-oriented analytical research. Still others are supported by industrial groups.

Information analysis centers typically acquire several forms of input. A library is frequently a portion of an information center, and it supplies the scientific and technical documents for information center staff members. Its holdings include books, journals, and published and unpublished technical reports. The library tends to be specialized, concentrating on the areas of concern to the center. Common input to information centers is raw or semiprocessed data. This is often in nonwritten form and consists of physical materials—graphic charts, paper and tape recordings, and other basic or semifinished data media. A third form of input is a verbal, characterized by conferences among information center staff members, informal private analytical and laboratory notations, and consultitions with members of similar information centers and subject area specialists. Input data, whether part of the center's store or specially collected, form the raw material from which the analyses proceed. Much of the research is substantively academic, involving intellectual analysis, laboratory experimentation, use of standard reference

---

* The terms information center, information analysis center, and information evaluation center are here used interchangeably. An information center that does not evaluate and/or analyze is a reference center, collection, or library.

works, and, sometimes, use of automated and machine techniques for data and material processing.

Document-handling functions at the information analysis centers differ from most of the other classes of organizations reviewed in this book. Collection efforts tend to be specialized and the cataloging, indexing, and other control procedures within the libraries often tend to be specialized because of the complex, highly technical, and diverse formats of the data stored. The typical data store consists in part of raw or partially processed physical material or nondocumentary representations of scientific input data. Storage, processing, retrieval, loan and exchange, and other handling of such data is special and does not typically follow library procedures. In general, information centers are only minimally machine supported. Machine support is most probable in an organization processing and exploiting a large literature data base.

Requests for services for information centers usually are conducted on a restricted basis. Requesting individuals or organizations must often be authorized to use the services. Other restrictions such as technical competence often are imposed. This is dictated by the high priority of analytical tasks forming the basic operation of the information center, which can be diluted through operation on nonspecific or nonessential analytic operations. High costs of the analyses also may impose restrictions.

Outputs of information centers typically are written analytical reports or the collations of data in a summary fashion. These outputs frequently are unscheduled reports in response to special requests. They may or may not be published technical reports. Outputs have included state-of-the-art reviews and publication of a journal covering reliability techniques. Some information centers produce announcements and other indicative media summarizing their production over a given period of time, but more often a current awareness listing of center holdings and a limited listing of newly produced reports are sent to users of the information center. The centers normally do not widely disseminate announcements or journals concerning their production.

The activities of the information centers in the federal sector tend to serve a specialized field of interest rather than a prescribed user group. The output therefore is not tailored to a user expression of need but rather to the generalized mission of comprehensive analysis and need. In contrast private information centers tend to be more directly user oriented. Among the information centers operated by private organizations may be cited the Smith, Kline, and French (SKF) Laboratories. Like many of the drug, chemical, and petroleum industry organizations, SKF Laboratories has determined that commercial competition is enhanced by adequate internal information services. Fruitful laboratory activities require preliminary literature search providing as many clues as possible to the potential value of the anticipated research or development. Not only must the literature be searched but analyses must be made by specialists. The staff of information evaluation centers is predominantly scientifically trained and in some cases alternates between the information center activities and the laboratory environment. In such companies the information specialist is a member of the project team and contributes to the technical execution of the project. The individual is assumed to be responsible for bringing to the attention of team members new concepts, techniques, competitive research, and products, as well as for preparing syntheses and special literature searches on request.

The output product of such an information center is tailored to limited needs and is not printed in quantity. It is distributed to recipients known to the center. Subsequent announcement and broad distribution are not ordinarily accomplished.

Among the more ambitious nonfederal "information center" plans now being considered is that of the Engineers Joint Council. As part of the EJC "Action Plan"—which involves descriptive abstracting and, where possible, role-and-link indexing prepared as much as possible by the source author—an information communication network under the aegis of the Engineers Joint Council is planned.

The configuration of such a system involves the aggregation of technical papers in a document storage and dissemination facility that would form the core of what is called "Information Central." Papers and reports distributed to specialized information evaluation centers for the production of special information products also provide an input to Information Central. To make access to the contents of Information

Central, the individual engineer seeks the assistance of his local or company library, which transfers his request for information through a regional switching center either to Information Central or to an appropriate subject specialist consultant. The regional network switching center is to perform referral functions based on its capability to interface between local and company libraries, Information Central, and the specialist consultants.

Implementation of the notion will involve extensive coordination among the individual companies who are potential users of the Information Central service. Information Central is to be equipped to offer printed and machine-readable indexes to engineering literature, lending and copy services for books and documents, automatic searching, bibliography preparation, selective announcement services for individual engineers, and referral service.

In the federal sector may be found the fifteen information data centers supported wholly or partially by the AEC. The Department of Commerce operates three data centers in the Coast and Geodetic Survey and, through the National Standards Reference Data Center, supports data evaluation activities at universities. Department of Defense maintains a comprehensive catalog of the approximately 300 data and information centers in DOD. Among the larger ones (for which direct costing can be obtained) are:

Defense Atomic Support Agency Data Center, in Santa Barbara.

Ceramic and Graphite Information Center, at the Air Force Materials Laboratory.

Thermophysical Properties Research Center, at Purdue University.

Defense Metals Information Center, at Battelle Memorial Institute.

Shock and Vibration Information Center, at the Naval Research Laboratory in Washington.

Counterinsurgency Information and Analysis Center, at the American University.

Human Engineering Information and Analysis Service, at Tufts University.

Military Entomology Service, at Walter Reed Medical Center.

Coastal Engineering Information and Evaluation Center.

Plastics Technical Evaluation Center.

The Department of Health, Education, and Welfare estimates that it supports more than fifty information evaluation centers. The majority of these are operated internally and range from a single individual to organizations with extensive bibliographic resources. The subject matter covered ranges from techniques of solid waste disposal to enteric phage typing. The Food and Drug Administration is setting up a comprehensive, machine-oriented information analysis system.

In the Department of the Interior, the activity of information analysis is not considered to be separated from the responsibilities of the technical and scientific staff. No organization considered to bear the title of "information evaluation service" is operated, but such activities are recognized to be performed. Publication of the results of any sort of literature analysis constitutes new reports entered into the conventional documentation system. The National Aeronautics and Space Administration supports seven information evaluation centers in addition to the comparable activities conducted by NASA research centers to provide information evaluation and analysis as service to the technical staff.

In general, the federal system has not evidenced as sophisticated a use of the information center or the application of as high a concentration of scientifically trained personnel as SKF or that being planned by the EJC. This in part is due to the more generalized mission of the federal centers.

Publication, Announcement, and Distribution Organizations

In S&T documentation an organization more often than not provides more than one service. Thus an organization categorized as a "library" could be categorized as a "publisher" when its services encompass preparation of major abstracting and indexing journals as do those of the National Agricultural Library and the National Library of Medicine. With respect to the functional categories previously established there exists a group of organizations that collectively are concerned with publication, announcement, and distribution of S&T documentation. These organizations are distinctive in that the services they offer are designed for the express purpose of widespread dissemination of information. Thus journal publishers usually accept manuscripts from any competent author and, space permitting, publish his material which is then publicly available. Distribution agencies

receive published materials of all sorts from a diversity of sources and announce and/or distribute the materials. Announcement agencies provide secondary representations of materials that usually were published elsewhere. In summary these organizations perform any combination of one or more of the following services: abstracting, indexing, copying, publishing, announcing, and disseminating materials they acquire.

This section describes a number of organizations visited during the course of the study which emphasize or wholly direct their efforts toward publishing, announcing, and distributing S&T documents. Both primary and secondary publications are considered. Table 2-7 indicates the categorization (neither paradigmatic nor mutually exclusive) used here and the most noteworthy features of the information activities described.

Table 2-7 Publication, Announcement, and Distribution Organizations and Their Characteristics

Publication Organizations

Association for Computing Machinery. Classified review journal, annual author permuted title indexes; development of integrated ADP system for acquisitions and reviewers' records.
American Chemical Society. Overall design plan for journal coverage, including staff-prepared technical news magazine; announcement and distribution of unpublished papers; research in photocomposition.
American Institute of Physics. Publication of cover-to-cover translated Russian physics journals; research in indexing and photocomposition.

Announcement Organizations

Engineering Index, Inc., and the *American Society for Metals.* Computer-based indexing pilot; role and link indexing; abstract text on perforated tape only for journal and catalog card publication convenience.
Chemical Abstracts Service. Permuted title index; computer-based system for literature of compounds acting on biological systems; magnetic tapes for both available with search program to subscribers; computer-based chemical compound registry being implemented; sequential card camera for indexes to *Chemical Abstracts.*
Biological Sciences Information Services. Four different computer-based indexing systems; computer-based acquisitions records pilot system; microfilm file of one-half million abstracts for use in experiment of direct (dataphone) service to individual researchers.

Table 2-7 (Continued)

American Petroleum Institute. Computer-based indexing system; "inverted" or "news story" abstract style; indexes and abstracts on magnetic tape by subscription (includes search and input programs); training courses for users; machine-produced "dual dictionary" for manual coordinate index search.
Society of Automotive Engineers. Extensive announcement and distribution of papers not published; elaborate papers' evaluation scheme; computer-based indexing system; guide to preparation of papers; market and user satisfaction studies.
Atomic Energy Commission. Comprehensive technical communication programs; processing essentially manual but based on superior business systems and procedures (flow and forms); experimentation with computer-based keyword index and with selective dissemination; sequential card camera index, EAM support for sorting index cards.
National Aeronautics and Space Administration. Extensive computer support in comprehensive indexing, journal production, and selective dissemination system; private organization operation of report literature processing; support to American Institute of Aeronautics and Astronautics for handling open literature; magnetic tape and search programs to be distributed for local search and selective dissemination of reports.
Cambridge Communications Corporation. Indexing avoided by elaborately hierarchical arrangement of abstracts; given text printed in full under alternate classifications if appropriate; looseleaf publication.
McGraw-Hill. Computer-based photocomposition system for directories and indexes; manual selective dissemination system for construction industry.

Distribution Organizations

Government Printing Office. Depository system; Linofilm photocomposition systems; experimentation with Linotron, computer-based photocomposition system.
Defense Documentation Center. Computer-based indexing and abstract file for 750,000 document titles in microform; abstract text output in response to computer search.
Clearinghouse for Federal Scientific and Technical Information. Pool of unclassified report literature offered for public sale; translations announcement journal; supporting development of government-wide reports index; abstracts text on perforated tape can be merged into DDC system.

Publication Organizations. Organizations whose primary mission is publication of a scientific or technical journal include the professional societies, trade associations, and commercial publishers. State and federal agencies and universities also

contribute to the serial population. Influential in this aspect of scientific communication has been the NSF's OSIS, which supports establishment of journals for fields not adequately served.

Estimates of the worldwide population of active serials in science and technology range between 22,000 and 35,000.* Of the 6200 journals published in the United States, 3470 are categorized as "technology," 1430 as "agriculture," 800 as "medicine," and 500 as "natural and physical sciences."

A 1963 study of a sample of some 211 journals in the United States indicates that the most common publication frequency for serials is quarterly. Circulation averages 4400 copies. On the average each of the sources sampled publishes close to 1000 pages (exclusive of advertising) annually, each page averaging 600 words. Fewer than half of the journals in the sample publish an abstract or synopsis with each paper. Approximately 30 per cent publish no abstracts or synopses. Of the abstracts published, 90 per cent are prepared by authors; half of these are not subjected to editorial control by the journal editor. Approximately 65 per cent of the journals publishing abstracts submit them directly and automatically to an abstracting service or journal. About 90 per cent of the journals sampled publish an annual author index, and 75 per cent publish annual subject indexes. Only 40 per cent of these journals publish cumulative indexes. Journals generally are printed on letterpress, although offset printing from typeset or typewritten copy also is employed. Journal publication cost averages about $0.075 per word. Use is estimated at an average of 100 readers per article.

In addition to the support by NSF in the study of the population of serial literature, individual societies and federations of societies study the population within their fields. As an example the Biological Sciences Communication Project of George Washington University has conducted a study of the characteristics of the literature of pediatrics. In this field 56 of the world total of 293 serials are produced in the United States. This constitutes the largest number for any individual country of origin. Of the 293, however, 101 are printed in the English language. In an additional five of the 293 journals, English is a secondary language. Quarterly

issuance predominates in serial literature of pediatrics, followed closely by monthly issuance.

The study of pediatric literature also indicated some of the duplication in coverage evidenced in other studies. For example, 28 of the serials are covered both by *Biological Abstracts* and by one or more other abstracting services; 38 are covered by *Chemical Abstracts* and by one or more other abstracting and indexing services; and 66 are covered by *Index Medicus* and one or more other services. *Excerpta Medica* covers 19 of the population which are covered by no other abstracting or indexing service. This particular study concluded that no one abstracting or indexing service covers more than 20 per cent of the population of the pediatrics serials and that therefore the desirability of a pediatrics abstract service should be studied.

The interface between the journal publication subsystem and the remainder of the S&T document network is that of the journal editor with contributors of articles and reviewers or referees. The journals can seldom be considered to have an interface—that is in the bilateral sense—with a user except to the extent that a user may consider the contents of the journal to be a principal motivation for remaining a member of the society producing the journal. A study of this sort of motivation of the recipients of journals is outside the scope of the description of this system; however, it cannot be ignored in terms of evaluating the source of lag between the needs or desires of the user and the techniques employed for the production of journals.

Journal publication policies of the American Chemical Society (ACS), for example, are oriented toward the article producer rather than the article user. This policy does not preclude experimentation by ACS with techniques for better serving the user. In any situation in which a conflict arises between the interests of user and the interests of contributor, however, the interests of contributor are the primary determinant of the policy. For example, when *Chemical and Engineering News* demonstrated that an authoritative, timely magazine format containing news of chemistry in sufficient detail to appeal to the entire membership of the American Chemical Society could be produced, ACS found itself constrained from including information that had not already been announced in a scholarly journal. That is, the demands of the contributor for prestige publication at the expense

* More detailed information about the world's serial publications may be found in Appendix 2.

of rapid dissemination were admitted. The situation does not seem atypical although few societies have been able to conduct as decisive an experiment in this factor as has ACS.

In contrast with the publisher of scholarly journals, the commercial publisher has the principal goal of developing an advertising medium of sufficient stature to attract the readers who may be considered appropriate potential customers for the products of his advertisers. For this reason commercial publishers demonstrate little interest in further expansion of responsibilities in S&T communication. Despite the volume of publication in science and technology, an organization such as McGraw-Hill remains conservative in attitudes toward experimentation and adoption of unconventional publishing techniques. Among the organizations contacted during the present study, two professional societies, American Chemical Society and the American Institute of Physics, are discussed in terms of primary or journal publication in that each is actively exploring unconventional media and techniques. Several of the federal agencies contacted are also primary publishers; e.g., the AEC publishes four technical review serials. Clearly the mission of the Government Printing Office is publication, but its characteristics are discussed in terms of a distribution mission. The one commercial publisher contacted during the study, McGraw-Hill, is discussed in terms of the announcement mission.

Comparatively typical of conventional publication activity is that of the Association for Computing Machinery centering around a quarterly *Journal of the ACM* and the monthly *Communications of the ACM*. A bimonthly review journal is published which is organized according to an hierarchical classification of the material considered to constitute the field. The organization of *Computing Reviews,* the cross references between sections, and the citation of a review under an average of one section in addition to that under which the review is printed had been considered a substitute for subject indexing. An author index and permuted title index are published annually. (Indexes for 1960–1963 have been published cumulatively.)

Machine support is being introduced into publications activities of the ACM. In addition to machine production of indexes for *Computing Reviews* (which is scheduled for monthly publication in the near future), the ACM is designing

an integrated system, scheduled for early 1966 implementation, providing for a single keyboarding of citation data as the basis for acquisitions processing, reviewer assignment, and followup. The *Reviews* covers approximately 2300 items per year, of which half are derived from some 250 serials obtained essentially through exchange; one fourth are books; and one fourth reports literature. Consideration is being given to expansion of the publication activity through introduction of a biweekly tabloid news style bulletin describing comparatively machine-independent applications of computer technology. ACM is introducing a reprint service, oriented toward items difficult to obtain, in conjunction with a repository established at the University of Pennsylvania.

The American Chemical Society (ACS) publishes 17 journals, exclusive of the activities of Chemical Abstracts Service. The publications group consists of 188 regular and contractural employees, 75 per cent of whom are professionally trained in chemistry. The total operating budget for the organization exceeded $6 million for 1964 and it is estimated to be just under $6.8 million for 1965.

Of the 17 journals published under the auspices of the ACS, one is prepared entirely by ACS personnel: *Chemical and Engineering News* (*C&EN*), a subscription to which is part of the membership dues in the ACS. Other publications are sold on the basis of individual subscription. A weekly news magazine, *C&EN* has a circulation of 115,000 and maintains field staffs in London, Tokyo, Frankfurt, and eight cities in the United States. ACS publishes annually an average of six volumes of the "Advances in Chemistry" series. The ACS publishes a review journal and is considering establishment of a journal of briefer reviews than have been provided in *Chemical Reviews*. The ACS is devoting a considerable effort to tailoring these various publications to particular audiences and has recently redesigned *Industrial and Engineering Chemistry* (*I&EC*) to produce a monthly somewhat newsy journal and three quarterly research journals.

Among the services that illustrate ACS efforts at unconventional pulication are the manuscript announcements in *I&EC*. With the consent of the author of a manuscript, an abstract is published in the *I&EC* before acceptance of the article for publication in any of the journals of

the ACS. An unedited, unreviewed copy is offered for sale through a coupon service—as a "private communication" from author to requestor. About 300 summaries are published each year, and about 3000 orders are placed for copies of manuscripts so announced. Most printing of ACS journals is done by rotary web-fed methods. Composition for journals and other publications amounts to some 40,000 pages per year. Special symbols, a good deal of tabular material, mathematical formulas, and chemical structures add to the complexity of composition for this field.

The American Institute of Physics (AIP) is noteworthy in its publication activities to the extent that its publishes cover-to-cover translations of eight Russian journals. The AIP and its member societies publish some 19 journals, each of which has its own editor and referees and submits manuscripts to AIP. A staff of 30 publishes and distributes the copies. Abstracts are required for all articles except short notes and letters. Copies of abstracts to be published are airmailed to *Physics Abstracts* and other secondary journals, such as *Chemical Abstracts* and *Nuclear Science Abstracts*. The translation journals are self-supporting, although their initiation has often been supported by the National Science Foundation. The budget for English-language publications is approximately $3 million annually and for translation journals, $500,000.

The AIP is particularly active in research in documentation techniques. One study, centered on 2000 physicists, resulted in the development of forms to help authors index papers before publication. The usefulness of these forms to indexers of varying ranges of experience is being studied. Preliminary findings indicate that the form is most valuable to the indexer who least understands the content of the paper. Other applications of the form by editors may be in suggesting title revisions, providing copy for composing microabstracts, checking on the content of an abstract prepared by an author, and providing the basis for synthesizing a "pseudo-index."

AIP has also conducted some experiments in citation indexing and bibliographic coupling.* Test results of the value of the citation index were inconclusive.

*Techniques for inferring relatedness of documents by common "predecessor" citations.

Announcement Organizations. **Organizations** whose primary mission is reannouncement of report and open literature may also be found among professional societies, trade association, federal agencies, and commercial services. Of the small sample of each category contacted during this study, a few generalizations may be made concerning characteristics of the products of each sponsoring category.

Professional societies traditionally are committed to discipline orientation; their abstracting and indexing services appear to be moving away from published announcement/retrieval tools toward centralized, custom services. That is, growth of literature in a discipline results in:

1. Inadequate coverage by the abstracting service whose income growth does not match the literature growth;

2. Development of a tool whose physical size defeats the goal of alerting users in favor of the goal of retrospective search; or

3. Fragmentation into multiple tools which reduces opportunities for casual or unplanned cross-disciplinary access and imposes additional costs to maintain the viability of the fragmentation.

In attempting to serve both purposes—announcement and retrieval support—the abstracting indexing service must trade off analysis cost and time. As the announcement function is subordinated, the requirement for publication is questionable. Alternatives are operation of a single central reference service or distribution of machine-searchable tools.

Abstracting and indexing services by sponsors other than professional societies are not subject to the same constraints. Fragmentation oriented toward a work mission is more clearly definable than is discipline fragmentation, and organizations and individuals constituting the user group more readily identifiable. The products of such services are marketable in terms of more direct application. The implications of this characteristic to the trade association is exemplified by the support of a central service for processing a core body of literature useful to all members of a given industry and fewer constraints on the format of the product (in contrast to the conservatism of scholarly, discipline-oriented services toward study of changes in communication techniques).

Among federal agencies offering announcement

services, mission orientation has encouraged experimentation in selective dissemination—a technique exploited for some twenty years by at least one commercial organization.

As an outgrowth of the work of the Engineers Joint Council in developing a thesaurus that might be the core vocabulary for families of announcement services and retrieval systems, the American Society for Metals and IBM entered into a cooperative arrangement with Engineering Index, Inc., to develop a machine-based system. The indexing technique is based on selecting substantive terms, which are part of the prescribed vocabulary, in sufficient number to ensure that retrieval on some combination elicits relatively highly relevant items from a file. The responsibility of EI in this overall program has been the development of a translator program for transforming the information entered on a work sheet by information analysts into the format appropriate for processing for the retrieval system. The personnel at ASM are developing the system for publishing the subject heading and author indexes to the *Review of Metal Literature* and to the *Engineering Index.* The *Review of Metal Literature* covers scientific, engineering, and technical literature concerned with the production, properties, fabrication, and applications of metals, alloys, and compounds. The abstract section consists of conventional abstracts arranged in 20 principal categories. The subject index printed in the copy of the abstract journal and the author index are prepared by a computer program and constitute computer printer listings photoreduced in a two-column layout. The principal side head or subject is overprinted for higher readability and titles are indented.

Engineering Index, Inc., is a nonprofit corporation whose president is also the director of the Engineering Societies Library. Thus the *Engineering Index* has close ties to the Engineering Societies Library and to the managerial control and advice of the United Engineering Trustees, Inc. It is through the mechanism of the United Engineering Trustees, as operators of the headquarters building in New York, where the secretariats for many of the engineering societies are housed, that the operations of the Engineering Societies Library is funded. *Engineering Index* included 47,000 abstracts during 1964 and exploits some 2000 titles, a selected group of government reports, standards issued by member societies, and conference and industrial reports not otherwise covered in open literature. The staff of 67 is approximately one-half professional personnel and one-half clerical. Most of the input materials for the *Engineering Index* are supplied through the Engineering Societies Library and directly from the member societies. An average of 1250 articles are abstracted and indexed per month. For two major sections—the Electrical/Electronics Section and the Plastics Section—abstracts and descriptor terms are prepared on special work sheets for use in the machine-based system. The abstract copy is prepared for pasteup in page layouts, photographic reduction, and plate making. The information written on work sheets is punched into tab cards. Each class of information bears a unique data class sorting number and the sort programs are run against these decks and against the source deck for development of the index.

After the resolution of discrepancies and errors, the updated index tape is listed for manual pasteup. The program is also being developed for writing a tape in which the two-column format can be assembled directly by the computer system to minimize manual handling in pasteup. The programs now under way provide an index in which the full title is printed under the term from the vocabulary. Formerly a program was investigated in which the abstract identification number was printed following the term. Such an index was prepared for the Society of Photographic Scientists and Engineers for the abstract journal for photographic science and engineering literature.

Abstracts for the material separately being handled in the experimental system based on fragmenting the electrical/electronics and plastics sections for machine processing are also published in the basic *Engineering Index* to avoid discontinuity should the experiment fail to develop to full maturity. The organization estimates that basic abstracting costs average $12 per item. For the materials being developed in the experiment, including the machine and program development costs, the item costing is between $40 and $45.

Chemical Abstracts Service (CAS) prepares several tools for the announcement and retrieval of chemical literature. The basic publication is *Chemical Abstracts* (*CA*), issued biweekly and encompassing 200,000 abstracts in 1965. It

includes material from some 10,000 journal titles from more than 100 countries and patents from 24 countries. CAS covers 95 to 97 per cent of the published literature in chemistry. Through the variety of tools produced, CAS skirts the trade-off between announcement and retrieval functions, but not without substantial investment. *CA* is fragmented, consisting of five parts, each dealing with a basic area of chemistry. A microfilm version of *Chemical Abstracts* from 1907 to the latest semiannual compilation is available.

In general, items are selected for analysis at Chemical Abstracts Service and are assigned to abstractors who are essentially volunteers working in the field of chemistry. The abstractor returns copy for the abstract, accompanied by keywords used in the issue of *CA* in which the abstract appears. Entries for the cumulative subject indexes are prepared at CAS by reanalyzing the abstract to develop a clause type index entry, sometimes called a "microabstract." The index prepared through the secondary analysis is a superior retrieval tool to the keyword index available with individual issues of the abstract journal.

Separately, the titles for articles selected for analysis are keypunched and read onto magnetic tape for development of permuted keyword-in-context (KWIC) indexes. Eighty thousand titles were published in 1964 in *Chemical Titles* (*CT*). *CT* is issued biweekly and provides for announcement of the paper prior to the appearance of its abstract in *CA*. *CT* is available on magnetic tape, enabling subscribers to perform searchers in their own facilities. CAS is also investigating the possibility of using these tapes for selective dissemination of announcements.

More than 3000 abstractors contribute to *CA* and some 100 section editors examine the constituents of the sections before publication. CAS has approximately 650 full-time staff members. Abstracts received from external abstractors are edited locally, keywords are checked, and the text is keystroked on electric typewriters for conventional publication production. Because the individual abstract issue is indexed only by the six (average) keywords supplied by the abstractor, the source item and abstract are subsequently provided to subject indexers who create six or seven entries which are dictated on tape recorders, then transcribed by typists on index slips. Subject clause index slips and any appropriate formula indexing entries, produced separately through checking the registry, are manually filed in order, awaiting subsequent typing on cards used in sequential card camera production of the cumulative indexes. Structural formula graphics are stripped into negatives of the indexes. The indexes are cumulative and issued semiannually as an author index, subject index, and the formula index. Each of these, plus the patent numbers index, is cumulatively published every five years.

Bibliographic data for papers cited in *CA* are punched, along with the name of the abstractor and the number of lines of abstract printed, to analyze: (a) the productivity of each of the journal titles; (b) the average length of abstract and the number of abstracts per section; (c) the completeness of coverage in terms of the introduction of material from journals previously not scanned, in terms of discontinuation of journals, and in terms of loss of individual articles or journals; and (d) for vocabulary investigation, by section, in conjunction with the section editor to ensure the viability of the individual section in terms of changes in the field covered by that section. The general system is called the Coden-based inventory, which is accumulated at the rate of approximately 700–800 abstract records per day. Abstractors' payroll information is developed quarterly from the same records. Of the total population of 10,000 serials from which abstracts are taken annually, 1000 of these serials produced 75 per cent of the abstracts printed in *CA*; 250 serials produced the first 50 per cent; one-third of all abstracts printed in *CA* are obtained from only 100 of the total of 10,000 serials scanned.

CAS produces a fully machine-based announcement/retrieval tool in *Chemical-Biological Activities* (*CBAC*), which is processed entirely in-house. The tool covers organic compounds that act on biological systems exclusive of the botanical kingdom, animal and microorganisms metabolism studies and *in vitro* chemical reactions of organic compounds of biochemical interests. Approximately 300 journals are covered to obtain material for *CBAC*. *CBAC* is provided in four formats: the digest section, which constitutes a bibliographic description and a specially formatted digest; a keyword-in-context (KWIC) permuted index; a molecular formula index; and an author index. Keyword from the title and from the digest are indexed

in the KWIC index. The general layout format for the digest provides that compounds are printed at the left margin of text. To the left of each compound term or referent is a registry number providing for retrieval on or derivation of the molecular formula for the compound term. Terms within the digest that are not compounds but on which the item is indexed are printed in all caps. Such terms are then printed in the KWIC index alphabetically on a fixed indexing position in the line and are in context with the remainder of the digest text line or with as much of the sentence as can be printed on a line of the index.

CA and its indexes are hard copy publications. CAS also is investigating the opportunities for producing microforms of the publications or portions of the publications in terms of satisfying requests for selective bibliographies. *CBAC* can be provided as a publication or on magnetic tape, accompanied by appropriate search programs. Searching is done on a character-by-character basis such that the KWIC vocabulary does not constitute a constraint. That is, despite the alternative uses of "hydrazide," "hydrazides," or "hydrazine," etc., the searcher may specify only "hydraz" as the basis for his search and would receive a printout of all lines containing that string.

Among the most recent developments of the Chemical Abstracts Service is the automation of the registry of chemical compounds. The basic operational feature of this system is the development of a linear description of the two-dimensional diagrams of chemical compounds, in which links are unambiguously identified. The resulting expression can be machine searched for principal structures and substructures and for comparison against potential new entries to avoid duplication on the basis of structure in the assignment of registry numbers. Coding sheets for keypunching compound descriptions are being prepared as compounds are encountered in the day-to-day abstracting and indexing. The entire file of more than three million compounds is expected to be in machine form within two years.

Although the American Chemical Society does obtain help from NSF and NIH in support of experimentation and developing some of the techniques now being applied in the Chemical Abstracts Service, the CAS considers itself a private enterprise and is concerned about implica-

tions of the development of standards such as the COSATI subject heading list. CAS is increasingly orienting itself toward machine support and hopes to be able to switch to machine-based formula indexing in or soon after 1967 by moving the keyboarding operation into the acquisition phase of the cycle. Subsequently author indexing is to be introduced into a machine-oriented system. Experimentation with the machine-based *Chemical-Biological Activities* and its machine-readable forms is directed toward expanding the coverage and toward shifting identifiable portions of *Chemical Abstracts* into a comparable machine-based system.

Analysis of the source item and establishment of policies and controls to ensure that source publishers provide abstracts in a format useful to CAS is considered a critical need. CAS expects to move toward agreement on standards on a case-by-case basis, however, rather than through arbitration and imposition by the federal government. CAS contends that specifications can be developed through independent negotiation, which will be precise enough to meet their needs and general enough to be useful to other abstracting services. With the policy of assigning an abstracting task to an individual working in the field, CAS anticipates no problem in finding the individual with multidisciplinary interests who is capable of abstracting multidisciplinary items according to a method useful to each of the discipline-oriented abstracting services to which the item might be of interest.

Biological Abstracts, published by Biological Sciences Information Services (BIOSIS), was founded in 1926 by the National Academy of Sciences, the American Association for the Advancement of Science, and the Union of American Biological Societies. BIOSIS is not, therefore, directly connected with any single professional society but does tend toward the academic rather than trade association or commercial announcement posture while aggressively investigating and adopting machine support. The organization publishes a conventional abstract journal produced by typing abstracts, manuscripted by external unpaid volunteer abstractors on electric typewriters for manual pasteup in galleys, for photoreduction and printing.

The basic abstract journal is organized in sections and individual abstracts are numbered sequentially within each section. The initial entry

in a given section is a "see also" notation. Policies of preparing the abstracts portions of the journal without adequate indexing put the organization in an unusual position when making some comparatively original decisions at the time machine support for indexing was considered. That is, the organization had not developed the sophisticated indexing format, classification, and vocabulary that might have hindered experimentation with and adoption of key-word indexing techniques.

At present, more than 100,000 abstracts are published per year—the number being determined primarily by the million-dollar annual operating budget of the organization. Each biweekly issue of *Biological Abstracts* contains a *CROSS* index, in which the name of each section head is followed by a posting of the numbers of every abstract to which that section name might be applied as a descriptor. (Note that this is not a uniterm index.) This type of index provides for cross referencing to avoid multiple printing of an abstract or some reference to the abstract in more than one section. The index is arranged in ten-column format to provide for coordination in searching for an abstract number on the basis of a search involving more than one term.

In addition to the section under which the abstract is originally printed, it may be cross referenced by multiple entries in this index. Since this index is produced by a machine program, its contents remain on a tape, available for cumulative merging as well as for individual searches in response to contract requests for bibliographies on intersections among descriptors.

Each issue of the abstract journal also contains an author index and biosystematic index organized into taxonomic categories and subordinately into organisms against which are posted the names of the section in which the abstract and its number were printed. Since the section name constitutes the descriptor, the search tool is comparatively powerful for retrieving the combinations of taxonomic categories, organisms, and general field of biology. As in the case of the other indexes, this material is in machine form and the possibility of accumulation for specialized searches will be examined as resources of the organization permit.

BIOSIS also publishes a permuted title index called *B.A.S.I.C.* produced in a KWIC-like program developed by BIOSIS. In preparing the copy for keypunching entries for this index, analysts augment the titles and ensure the usefulness of the indexing point by binding terms to avoid spurious index entries. As a visual aid to the use of the permuted index, the copy to the left of the indexing position on the line—which is twenty-five characters to the right of the left margin—is covered with a screening (acetate sheet on which has been printed a dot structure to create an overall appearance of a gray tint block).

This permuted keyword index may be subscribed to without subscription to *Biological Abstracts*. By making this available, BIOSIS hopes to appeal to individual users who would not necessarily be customers for the abstract journal but would have access to it in a library. The user of *B.A.S.I.C.* who wishes to maintain a file of individual abstracts selected on the basis of analysis of the permuted keyword index may order microcard versions. A charge of $6.00 is made for ten abstracts or fewer; each additional abstract being $0.50.

The constraint to remain at approximately 100,000 abstracts per year has resulted in a backlog of material considered to be of lower productivity to the maximum user group. To ensure that this material is at least announced to the field of biology, NSF-OSIS has provided support for production of a permuted keyword title index such as *B.A.S.I.C.* During 1965 the supplement *BioResearch Titles* is to be distributed as part of the subscription to *Biological Abstracts* and will provide announcements of an additional 5000 titles in each monthly issue.

In addition to the permuted title, this document will contain a bibliographic entry—not a complete abstract. Entries will be listed by source journals, which are to be arranged by title. Each issue will also contain an author index. Beginning with the end of calendar 1965, *BA* intends to publish cumulative author, *CROSS*, and biosystematic indexes to *Biological Abstracts*, each of which will be available as a separate subscription.

In becoming more oriented toward production of indexes using machine support, BIOSIS is experimenting with a variety of information services, which accounts for the change of the name of the organization from "Biological Abstracts." Some investigation is being made of the opportunities for selective repackaging of the abstracts developed for publication in the journal. The organization has on microfilm the abstracts published during the past six years,

one abstract per frame. Manual and computer techniques have been used in determining abstract identifications appropriate to a particular search and the subsequent microfilm search and printout of required abstracts. In a novel experiment BIOSIS is accepting and servicing requests entered directly by researchers through a communication system terminated in Electrowriters. During the first three months of experimentation, some 500 requests have been handled, one involving nearly 3000 individual abstracts.

Of particular interest in the field of announcement and retrieval services is the outstanding effort of BIOSIS to develop a sound computer-based acquisitions records system, not only for management of acquisitions but to provide appropriate machine record support and to eliminate duplicative clerical efforts as an item passes through the processes to be included in an announcement service. The field of biology is supported by the Conference of Biological Editors, a group that meets annually to discuss the problems and new developments in the field of editing primary and secondary journals for the support of the field of biology. Through the medium of this organization, the producers of secondary announcements media can and do develop coordination and cooperation with primary sources in terms of the provisions of suitable abstracts.

The American Petroleum Institute (API) membership consists of petroleum industry corporations, each of which supports an internal information service. Eight years ago Institute membership agreed that some core of the literature then being searched and analyzed separately and redundantly at various organizations could be processed centrally more economically. The Central Abstracting Service for the API was established and now covers approximately 150 journal titles from which are derived an average of 12,000 abstracts annually.

Guidance for the selection of journals and feedback relative to system services is provided by a committee of representatives of ten of the major petroleum organizations. A staff of approximately 36, operating on a budget of about half a million dollars per year, produce the visual and machine form announcement and retrieval tools. The service is self-supporting, with 40 subscribers to the literature abstract, 20 to the patent abstracts, and 18 to the indexes of both. The indexes are generated by a computer-based system and may be obtained on magnetic tape for local search. In addition to literature abstracts, the service publishes a journal of abstracts for some 11,000 patents each year.

The abstract journals are issued weekly and contain author indexes. Subject indexes are issued monthly and cumulated semiannually. The subject index consists of the title plus subordinate subjects and an abstract identification number, listed under major subjects. Abstract identifications are also posted in an inverted printed index, two copies of which are supplied for manual coordinated searches. The dual dictionary inverted coordinate index is issued three times a year and cumulated in the second and third issues. Magnetic tape versions also are available three times a year and cumulated for the second and third of the three issues.

In the monthly subject indexes to the abstracts of refining literature, the identification number of the abstract is indicated with the title and subordinate or minor terms. In the inverted index, roles and links are also indicated where they have been assigned during indexing process. Among the roles that may be specified are "agent," "product," "intermediate," "catalysts," "catalyst-product," "prior treatment," "medium/solvent," and substance analyzed." These additional qualifiers to the item identification number are also written on magnetic tape for machine searching of the inverted index.

The subscriber to the magnetic tape service is also provided with a 1401 search program, a 7090 input program, and the opportunity to send an individual from the company's computer group to the API abstracting service for instruction in the exploitation of the tapes. The assumption is that in undertaking the use of the magnetic tapes, the individual organization will also prepare the abstracts and indexes for materials in which they are individually interested in accordance with the formats and requirements of the central service system. The service conducts a training program for individuals who are to use and develop these tools in the various subscribing organizations. A guide to abstracting and indexing policies and practices is available for new personnel.

Each major petroleum industry organization abstracts an additional 300 to 500 journals to meet individual goals, yielding an additional 10,000 abstracts per year. The API does not seek to expand its coverage to include these journals, however, but rather to process a core set of journals maximally productive to the entire subscriber group. The present emphasis is on

refining. An experiment has been conducted at the University of Tulsa on the possibility of separately covering exploration and production aspects of the industry. Similarly, a separate journal covering transportation and storage might be appropriate although these aspects are now partly covered in the refining journals. Establishment of specialized field journals depends entirely on concurrence by the industry, through the committee in the Institute, that a market or need exists for the journals.

The goal is to serve a current awareness need by preparing abstracts in a style considered easier to read than are conventional abstracts. The principle of this "inverted" style is similar to that of news reporting in which the lead (first) sentence consists of the main thought of the article. Because in technical literature and patents this main thought is commonly expressed in the title itself, the inverted abstract often begins with the words of the title in a sentence. Citation information, such as the name of the author and corporate source, is printed at the end of the abstract. The development of techniques now in use by API is a consolidation and exploitation of techniques developed in several of the major companies belonging to the Institute. The adoption of any given technique is controlled by the advice of the committees of the Institute which reflect the interests of the Institute membership at management level.

Management of the API abstracting service considers the significant goal to be selection and reporting of information that is slanted to the application of petroleum technology. In general, the direction and extent of the service of the API has developed from the pragmatic point of view that policy and financial decisions are involved in information support. This warrants the attention of management personnel in the petroleum companies. The service, therefore, develops on the basis that the support to be provided plays a key role in the productivity of the organization.

The principal goal of the information services of the Society of Automotive Engineers (SAE) is current awareness for its individual and corporate membership. The contents of the *SAE Journal* therefore are comparatively less theoretical and are interspersed with news of the industry and of government activities having an impact on the industry. The Society of Automotive Engineers offers its 32,000 members several ser-

vices in addition to conventional publication of a primary journal. Among these services is the redistribution of reprints and copies of papers (a) submitted but not accepted for publication in SAE serials or (b) presented at SAE meetings. Papers are announced through the publication of a brief summary in the *SAE Journal* accompanied by an order blank. Prices are $0.75 per copy to members for most items, although a few titles may cost as much as $15.

As an example, the July 1965 issue announced availability of copies of 81 papers. Summaries are indexed on an average of three terms. The index consists of terms, each of which is followed by the six-digit identification number for each item to which that descriptor applies. Because the SAE believes that the customer of these papers is often an organization rather than an individual, it will soon offer copies on microfiche on the assumption that various industrial organizations are equipped with microfiche readers.

Using the basic technique of descriptive abstracting advocated by the Engineers Joint Council, a summary is prepared for each piece of literature issued by the SAE for inclusion in an annual abstract compilation. Those items that have appeared in the *Transactions* are noted along with the names of discussants. Subject and author indexes are prepared for the abstract issue, in which the descriptor term is printed in boldface followed by the title and abstract number for any item to which the descriptor has been assigned.

The basis on which papers are accepted for publication in an SAE serial is a formal critical review technique. Each paper is reviewed by a minimum of nine judges who are experts in the subject content of the article and who independently assign to the article a review score or rating. In rating the individual paper, each judge is provided with a tab card offering the option for his rating as "excellent," "good," "fair," "poor," or "waive" for each of the following factors:

1. Contains new information or comprises a measurable contribution to the technical area involved.

2. Has data and theory useful for several years.

3. Has specifically stated conclusion directly supported by facts.

4. Clearly states its objective at the beginning and develops information concisely, completely, and logically to reach the stated objective.

5. Has clear tables, graphs, and illustrations.

6. Adequately references outside data used.

7. Is free from commercialism.

In developing the score for a paper based on the composite of reviewers' analyses, the various classes on which it is rated are weighted to derive a numeric score. A score beneath a threshold level results in rejection of the paper. Papers scoring within a middle range are published in the *SAE Journal*, whereas those with the highest scores are reserved for development of documented discussion and publication in the *Transactions*. Contents of the latter are "judged to be of exceptional value to the permanent literature."

The ranking of a paper is available to any of the membership requesting it and to the organization by whom its author is employed. Management of the SAE publication activity considers the development of this paper rating system to have been influential in significantly improving the quality of the literature of the field. The contributor of a paper is advised that his paper will be subjected to critical review and is in fact provided with a twelve-page guide to the preparation of his paper which, in addition to providing guidance on style and format, explains the rating system.

Also of particular interest in SAE is the continuing sampling of user response to the *Journal* and the SAE services. Although individual samples appear to be small, sampling is conducted regularly and the results are used as guides to changes in the content or emphasis of the *Journal*.

The Division of Technical Information of the U. S. Atomic Energy Commission (AEC) has the mission of collecting and making available the worldwide literature in atomic energy and nuclear science. In addition to providing conventional library services in support of the 6800 direct employees of the AEC stationed in Washington, Oak Ridge, and field offices, the Division acts as a clearinghouse for AEC-initiated report literature. It publishes:

1. An announcement/retrieval tool for journal and report literature.

2. Primary journals in nuclear safety, power reactor technology, reactor materials, reactor fuel processing, and isotope and radiation technology.

3. Technical books and monographs, and offers educational services including exhibits and demonstrations.

The AEC also provides partial or full support to 15 information and data centers.

Report literature in the field approximates 14,000 titles annually. Nearly 100,000 requests for copies of such reports are serviced for qualified requesters each year. Annually an additional 100,000 requests are received for educational material and two million items are distributed in response to these requests.

The AEC's major announcement/retrieval tool is the journal *Nuclear Science Abstracts* (*NSA*), published biweekly as the principal guide to unclassified world literature on atomic energy. In addition to *NSA* the Division of Technical Information publishes *Research and Development Abstracts of the AEC, Abstracts of Weapon Test Reports, Abstracts of Classified Reports*, and lists of reports for civilian application.

Reports produced in execution of AEC-supported contracts and grants are distributed by source organizations in accordance with standard distribution lists developed by and published by the Division of Technical Information. Among the recipients listed are the Division of Technical Information itself and, for unclassified and limited materials, the Clearinghouse for Federal Scientific and Technical Information. Of the copies received at the Division of Technical Information Extension, Oak Ridge, 200 are distributed to AEC depository libraries around the world. Unclassified unlimited documents may be purchased from the CFSTI or in microform from Microcard Editions, Inc., by individuals who are not qualified to receive them free from the AEC.

When received, the report is analyzed to determine restrictions with respect to patent disclosure or international agreements limiting the dissemination of contents. The item is then evaluated to assign it to appropriate subject categories and to specify subsequent processing. In addition to the 14,000 reports from the United States and foreign countries, the evaluation group analyzes some 800 translations, 1500 patents, 800 books, 13,000 conference proceedings, and 17,000 journal articles. More than 700

journals are regularly scanned and another 700 titles provide irregular inputs to the abstracting and indexing service. From this data base, items are selected for abstracting and indexing. Items are designated:

1. Acceptable for inclusion in *NSA*.
2. Acceptable for inclusion in the classified abstract journal.
3. Outside the scope of AEC interest but to be retransmitted to another agency.
4. Outside the scope of *NSA* but to be noted in the card catalog for bibliographic support to AEC personnel and contractors.
5. Rejected.

An authority file of approximately 14,000 main subject headings, under close control by subject heading specialists, is a basis for organization of the abstracting journal and its indexes. An average of slightly fewer than four access points is provided in the subject index for each item appearing in *Nuclear Science Abstracts*.

A staff of approximately 50 professional and nonprofessional personnel, at a cost of somewhat less than $600,000 per year, produces *Nuclear Science Abstracts*. In 1964, 45,000 items were covered in 24 issues and distributed to a total circulation of 8000.

Descriptive cataloging is prepared by subprofessional personnel prior to abstracting and indexing. Tape-perforating equipment recently has been introduced into the descriptive cataloging activities for the development of a machine-readable record and subsequent machine development of retrieval and announcement tools.

The abstract copy and index entries are prepared by the same individual for a given item. In addition to the subject index entries prepared for use in the issues of *NSA*, a list of keywords or descriptors is prepared for each item for keypunching and subsequent use in an experiment in selective dissemination being conducted by the AEC. Abstract text is composed on electric typewriters. The composition group prepares approximately 200 abstracts daily. After the cutoff date for publication of a given issue, individual abstracts are numbered, based on the section in which they are to appear. Hence the index line card is not punched and sorted until after this phase of the journal preparation.

Indexes are cumulated quarterly, semiannually, annually, and quinquennially. Then after sorting, listing, and preparation of repro negatives, the index cards are separated from header cards and set aside for cumulative index preparation.

Nuclear Science Abstracts receives advance page proofs for more than fifteen of the journals regularly scanned. Other journals provide advance abstracts of articles prior to journal publication. An additional group of journals is airmailed directly to *NSA* in advance of publication date of the primary journal. The AEC is presently negotiating to receive abstracts and index material from foreign sources in English and in the style and vocabulary of *NSA*.

The section organization of *Nuclear Science Abstracts* echoes the organization of the standard distribution lists evolved through extended experience with the field and the user group. The Division of Technical Information Extension therefore is cautious about the possibility of its exploiting the COSATI subject category list and its fields and groups organization.

In the area of announcement tools the National Aeronautics and Space Administration (NASA) probably has been the most active of the federal agencies in developing selective dissemination of information (SDI) techniques. Report literature in the aerospace field generated as a result of NASA's sponsorship or through acquisition on the basis of interest by the community is received at NASA's Scientific and Technical Information Division for screening. Reports considered to be applicable to the space mission are transferred to a private organization, Documentation, Inc., for processing. Processing results in the preparation of the abstract journals *Scientific and Technical Aerospace Reports* (*STAR*) and its counterpart, *CSTAR*, in which are announced classified or restricted reports. *STAR* is expected to cover approximately 30,000 abstracts for the fiscal year 1966. During fiscal year 1965, 5000 of the abstracts represent reports originated through NASA; 11,000 were items from other sources in the United States; 4000 were from Russian sources; and 3000 from other foreign sources. Circulation for *STAR* is approximately 9000 copies, and for *CSTAR* it is approximately 3000 copies.

The contents of *STAR* are organized into 34 subject categories covering 8 disciplines, 18 different areas of engineering, and 2 interdisciplinary categories. Few of the categories actually

are mutually exclusive. Scope notes are provided to guide the user to alternative or related categories. In addition to the regular publication of the abstract journals, NASA publishes continuing bibliographies, which are selected compilations of abstracts previously published. These compilations are indexed comparably, using the information provided at the time of original publication of the abstract.

Reports transferred to Documentation, Inc., are analyzed by subject specialists who prepare an abstract and a "notation of content," used in the index as an entry under the index term selected for the item. An average of four or five index terms is selected for indexing the individual issue. The index entry also contains the corporate source number, the abstract number, and the number of the section in which the abstract appears.

In addition to the notation of content and the selection of index terms to be published, the analyst prepares lists of uniterms which are the basis for retrospective search and selective dissemination. Between 12 and 20 uniterms are selected for each report against which are posted accession or abstract numbers in an inverted file. A vocabulary of approximately 13,000 uniterms is involved and a guide is available for developing search strategy. The guide itself is in machine form but listed on a 1403 in a program which makes no differentiation except overprinting of the index term and indentation of "see," "see also," and "confer" (related or associated concepts) references. The copy for the abstract section of *STAR* and *CSTAR* is prepared on Justowriters for Photon photocomposition. The issue index is also prepared on tape perforators to be read into the computer-based system which sorts entries and generates the index tape. In addition to the subject index each issue contains a corporate source index, a personal author index, a report-accession number index, and an accession/report number index. The latter are generated as byproducts of the program that writes the basic subject index.

A parallel analysis of aerospace literature available openly is conducted by the American Institute of Aeronautics and Astronautics using the same general techniques used in NASA's publications. The abstract journal covering open literature is *International Aerospace Abstracts* (*IAA*). During fiscal year 1965 *IAA* contained abstracts to 10,000 U. S. citations, 3000 Russian citations, and 5000 other foreign articles. Circulation of *IAA* is also 3000 copies. *STAR* and *IAA* are published biweekly on an alternate schedule. Although the contents of *IAA* are prepared by the American Institute of Aeronautics and Astronautics, the machine record of its contents is available for searching in conjunction with searches of the report literature records.

The records on magnetic tape are searched daily in response to 600 to 700 requests received. NASA distributes one million full-size hard copies annually and 4.5 million microfiche copies of documents. Approximately 500 bibliographies and literature searches are prepared annually. NASA supports the preparation and announcements of approximately 600 scientific and technical translations per year.

Regular automatic distribution of report copies of microfiche is made to approximately 4000 recipients in NASA research centers and contractor organizations; 700 U. S. Government agencies and their contractors; 200 universities and major public libraries; 550 foreign government agencies, institutions, and professional societies; and 5000 industrial and U. S. business organizations.

The selective dissemination program introduced by IBM and tested internally for support of their engineering personnel also has been under intensive study by NASA for support of NASA personnel and contractors. During the past two years the experiment has developed into a pilot operation now servicing more than 700 participants in the various NASA laboratories.

When a report is analyzed, the uniterms selected and notation of content are introduced into the machine system. The selective dissemination program is run on the machine file for the contents of a given issue of the abstract journals. Each of the 700 participants has provided a list of uniterms believed to constitute his interest profile and this record is run against the uniterm index for new abstracts.

Hits (matches between user and document profiles) are written on an output file which is sorted on the basis of individual identification and then printed as a deck of portapunch cards, one half of which contains the notation of content, abstract number, and uniterms. The other half of the card constitutes an order and an indication of the recipient's interest in any item for which he has received notification but which he does not wish to order. Return of the card

permits analysis of the effectiveness of the individual profile and the degree to which matches are being obtained in rerunning the selective dissemination program.

The requester of a document may specify a preference for microfiche or hard copy. Although he returns the response card through his local laboratory library to NASA, the required copies are distributed by Documentation, Inc. During the operational phase, which began in the last quarter of 1965, Documentation, Inc., provides stocks of microfiche to the local libraries for decentralized distribution. There is also a plan to provide the magnetic tape record for each issue of the abstract journals to the local laboratory for local development of full-scale SDI service. Ranges of interest of the laboratories cluster and differ from one another sufficiently to expect improved efficiency of the search at the local level.

A separate division of NASA, the Technology Utilization Division, has undertaken the preparation of an abstract journal called *Tech Briefs* for reports created by NASA laboratories, which are suitable for exploitation by industry and are in no way limited. The journal consists of a citation and a very short abstract; its preparation apparently is not correlated with that of *STAR* and *IAA*. Its apparent overlap with the audience and goals of the CFSTI are probably justified as a "public relations" need for the sponsoring agency.

One of the small private abstracting services, Cambridge Communications Corporation, was briefly studied. Since 1957 the Cambridge Communications Corporation has been publishing a series of abstracts covering materials, metallurgy (30,000 abstracts), solid state physics (29,000), devices (13,000), electronics, computers, and aerospace. Originally it offered catalog cards in various subject areas. Recently the card service has been discontinued in favor of looseleaf, page-form publication. The organization of each subject area is hierarchical. In general the hierarchical organization of the abstracts on the basis of conceptual relationships is considered to minimize the requirement for indexing. Indexes therefore are minimal and tend to differ from a table of contents in that entries are alphabetized in a given major heading.

The corporation also is attempting to develop personal-interest profile services based on special packaging of material published otherwise in page form for inclusion in the various abstract

binders. Publication techniques are conventional. The organization claims approximately 2000 users, half of whom are outside the United States.

Although McGraw-Hill is a primary publisher of both serials and books in science and technology, the aspects of its activities pertinent to this discussion center around announcement services. For it is in the directories and index area that McGraw-Hill is experimenting in computer support and photocomposition.

For 1965 McGraw-Hill processed *The Electronic Buyer's Guide* by computer. The text for the manufacturer's section and code numbers for products made by each manufacturer were keyboarded on tape-perforating typewriters. The computer used this input for the composition of the product section without additional keyboarding.

McGraw-Hill investigated both the Dura Mach 10 and the Flexowriter as input devices. The Dura was used because the (Selectric) type ball offers higher potential input rate. Experience with the system revealed that the higher typing speed is not always attainable in practice because the shift key does not necessarily punch its corresponding code when the typing speed is high. In contrast, the Flexowriter requires a deliberate down shift for a change in case, which is more reliable in the punching of the shift code but is also much slower in operation. The McGraw-Hill system uses a Honeywell 200 computer.

Photocomposition machines, considered to be inherently more accurate than hot-metal casting machines, are preferable for computer-based typesetting in which one of the goals is avoidance of proofing the final copy. McGraw-Hill uses the American Type Founders B-8 which is slow but reliable. Line printer proofs of the results of the input of copy and corrections are pulled. After the input of corrections based on proofreading the listings, the system punches output tape for actuating the ATF B-8. Ten hours of computer time are necessary to drive the 100-character per second punch producing the eight-channel tape for the ATF for the manufacturer's section. An off-line converter could have been used.

Thirty hours of computer time are involved in producing the product section in which the manufacturer's data must be repeated under the heading for each manufacturer's product and in

which a change in type font identifies advertizers, The ATF B-8 machines run at about five characters per second, producing repro negatives from which positive prints are pulled. Repro proofs and ad proofs are dummied and photographed for making offset press plates. The input data used for production of the directory is written on magnetic tape which is to be stored, updated, and used subsequently for the next annual issue.

In its commercial activity known as the Dodge Reports, McGraw-Hill is operating a system conceptually similar to what is now called "selective dissemination of information." The Dodge Reports have been in existence for some twenty years and were purchased four or five years ago by McGraw-Hill. The principle of this system's operation is the scanning of open literature (primarily news and special purpose literature related to construction) and the preparation of announcements according to a prescribed format. These announcements are distributed to subscribers on the basis of their selected areas of interest, including project size, geographical location, or of construction features such as medical centers, aquariums, post offices, apartment buildings, bridges, etc. The subscriber may indicate that he is interested only in certain stages of development such as "contemplated," "planning," bids and awards relative to carpentry or glazing, announcement of architect selection, and general contract award.

Some 500 million individual announcement slips are published annually. Service on the subscriptions is daily to the extent that the material has been analyzed appropriate to the stated interests of the given subscriber. Some 1400 analysts gather this information at 19 centers, primarily in the east and midwest. In general the service is manual, although the center in Boston is investigating the possibility of machine support.

Distribution Organizations. Organizations whose primary mission is distribution serve a function for report literature that is performed by the serial dissemination to the interested user, usually through a medium of publication or reproduction. Report literature currently approximates the volume of published serial literature. To announce acquisition and availability of reports, distribution agencies publish secondary media and are developing unconventional re-

trieval tools. The choice of describing the Government Printing Office, the Defense Documentation Center, and the Clearinghouse for Federal Scientific and Technical Documentation under the category of "distribution agencies" arises from the requirement of these organizations to maintain supplies of documents or reproducible masters with which to respond to requests or orders from user groups. Announcement media (abstract and index tools) produced by each are also summarized.

The Government Printing Office (GPO) is charged with printing and distribution for the entire federal government. The GPO receives manuscript copies from various agencies, determines on its own initiative or on the advice of the source organization that the document should be announced and made available through the GPO distribution system, and publishes and distributes as appropriate. The GPO publishes special bibliographies that are also intended to be price lists for publications that are popular—and for those for which additional promotion is considered desirable to reduce inventories. Announcement and distribution are activities of the Office of the Superintendent of Documents.

All federal documents, whether or not reproduced for separate distribution by GPO, are announced in the GPO *Monthly Catalog.* The source organization is considered the publisher of the document distributed by the GPO. The catalog is organized by item source, which is revealed by the code assigned to the item. Information on availability, either from the GPO—with the GPO distribution price—or alternate sources, is provided with each of the item descriptions.

The catalog lists an average of 1700 entries per month. A staff of over thirty produces the descriptive cataloging for, and the index to, the *Monthly Catalog.* The slips of paper constituting index file entries are cumulatively interfiled for preparation of an annual index. Approximately one subject entry per item is provided in the index.

GPO has the responsibility to distribute a copy of every document it prints to a list of depository libraries. Each representative and senator may designate two such depositories, although none may be removed from the list arbitrarily by changes in the legislative personnel. The theoretical maximum number of authorized

depository libraries is 1340. GPO management estimates that slightly more than 800 are authorized. The designation continues until the depository "vacates the privilege" at its own request or until the Superintendent of Documents removes it from the list for failure to abide by the requirements of the program.

Regional depositories (two per state) must take and keep either a microform copy, made at its own initiative and cost, or the hard copy of every GPO document. Within the region it serves, a regional depository must provide interlibrary loan, reference service, and assistance for regular depository libraries in disposing of unwanted government publications. Regional libraries therefore act as a redistribution point between other depository libraries to provide for exchange prior to authorized disposition of unwanted materials. Issuing organizations may preclude the distribution of an item to a depository by designating the item to be for official use or administrative or operational purposes that have no public interest or educational value and through the mechanism of military security classification. The items that are to be sold through the CFSTI are also considered unavailable for deposit in the depository libraries. On the other hand, some items not available for sale through the GPO are sent to a depository library.

Actually, depositories (except regional) may be selective in regard to the materials sent to them. The depositories are sent lists of available classifications of materials and duplicate cards, the return of one of which constitutes the selection of that class of material for the library. When forwarded to a depository, government publications must be made available for free use by the general public. Depository libraries in executive departments and independent agencies must offer items to the Library of Congress and to the National Archives prior to disposing of unwanted items.

The GPO has a program of surveying depositories to assure that the materials sent are not simply being stored in "shoeboxes." Funds for this activity are limited, however, and seldom are more than a half dozen of the depositories examined each year.

Internally the GPO uses primarily offset rather than letterpress printing, except for congressional documents and certain specialty printing. At present the GPO estimates that about one-half of what is printed over its imprint is actually subcontracted by outside printers. Both typecasting and photocomposing machines are in use.

Again of particular interest to material of science and technology is the use of the Linofilm photocomposition equipment for setting the pages of the *Technical Abstracts Bulletin* (*TAB*) of the DDC and the U. S. *Government Research and Development Reports* (*USGRDR*). This equipment operates from perforated tape which is produced through a conversion process from the perforated tape produced on Flexowriters and Syncrotape machines by the DDC and CFSTI in their present method of preparing copy for their abstract journals. The Linofilm is photocomposing equipment similar to the Photon and is capable of accessing 18 different 88-character grids and operating at a rate of 10 characters per second in composing on a line-by-line basis.

One of the first experiments with the Linofilm, using the RCA 301 and tab card input, was conducted by the GPO and the Patent Office in producing the *Attorneys Roster*. The names and addresses for some 8000 attorneys eligible to practice before the U. S. Patent Office had been punched and, since 1949, had been listed on EAM equipment. Press plates were made photographically from pasteups of printer listings. The resulting publications amounted to approximately 100 pages in three-column format.

In the keypunch-listed versions, periods had been eliminated following initials. To restore the more common typographic policies, the program introduces a period after any initial that stands alone. Instances that fail to fit into the logic as outlined (D'Amico, St. Amand, etc.) are corrected in galley after the photocomposition unit has produced its output.

The program introduces information concerning the width value for each character, since—in contrast to the constant character spacing of EAM equipment and standard typewriter—characters in Linofilm fonts have various widths. One of the principal motivations for the development and exploitation of a photocomposition system using machine-readable copy from a computer-based system is the reduction in paper, shipping, and press setup cost—type density of graphic arts fonts being 30 per cent higher than that of comparable size computer printer listings. The GPO is actively pursuing development and acquisition of computer-based photocomposition equipment.

The primary functions of the Defense Documentation Center (DDC) is the distribution of copies of reports generated by defense contractors and military organizations. To fulfill this mission, DDC receives copies of report literature, analyzes these to produce abstracts and index terms, all of which are keyboarded on a tape-perforating system for input to a computer-based file. This information is then organized for publication in the *Technical Abstract Bulletin (TAB)*. Each report is microfiched* to provide for reproduction of copies on request.

The incoming item is analyzed to determine whether it is unclassified and otherwise unrestricted, in which case it is transferred to the Clearinghouse for Federal Scientific and Technical Information for processing. Items that are in any way classified or restricted are processed by DDC. The division between restricted and unrestricted reports is approximately 50–50. DDC estimates that the 55,000 reports received per year (1964 estimate) constitute more than 70 per cent of all formal DOD reports, and that the maximum the system would process is 90 per cent. Among the 10 per cent it does not anticipate handling are those classified top secret, cryptographic items, intelligence documents, contract proposals, and administrative reports.†

Recently DOD has issued a directive requiring submission of an abstract and index terms with each source item. Analysis includes the assignment of descriptor terms from the 6000-term vocabulary. The *ASTIA Thesaurus*, which has undergone continual development since its second issuance, is expected to be further affected by the release of the COSATI subject category list, to ensure compatibility with its field and group organization.

The copy for the abstract and the indexing terms is keyboarded on Synchrotape tape-perforating typewriters. The machine-readable copy is then used to produce camera-ready master galleys for publication of the buff section of *TAB* and for merging into the computer memory. The orientation of the DDC operations is toward updating the computer record. This fundamental policy guides the choices made in terms of the visual announcement/search tool—the *TAB*—and emphasizes a source of incompatibility between the tool and the COSATI descriptive cataloging standards, which are oriented toward the catalog card prepared as a visually searchable unit record.

Beginning in fiscal year 1966, the perforated tape is being used as input for the converter that produces tape for activating the Linofilm photocomposition system. As described previously, this activity is conducted by the GPO, which publishes and distributes some 17,000 copies of *TAB* biweekly. Each issue of *TAB* contains more than 2000 abstracts and an annotated subject index consisting of 3 of 4 of the terms selected for indexing the report. An average of 15 terms is assigned and available for computer search. Subject and corporate author indexes are accumulated and published semiannually. In addition to demand bibliographies, DDC prepares bibliographies on frequently requested subjects. Such bibliographies are assigned AD numbers and announced in *TAB*.

In serving the mission of redistributing copies, the DDC operates a printing plant capable of reproducing from microfilm or microfiche the copies requested. DDC now encompasses more than 750,000 titles on microform, 100,000 in hard copy stocked for immediate response to requests. As in the case of the reports themselves, requests for reports that are in no way restricted are transferred to the CFSTI for handling. Nearly 7000 requests are received per working day. Approximately 800,000 documents are distributed annually by DDC. An additional half million requests per year are transferred to and serviced by CFSTI. Nine per cent of the requests received by DDC are not filled because the requester is ineligible for the document requested or because the document is unavailable.

Requests are accepted from qualified users for whom subject area information is on file in the Field-of-Interest Register. Registered for DDC services are 3700 military organizations, 300 federal agencies, and 2000 industrial and educational organizations. Qualified users are provided with tab cards on which is punched an address code and which is used by the requester to obtain copies of AD reports. Requester eligibility is also processed in the computer-based system to validate requests. Qualified requesters receive reports without charge. Requests also may be made by teletype directly from any of the seven field offices to DDC.

The number of requests for bibliographies has been rising steadily and has recently approached 90 per day. On the average, 120 citations are

---

* Prior to fiscal year 1966, microfilm was used.
† DOD is developing a separate information system for contracts and related documents.

output per search request, each citation constituting 30 lines of printing. DDC is working on a refinement of the search strategy to allow a requester to specify the type of information he seeks; that is, to limit the output printing to some fragment of the total machine record rather than to output the entire abstract and descriptive cataloging information. The input record for the system, prepared on tape-perforating equipment, is complete with signals for upper and lower case, but the output printing is done in all upper case on 600-line-per-minute printers.

The Clearinghouse for Federal Scientific and Technical Information (CFSTI) is a part of the Institute for Applied Technology of the Department of Commerce. Its functions are an extension of those previously performed by the Office of Technical Services (OTS). Greater emphasis is now placed on the clearinghouse or redistribution functions, with certain of the OTS research functions remaining in other units of the Bureau of Standards. CFSTI has approximately 300 employees and an annual budget of more than $5 million. Half of this budget is transfer funds from other agencies to support the CFSTI in announcing and redistributing reports prepared by, or in the interest of, these agencies. The enabling legislation for the CFSTI is broad in terms of the audience to be served and the functions to be performed.

One of the major portions of the CFSTI collection is the report literature from DDC which constitutes unlimited unclassified reports from military organizations and defense contractors. In addition, the CFSTI handles comparable report literature from NASA, the AEC, and 30 other federal agencies. Only scientific, technical, and engineering reports resulting from efforts supported by federal funds are acquisitioned. Subject guidelines are adopted from the new COSATI subject category list.

For the fiscal year 1965 the CFSTI processed the following volumes of materials from the organizations indicated:

Department of Defense	16,000
Atomic Energy Commission	8,100
NASA	5,900
PB Reports	1,900
Technical translations	22,400
CAPE drawings packages (AEC)	500
Patent abstracts	900

Depending on the treatment given at the source agency, an input report may be reanalyzed for CFSTI cataloging or the material provided may be reviewed and modified as appropriate to conform to the CFSTI formats.

Items input to the CFSTI are analyzed and abstracts are produced on tape-perforating equipment. The tapes are supplied to DDC for publication as the white section of *TAB*. The abstract section produced by CFSTI remains an entity and is also published in *U. S. Government Research and Development Reports* (*USGRDR*).

The incoming report is microfiched and, at present, also microfilmed if it is not accompanied by at least ten copies. It is analyzed using a mathematical prediction model to estimate its sales potential. Reports that are estimated to be salable in quantities greater than the number provided by the source are microfilmed for use of the Copyflow technique, which produces electrostatic image offset masters for reproduction. The initial press run, produced during this phase, is stocked and a record is maintained of the activity on the stock as a means of modifying the prediction model.

Supplementing the stock printed locally by CFSTI of reports considered to be within the scope of their distribution activities are bulk quantities of overruns of S&T information published by the GPO for other federal agencies. In distributing these items, the CFSTI acts as a bookseller, distributing material at the prices assigned by the GPO. Pricing of items produced locally by the CFSTI is assumed to cover only the actual reproduction cost. Budget authorizations and transfers of funds from other agencies cover CFSTI analysis and overhead costs.

Besides supplying documents on demand at the fee or price listed in the announcement bulletins, the CFSTI prepares special bibliographies on a contract or fee basis, in conjunction with the Library of Congress, Department of Agriculture, and Department of the Interior. It also initiates certain bibliographies on comparatively popular subject areas that may be considered to be price lists or secondary announcement media for the basic report literature store. The CFSTI also publishes *Technical Translations* bimonthly.

In addition to the approximately half million requests annually transferred by DDC, the CFSTI services approximately 2000 direct customer requests per day (for fiscal year 1965).

This figure was expected to increase 50 to 75 per cent during fiscal year 1966. CFSTI supplies either hard copies or duplicate microfiche. In the reproduction of incoming documents for its own use in making hard copies and in supplying duplicate microfiche, the CFSTI will produce more than a million microfiche during fiscal year 1966. Of the total output of documents requested, 97 per cent can be filled from stock, which is developed on the basis of the prediction model mentioned. A remainder of some 600 items must be supplied by single copy reproduction from microfiche.

One of the principal efforts of the CFSTI at present is the development of potential sources for documents and the negotiation for acquisitioning such material more directly and rapidly than in the past. Where adequate distribution mechanisms already exist, the CFSTI expects to undertake announcement of availability rather than responsibility for duplicative or substitute distribution. A single point of contact for industry and the technical community is the goal of the organization.

The current annual rate of translations and foreign reports is approximately 2500. The CFSTI is hoping to double their input rate of this kind of material. The CFSTI expects to seek the support of the Federal Council for Science and Technology toward compulsory registration of significant translations made or planned by any other federal agency in order to develop a closer control and interchange of the translation effort.

The CFSTI is looking toward the establishment of a separate journal for the announcement and index coverage of some 20,000 patents per year considered of interest to industry and government. Similarly, an attempt will be made to develop a journal for announcing materials such as engineering drawings available from AEC, DOD, and NASA. A journal called *Research in Progress* is to be established in which announcements of ongoing research developments projects will be published. Such information is generally obtainable from the Science Information Exchange. However, the SIE has not attempted to serve the public to be accommodated by the CFSTI. *Research in Progress* is to contain some 65,000 items per year. The CFSTI is also interested in becoming the source of standards for the description and analysis of technical documents which would include docu-ment organization, descriptive cataloging, abstracting, indexing, report numbering, and transliteration. The CFSTI has established an index to all literature produced by Government funding. The index contains subject, author, source, and report number sections.

Document Generators and Users

As stated earlier, all organizations generate or use documents. There is a community of typically mission-oriented organizations, however, which, with respect to document and information services, may be characterized almost exclusively as the generators or users of documents. These organizations, which include myriad contractors, universities, government laboratories, and industrial organizations, are often involved to some degree in other aspects of documentation and information processing. For example, they may operate a technical library which becomes the major interface with the rest of the information system. But the library is often a support service, auxiliary to the major purposes of the organization. This section focuses on the generation and use of documents within such organizations with particular emphasis on report literature.

In connection with contract performance, research programs, and similar efforts, documents and reports are issued regularly. These typically include periodic progress reports and end-product documents representing major milestones or task completions. Collectively these activities may be called document generation. For most contractors the contract or related administrative document usually specifies the minimum number of documents to be produced as well as the distribution of those documents. It is common for the contracting agency to control distribution, sometimes taking on the task of physically distributing the reports (especially in such cases as DOD, NASA, etc.). This tends to limit distribution and impede rapid dissemination. From the generator's point of view his documents go to three places: the in-house "library," the contracting office or agency, and a specified but usually restricted primary distribution list. The contracting agency may—but often does not—announce the document and assume responsibility for subsequent distribution and efforts designed to bring the document to the attention of the larger scientific and technical

community. This tends to cause delays. A similar set of events occurs with respect to documents produced at government laboratories or facilities except for the minor point that the laboratory or facility does not usually operate through a contracting agency.

The most immediate manifestation of these procedures is a delay in injecting the information into the larger scientific and technical community, including significant delays in current awareness. Many government organizations provide for announcing the documents received in such media as DDC's *TAB* and NASA's *STAR*, but again there may be restrictions concerning what is announced, and delays are a certainty.

Some portion of the information produced will find its way into journals and/or books. This is especially true when the document generator is a university, although contractors also produce a significant amount of journal articles and books. If the material being produced has no restrictions on its publication, then the problem of delay—that is, the time lags previously described—in publication obtains. This may be as long as two years (see American Psychological Association Study in Chapter 4). If there are restrictions, as in many DOD contracts, then prior approval must be obtained from the contracting agency. This adds additional time (usually a few months but sometimes as much as a year or more) to the process.

The in-house procedures in the production of documents vary considerably among organizations and are of little concern here with the exception that the diverse formats required and the multitude of report requirements imposed by contracts or other devices tend to further impede the dissemination of scientific and technical information. As in journal publishing, almost no consideration is given to user requirements in generation of reports.

There is also concern here with the use of documents at some ultimate consumer level such as the individual scientists in an industrial or government laboratory or production facility. Two points are of particular interest: current awareness and retrospective search and retrieval.

The user may remain currently aware of documents and information of interest in a multitude of ways. These are reported elsewhere in this book and include local announcements, published abstracts and indexes, journals or other appropriate literature, primary distribution, and verbal or nonpublished communications. Most users employ many if not all of these media. What is perhaps surprising is the report from user studies about the lack of awareness on the part of the users about current awareness media. For example, the Auerbach Report indicated that 53 per cent of the sample of DOD contractors and in-house engineers and scientists did not use the DDC *TAB*. Of these, 21 per cent were not aware of its existence. This is in part mitigated by the fact that the technical library acts as a buffer and often it, rather than the ultimate user, has access to and makes use of the *TAB*. What is apparent from a review of current awareness practice is a great deal of inconsistency and unevenness, so that even within a single large organization the practices vary considerably. This is in part a function of user education, but also relates to the lack of adequate practices and the need for introducing standards for user awareness practices.

The classical method of retrospective search and retrieval involves the use of some library tools such as a subject catalog to ascertain what is in the collection and then to request the appropriate documents. Such practices, although still in use, are rapidly becoming outmoded for present-day science and technology activities. Newer procedures including machine searches, selective dissemination, and the use of many secondary sources are assuming a position of greater prominence. For example, the Foreign Technology Division of the Air Force (in the federal sector) and IBM (in the nonfederal) disseminate materials or notifications to selected users based on user profiles which are modified with experience. This does not eliminate the time consumed by users in search activities, but greatly reduces it. Current awareness also is greatly facilitated. These, however, are among the more advanced techniques. Two more commonly used techniques are the use of secondary sources and machine searches.

Secondary sources such as *Index Medicus, Engineering Index,* and *Nuclear Science Abstracts* have been described in detail. These sources are a basic tool in the retrospective search for many areas of science and technology today. The user (a librarian, for example) can rapidly examine the secondary source materials and ascertain what may be of value. Most often the documents are not immediately available but must be ordered. Many systems provide facilities

(e.g., the order forms and standard procedures used by DDC) for reasonably short response times to requests. Even so, a one-week delay is frequent and delays of three or four weeks are not uncommon. For secondary sources greater delays often are encountered, especially where the source of the document must first be determined. The greatest single delay, however, is that incurred in the process of getting the materials announced and reported in the secondary source, which may take months to accomplish.

Such devices as descriptor terms to produce a list of candidate documents are used widely today in machine retrieval of information. In some instances, such as DDC, extensive special bibliographies may be prepared on this basis. There is still the delay of processing the request and distributing the product. There is also the restriction imposed in many instances by limiting the system to qualified users such as DDC. Machine retrieval also imposes the task of providing definitions in a dictionary or thesaurus which are acceptable and workable in the area of interest. Familiarity with such tools of course is implicit.

Administration, Policy, and Support

The activities of organization in this category are quite diverse. One attribute they share, however, is that they are not directly involved in the processing or manipulation of documents and information (except for their own use). As such, there is little to describe in the way of operations pertaining to the handling of S&T information. But their functions with respect to administration, policy, and support of information and documentation practices significantly influence these practices, and those functions are reviewed here.

Two modes of administrative and policy development and implementation exist within the executive departments and agencies in the present system: (a) the direct administrative or line responsibility; (b) the indirect by means of recommendations usually proffered by committees.

The several departments and agencies allocate resources and budgets to the appropriate divisions thereby exercising an important means of administration and control. The departments and agencies typically do not get involved, how-

ever, in the technical problems of document and information handling. Instead they rely on the document system organization to do so. They do exercise review.

The major control exercised by the President's office is through the Bureau of Budget (BOB). BOB is more likely to concern itself with total department or agency budget rather than subordinate unit budgets. The exception to this is when large discrete organizations such as DDC can be readily identified.

Indirect control on policy formulation is exercised in several ways. Interagency ad hoc committees such as the Federal Library Committee are formed. PSAC and FCST are sources of such influence. The influence of the Library of Congress on the library community has already been described. Standards and similar developments by professional societies form still another method. But perhaps the most significant activity in this realm today is COSATI. This organization, operating through the FCST in the Executive Offices of the President, has been specifically charged with review, analysis, and planning functions concerning the present and future S&T information system. Although they act as a committee and do not exercise any direct control, their membership is such that their recommendations may carry a great deal of weight and result in actions on the part of several departments and agencies represented in COSATI. For example, COSATI recently devised a scheme for standardization of microfiche which is now being widely adapted throughout the federal sector.

Several organizations influence the activities of the present system by virtue of the support they provide in such areas as research and development, especially in the development of new technologies. Organizations of both the federal and nonfederal sectors are so involved. Of particular significance in the federal sector is the OSIS of the National Science Foundation. As described elsewhere in this chapter, OSIS is involved in support of both research programs and direct subsidy or grants for journals, translations, and the like. Although this may at times result in direct control of some elements of the system, OSIS tends to operate in a laissez-faire manner. OSIS also provides support by virtue of funding a number of activities such as SIE and NRC which are operated elsewhere in the government.

In the nonfederal sector support is not as

clearly defined. Several of the professional societies and industrial associations, however, have
involved themselves in activities likely to ramify
throughout the system. Some of these organizations have been active in research activities in
the information sciences. Others have been active in developments including the establishment
of operational systems that exist to serve particular user groups but which also serve as a basis
for major portions of future system developments. For example, the Engineering Joint
Council has been active in establishing the *Engineering Joint Index* along with associated tools
such as the *Engineering Thesaurus*. This has
potential for broader application than exists
today.

PROBLEM AREAS

A major effort in the study of the present system was the identification of problems. This
identification, as reported by respondents or as
problems emerged from analysis of current practices, is important in understanding current operations and provides an important basis for the
requirements discussed in Chapter 6. Three
problem categories relating to implications for
a system design were identified: (a) administrative and organizational; (b) operational and
functional; and (c) support. Seventeen specific
problem areas, each falling into one of the three
categories indicated in Table 2-8, were isolated
and are reviewed here. These reviews represent
a distillation of the problems reported earlier
in this chapter. The problems—briefly summarized here to provide an integrated perspective of areas that require attention—are not as-
cribed to specific organizations. Instead they are
related to the organizational categories used
throughout this chapter where appropriate.

Administrative and Organizational Problems

Administrative and organizational problems
concern operational activities and services other
than direct manipulation and processing of documents and information. To a large measure
they tend to be system problems—that is, problems relating to all portions of the present system as opposed to individual organizations or
aggregates thereof. This is particularly true in
terms of the requirements derived from these
problems.

Table 2-8   Problem Areas

Administrative and Organizational Problems
  Reporting and records
  Funding patterns
  Personnel and training
  Legal aspects
  Facilities and locations
  Proprietary and other constraints
Operational and Functional
  Subject area coverage
  Users and user services
  Dissemination
  International operations
  Representation
  Collections
  Processing
  Compatibility (convertibility)
  Analysis
Support
  Application of advanced technologies
  Evaluation tools and techniques

Reporting and Records. It was difficult to obtain
good data about the documentation and information services provided by any of the agencies and organizations visited. Records often
were geared to organizational or budgetary requirements rather than documentation or information services. Use data often were lacking
or incomplete. Similarly, often one could not
ascertain actual operating costs. For example,
overhead or capital investments are not commonly reported as information services costs yet
they may be a major element in such costs. Furthermore, it is not possible to make direct comparisons across or within agencies since the
forms and records are not consistent and the
data contained are not standard. These problems
were particularly intense in the several federal
and nonfederal library organizations.

Funding Patterns. Like records, budgets do not
always relate to document and information services and operations. They are often related to
other aspects of the agency or organization. This
causes difficulty in maintaining adequate records
(see preceding) with respect to controlling or
maintaining efficient operations in documentation and information. This problem applies to
almost all organizations where the document services are provided as an integral part of a large
entity—for example, libraries within operational

agencies. On the other hand, this appears to be much less a problem for organizations whose operations are exclusively document or information oriented (e.g., CFSTI, DDC).

Personnel and Training. There is a lack of properly qualified personnel including information specialists, librarians, and clerks. Additionally, there is a high personnel turnover along with its concomitant costs in a number of organizations. This is especially true of clerical personnel who require special training and qualifications beyond that required of most clerical personnel. Educational requirements are generally standardized, but performance criteria are lacking. These problems apply particularly to nonfederal libraries, somewhat less to federal libraries and to generator/user organizations.

Legal Aspects. A multitude of diverse statutes, administrative rulings, or other legal requirements establish the legal basis for the information activities of the several organizations (see Appendix 3). These statutes and requirements have developed independently and result in different legal bases for the several information activities, which may produce inadvertent damage performed by one element of government upon others and present problems for any plan attempting to integrate the activities of several organizations. This problem applies directly to all federal and other government organizations and has implications for certain nonfederal organizations because of their dependency on the federal sector.

Facilities and Locations. There is often failure on the part of federal agencies to share facilities even where two or more organizations operate similar services in the same area. There also is a great deal of concern about future storage requirements and future microform facility requirements. It is likely that changes will have to be made to allow for the very large expanding volume of materials expected over the next several decades. Although the problem impinges on all organizations in the sense that any organization might be concerned with sharing facilities or with storage of materials, it is primarily an administrative matter and relates to the development of policy and procedures.

Proprietary and Other Constraints. A large volume of scientific and technical information is excluded from the information "marketplace" because of constraints on the flow of certain information. These include proprietary restrictions, security restrictions, and similar limitations. Although the need exists to protect proprietary and security information, there is a feeling throughout the community that much of the information is unnecessarily classified or controlled resulting in excessive waste and inefficiency. Particularly there is a problem with respect to determining what constitutes proprietary information. Another general problem is that of classifying entire documents (i.e., security classification) while only small portions of those documents are, in fact, classified. The problem of constraints is manifested primarily in mission-oriented organizations producing documents for DOD or certain other government agencies. The problem impinges, however, on almost all organizations that must process such documents, especially the libraries and information analysis centers, and generally limits use of much valuable information.

Operational and Functional Problems

Operational and functional problems relate to the processing and manipulation of documents or information and related services. Although they often apply to the overall operations of the present system, they also frequently apply to individual organizations or aggregates of a few organizations. The requirement implications therefore vary from broad system to specific organization requirements.

Subject Area Coverage. There is much concern with duplication and overlap in subject area coverage. Some of this redundancy is deliberate and desirable; some of it is unknown. There are also omissions and gaps reported in coverage, although much of this relates to specific organization mission wherein complete coverage is not appropriate. The problem here is our lack of knowledge concerning the extent of overlaps and omissions. A need exists to assess the overlaps and duplications as well as the omissions and gaps to ascertain: (a) what is unknown, and (b) what is undesirable. These problems relate primarily to libraries and publication, announcement, and distribution organizations.

Users and User Services. There is a lack of awareness and skills on the part of the users concerning the services and resources available.

There is also some question concerning the utility of certain user services—for example, the myriad announcement bulletins, indexes and abstracts, etc. Another problem in this area is the frequent lack of effective feedback mechanisms for modification of available services. Document source organizations, for example, are not sufficiently aware of the effect or utility of their services. Although such problems are concerned primarily with users, it is incumbent upon all elements of the system to better "advertise" their resources and services.

Dissemination. The dissemination patterns do not always reflect needs. Many delays have been reported, particularly with respect to secondary materials. There is conflicting testimony (partly due to changes now underway), however, as to how bad these delays are and what effect they may have. The question of applicability of selective or active dissemination with positive feedback is frequently raised and requires attention on an individual organizational basis. Dissemination problems apply across the entire spectrum of organizations, focusing perhaps on the users.

International Operations. A number of agencies are directly involved in acquiring material from overseas sources. Coverage is often redundant. Several government agencies and private organizations may purchase the same materials independently of each other. This is particularly inefficient because of the difficulties in effecting purchase and exchange operations in many countries. At the same time, coverage is incomplete and significant gaps have been reported in particular foreign materials. There also are a number of international exchange agreements in effect which are deficient in their operation. This is a problem for libraries and publication, announcement, and distribution organizations.

Representation. Several distinct problems exist in this area. First is the question of the utility of various forms of representation such as traditional catalogs, indexes, and abstracts. Second is the question of cooperative arrangements with respect to representation, such as arrangements for cataloging. Third, there is a lack of standards for various forms of representation, as well as a lack of indications concerning the desirable levels of representation for various applications or uses. Finally, there is the problem of repeti-

tive representation (described in greater detail in the next chapter). Representation problems extend primarily to publication, announcement, and distribution organizations. To some extent, however, they also extend to the document generation organizations in that the originators of documents are often required to provide abstracts or other forms of representation and the responsibility for representation is shifting toward the document originators.

Collections. A number of libraries and facilities do not know precisely what is in their collections. This is due in part to the backlogs of unprocessed material. Even when the contents are generally known (e.g., serials that have not yet been processed), access and retrieval becomes a problem. There are deficiencies both in acquisition and purging policies. Acquisition policies often do not reflect use patterns. Purging policies are noticeably absent. These problems were found in most libraries and information analysis centers.

Processing. A number of problems have been identified with respect to processing (here defined as all of the manipulations to which a document is subjected before being made available to a user) of documents and information. The procedures by which documents and information are processed vary from place to place and are uneven in their efficiency. There is the question of utility of machine systems as a tool in such processing. There is a special problem with respect to certain information services, for example, computer programming. The same materials may be reprogrammed when existing computer programs (which are not generally available) have already been developed and paid for by the government. There is also the costs associated with repetitive keyboarding in the generation and subsequent processing of documents. Except for repetitive keyboarding—a problem for document generators—these problems apply to libraries; information analysis centers; and publication, announcement, and distribution organizations.

Compatibility. Many document and information system tools, such as indexes, catalogs, and thesauri, are not compatible or convertible. This imposes difficulties in effecting efficient cooperative activities between organizations. This problem is related primarily to libraries and distribu-

tion organizations but also extends significantly to the generators and users.

Analysis. A basic problem is the lack of formalized criteria for establishing information analysis centers, except in the case of DOD where published directives exist. There is also a lack of awareness about services available. This problem, although concerned with operating the information analysis centers, is also an administrative problem in terms of planning, conspicuity, and training.

Support Problems

The support problems are not concerned with operational activities per se. Rather they are problems that relate to developments external to system operations which may in some manner influence those operations. The cases cited are in the area of research and development.

Application of Advanced Technologies. The applications of advanced technologies are sporadic and uneven. There is also a lack of information concerning research and development innovations. There is a lack of R&D activity in certain significant areas. For example, relatively little effort is devoted to use of computer technology in most library operations. This problem extends to most organizations visited.

Evaluation Tools and Techniques. A particular area of deficiency is the development of evaluation tools and techniques with respect to information and document services. Especially there is a lack of standards and criteria for system performance evaluation and the tools and techniques by which such standards and criteria may be developed. This is a significant research problem of concern to the organizations that provide research support.

Chapter Three

The Present System: Document Flow

The preceding chapter reviewed the organization and operation of the current system. This chapter focuses on the document and the events in its generation, transmission, management, and exploitation. It describes techniques for generating and controlling documents and the technology that is shifting emphasis from discrete, uncoordinated events to integrated flow.

There exists a sequence of events from the generation to the ultimate exploitation of S&T information. These events and the flow of documents through the present system are depicted in Figure 3-1. The elements and functions of that network are described in this chapter.

In the processing of the S&T information, documents flow through the network facilities where they are subjected to various processes. For example, representations are generated and disseminated. Many of the processes are performed repetitively and such repetitive functions are described later in this chapter. The argument is presented that the functions can and should be integrated for maximum exploitation of the information at least cost. In practice, this hypothesis is already being tested, often without conscious direction, and its validity is being demonstrated in such shifts as chronologically earlier generation of representations. Also, services formerly considered closely related to the reference function of a library are now being elaborated to become those of an information center. Such developments, which attempt to offer services more closely tailored to user needs, are included in this description of document flow in the present system.

ELEMENTS OF THE DOCUMENT NETWORK

The relationships and variations in the current system may be loosely modeled as a network as illustrated in Figure 3-1. The basic unit is called the *report*. Into this class we place a document that is originated and enters the system as a unit and which contains the chronologically earliest report of scientific or technical work. Some million S&T reports are prepared each year in the United States, either as a result of requirements imposed by a contractor or on the initiative of the three million individuals or twelve thousand source organizations to record the methodology and results of work in which they are engaged.

To broaden the range of dissemination of information documented in reports, at least a million papers are prepared and accepted for journal publication or for oral presentation. A *paper* is a unit introduced into the network as a member of an aggregation. The network thereafter must process both the aggregate and the member unit. Ordinarily less detailed than the report, the paper (including technical letters and releases) usually is subject to editorial and technical screening outside the source organization.

Because information presented orally may not be identical with that documented for presentation, the evaluation of oral presentations is considered less reliable than that imposed on source items destined for primary publication. Consequently the 30,000 serials (some 6000 published in the United States) are preferred above the

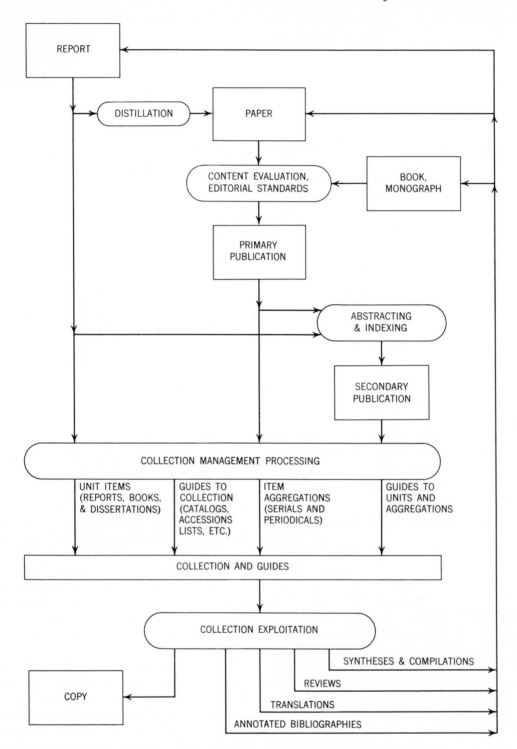

Fig. 3-1 The document network.

report or conference paper, both as a source and as a medium for dissemination, despite the delays associated with refereeing and publication.

To provide information about what is avail-able in report and journal literature, the fourth major element in the documentation system ap-pears: the nearly 400 U. S. abstracting and in-dexing services. With the goals of (1) announc-ing the existence of a document unit in one of

some collection of unit aggregations, and (2) simultaneously creating a tool for retrieving document units pertinent to a user need, these services adopt and create restricted, constrained, and controlled referential or indexing vocabularies—ostensibly tailored for effective use by specific user populations. The product of abstracting and indexing has been exclusively a publication until recently. The network must process this *secondary publication* as a unit.

The fifth major element in the documentation network is the 10,000 *collections* the information user tries to access. Each collecting organization creates additional announcement and search tools.

The catalog is the principal search tool for a collection and also uses a constrained vocabulary. Also, until recently the catalog has consisted of a deck of unit records—three-by-five cards. Decks of cards require maintenance in terms of filing. Filing rules—a collection organization constraint—can be a communication impediment as much as an aid. The catalog that is available in page form may not suffer the weaknesses of a card catalog (human inconsistencies in filing, etc.), but—worse—it may not match the collection. Publishing frequently enough to keep the catalog as current as the collection may be economically unfeasible.

The collection for scientific and technical information is assumed to function as a redistribution and exploitation point (rather than an archive). Redistribution involves copying or circulating the document. The products of exploitation become input units to the system: documents consisting of analytic (in some cases, periodic) reviews, syntheses, translations, and annotated bibliographies.*

When the document meets certain variable specifications such as size and cover material, it is designated a *book* or a *monograph*. Like the journal, appearance of the book is a primary publication. In terms of managing the collection, the book is a unit item.

Next we shall cover some of the highlights in the generation and transmission of documents and their representatives through the overall network. Later in this chapter we consider the technology and decision parameters at principal points in the overall network in enough detail

to indicate the implications to coordinated management of an overall network of a scientific and technical documentation.

A GENERALIZED PATTERN OF INTERACTING FUNCTIONS

For each unit with which the system must cope, we can generalize the minimum pattern of preparation, distribution, announcement, and collection. Each of these functions results in separate "documents." *Preparation* creates the source item containing some substantive fact or opinion. *Distribution* requires preparation and collection of recipient data "documents" or records—including qualification with respect to receipt of source item substance. *Announcement* requires preparation and collection of records of source items, and preparation and distribution of announcements.

By going through this pattern only once, we can begin to suspect that the system is generating more documents than it is managing. One goal of improving the system should be to ensure that any document generated is doing a job not done by any document already part of the system. The subsequent discussions will follow the multiple continuous paths of a document through the network of Figure 3-1, summarizing how each of the four generalized functions is performed on each of the major elements. Wherever practical we will point out the parameters guiding the choices in performing required functions through application of typical and novel procedures and equipment. We will also see how applications of novel procedures and equipment create opportunities and implications for the network distribution of functions.

The Initial Cycle

The documentation system "begins" with the originator of scientific or technical information. In spite of his own identification as a user of technical or scientific data, the originator of scientific or technical data seldom considers the interest of the system providing for its use. In part he lacks direct knowledge of the most probable using system, and in part he simply denies that document preparation and management are specializations encompassing knowledge of goals and techniques that his use of language does not alone prepare him to share. The documentation system therefore interacts with systems

---

* Unannotated bibliographies constitute selective announcement bulletins and are guides to—not exploitations of—the collection.

historically or chronologically before the originating system; that is, the education and experience of the originator are indirectly part of the documentation system. The burden falls on the documentation system to compensate for these pre-documentation factors.

To get down on paper the concepts and correlations being originated costs an average of $3 per word of direct labor (if all S&T personnel are considered) before the information system becomes involved. This gross average is based on an annual volume of 2×10^6 units (reports plus paper) each containing an average of 6×10^3 words, produced by 3.6×10^6 individuals, each earning an average of 10×10^3 per year. That is, a direct labor investment of 36×10^9 yields 12×10^9 words. Examining particular kinds of papers, in particular fields, and reducing the population to authors (rather than total S&T personnel), and basing investment on program costs that include laboratory support equipment (but not necessarily overhead or burden costs) lead to ranges in the cost per word from $0.10 to $50.

The document originates with draft keyboarding, most often on a typewriter. To maximize exploitation of the keyboarding labor, despite iterative review and modification of document contents, some source organizations use equipment that produces a machine-readable copy along with draft copy. As the draft is revised, any text that has not changed is recreated automatically, thereby minimizing keystroking. Systems in which machine readability is mechanical—such as tape-perforating typewriters—suffer from text formatting constraints. For example, the existence on such tape of a carriage return code makes awkward the introduction or deletion of text. Additional operator time is required to erase (overpunch) the carriage return codes and introduce new ones. Nevertheless, the "reuse" of text reduces the burden of proofreading.

Some work has been done in the development of computer-based systems for the preparation of documentation at the source, in which the computer program handles such changes in format. The Applied Physics Laboratory of Johns Hopkins University has done some experimentation in this area, as has IBM. When text is input through a keypunch, sequences of punch codes identify for the program the shift from upper to lower case and other typographic data.

Clearly such control codes involve additional, nontextual keystroking.

The source organization may impose standards for editorial review or support and for controlling the information that may be made available in the document. We will not discuss documents that remain entirely internal to an organization—for example, those whose technical content is proprietary or organization sensitive and which are not eligible for input to any system outside the source organization. Techniques for controlling such documentation cannot be ignored in considering processing applicable to items released into the networks of scientific and technical documents with which libraries, journals, and abstracting and indexing services may cope. Rather, the similarities in the requirements for document control regardless of document content or destination deserve a more objective consideration than the community of librarians has given them.

In the worst—and most common—case, the document is prepared for reproduction, appropriate to the organization policies, with little regard for its control. Bibliographic control data such as a series number may be included as part of the content of the report. Equally commonly, however, the author's name, a title, and the report date constitute the total original control data. A copy of the document is then made available for internal control, perhaps in the equivalent of a special library or document management system.

To create guides to a collection of such documents, this group in the source organization may assign additional bibliographic control data which may or may not accompany a copy or copies of the source item when they are released into the network. The internal organization may prepare an announcement bulletin for alerting other members of the organization to the existence of the document. Development of control records and of announcement bulletins represents additional investment in keyboarding and file maintenance.

The final document is made available through a distribution list, usually prepared and maintained by another group in the source organization. The content of the distribution list must be keyboarded and updated as changes occur in addresses or identifications of intended recipients. When required as part of a contract commitment, the document may be accompanied

by certain cataloging or control processing information (at one time even including a catalog card set)—information constituting the next major representative of document contents. Thus, before it has been released outside the source organization, the document's identification has been keystroked not only for purposes of preparing it, but also for controlling it in terms of a document collection or management system and in terms of a distribution system.

Subsequent Cycles

At the receiving organization the document and its bibliographic information are examined to determine the adequacy with which the source organization has complied with recipient's needs or specifications. This analysis involves control files of policies (specifications) and of item representatives (catalog or shelflist) on the basis of which the recipient accepts and identifies the document. Redistribution is assumed to be the mission of the receiving organization. Control processing by a recipient solely to hold or use the document is implied but not explicitly examined. The primary journal, the clearinghouse activity, and the collection activity all redistribute the original document contents and announcements of those contents. In creating the file(s) of representatives (catalog or index), document identification is repetitively keyboarded as required.

To generate representatives of a source document, the receiving organization creates and maintains a referential vocabulary and a set of processing procedures. For clearinghouse and collection activities, more than access vocabularies is necessary. Anticipating that among recipients of the announcement of its accessions are potential users of documents, a receiving organization establishes a storehouse of documents or document images, inventory control systems, and request control and distribution systems to enable it to respond to requests for copies of the item.

The document, distributed and announced as described, goes to more than one organization, some of which are only indirectly involved in the use of the document. Each of these establishes input evaluation, storage, and announcement policies and maintains various files of document representatives. For example, a report bearing scientific and technical implications, produced by a source within the federal government, might be published initially by the Government Printing Office (GPO) and made known through its *Monthly Catalog*. The report would also be announced, following appropriate processing, through the clearinghouse for Federal Scientific and Technical Information (CFSTI), in its announcement journal.

The rationale for such duplication of announcement and processing is that users of the GPO catalog and those of the abstracting journal put out by the CFSTI are not identical, and information about the existence of the item must be made known to all potential users. In some cases, work duplication is minimized by copying document identification data and/or representation from one announcement medium to another. Each announcement medium must be separately indexed, however, because of disparities in vocabulary between the announcement services and differences in depth to which an item may be indexed by various services—both factors being determined ideally by the specific needs of the group of users served by a particular announcement medium.

The distinction was made between papers and reports to indicate differences in the channels for these two kinds of source document. The document prepared for oral presentation or publication in a primary journal may receive editorial review internally by a source organization comparable to that required for the contract report. For handling within the source organization document management system, the paper may be assigned certain cataloging information. To the degree the journal imposes requirements, this information may accompany the document as it is released to the journal.

Primary journal publication has changed little during the last several decades. The manuscript received by the journal is subjected to editorial and technical review, then keyboarded on typesetting or photocomposition equipment. Indexes to the contents of a primary journal are prepared essentially manually, with possible addition of sequential card camera techniques for the compilation of cumulative indexes. Primary journals increasingly are making a practice of including with a paper the text for an abstract, usually prepared by the author, perhaps with editorial assistance or guidance.

Introduction of the use of photocomposition equipment in the production of primary journals was the first point at which the keyboarding

for publication produced a machine-readable document record—as a perforated paper tape. Until recent experiments, however, these tapes were used only for control of composition equipment and were not processed, for example, to derive indexes automatically.

Equipment otherwise available for producing machine-readable document records in manuscript form (e.g., the Flexowriter) is not considered adequate for primary journal publication because of limitations in the number of type fonts and graphic control codes and because of unreliable operation of the input devices. Whereas a source organization exploiting only a fraction of the maximum character per minute output capability of a typewriter or tape perforator can absorb a corresponding fraction of "downtime," the journal publisher cannot afford this source of increased cost per character, output delay, and processing discontinuity.

Like the report, the contents of the primary journal constitute input material for the abstracting and indexing services.

In attempts to reduce the delay between the date of publication of information in a primary journal and the announcement of its publication through the medium of an abstracting and indexing service, these services are increasingly depending on varying degrees of machine support. Of the services briefly studied during the course of this investigation, none creates the text—for what is ultimately published by the service—initially on equipment producing a machine-readable record. In a more recent experiment sponsored by the National Science Foundation, however, a method was developed by which all text items in a machine record can be functionally identified so they can be processed to any secondary form. The researchers also developed a computer program system for automatically converting the machine record into various forms. Thus all the information that may be required in subsequent processing is recorded during initial keystroking. The difference between this and other textual data recording is that the text item content—rather than its typographic form—is recorded. This procedure allows the primary record to be directly processed into a variety of secondary products, regardless of their typographic forms. For example, operating from a single input manuscript record, such diverse forms as typesetting tapes for the primary publication, author index, and

abstract journal entry may be produced simultaneously.

Text is usually handwritten on a worksheet, then separately typed one or more times before being keyboarded on tape-perforating equipment, from which reproducible copy is typed. The copy is pasted up into camera-ready page layouts, and the machine-readable tape is discarded or stored. It does not ordinarily become the basis for further machine processing. With few exceptions the announcement tools are publications. Thus the secondary service available in support of attempts to search the collection is, in fact, an additional item for the collection. The exceptions are secondary services to which the customer may subscribe, in which the delivered product is a magnetic tape containing full text and/or indexes.

Experiments into the automatic production of the indexes to the contents of the abstracting journal are based almost entirely on separately keyboarding the title, or various groups of descriptor terms, and the abstract identification code on punched cards, then sorting the cards mechanically or using a posting or index assembling computer program. A minimum of analysis is devoted to producing such indexes, on the basis that the announcement function is best served by rapid availability of a number of units small enough to be used, if necessary, without an index. For retrieval indexes to abstracting journals such as *Nuclear Science Abstracts* and *Chemical Abstracts*, formal analysis produces a special index form, sometimes called a "microabstract," which is keyboarded on cards useful for sequential card camera techniques.

The organization collecting source items and their representations, which constitute search tools, generates independent announcement tools serving the community of users of that collection. Again identification of the item may be keyboarded—in general, on typewriter equipment, without regard to any attempt for machine processing of the information. Some private industrial collections, small in terms of those supported directly by agencies of federal government, are generating machine form representations for items accessioned into the collection—for example, Lockheed, Douglas Aircraft Company, and the Applied Physics Laboratory.

The final major activity in the network can be classified as exploitation and is formalized in the development of information and data

Table 3-1   Principal Documentation Functions

Element	Functions			
	Preparation	*Distribution*	*Announcement*	*Collection*
Reports a unit basis	Original keyboarding, increasingly on equipment producing machine-manipulable characters, permitting editing and insertion of graphics by computer program and permitting transmission and remote composition and publication. Duplication for review and distribution using xerography, microreproduction, offset presses.	Involves maintenance of recipients file amenable to machine support including printing of mailing labels.	Internal announcement may be combined with ordering copies. Announcement bulletins may be generated from keypunched titles, using an index assembling program.	May utilize inverted indexes for report literature, in manual card system, "dual dictionary" system, or optical coincidence cards. May use machine support for production of page form catalogs or printing of catalog cards. KWIC and KWOC.
Papers and journals primary publication	Subject to close editorial control and technical review. Elaborate judging scheme of SAE. Publication delays. Photocomposition used increasingly, involves machine-readable character codes.	Conventional, by mail, by subscription.	Index functions as "announcement." Journals may contain announcements of papers received but not reviewed, or not accepted for full publication, copies of which sold direct to requestor at cost.	No collection activity.
Abstracts and indexes secondary services	Variations in abstract style—indicative, informative, telegraphic, inverted, extracts, and digests.	Conventional.	Indexing versus classification and cataloging. Indexing vocabularies, thesauri. Index "displays" including sequential card camera techniques, current contents, citation indexes.	Acquisitions records machine-oriented system.
Library collection	Acquisitions records. Problems of variety of forms for various sources. Computer-supported serials acquisition system. Catalog card replication and filing. Page form catalogs and increased filing points. Finding lists and multiple copies. Optical coincidence and inverted indexes.	Machine-supported circulation control systems.	Broadcast announcement via accessions lists. Selective announcement via computer-based descriptor matching.	Purging policy problems.
Copies	Microform masters for reprography—reels, fiche, and aperture cards. Photochromic microreduction. Video storage and display.	Volume distribution requires inventory control on stock of micro reproductions and hard copies. Files of requestor qualifications and billing records.	Comparable to that of abstracting services.	Inventory control techniques.
Exploitation critical syntheses and translations	Development and variety in information and data centers. Emergence of the "information specialist." Service orientation. Cover-to-cover translation. Machine translation.	Trend toward man-machine negotiation, search of natural language data base in ADP systems.	Comparable to reports announcement.	Comparable to library systems.

centers whose mission is analysis, evaluation, synthesis, and repackaging of either representations for, or fragments of, source items. During the last five years the differentiation of this activity from library reference activities has been growing to the point of use of new terminology for the work and its possible realignment as a research support activity.

The strength of the center lies in its relationship with a user group that it can clearly identify and whose needs it can determine and meet. This ideal is not necessarily achieved in many existing centers. Established without criteria for measuring user needs and satisfactions, the center can become another vacuous generator of redundant documents about documents.

The obvious observation to be drawn from this overview of the network of document handling is the investment in labor and equipment systems for creating representations of a given source item. We will next examine more closely some alternatives of preparation, distribution, announcement, and collection for each of the major elements. A brief overview of these alternatives is provided in Table 3-1.

THE REPORT—THE UNIT BASIS

In the previous discussion the interacting functions of preparation, distribution, announcement, and collection were identified. The balance of this chapter is devoted to these four functions as they are accomplished in the creation of each of the major elements of the documentation system. Preparation techniques or considerations relative to the preparation of each element are described. Parallels are drawn and, to the extent possible, redundancies pointed out. Examples are given of particularly effective techniques of application of technology to the execution of these functions by the producers of the individual major elements.

Report and Paper Preparation

Almost universally, the originator of the contents of a document is indifferent to and ignorant of the processing to which his efforts are subject. Efforts at augmenting educational programs, particularly at the undergraduate level, to improve the individual's ability to prepare written presentations of his work appropriate to given materials and audiences, are limited— principally by the pressure of increasingly con-

centrated curricula oriented toward a technical subject specialty.

Once he has given birth to an intellectual effort, the originator delegates responsibility for its documented debut—almost as a triviality that interferes with further "productive" efforts— while lamenting the failures of the "system" to fill his own information needs. Those responsible for serving such needs find that they are working without the support of, and even in spite of opposition of, those who need and who are originating information. The increasing complexity of documentation systems has aroused user criticism, paradoxically, because the systems are being developed without his participation. Responsibility must be shifted increasingly to the originator to prepare his materials suitably for the audience he expects to satisfy and the system in which his document will be entered for transfer through the network of scientific and technical information.

Preparing the content of a source item includes:

1. Keyboarding review draft(s).
2. Imposing editorial support and control and technical review.
3. Graphics production support.
4. Keyboarding and preparation of final master copy appropriate for publication, duplication, and distribution.

The gross cost comparison that follows for various techniques is based on some arbitary assumptions derived from publication system experience. Regardless of whether this experience corresponds to that of more than one organization, use of the same base facilitates costing comparison. The cost of overhead or other administrative price burden is not included.

Keystroking, Editing, and Graphics. A minimum theoretical rate for keyboarding is estimated at $0.0001 per keystroke, for a $1.50 per hour operator producing 250 keystrokes per minute. Average cost of draft keyboarding is approximately three times that figure, and final master preparation keyboarding is approximately $0.0005 per keystroke. Assume the average document page is to contain 2000 keystrokes including spaces, text characters, and typographic control strokes such as case shifts and carriage returns. Keyboarding the first review draft on a typewriter would cost an average of $0.60.

Alternative to typing directly on a typewriter is the preparation of manuscript copy on:

1. A tape-perforating typewriter such as the Flexowriter, Synchrotape, Dura Mach, or IBM 1050.

2. Card-punching equipment or equipment consisting of a typewriter with slave keypunch, such as an alternative configuration of the model 1050.

3. Magnetic tape-recording equipment such as the IBM magnetic tape Selectric typewriter (MTST) system.

4. Direct on-line terminals in a computer-based system, where terminals may be keyboards such as the 1050, the modified Selectric typewriter, or teletype equipment.

The type font used in preparing the original copy normally is not selected; whatever is available on standard office equipment is used. When an attempt is made to salvage unchanged material with minimum rekeystroking, and when volume of printing is high, the type font may be selected for graphic arts quality on the combined basis of esthetics and higher type density. The newer electric typewriters offer not only comparatively well-designed typefaces but the variable character width that provides higher character density. Some offer selection of typefaces. The VariTyper, for example, may be equipped with any of a wide range of typefaces and sizes, two of which are installed on the equipment at the same time for comparative ease in change of face. The Selectric uses an interchangeable ball on which the type is cast. All characters in the face, however, occupy the same amount of space on a line.

Among the tape-perforating typewriters, the Flexowriter provides a comparatively good graphic quality type font, including the option of differential spacing for characters. The IBM 1050 and Dura Mach, since they use the basic Selectric type ball carrier, can be equipped with the desired face. For making typeface selection when the input is prepared on card-punching equipment, special punch sequences must be used activating the output equipment to make changes in the type, as for upper and lower case. Inasmuch as the MTST system uses the Selectric, the original input and output are in any desired face available with the system. On-line terminals offer some variation in typeface

availability. The Selectric again offers the changes among those balls provided, where the material prepared at the terminal or automatically through the terminal will be used for final copy. These computer-based systems are most effective, however, when used with high-speed output printers, which are not ordinarily available with the selection of typefaces desired. For example, the output printing chain on computing equipment is not available with differential character spacing and, unless an available typeface is selected, must be designated specifically for the application. Teletypewriter equipment is now being offered with some variation in typeface, but it is ordinarily all caps and in a sans serif face.

In discussing the variations in costing for preparing the contents of a source document in each of these types of systems, the cost per keystroke includes setup time, as in the loading of the MTST system with its reels or loading the tape-perforating equipment with tape, etc. Some cost comparisons for various input devices are offered in Table 3-2.

Keyboarding an original first draft on a tape-perforating typewriter averages slightly less than double the cost of keyboarding on a conventional typewriter, primarily because the equipment capability is lower. Although this is not entirely true in the 1050 system, because the keyboard itself is as responsive as the best of the electric typewriters, the effective speed of the tape-punching system remains comparatively low. The cost range listed for tape-perforating systems covers the option of running the final tape through a unit that introduces spacing between words to produce an even right column margin. This is done at top machine speed of ten characters a second at $0.0001 per keystroke additional labor.

Card-punching costs are about double average typing costs. Further, because preparing punched cards involves double the number of keystrokes of typing in order to verify the original punching, an immediate doubling in keystroking costs is involved. In Table 3-2 the estimate for control strokes is the same as the typing case. But preparing text for processing by a powerful computer-based system, which produces upper and lower case or otherwise augmented character set output from a high-speed printer, requires a far higher ratio of control keystrokes to text keystrokes. Ten to 15 per cent

Table 3-2 *Comparison of Minimum Costs of Preparing a Single Document Page° Using Various Input Devices*

Activity	Typewriter		Tape Perforator		Magnetic Tape Selectric		Keypunch and Verify		On-Line Computer-Based	
	Text	*Control*	*Text*	*Control*	*Text*	*Control*	*Text*	*Control*	*Text*	*Control*
Original keying	(1625)†$0.49	(375)$0.11	(1625)$0.81	(375)$0.19	(1625)$0.49	(600)$0.18	(3250)$1.95	(750)$0.45	(1625)$0.49	(600)$0.18
Proofing and format	0.16	0.04	0.16	0.04	0.16	0.06	0.16	0.04	0.16	0.06
Revised draft	(488) 0.15	(112) 0.03	(268) 0.13	(62) 0.03	(268) 0.08	(99) 0.03	(536) 0.33	(124) 0.07	(268) 0.08	(99) 0.03
Final keystroking	(1625) 0.81	(375) 0.19	(650) 0.33	(150) 0.08	(358) 0.11	(132) 0.04	(715) 0.43	(165) 0.10	(358) 0.11	(132) 0.04
Final proofing	0.16	0.04	0.09	0.02	0.06	0.02	0.06	0.02	0.06	0.02
Labor exclusive of author	1.77	0.41	1.42	0.36	0.90	0.33	2.93	0.68	0.90	0.33
System equipment	$0.04		$0.40		$0.35		$0.13–1.00		$1.10	
Text preparation	$2.22		$2.18–2.40‡		$1.58		$3.74–4.61		$2.33§	

* A "page" is defined as 25 lines of 80 characters each, averaging 13 words per line, and each line averaging one case shift plus one carriage return.
† Numbers in parentheses indicate keystrokes.
‡ Higher figure is for right justified copy.
§ Same for right justified final copy.

more control keystrokes are required for producing a document on a magnetic tape writing or an on-line computer-based system over those needed for a conventional typewriter.

Assume that once the draft has been originally typed, it is proofread (resulting in 5 per cent corrections) and reviewed by the author (resulting in 10 per cent changes). Preparing a reasonably "clean" (but not necessarily perfect or completely retyped) second typewritten draft for technical review involves an average of twice the number of keystrokes required directly for correction to accommodate reformatting that results from addition or deletion of text.

This requirement is eliminated in the more capable of the keypunch-based systems (such as IBM employs internally for the production of instruction manuals) and in the on-line computer-based system, in both of which the computer program takes over the responsibility for readjusting text for formatting corrections. Therefore, when text is originally recorded on magnetic or perforated tape or on punched cards, keystroking to reformat for draft review is minimum—perhaps 10 per cent of the volume of correction keystrokes.

The base price assumed for proofing is $0.0001 per keystroke. The rationale for the derivation of costs for proofing and format control is based on the number of keystrokes in that, as the proportion of distinct control keystrokes rises, the time for proofing (labor) apparently rises linearly. That is, proofing material keypunched for input into a computer-based system must be done more deliberately than that involved in checking a conventional manuscript because the control codes are not natural language and are not as readily recognized by the proofer as patterns. For example, rather than being concerned with whether a given sidehead is initial cap or italic, the proofer must check whether the control code associated with the sidehead text specifies the appropriate level, which code the computer program recognizes as an order for a particular sidehead style. Transferring these tasks to the computer program results in higher consistency in spelling, formatting, and other mechanical aspects of editing, and provides the opportunity for automatic derivation of document elements such as the table of contents and indexes.

We assume, conservatively, that 20 per cent of the text submitted is changed in editorial and technical review. For input prepared on a typewriter, the entire manuscript must be rekeystroked at the higher final keystroking cost as indicated. For perforated tape input, the 20 per cent that was changed must be keystroked plus 20 per cent additional for corrections to format. For the magnetic tape system and either the keypunch or on-line terminal computer-based system, only an additional 2 per cent corrections need be keystroked.

Notice that we have assumed a comparative minimum of keyboarding. That is, practice in most organizations would require complete retyping for various drafts, thus increasing the differential in cost for the source item produced on a typewriter as opposed to one produced in any system providing for the capturing and "reuse" of any keystrokes that are not changed in draft correction iterations. Concomitant with such keystroking costs are those of proofreading corrected or changed material. Where policies

require complete retyping, they entail the cost of additional proofreading. Retyping policies also are guided by the proportion of changes to be made in a given page. Where the changes affect half the total number of lines on the page, retyping the whole page is more economical than making corrections (when the document has been prepared on the typewriter). The cost saving in such cases is obvious for any system that captures the keystrokes.

In addition to the labor costs for producing each page of the source item, the figure indicates some approximations of equipment costs. The basis on which these may be considered minimum, however, varies between systems. Rental cost is based on a 176-hour month, with the character load per hour geared to the output of the keyboard operator as indicated in the labor breakdown. That is, the average cost per keystroke derived as $0.0003 is based on a certain output per hour and a given hourly rate. The same character per hour is used as the load capability of the equipment.

The typewriter is clearly the least costly of any of the input devices in itself. Keypunch and verification equipment is similarly inexpensive. The costs for tape-perforating or magnetic tape-recording systems appear to be comparable to each other, whereas the computer-based system is clearly the most costly even at maximum load utilization.

In costing the labor for the keypunch and verification scheme, additional control keystrokes were included on the basis that the cards produced might be used in a computer-based system. The cost for equipment for the keypunch-based system, therefore, ranges from $0.13 (where card decks are listed, as is, on EAM equipment) to an order of higher magnitude. The latter figure is based on an hourly rate for a computer system such as the 7094, where the system is not used solely for documentation processing. Costs of the on-line computer-based system are based on the assumption that the terminal capability is used to the maximum.

The *page* has been used as the unit for deriving these cost comparisons. The typewriter alone of the devices listed is "open-ended" with respect to its efficiency in terms of the number of pages that may be produced; that is, the cost per page is the same regardless of the number

typed. In contrast, the rental cost on the equipment of the other systems ranges between $600 and $15,000 regardless of use—even if only one page were produced per month and both the keyboard operator and keyboard were idle the balance of the month.

The tape perforator involves some costs for changing reels of tape and for locating particular points in a given tape once it is perforated in order to make changes or corrections. The magnetic tape Selectric system involves an electronic search for specified locations on a reel. Because the reel can contain only 24,000 characters, however, the time for selection and loading of the correct reel reduces the maximum system output.

Although keypunching is open-ended with respect to the document units, processing in a computer-based system is constrained by the economics of operating the computer system. Unless the processing does exploit the capability of the computer for formatting and other editorial functions, and the document volume being processed on a given computer pass takes advantage of the high speed of the processor and printers, the computer-based system suffers economically. Of course in any computer-based system, it is not necessary to assume that the entire workload of the system at any given time will be devoted to documentation ultimately destined for introduction into the system of scientific and technical documentation.

This summary of the keystroking portion of the document production has not covered consideration of the number of review copies that might be required. The implication was that only one review copy was prepared and that it alone was returned with corrections. Actually many systems involve distribution of more than a single copy for technical or policy review, and additional production problems and costs are created in this phase. These costs are described in the paragraphs on "Production and Duplication."

The use of typographic changes as themselves bearing information cannot be overlooked. That is, when we underline a word or set it in italics, we provide the reader with additional information about our intention concerning that word. We wish him to note it especially or we imply that it plays some particular role in the text, such as the label for a section or the name of some other portion of the document. Unless he

is familiar with the considerations of publication, the reader seldom realizes the number of different typefaces used in the material he encounters. His habits of inference of the information content of such typographic data appear to be subconscious.

For the producer of the source document, the choices of use of such signals must be based on knowledge of the interpretation to be given them by the reader. The document-handling community in general believes that the variation in type and the information contained by the use of various type fonts require availability of some thousand unique characters in the set for production of scientific and technical documents and in their representations—for example, abstracts, indexes, and catalog cards. Clearly the document manuscript, when originally typed or prepared on any of the input devices described, does not contain 1000 unique characters. Variations in characters are indicated by such devices as hand-drawn graphics, straight and wavy underlining, and marginal notations.

To select the printing or duplication method for a given source item, the source organization must specify the number of different characters required by the text, the number of copies to be printed, the frequency with which a given document may be republished in modified version, the size of the document as a whole, the degree to which typographic information will contribute to or support the content of the document, and the combination of graphics and text, or other techniques for making ready the printing itself.

In addition to the text that must be prepared for inclusion in a document, graphics of various kinds must be prepared. The choices made relative to the techniques used for graphics are related to the methods of production available for final printing and to the characteristics of the graphic material.

In manuscript, graphics are indicated by captions, and space may be left within the body of text for the introduction of the graphic at the appropriate point in the production of the document. Most commonly the graphic is prepared separately and merged with text either photographically or on the camera-ready pasteup copy. To develop a document and its graphic compatibly in a computer-based system has been the goal of several new equipment developments. In general, the direction has been toward scanning the graphic image linearly and digitizing the resulting modulated signal. The digital string can be stored and then reformed on a graphic display device such as a cathode-ray tube for introduction into the correct position in text.

In one program developed by IBM for preparing source documentation, a limited degree of graphic capability is offered within the symbol representation used for inputting text. For example, certain keypunch code sequences identify graphic elements such as an outside right corner, an inside right corner, intersections, and individual line elements. The ingenious editor can create from sequences of such codes a graphic for introduction in the main text stream as needed to produce tables and elementary graph forms. A comparable technique is being investigated for use in preparing the graphic or structural diagrams for chemical literature.

Systems in which the graphic is converted to an analog signal that is digitized are capable of accepting the original in, for example, aperture card form, the image on which is scanned as described. When displayed on a cathode-ray tube, the image may be modified and restored in the computer memory in modified form or photographed as modified from the face of the cathode-ray tube.

Image displays have been considered by document handlers as a technique primarily for assembling the image constituted by a full page of text for use in image storage systems. Primarily oriented toward retrieval, such systems are covered later in this chapter under the heading "The Copy."

Production and Duplication. The document that has been approved for distribution or release by the source organization is now available in some form considered a master for reproduction or duplication, printing, and distribution. The choice of techniques available for reproduction is based on the number of copies to be distributed and, to some extent, the type of graphics involved in the document. The most elementary technique involves preparing carbon copies when the document is originally typed. This technique provides very poor secondary copies and does not allow convenient introduction of graphic material. Combinations of

preparing text on paper masters and photographically preparing paper or metal masters of graphics for offset printing are commonly employed.

One of the problem areas in the reproduction or duplication of a source item centers around situations in which fewer than 25 copies are to be prepared. Setting up an offset press for fewer than 25 copies raises the cost per copy to close to the cost of diazo dye or other unit reproduction methods—approximately $0.03 per impression. The electrostatic image reproduction (Xerox) process proves to be economical for fewer than five copies but is generally uneconomical for larger quantities.

Where certain sacrifices are tolerable in the size and legibility of the image, the document may be photographed on a microform such as an aperture card or microfiche which may then be used in reproduction equipment such as the 3M Quadrant from which individual impressions may be pulled at a cost of approximately $0.02 each. Other low-volume copying techniques cost from $0.08 to $0.30 per impression. Beyond the parameter of base cost, the choice of reproduction method is influenced by the workload imposed by this activity and the possibility of exploiting the method. For example, an aperture card system that costs $0.15 for the master card and $0.08 for each print offers a basis for machine sorting the card containing the image, for selective retrieval or elimination of manual filing. Costing the reproduction alone therefore does not provide a complete picture of the basis for method selection. On the other end of the scale of costs and of techniques available for printing are source items to be distributed in volume over one thousand. For runs as high as a thousand impressions, multilith presses are uneconomical and provide poorer quality than is achieved with rotary presses. Because the source organization does not commonly print such volumes, the methods for high-speed reproduction are covered in a later section under the heading "Typography, Composition, and Printing." Regardless of the press considerations of duplication and printing, the copy to be reproduced may be introduced on the master directly and automatically where the copy has been prepared in machine-readable form. That is, the typewriter actuated by perforated tape, by magnetic tape, or by the contents of a computer memory can be loaded directly with paper offset press plates. Similarly, where the computer-based system is utilizing a high-speed output printer, the printer may be loaded with fanfold multilith masters.

Report Distribution

Distribution of the original reports may be as informal as its transmittal by the author, with a letter to one or more professional associates. More formally, the report may be distributed to a list of recipients on the basis of contractual requirements, author prerogatives, and expressed interest of recipients. The management of these distribution lists constitutes the creation of a file and the production of elements such as mailing labels.

Transmission. Most commonly, transmission of the documented information is by delivery through the postal system. Considerations of the cost of such transmission as well as its lack of speed have resulted, in certain instances, in investigation and adoption of alternative transmission methods. Among the alternatives is the use of the telephone lines. For the latter, text must be in machine-readable form. Such form may be the perforated tape that is utilized with teletype equipment, or it may involve digitizing for data phone transmission.

Although not an example of report transmission, the techniques being used for managing the documentation necessary to maintain test stands for missile launching exemplify the use of keypunch input, which actuates line transmission equipment. At the receiving end, cards are punched bearing the information transmitted, and are introduced into the deck representing the body of text for given document units. The revised deck of cards can be listed for local production of required copies.

As an alternative to delivering hard copies, some organizations are studying the potential for delivering microform copies. This trend is evidenced particularly in large organizations that are contractors to NASA or the AEC, both of which are increasingly using the microfiche form for the transmittal of copies of reports. As indicated in the description of report preparation, when the microreproduction of the page image offers the opportunity for economical distribution of copies within an organization geographically scattered and/or responsible for the

provision of copies to a large distribution list of co- or subcontractors, the production of microfiche is attractive. The features and cost of various microforms are described later in this chapter.

Transmittal. The management of a file of addressees for transmittal of copies of reports is being studied increasingly from the standpoint of machine support. For example, a source organization is often responsible for distributing copies of reports on a number of contracts each of which has a required distribution list, some entries on which are common to more than one. Although the activity on the file may be low, changes are randomly distributed. The cost of rekeystroking the entire distribution list responsively to individual changes, despite the high percentage of repetitive use of a given record, is leading to investigation of the applicability of machine support for the production of such lists.

An organization such as the AEC depends so strongly on the control of distribution of copies of reports that its Division of Technical Information Extension publishes a document in which a standard distribution list for each of the principal subject categories for report literature is reproduced for contractors' use. The production of this document in itself is an opportunity for machine support inasmuch as the addressee's identification appears in many more than one of the subject category listings.

A comparatively simple machine technique involves keypunching or preparing perforated cards. The latter are produced on tape-perforating equipment, but the text is punched on card stock on which the information may also be typed for visual selection of the card from the file in assembling needed distribution lists.

Mailing labels or shipping lists can be produced from such machine-readable records. The perforated card actuates a Flexowriter or similar equipment which has been loaded with gummed paper stock or labels. Keypunched decks can be listed on EAM equipment. In fully computer-based systems, the output printer can be loaded with fanfold stock consisting of preprinted gummed labels on which addresses are printed selectively from a master tape record, based on identification of the subset of recipients for the document being distributed.

Report Announcement

Techniques for announcing to other members of a source organization the availability of an internally produced report range widely in the degree to which report identification is repetitively keystroked. As an example of a system in which the keystroking performs two functions, at System Development Corporation the announcement tool is simultaneously a report order. That is, each of the reports released during the previous day is listed on a daily announcement bulletin. By returning the announcement bulletin appropriately completed with respect to name, location, and charge budget number, the employee orders a copy of any report of interest to him. At Lockheed the monthly announcement bulletin is produced by keypunching the titles of documents and using a permuted title index program. At IBM in Los Gatos, California, the announcement bulletin—prepared in the library—is keystroked on the Administrative Terminal System. The text is not manipulated inasmuch as the number of entries does not warrant indexing or classification.

Collections of Reports

In the source environment, reports may be collected by a special library group. The techniques for managing the collection are described later in this chapter. The local collection, however, is the point at which a bibliographic record may first be created for the source item. Unfortunately this bibliographic record is seldom transmitted with the source item for exploitation by any other recipient. Clearly, progressive collection organizations within source organizations that have developed computer-based systems for support of their activities would not necessarily find economical or convenient the exploitation of such records were they available.

One of the source organizations that has implemented machine support extensively in library operations is the Douglas Aircraft Company in Santa Monica, California. The program for introducing machine support was first geared to the machine development of coordinate indexes. Subsequently the backlog of uncataloged items has been made available through a permuted title index bulletin and cataloging has proceeded to include full machine support for production of catalog cards and inverted de-

scriptor indexes, for retrospective searches, and for generating individual announcements of the receipt of items judged—by matching descriptors characterizing a user and those characterizing the document—to be of interest to principal technical personnel.

It is in the management of the report literature that the source organizations have proved most progressive in exploiting the machine support. In contrast to the processing traditionally applied to book literature, report literature has been managed through extensive indexing and minimized subject classification. Most commonly, report literature is handled on the basis of the source organization's identification number for the item. Access to the physical copy, identified as satisfying a search based on authorship or subject content, is made through use of an index rather than through a conventional catalog.

The source organization library with limited resources for the analysis of incoming items can exploit machine support in preparation of a permuted title index. Based on the assumption that the author of a technical report selects a title that contains substantive clues to the contents of the report, a computer program accepts the keypunched title—and supplementary terms that might be assigned by the library—and: (1) generates for each term in the title that does not appear on an exclusion list (e.g., "and," "the,") a repetition of the title; and (2) sorts the copies in the alphabetic order of the substantive terms.

Two variations of the program are available. In one, a particular physical position on the index line is considered the indexing position, and the title is permuted to create repetitions in each of which a different substantive term is located in that position. All copies of the line are then alphabetized on that position. Alternately the program may repeat the substantive term as a left margin header under which are listed all titles, in their natural order, for which that term was assigned or that contained the term or some acceptable variant. Both variations on permuted title indexing depend on the user to make discriminations among reports containing the same substantive term by inference from the context in which the term appears. The best-known program, developed by H. P. Luhn, is called the "keyword-in-context" or KWIC program.

In contrast to the use of context for discrimi-

nation is the use of coordination among more than one word or term to identify reports responsive to a given search. Also on the presumption that terms or individual words constitute significant clues to the "meaning" or content of a textual item, report literature has been indexed in what has been called an *inverted coordinate technique*. The conventional library record for an item managed in the collection contains all information about the item that the library chooses to extract. A duplicate copy of the full record is interfiled in a catalog in enough locations to afford access to the item in response to author and subject requests. The catalog is a "direct" file. An "inverted" or "aspect" file is one in which each individual entry in the file represents the entire collection with respect to the term for which that entry is made. Evidence of the applicability of the term to any item in the file is indicated by the presence of the item identification number on the record for the descriptor term.

In completely manual systems the descriptor record is often a table of document identification numbers, organized into ten columns for convenience in coordinating among more than one descriptor to identify items satisfying the search prescription. The search prescription consists of a set of terms selected from the directory, if one exists, used for indexing and considered descriptive of the desired document. A fully computer-based system often uses this type of organization. The descriptor term is followed by the identification number in machine form for each of the documents to which that term applies.

The ASM/EI computer program system is considered to encompass the feature of both direct and inverted file organization. The information derived from search is a list of document identifications—usually a numeric code. To derive any additional information—such as the name of the author or title of the document—requires a pass through a file organized on the basis of identification numbers. The *serial* or *direct file* has the advantages that all data on an item are available at the point of access, and descriptor relationships are easily expressed, but all file items must be examined relative to each request.

Machine searching an inverted file is attractive since only the pertinent portions need be processed. The information retrieved by the search,

however, is only a set of item identifications. High-density terms load the file, and descriptor relationships are difficult to express. Searching an inverted coordinate file manually is extremely tedious and error prone. Except where the size of the collection and the size of the vocabulary for representing the collection are of comparable size, the inverted file is longer than a direct file (in machine systems). Inasmuch as a vocabulary between 10,000 and 15,000 terms can adequately represent the contents of a collection of a million or more items, a direct file consisting of item numbers followed by descriptors or their codes is shorter than that consisting of descriptors followed by item numbers.

Tape-perforating typewriters have been discussed in terms of application to the preparation of the source item. Such equipment is used in the source organization library to create the machine record for catalog cards. Multiple reproductions of the contents of a perforated tape are more economical than rekeystroking of the same information for multiple filing into the catalog. Where the source organization library does utilize machine processing for any other support operations, keying the report cataloging information on a tape perforator produces machine-readable copy simultaneously with preparation of the visually accessible copy. The Douglas Aircraft Company system, the Argonne National Laboratory, the ITT Communications Systems, Inc., and the University of California Lawrence Radiation Laboratory are among the organizations utilizing the Flexowriter for input keying of the information to produce catalog cards and for subsequent machine processing.

THE PAPER AND THE JOURNAL— LESS DATA, BETTER BUT LATER

As indicated earlier, the "paper" is distinguished from the "report" in respect to the distribution mission. Because the paper is intended either for oral or journal publication, it tends to be less detailed than the report and is seldom reproduced in quantity inasmuch as it is to be published in a primary journal or proceedings of a conference. It is also a unit document in terms of the network but it is not destined to be handled as a unit.

Primary publications are journals and other serials in which appear collections of papers on a common subject or presented at the same conference or meeting. Input items are papers which are subjected to editorial and technical review. Those accepted are composed for printing and distribution in a volume ordinarily far higher than the volume of distribution for the individual report. The combination of the review cycle and the form of publication usually results in a delay of at least six months between transmittal of a paper from author to editor and its appearance in a publication. For 45 per cent of the journals produced by professional societies and for 36 per cent of those produced by commercial publishers, the delay has been estimated at more than seven months. Twenty-three per cent of the society journals and 20 per cent of the commercial journals are able to publish materials within five months of the time of receipt. Of a sample of 211 journals studied in 1963, the remaining 40 or more per cent of the journal required more than seven months between receipt of paper and its appearance in an issue. A salary or honorarium is paid to approximately 75 per cent of the editors for journals in chemistry and engineering produced by professional societies. Only 7 per cent of the editors of mathematics journals receive any compensation.

Table 3-3 lists the frequency of publication for a sample of 219 journals studied in 1963.

Serial Preparation

Preparation of the contents of a serial consists of review for technical worthiness and editorial control. Marked manuscript copy is provided to a (usually commercial) printer for typesetting and press work.

Reviewing and Refereeing. One of the principal obligations of the journal editor is the establishment of a group of reviewers and referees who assume responsibility for analyzing the content of each paper and making selection for inclusion in the published medium or the oral presentation. In general the competence and professional rank of these reviewers and referees tend to correspond to the reputation of the journal as an authority in its field and as a reliable screening mechanism, "protecting" the reader from papers of low technical quality. At least one journal has established an elaborate judging system, partly in an attempt to improve the quality of

Table 3-3   Frequency of Journal Publication

Number	Discipline	Mean Number of Issues per Year
90	Biology	6.7
12	Chemistry	9.3
8	Earth sciences	7.4
18	Engineering	7.1
18	Mathematics	5.2
13	Physics	13.5
42	Social sciences	5.1
18	Miscellaneous	5.2
219 (total)		6.8

papers in the overall field. As described in Chapter 2, the Society of Automotive Engineers distributes copies of each paper being considered to judges who rate the paper on several weighted characteristics. A composite score is computed and any source item scoring below a minimum threshold is rejected. Papers with highest scores receive special attention and are published in a more prestigious journal.

Reviewing is not ordinarily so formal although most journals of good reputation obtain reactions from two or three referees for each paper. As a result of the reviewing activity, it has been estimated that only a fraction between one-tenth and one-third of all papers submitted to journals actually are accepted for publication. In view of the practice of authors to resubmit papers to other journals when they have been rejected by one, the statistics relative to acceptance are extremely difficult to quantify validly.

Typography, Composition, and Printing. For a circulation of 7000 copies, journal production costs average $420.00 per paper. One of the considerations in large printing runs is the density of type on a page, for minimum paper and press setup time. Of greater consideration to the publishers of a primary journal than the density of type on a page is the need for the wide variety of alphabets and special symbols. Although journal publication is comparatively conventional and, in general, minimally supported by computer techniques, organizations such as the American Chemical Society are using direct line transmission from the point of editing and manuscript preparation to the printer geographically

distant. This is done by keying the text on teletype equipment. The American Institute of Physics has experimented with the composition of primary journals using Flexowriters to produce perforated tape to which can be added signals for typographic information such as change in typeface and so on.

Conventionally, type for printing is set by a compositor using typesetting equipment such as the Linotype, Intertype, Monotype, and Ludlow. On the basis of the key struck by the operator, a "matrix"—a brass die or mold, the face of which bears the desired character—is selected from the channels in which the matrices are stacked. As the keys are struck, the matrices are assembled in a line. Striking the space key introduces a wedge-shaped element called a spaceband. When the operator strikes the "line-completed" key, the spaceband drops to fill the line out to the selected length. Molten metal is forced against the faces of the assembled matrices. The hot lead hardens to produce a solid line, called a slug, with characters in relief. The matrices drop into a carrier which returns each to its channels into which it falls on the basis of a mechanical key ground into its sides. The slug is removed and trimmed mechanically.

Type slugs are arranged in a galley—a rectangular pan or tray open at one end—inked, and a proof taken. After proofing and the removal and replacement of lines containing errors, a revised proof is pulled. If offset presses are to be used, a repro proof is pulled from the type for camera processing. The type slugs are used for low-volume letterpress printing. For high-volume press runs, the lead slugs may be used to create an electrotype or a stereotype plate. For an electrotype plate, an impression of the type is made in an easily molded material such as wax. Metal is deposited by electrolysis on the molded surface to form a thin shell. This shell is then used as a master mold. Stereotyping involves impressing the type image into a felt or cork blanket under pressure. The resulting mold is also used for casting a solid metal printing plate.

Offset presses are approximately twice as fast as flatbed cylinder letterpresses. The startup or make-ready time of the offset press is a fraction of what is required on a letterpress. The flatbed cylinder press involves feeding paper down the cylinder and across the face of a flat type plate.

The offset press involves transferring ink from the plate to an intermediate blanket which deposits it on the paper stock.

We have discussed tape-perforating equipment as an input device for creating the document. It is also a composing machine. Special codes may be inserted in the text stream on a tape-perforating typewriter which are not themselves printed but which can be recognized for controlling typefaces when the tape is used in conjunction with other text composing machines.

Composition may utilize hot lead typesetting such as already described, but under the control of a perforated tape. During the last decade, increasing use has been made of photocomposition equipment in which either direct keyboarding or the actuation by the perforations on tape causes the exposure onto film or photosensitive paper of the image of the character represented by the code on the perforated tape. More than a thousand unique characters are available on one such equipment which operates at a speed of approximately ten characters per second. Alternative systems offer fewer unique characters and operate at approximately the same speed. Photocomposition based on sequential card techniques is summarized later in this chapter in the section on secondary publications, inasmuch as its role as an index display technique is more novel than is its technique in terms of printing and composition.

The characters available for composition are generated either: (1) photooptically by passing light through or reflecting it off a matrix plate on which the character images are engraved; or (2) electronically through the mediation of an electronic beam passing through or reflecting off a stencil-like matrix. In the latter, the text image projected on the face of a cathode-ray tube is photographed. Composition can be accomplished at the rate of 17,400 characters per second. Rather than creating a negative for photographically making a press plate, the page image may be projected on a plate for electrostatic reproduction and preparation of offset masters. The latter technique allows the use of only 64 unique characters and therefore is considered inadequate for most high-quality printing. It is used for high-speed composition of computer generated data, particularly when composition is not to be exploited in high-

volume press runs. For large printing runs the density of type on a page is a serious consideration. The comparatively low density of a computer printer listing results in an excessive volume of paper and a subsequent expense for a long printing run of such a document.

A recent development promises to make available a high-quality, graphic-arts, high-speed composition system offering more than 1000 unique characters in any size from 5 to 18 points which will compose 600 pages per hour. The GPO prints and makes available copies of reports produced by the federal agencies and is conducting extensive experimentation into the use of photocomposition and computer-controlled composition. The acquisition of the Linotron computer-based composition equipment will make possible the acceptance of machine-readable copy (e.g., Flexowriter tapes, punched cards, and magnetic tape) for conversion using a special program that introduces typographic codes for changes in typeface, line leading, and so on.

Distribution of Journals

Distribution of serials and periodicals by scholarly and professional societies utilizes mailing techniques such as addressograph plates. Maintenance of the deck for producing mailing labels on demand are conventional and comparatively low speed.

Average circulation is 4400 copies. Journals in chemistry, engineering, and physics average slightly more than 7000 copies in circulation. Maximum circulation is achieved in engineering by commercal publishers. Approximately one-fourth of the total circulation is to foreign recipients.

The costs to the subscriber for journals range from a low of $3 per year in biology to a high of $45 per year in chemistry, for journals produced by professional societies. The cost per 100,000 research words is lowest in the field of physics—$0.67—where the highest number of research words are published at an average domestic subscription rate of $21 per year.

Journal Announcement

Announcement of a primary journal may be considered to center in the preparation of indexes published either with the individual issues

of the journal or at some regular interval. The study cited previously of some 211 journals indicated that annual author and subject indexes are not published until six months or more after the end of the year. In some cases the index appeared as much as fifteen months after the end of the year in which the article was published.

The primary publisher increasingly is offering certain other announcements services in conjunction with appearance of a source item. For example, *Industrial and Engineering Chemistry* announces the existence of papers that are not yet edited or reviewed, but copies of which *I&EC* supplies, as a direct communication from the author to any interested reader, for a small charge covering reproduction. A similar service on a somewhat broader scale is offered by the Society of Automative Engineers. A recent issue of the *SAE Journal* announced availability of copies of 81 papers, at an average cost of $0.75 per copy to members. This technique provides for the availability—in the case of this society— of reports not necessarily qualified for publication in the society's journal. Further, because the volume of announcement is so high, indexes to the announcements are provided.

Collections by Journal Producers

The primary publication enters one of two types of collection: (1) that from which, as a total item, it is routed, circulated, and retained; and (2) that from which it proceeds into the secondary services cycle. Figure 3-1 shows a simple two-option path into the abstraction labeled "collection management processing." The problems of acquisitioning journals for preparation of a secondary publication are essentially those of any large library. In the environment in which the primary journal is produced, however, consideration of collection is comparatively trivial.

THE SECONDARY PUBLICATIONS

"Secondary" publication is the label assigned to the publications and services derived from analysis of report literature or of the contents of primary serials. The goal of the secondary publisher is service to a particular user group, ordinarily oriented toward a single scholarly discipline but occasionally oriented toward a mission or industrial product.

A list compiled by the Library of Congress in 1962 reveals that there are some 1900 abstracting and indexing services in the world. As in most of these statistics relative to the documentation area, some 10 per cent of the total world services create approximately 90 per cent of the products. For example, one million of the nearly two million abstracts published in the United States appear in 13 abstract journals. Because each of these secondary services is motivated to serve a particular user group and since discipline orientation increasingly tends to overlap in the application of scholarly work to various technological development, the overlap among abstracting and indexing services is quoted as both inadequate and excessive. That is, although only one-third of all of the world's serials are abstracted, any given journal is abstracted an average of three times by the various services.

Until recently, secondary abstracting and indexing services were entirely in publication format. The principal aspects of the preparation of the published product are:

1. Analysis of input items.
2. Classification for the organization of elements within the publication.
3. Development of an indexing vocabulary.
4. Display variations in the publications.

The choices made, the history of the development of present practices, and the wide range in analysis, vocabulary, and display techniques appear to evidence the ingenuity of the producers, if not necessarily the range of needs of the users.

Preparation of Announcement and Retrieval Tools

Among the secondary publications prominent in the scientific and technical documentation system are discipline-oriented services usually provided by professional societies, mission- or project-oriented services usually provided by professional societies, and mission- or project-oriented services provided by industrial and trade groups and by the federal government. The analysis techniques employed by these major sources of secondary publications differ on bases of:

1. Motivation of the user in using a particular service.

2. Precedence in service for a given source.

3. Differences in the vocabularies and syntax of the technical languages of the field covered by each service.

The discipline-oriented secondary publication must rationalize a subclassification or organization of the field considered to constitute the discipline. In the present situation of burgeoning cross-disciplinary developments, given categorization or classification is likely to be unstable or inadequate. In response, the secondary publication may find necessary the use of extensive cross-referencing, resulting in a physically large document, awkward for the user to handle. Notice that this does not necessarily constitute a use hazard as long as document organization is completely clear to the user. An alphabetically arranged telephone book of unlimited size is no more difficult to use than a small similarly arranged document. Nevertheless, physical handling difficulties limit the size of even a well-organized document. The largest of the secondary services, therefore, are investigating and implementing policies of separate publication for sections of the total journal.

Analysis results in two products: identification of the document and its source and a representation of the contents, which constitute the abstract entry, and a further distillation of the representation to create indexes to abstract entries and/or the literature abstracted. The development of the abstract may be delegated to a member of the discipline, who virtually contributes his services in providing his field with a tool for the announcement and the subsequent retrieval of its literature. Alternately, abstracts may be prepared by the staff of the secondary publication, in some cases with the support of a document describing the policies and techniques for the preparation of the kind of abstract used by the given secondary publication.

Late in 1963, Engineering Index, Inc., contracted for a study of its operation by Battelle. The study determined that on the average, when the entire article was used as a basis for indexing, 20 to 25 minutes of indexing time was involved. A comparable time is involved in abstracting. When both activities are undertaken by the same analyst at the same time, however, they can be accomplished in 30 minutes on the average. When indexes are drawn from abstracts alone, three minutes or less is necessary.

The principal mission of abstracting is the representation of the document and/or its contents to the degree necessary to guide a user in evaluating the potential applicability of a given document to his information needs.

There are several varieties of "abstract." Journals such as *Nuclear Science Abstracts, Chemical Abstracts,* and *Biological Abstracts,* tend to prepare summaries of the contents of the original article. In general, such summaries may be considered to be a reflection of the viewpoint of the author and, in the best examples, indicate the methodology, hypothesis, and results of the work described by the paper. Effectiveness of this type of condensation relies heavily on the subject specialty competence of the abstractor. Called "informative abstracts," these condensations seek to present conclusions and results in enough detail to minimize the necessity of the reader referring to the original article.

In contrast, the second major type of condensation, called the "indicative," "descriptive," or "annotative" abstract may be considered a description of the document and what it is "about." Such an abstract does not contain the information provided in an informative abstract. During the past two or three years, use of the descriptive abstract has increased partly on the impetus of the Engineers Joint Council and their "action plan" for information services. The technique of preparing a descriptive abstract is recommended on the basis that a lower competence in the scientific specialties of the specific documents is required, and keyword indexing, augmented as appropriate with "role" and "link" tags, is facilitated with the use of this type of abstract. The indicative abstract more often is intended as a document retrieval tool, whereas competently prepared informative abstracts may be considered a low level information retrieval tool. Abstracts may of course combine both features.

A condensation consisting of statements in the author's own words is called an "extract." Extracting is the basis for present experimentation into producing "abstracts" automatically through computer-based systems.

An alternative condensation is the "digest," which does not use the author's words but derives condensed statements from particularly information-rich statements in the source article. Some rearrangement of thoughts and concepts may be achieved in producing the digest.

An increasing trend in the preparation of material for the publication of an abstracting journal has been the use of abstracts prepared by the author of an article. Seldom, however, is the author provided with a background in the distinction that may be made between types of abstracts and their goals as documentation or retrieval tools. Thus, if we find a problem in the author's lack of information about the usefulness of his overall document and a weakness, therefore, in the document as an information transfer device, we can hardly expect the abstract itself to perform with greater effectiveness the announcement and retrieval tool function. Nevertheless, because of rising costs of production of secondary publications and the maintenance of abstracting and indexing services, both the discipline-oriented and the agency-supported, mission-oriented abstracting services are depending to greater degrees on author-produced abstracts.

The weaknesses of conventional abstracts and a desire to produce an index that was machine searchable and, therefore, required rigid control, led Western Reserve University and the American Society for Metals to develop an elaborate scheme for "telegraphic abstracts" in the late 1950's. The telegraphic abstract actually was constructed not from the source item but from the index prepared for the item. A "semantic code" was used in indexing to indicate not only the identification of the concept but of the implication within the source document. As an example, the code "M CH" covers the concept of machine or device. In the blank space an infix letter is introduced to differentiate source document use of the concept. In addition to these infix codes, "role" indicators were assigned.

A narrative abstract was written for publication in the *Review of Metal Literature* from the telegraphic abstract prepared to create a machine record of index terms that might be searched automatically. During the course of some six years in which the technique was used, a file of 160,000 documents was written into machine form. A preliminary analysis made of the efficiency of role indicators revealed that certain of the indicators were used heavily and that the value was questionable. The scheme has been replaced by use of the descriptive abstract and role-and-link indexing techniques of the EJC.

The American Petroleum Institute uses an abstract style that may be either "indicative" or "informative" but is characterized by placement of citation information (title, author, corporate source or journal, volume and page numbers, etc.) at the end of a text block that begins with a sentence revealing the main thought of the paper. This lead sentence often, therefore, contains the words of the title (in upper case) when it is a succinct phrasing of the principal "fact" of the article. Such "inverted" abstracts have a newsy flavor inasmuch as their structure is reminiscent of that of a newspaper story.

Distribution of Announcement and Retrieval Tools

The techniques for managing the distribution for secondary publications and the machine-readable versions of the secondary services are conventional and involve maintenance of the file of identifications of recipients.

Among the more interesting schemes for distribution is one illustrating the shift from secondary publication to secondary services. The Biological Sciences Information Services (in Philadelphia) is conducting a pilot operation to provide searchers of some half a million abstracts, or individual frames of microfilm reels, on direct request from members of the staff at Walter Reed Hospital (in Washington) through a phone line terminated in Dataphones and Electrowriters. Because BIOSIS has its indexes on magnetic tape, both machine and manual searches have been conducted. For the initial three months of the one-year experiment, some 500 requests have been serviced, each yielding an average of 60 blowbacks of published abstracts which are mailed to the requestor. The implications of such direct service to the subscription and, therefore, publication activities are complex and are being studied before the service is offered more broadly.

Announcement Function of an Index

As in the announcement tool for primary journals, we consider the announcement function for secondary journals to be performed by the indexes published with the individual issues of the journal and the cumulative indexes published less frequently.

Vocabularies. Our purpose is not to discuss the philosophical basis for the differences in the indexes produced for various secondary

publications and for use as retrieval tools for collection. M. E. Stevens has comprehensively described the development of variations in indexing philosophies in a National Bureau of Standards Monograph dated March 1965[14]. Our purpose here is to point out the kinds of files that must be maintained to produce an index.

When the index terms are not simply extracted from the substantive words in a title, an index can be developed only through the use of an authority list, dictionary, or thesaurus. Among the most comprehensive technical thesauri are the *Chemical Engineering Thesaurus,* the *ASTIA Thesaurus,* and the Engineers Joint Council *Thesaurus of Engineering Terms.* In conventional subject authority lists or classifications schedules, the subject matter of a collection is rationalized into a hierarchy and the codes representing subject fields echo the organization of the field.

In contrast, indexes ordinarily are considered to be free of hierarchial constraints, thus countering the argument that the assignment of a code reflecting a relative position of some subject in a field to the others breaks down as science advances into cross-disciplinary areas. Nevertheless, in preparing a thesaurus the scope notes that assist both the indexer and the seracher in determining whether a given term will be fruitful in response to a given request codify term relationships.

Index Displays. Conventional index "displays" consist of typeset copy organized alphabetically on the index term, under each of which are titles or qualifying phrases and document identifications. Indexes being compiled by computers exhibit a range of display characteristics.

The compilation of cumulative indexes for announcement media may center around a technique in which the index is typed on a card designed for mechanical sequencing through a camera that photographs each line as a unit. Text is typed in a fixed position on the cards which are punched to accommodate the feeder fingers on the card sequencer. The card may be interfiled manually on the basis of the text content, or some gross sorting code may be punched in the nonprint areas of the card. The code identifying the document or announcement number is punched also in a nonprint area of the card. The cards then may be sorted on EAM equipment and visually checked for order before the photographic process. The camera operates at rates between 7000 and 14,000 cards per hour. The text is keystroked on equipment such as the electric typewriter or VariTyper to obtain variations in type font, improving the readability of the index. Text content, keystroked at the character rate and costs listed earlier for final copy plus the cost per line for the use of the equipment, produces a total cost for this process of an average of $0.15 per line.

Two other indexing tools that should be mentioned are tables of contents listings (compilations of reproductions of the tables of contents of journals sharing a particular subject field) and citation indexing. The latter technique has been used in law and is now being applied to the literature of science. The citation index consists of lists of cited articles associated with the articles that cite them. The development of a comprehensive citation index requires machine support to be practical.

Such a retrieval tool provides for following, both forward and backward in time, the course of development of the information contained in a particular article. The index compiler capitalizes on the intellectual judgment of an article's author; there is no requirement for interpretation of an article by an indexer. Although the citation index does not suffer from discrepancies between an indexer's perception of the subject content of an article and the user's perception of that content, it does suffer from the inconsistencies with which citations are used in the literature. On the other hand, the cross-fertilization taking place in scientific fields is revealed more clearly in the citation index than in other display tools. Also, despite changes in the terminologies of different fields, relationships between articles are revealed through the medium of mutual citations.

The citation index serves the announcement function to the extent that articles or authors in which a user is interested are cited in the current literature.

Collection by Secondary Publishers

As mentioned in the discussion of the collection for the primary journal, the collection activity in the secondary publishing organization is, chronologically and in terms of material flow through the system, the input of the various journals from which articles are to be selected for abstracting and secondary announcement.

The management of a serials collection is somewhat more complex than is management of a unit item collection (books, reports, etc.). A principal source of the difference is the anticipated continuity of publication of the serial and the consequent need to assure that each of the issues in a volume is received. The frequency with which journals are issued varies. Among the organizations contacted during this study, none was exploiting machine support for the management of a serials collection, although Biological Sciences Information Services is designing a machine-supported system that includes acquisitions records. One extensively machine-supported system is in operation in a source organization. Serials handling therefore will be considered in the following discussion on the preparation of the collection.

THE COLLECTION

With casual consideration the analyst of the scientific and technical document-handling network tends to focus attention on the collection (i.e., the library) and its management. Earlier in this chapter we indicated that the kinds of activities carried on in collection management are involved in the preparation of the source item, the primary publication, and the secondary publication. This viewpoint suggests that alternative methods might be worthwhile in which some of the work done chronologically before an item becomes eligible for a collection might accompany the item to make more rapid its introduction into a collection.

Preparation of the Collection

Preparation of the collection consists of the acquisition and cataloging of the aggregation of unit items and of serials, proceedings, secondary publications, and supplementary collection announcement and retrieval tools.

Acquisition. Acquisition consists of a subsystem involving purchasing, ordering, and receiving at the collection input. The inputs to the acquisition function are requests from the user population, suggestions by a library staff concerning suitable additions to the collection, and the input of the items ordered and received on regular distribution. To manage the input of documents and the output of orders requires control files.

For the source organization collection, the acquisition function is the first point at which a bibliographic record can be started. It may be based on information provided by a requester, supplemented by support information from directories and catalogs from vendors or document suppliers, and can be augmented as additional information about the item becomes available.

Machine support in the acquisition function is impeded in part by the variety of forms required by vendors and document suppliers. For example, for the source organization that is a qualified requester of materials from the Defense Documentation Center, the order form consists of a tab card that must be completed and returned to DDC. Many source organizations must acquisition materials from combinations of federal agencies (NASA and AEC, in addition to DDC) and for each must be supplied with the correct forms. Hence even the system that does employ machine support in its collection management must duplicatively keyboard the document identification and other data. The acquisition of an item in response to a request by a requester also ordinarily involves the maintenance of a control file. That is, the requester may supply a form completed with information he has about the item he requests, and the library is required to maintain a file of such open or outstanding requests after an order has been placed with a potential supplier.

Variations in the requirements for processing acquisitions are based not only on the variations in forms that are required by certain suppliers but on the characteristics of the item. That is, for serials acquisition, extensive followup is necessary to ensure that every copy received for a periodical is noted, both for cataloging and for claims purposes. One of the most comprehensive of machine-supported serials-handling systems is in operation at the University of California at San Diego. Approximately 5000 titles are handled. In most cases a single copy of each title is obtained for the collection (there is no routing). For some science titles, however, multiple copies are ordered to provide access in the branches of the library. A computer program was written to produce daily receipts lists, a complete holdings list, partial holdings list, bindery records, and an arrivals file. A manual search is made through this latter file when a serial is received. Cards matching the incoming serial are transferred to the processing function

to produce the receipts lists and to update the holdings tape. Cards that remain in the file are used as the basis for claims followup. A subroutine of the program also provides some statistics including the volume and issue numbers, the year, and other data for punching the cards that constitute the arrivals file held in receiving, awaiting the next expected issue of the periodical. The program alphabetizes and prints out the full title from a mnemonic for the title which is punched into the card. Multiple copies of the list are prepared to supply each of the branch libraries.

Catalogs to Indexes. The cataloging function comprises three principal activities: classification cataloging, descriptive cataloging, and subject cataloging. Descriptive cataloging is the comparatively mechanical task of recording the information about the item in a standard format. Classification and subject cataloging involve a partial analysis of the contents of the item to assign classification codes and one or more subject tracings. Before either activity is undertaken, it is necessary to check a control file, such as the catalog for the collection, to determine whether the item in hand has already been cataloged. Even if it has not, the existing catalog may provide guidance to the cataloger to ensure some consistency in the treatment of items that are similar in subject matter. Because of the need for the cataloger to access the catalog for guidance in the cataloging operation, and because ordinarily only a single set of catalog cards is maintained, the card catalog is tied up simply for library processing. To relieve the library personnel of some of the clerical or mechanical aspects of cataloging, machine systems are being explored.

As indicated previously, the tape-perforating typewriters have been used in collection management to produce the text for catalog cards, since the perforated tape can be used repetitively to print enough copies of the catalog card text for each of the tracings.

In a study done at Lockheed, descriptive cataloging was analyzed as taking an average of 10 minutes per item. Inasmuch as the average output for cataloging activity commonly is considered to be about 10 items per day per cataloger, the remainder of the time is involved in making reference to the existing catalog and determining the appropriate subject classification and term

selection. IBM estimated that in changing from a completely manual cataloging effort to the use of EAM equipment to support cataloging, some 17 man-hours were saved per hundred items cataloged. Similarly, the estimate of a reduction from 6 man-months to 3 man-days per year was made in respect to the Argonne National Laboratories Library processing of journal renewals alone, using EAM support, for a holding of 2000 subscriptions.

Lockheed uses an EDP system that produces cards but minimizes the manual handling by printing the tracing under which a given copy of the record is to be filed at the top of the card and in the order in which they will be filed into the card catalog. Nevertheless the constraints for manual filing ordinarily result in a policy of only two or three tracings for card catalogs. In contrast, the sheet or page form catalog can be produced without the manual filing effort and therefore is characterized by a higher proportion of tracings or access points. With the capability of automatic data-processing equipment to produce completely sorted catalogs printed in sheet form, this technique is becoming popular for large collections. Clearly a card catalog for a one-million volume collection is quite massive and subject to a high percentage of filing errors. A comparable sheet form catalog is both more easily checked for filing errors and, once corrected, remains in the correct order.

Management of small collections (such as may be accumulated in the analysis of very limited subject field by an information evaluation center) may involve the preparation not of conventional catalog cards but of inverted indexes. The basic technique was described earlier. In addition to the eye-legible version consisting of a table of ten columns of document identification numbers posted on a descriptor term, the inverted technique is used with what are called optical coincidence cards. The latter medium involves the representation of a document not by its identification number but by a position on a grid on the descriptor card. When a given descriptor has been assigned to an item in the collection, represented by a given position on the descriptor card, the hole is punched from the card in the appropriate position.

Several systems are available for implementing the optical coincidence technique of indexing and retrieving. In general, collections of 10,000 items can be represented by a given optical

coincidence system. There are, however, systems accommodating up to 40,000 items. Since the vocabulary for a collection of between 10,000 and 25,000 items may amount to about 7000 terms, the total index for the collection indexed on the average by 10 to 20 terms consists of the 7000 optical coincidence cards. In contrast, a conventional card catalog, with perhaps three to four "tracings" or access points per item in the collection, would consist of as many as 100,000 cards. Retrieval of the identification of items responsive to a given search specification is comparatively rapid. Optical coincidence cards for the terms in the search are aligned physically in a holder. Light passes through the hole(s) for any document to which all of the terms in the search question have been assigned. Punching the holes is subject to error that is not easily detected except in failures of the system to retrieve adequately.

Some of the opportunity for error in retrieving from a conventionally posted, 10-column display of inverted coordinate index terms is alleviated through the use of the "dual dictionary." This amounts to no more than the provision of two identical copies of the index, bound, for instance, with spiral binding to facilitate the access to two different portions of the index—each containing one of the terms responsive to the search specification—at the same time. The inverted index that must be updated manually is particularly subject to errors of posting which are not easily detectable. The "dual dictionary" technique is used by the Pacific Aeronautical Library and by the American Petroleum Institute. In the latter the dictionary is generated as part of a computer-based index-assembling system.

One of the tedious problems in designing a computer program to generate catalogs in either card or page form, but one that results in extended negotiation between the collection manager and the program designer, is that of designing the representation for the author's name and, in catalogs that cover report literature, the corporate author's name and any codes supplied by the source for identification of the item. For example, in a conventional card catalog, filing conventions develop with the greatest possible correspondence to the library's notion of the significance of certain portions of a name. The choice of filing point for "Beethoven" is colored by considerations that go beyond the alphabetical order of the letters constituting the name; that is, in a given system, the "von," which legitimately might precede the name "Beethoven," is ignored because the name is of foreign origin and the prefix is considered less a name than a preposition. In contrast, the same catalog might provide for the filing of the name "Von Braun" under the letter "V," despite the foreign origin of the name and the person to whom it refers, on the grounds that the man is now in and out of the United States. Such distinctions are impractical in an automatic data-processing system.

In addition to eliminating manual interfiling of catalog entries and providing that more than one citation can be scanned at a time, the page form catalog allows multiple copying for distribution in various functions of the collection related to its management and to various user populations. Nevertheless, widespread distribution of copies of a page form catalog may, in turn, create costs that preclude multiple reproduction of the total bibliographic data at every access point. Such catalogs are then called "finding lists" and the full bibliographical citation is provided at only one access point—usually the author's name. Subject indexes and various numerical indexes contain the portion of the bibliographic data that is most likely to be useful to the user searching that particular list. A finding list for subject browsing may contain, alphabetically arranged by subject, titles and other subject entries as well as the library identification number for the item.

Freed from the need to interfile individual cards for every subject entry selected, collection management can adopt the policy of increasing the number of tracings for a particular item. Consequently the finding list is more responsive to requests for more specific information. This proliferation of tracings is more commonly referred to as indexing. The indexer is given the opportunity to select as many as 20 terms appropriate to a document. The responsibility for selecting a single correct descriptor or for ensuring the correctness of any one descriptor therefore is minimized.

Distribution in the Collection Environment

The distribution functions in the collection organization center around circulation. For a collection on which a strong control policy is exercised concerning the return of items within

a specified period, machine support has been investigated and implemented. The circulation problem of a university library is probably the most severe of any classification of collection agency. At the main loan desk at the University of California at Los Angeles, some 363,000 volumes are circulated over a year. Before the introduction of machine support, however, the turnaround delay between receipt of a book from a borrower and its return to the shelf for subsequent circulation was as much as several weeks. Books waiting for discharge of records therefore required allocation of space that was "unproductive" while each waited for its charge card filed by due date and its book check filed by call number.

To reduce manual handling of records and to speed turnaround, UCLA established a punched-card system. Transaction numbers are prepunched into two parts of a separable 80-column card. The borrower fills the data in on the left portion of the card (author, title, call number, borrower name, address, and status), which is date-stamped at the charge desk. The daily deck of cards is gangpunched with the due date code and loan code. The call number and borrower status are keypunched individually. The deck is reproduced and interpreted to generate separate charge and transaction files, each of which is analyzed statistically and sorted. The sorting technique is an empirical determination of the best tradeoff between manual filing and mechanical filing. A gross mechanical sort is made, followed by a manual sequence check.

The second (right) half of the card filled in by the borrower remains with the book. When the book is returned, it can be discharged to the stacks while the stub is used to purge the transaction and charge files. Although the system does not require as many charge desk personnel, it uses more shelves because of the reduction in transaction time and the resultant increase in circulation pattern. The turnaround time has been reduced to approximately twenty-four hours as a result of this system.

Announcement by the Collection Activity

The announcement function of a collection management activity centers in the production of accessions lists and in experimentation with what is called "selective dissemination of information" (SDI).

Broadcast Announcement. Preparation of accessions lists distributed to all potential users of the collection involves keyboarding and distributing the accessions list. A few of the alternatives of announcing new accessions to a collection were mentioned earlier in this chapter. Other techniques have been used, including the shingling of strips, each of which contains some portion of a citation, which are assembled into some preferred order—such as by field subclassification—and photographed or reproduced by electrostatic reprography for publication and distribution.

Selective Announcement. Preparation of selective announcements is practical only in a large system with some machine support. Such a system depends on the proliferation of indexing terms and the mechanical or automatic matching of the terms characterizing a document with terms characterizing a user's interests. The selective lists of accessions are organized by user identification and may be provided either in sheet form, with or without a copy of the abstract text, or on cards. IBM has experimented with providing both of these physical tools and has determined that the sheet form distribution is superior. NASA is conducting a pilot operation in distributing announcements and copies of report literature to a population of 700 scientists participating in the program.

The bibliographic record, including index terms for an item to be accessioned, is punched into cards or tape to be processed by machine. The list of user interest terms is similarly punched and entered into magnetic tape records. The bibliographic record tape is matched against the user profile tape and when a match occurs in which the percentage of terms in the source item is high enough to justify its being considered to match the profile, the bibliographic record is read off onto another tape with the identification of the user for whom it is considered to be a match. This latter tape is sorted and used to print either page form listings or duplicates of a card distributed to a user to announce the information and to afford the user the opportunity of either ordering the item or assisting the library to maintain a correct and current profile of his interest.

The IBM Technical Information Center at Poughkeepsie (New York), NASA, and Douglas Aircraft Company are investigating systems of

this kind using a punched card offering the user the option of punching a hole on the card corresponding to whether he: (1) has seen the report on microfilm; (2) wants the document; (3) does not need the document despite its interest to him; or (4) has no interest in the document. Before servicing a request submitted on one of these portapunch cards, the system keeps records in order to analyze statistics relative to the efficacy of the user profile, the activity on the system by the user profile, and the activity on the system by the user group.

The dynamic nature of profiles for individual users is a source of problem in the design and operation of a system for selective announcement of accessions. There is also a problem of correlating the indexing or assignment of descriptors with the range or depth of interest of the user. The latter problem may result in failure of the system to notify a user of an item that has some interest to him. IBM contends that the effect is minimized by the use of a large number of descriptors and by further providing a conventional announcement bulletin from which a user may also order items. As in the return of the portapunch card, orders from the announcement bulletin are analyzed statistically to help develop better understanding of the discrepancies in the user profile.

Collection Functions and Problems

With the responsibilities for collecting and redistributing documents, a responsibility exists to maintain the viability of the collection by purging the materials no longer used. This theoretical obligation seldom is implemented, however, and even less is machine support involved in such a function. In an attempt to develop a basis for a purging policy, the document library at the Applied Physics Laboratory is instituting a program in which a checklist is provided with each document distributed. The user of the document is asked to rate the document on a 10-point scale concerning the significance of the document to the field for which the descriptor terms have been supplied. He is also asked to rate the document in terms of his estimate of its probable useful life. That is, judgment of the value of the report is to be correlated with the estimate of length of time during which the contents may prove useful. No results are yet available on this study which is just beginning. It is anticipated that over an extended period, sufficient information can be gathered to

provide a strong guidance tool for a purging policy. Were such a policy available, a record for the item could be maintained in a machine-based system, which would alert the operators of the system at regular intervals to the appropriateness of retiring a given document to some level of a storage hierarchy such that the documents needed most were most readily accessible.

THE COPY

As the scientific and technical document has passed through the network and representations of it have been prepared for purposes of announcement and retrieval, it is often copied either for reference by the individual creating the representations or for the creation of a collection oriented to a particular purpose. In the abstract sense the report must become part of some collection before being copied. In the overall network of relationships between the original document and its representations, the copy can be considered to constitute the basis for exploitation and possibly the initiation point for subordinate cycles or iterations through portions of the network.

Preparation of Copies

A few of the techniques for preparing copies of documented information have been summarized in conjunction with the preparation of the report and its review iterations. The copies produced after the report has been released into the network, however, are increasingly taking the form of microreproductions. Therefore in this selection we will summarize some of the characteristics of microform systems and of their possible electronic successors, videoforms.

Microforms. Microforms are created through photographic reproduction. Reduction ranging from a ratio of approximately 12 to 1 to as high as 200 to 1 may be achieved. The result of the photographic process may be a roll or cartridge of film containing up to 2000 images, a unitized or aperture card bearing a film chip on which there may be several page images, or a microfiche providing for as high as 60 to 90 pages on a single transparent sheet.

For collections to which documents are added serially rather than merged into the whole, roll film is an effective microrecord. In addition to its convenience for storage and some capabilities for automatic mechanical indexing on individual

frames, roll film provides for storage of between 1000 and 2000 document pages per 100-foot reel.

The cost per page image ranges from less than four-tenths of a cent to approximately $0.10 for the most common systems. Per image costs exceed $0.35 for systems on which individual records or frames are selected optically or electronically. Duplicate reels in all cases can be made for $7.50 per 100 feet. A typical roll film system is in use at IBM's Technical Information Center in Poughkeepsie, where the contents of both internal and unlimited external reports are microfilmed in conjunction with semiautomated index production. Copies of the reels are distributed to the multiple laboratories. The announcement bulletin indicates reel and frame numbers on which the document is photographed.

For collections in which binding the retrieval of a document image to a serial location on a reel is a constraint, but in which the individual document consists of more than three or four sheets, the microfiche is the most convenient microform. The microfiche is a film negative in sheet form, ranging in size from between 3-by-5 inches to 5-by-8 inches. The fiche may be produced by using roll film originally and cutting and pasting strips of roll film to produce a master from which the fiche negative is made. Alternatively the document may be photographed by a step-and-repeat camera that automatically positions the image on the microfiche sheet. Cost of a microfiche master ranges between one and two dollars, depending on volume. Cost per page image for an average 20-page report is $0.05 for the master. Duplicates of the fiche can be made at between $0.09 (at quantities over 200) to $0.45 each.

The third major type of microform is the aperture card. The card is die cut to permit mounting a frame of film, usually 35mm, on which may be photographed up to four page-sized images. The card in which the chip is mounted may be written on, keypunched for EAM processing, or edge-notched for pin-sorting.

In addition to the three principal types of microform, microcards have been used. These are positive prints prepared from either strip or roll film masters. Film strips may be used in which original photography is done on roll film, which is cut to up to 5-inch lengths, each containing up to 10 page images. Strips have been used to some extent in certain business applications.

Access to a microfiche is made by a visual or manual search based on reading a header line separately photographed at full text size across the top of the microfiche. Roll film may be accessed by manually passing the roll through a reader, by mechanical indexing on the basis of an optical signal photographed between image frames, or by a semiautomatic optical selection system. The latter equipment is actuated by keyboard selection of the code options representing indexing classes which were selected when the document was analyzed and were photographed as text image search tools in sequence with or physically parallel with the image constituting the text.

Aperture cards may be retrieved mechanically using EAM equipment, where the index codes for the image contents have been keypunched into the card, or by mechanical actuation of keyboard-controlled trays holding edge-notched cards. Alternately an equipment is available for selecting aperture cards from a store that consists of a drum containing 20 pockets, each of which holds 50 cards. Each card can be individually addressed and retrieved.

Each of the microreduction techniques described allows reproduction of the original image as a "hard" copy. As indicated elsewhere in this chapter, microforms can be used to generate offset plates. Readers and reader printers that provide for the reproduction of the image at a reading size are available for all three major types of microforms. The quality of the resulting print is subject to criticism. The legibility is adequate, however, considering the rather transient nature of the use of the copy.

Completed aperture cards cost approximately $0.08 each and may be duplicated at a price of $0.05 each. Hard copies taken from aperture cards range in price from $0.02 to $0.15 each. Producing the master of a reel or roll film microrecord may be as inexpensive as $15 for 2000 frames where no indexing or search guides are provided by the introduction of interframe optical coding.

Sixty images, arranged in 5 rows of 12 images each, may be contained on a 4-by-6-inch microfiche, using an 18 to 1 reduction ratio. Federal agencies are adopting this standard proposed by COSATI. Three of the 60 images are reserved for eye-legible information. Since most technical reports average fewer than 60 pages, they may be contained on a single microfiche. A special camera is used to photograph title information

identifying the fiche, which can be read without enlargement. Each fiche is produced with a resolution guide frame to aid the user in establishing variations in the quality of output of his equipment.

Duplicate microfiche commonly are made using diazo film, which is less expensive than silver halide film, makes duplicate negatives from negatives, and incorporates the emulsion into the negative so that the image is not easily scratched in use.

The photochromic microreduction technique of National Cash Register Company deserves comment inasmuch as the extremely high reduction ratio (200:1) provides that a 300-page book may be reduced to occupy approximately one square inch of film. The images contained in the book occupying 270 miles of shelf space in the Library of Congress would fit in six filing cabinets on photochromic microslides. In contrast with the silver halide or diazo emulsion of standard microfiche and aperture cards, the photochromic technique is based on an instability of certain dyes under ultraviolet light, which allows the erasure and reuse of an image area on the base. This capability appears attractive for systems in which documents might be retired from one level to another of a storage hierarchy, based perhaps on the frequency of access or activity history of use of the image. It also provides a basis for updating or modifying documents in microstorage.

Videoforms. The most recent introduction to the techniques of image storage is that of the video file. Systems have been developed primarily for military application but are expected to become available for commercial application. The system consists of a television camera, one or more tape recorders, one or more desk-top television units and printers, and various system equipment interconnecting these main units. Using the techniques of electronic scanning employed in television, this system reads the image, creating a modulated signal that is digitized and stored on tape. The resolution is 1028 lines per inch—twice that of conventional television. Six page-size images are recorded on an inch of magnetic tape. Reels of 7200 feet are used, providing for storage of a maximum of a half million page-size images per reel. Actually, since the page images are organized into record length separated by interrecord gaps, this maximum is not necessarily achieved. The entire reel can be searched

in one minute, based on numeric addressing of the individual record. Up to five desk-top reader units may be serviced simultaneously through the buffer from a single tape-recorder store. The image projected at the desk-top unit can be retained indefinitely while it is being read. Despite the high cost (on the order of $1 million per installation) of the initial development for this system, the technique is attractive from the standpoint that the signal is suitable for long-distance transmission.

Copy Distribution

The growth in the emphasis on copying elements of a collection using the techniques described, in terms of source item reprography and microreproduction, is particularly evidenced in the distribution activities of agencies such as DDC, the Clearinghouse for Federal Scientific and Technical Information, the AEC, and NASA. In this activity the documentation system takes on the characteristics of a mail-order sales organization.

Inventory Control. In receiving and redistributing document titles, primarily in the report literature, federal agencies have found it necessary to set up stocks and inventory control comparable to that of a merchandising operation. At the CFSTI a prediction model has been developed of the potential for redistribution of a report on the basis of its subject content, its author, etc. Based on the use of this algorithm, the CFSTI prints and stocks a quantity of copies sufficient to meet anticipated requests. By constant updating of the supply record, the CFSTI not only modifies the prediction model appropriately but expects to ensure the most rapid possible response to requests. In agencies such as the AEC and NASA, inventory is more commonly in the form of microfiche stocks. The same general control problems exist, however, in managing the stock and providing for its replenishment as required. Distribution patterns are more determinate for the AEC and NASA than for the CFSTI.

Requesters and Requests. Where an organization is distributing copies of report literature in volumes sufficient to involve inventory control and prestocking, it can anticipate the problems of managing the files concerning qualifications of requesters and files for followup of request processing. At the Defense Documentation Center, the registered potential requester is supplied

with prepunched tab cards which he uses to order items. The prepunched information provides for a computer analysis of his qualifications for receipt of the requested document, as well as the basis for servicing the request. The NASA system also provides for machine support in the servicing of requests.

Machine support is not used in this aspect of the AEC system. In contrast, the forms for ordering reports have been designed to facilitate the handling of the orders at the Division of Technical Information Extension.

THE EXPLOITATION PRODUCT— BOOK, PAPER, AND REPORT

Documents assembled in a collection, the organization and contents of which are known to a potential user on the basis of catalogs and indexes, is the basis for the development of exploitation products. At this end of the system, closest to the user, services are changing most rapidly to be responsive to user needs and to close gaps in the existing documentation system services.

Among these services are the information analysis centers, increasing review publications, and translations publications. Each of these is an elaboration of a phenomena of long history. The information and data analysis center, the critical synthesis or review, and the translation are not responses to new needs but institutional responses to long-standing needs that have crystallized in the environment of technological competition and increasing volume of scientific and technical information.

Characteristic of this institutionalization has been development of specialized literature data bases, searchable by novel and specialized tools, some machine supported.

Preparation

The preparation of an exploitation product is obviously the same as that of an original paper, report, or book. Of greater interest than the techniques for preparation itself is the increasing development of organizations such as the information center and of services such as translations.

Information Centers. Chapter 2 discussed at some length recent developments in information analysis or evaluation centers. The information centers were depicted as a major development in the exploitation of information which emerged largely from the inability of libraries to cope with the increasing demands for information by the S&T community.

The exploitation function of information centers focuses on their use of subject area specialists, working in close conjunction with a library or other collections, to provide detailed syntheses of information tailored to the users' needs. Such syntheses may include compilations of data, critical or substantive reviews of literature, or detailed analyses which may be supplemented by special information such as tests or laboratory data developed by the center.

Among the more advanced developments for exploitation described in Chapter 2 was the Smith, Kline, and French Laboratories where not only is information produced upon user demand but the Center actively pursues bringing appropriate information to the attention of the S&T personnel.

Although the exploitation level of such centers is quite high—particularly when compared to more traditional uses of libraries—the dissemination of such information often is quite low. The products often are produced for very limited audiences, and subsequent announcement and distribution usually is equally restricted.

Translation. Exploitation of the non-English items in document collections involves translation and the production of a new document constituting the translation. Despite some activity supported primarily by the military for automatic translation, the bulk of scientific and technical translation may be considered to be done manually. In terms of the analysis of its role in the total document network as now constituted, introduction of foreign language material into various collections and the production of translations that are not necessarily centrally correlated has resulted in duplicated effort and some agitation by critics for improvement in the system. The Clearinghouse for Federal Scientific and Technical Information is responsible for publishing an abstract bulletin announcing the existence of translations prepared by government agencies and those prepared by special Libraries Association through the John Crerar Library. The resulting abstract journal, *Technical Translations*, also indicates the price of a copy of each translation. The CFSTI is attempting to obtain sufficient authorization from the Federal Council for Science and Technology to

impose the requirement that the CFSTI be alerted to the intention of an agency to acquire a translation as well as the provision of the resulting translation to the CFSTI for further distribution.

Translation services are performed or acquired by some 89 federal agency information services, partly through the Joint Publications Research Service. The JPRS retains 2000 translators on a contract basis. Under Public Law 480 (the Food for Peace Program) translations are obtained for seven federal agencies. This latter program is administered and coordinated by the National Science Foundation for the Departments of Agriculture, Commerce, Interior, and Health, Education, and Welfare; and NASA, AEC, and the Smithsonian Institution. The program now involves groups of translators in Israel, Yugoslavia, and Poland.

Private exploitation of the foreign literature is typified by the activity of the American Institute of Physics in cover-to-cover translation of Russian physics journals (originally with NSF support) and in the services offered by the Engineering Societies Library for the translation of individual articles on a contract basis. In the former the translated journal is sold by subscription; in the latter the translation becomes the private property of the individual contracting for its translation. Therefore it may never enter the documentation system. Translations undertaken in pursuit of the mission of national defense and strategy planning often are treated almost as though a security classification had been assigned to them, despite their original appearance in an unclassified, open source.

An estimate of some $3 million per year has been made as the cost of translations, not including classified translations or research on automatic translations. The average cost for translation is considered to be $16 per thousand words.

Machine support in translating foreign literature has been investigated for some fifteen years. The present most productive experimentation is directed toward support of the military mission and is based on a goal of rapid translation of maximum volume. Computer-produced translations are polished and otherwise edited by professional translators. The most recent estimate of automatic translation costs puts it at double (approximately $33 per thousand words) that of conventional translation. In exchange for the additional cost, the volume of translated ma-

terial is far higher than that which can be obtained through conventional means.

Distribution of Information and Documents

The distribution function in terms of exploiting the contents of a collection may result in unconventional interface between the user and the system when the system has machine-readable search tools. Specifically, collections in which indexes are on magnetic tape are being studied for the possibility of displaying the contents of a tape as an image on a cathode-ray tube, portions of which the user may specify as of interest. For those portions the system then presents additional information on the face of the cathode-ray tube. Such a system is being studied at Massachusetts Institute of Technology as part of Project MAC and at System Development Corporation in the BOLD (Bibliographic On-Line Display) system. Details on this type of operation are provided in Appendix 1.

A SHIFT AND CONSOLIDATION

In summary we have examined the processes to which original documented material is subject in the course of passing through the cycle once. The report is available for distribution at a cost of approximately $3.50 per page. The identification information (estimate 400 keystrokes) on one of the pages costs $0.15 at the source. Because it is not available in a form useful for secondary services and collection management, each of these elements of the network spends an additional $2 replicating the data. Processing within an indexing and abstracting service costs, on the average, $18 per document. The minimum time lag between the generation of a report and its entry into a redistribution point is a few days for a report handled by a federal agency. But until it is announced, it is virtually not available. Therefore an additional two months must be added to the minimum access time. For a paper, primary publication adds from six months to two years to the delay between the generation of the paper and its accessibility through a collection. Where the user depends on secondary services as a retrieval tool, the delay is an additional three to six months.

To reduce these lags, sponsors of primary publications are attempting to preannounce articles and to provide comprehensive indexing services. Possibly, for individual fields, we may see a

diminution of the need for separate secondary services. This may occur particularly where the primary publication is aggressive in the introduction of machine support and the production of machine-readable copy for exploitation through a collection function.

The provision by the primary publisher and the report generator of an abstract and of indexing terms that are part of the vocabulary of the secondary service may be another factor contributing to a reorientation in the secondary services.

It is in conjunction with the deep indexing associated with secondary services that the selective dissemination of accessions is being studied. Therefore the shift is away from the collection function to that of the secondary service for more rapid dissemination of selected information or documents.

Management of the scientific and technical collection cannot avoid changing its character responsively to the increasing discrepancy between the size and importance of the book collection to the size and activity on the documents and serials collections.

We began this summary of the generation, transmission, management, and exploitation of scientific and technical documentation on the general conviction that a rationalization of the individual organizations contributing to the system is not practical and that, instead, we might learn more about the entire system by summarizing the technology at each of its major functional points. Although the interrelationships of some of these functions are more clearly stated in terms of this type of description, we have seen as we progressed through the network that various organizations are accomplishing each of these tasks with varying degrees of machine support and with varying degrees of commitment to particular functions. The milieu provides little indication that any trends toward clear definition of subsystems and consolidation of functions exist or can be predicted. Completely clear is the fact that the milieu is changing rapidly and, hopefully, responsively to the increasing demands placed on information services by the scientific and technical community.

REFERENCES (Chapter 2 and 3)

1. American Library Association, *American Library Association Directory*, New York, R. R. Bowker Co., 1964.

2. Committee on Scientific and Technical Information, Federal Council for Science and Technology, *International Data—Exchange Agreements and Arrangements of Agencies of the United States Government*, Washington, D. C., 1964.

3. Evans, L. H., et al., *Federal Departmental Libraries*, Washington, D. C., Brookings Institute, 1963.

4. U. S. Congress, "Hearings before the Ad Hoc Subcommittee on a National Research Data Processing and Information Retrieval Center of the Committee on Education and Labor on H. R. 1946, A Bill to Amend Title X of the National Defense Education Act of 1958 to Provide for a Science Information Data Processing Center to be located at one place in Chicago, Illinois." Appendix to Vol. 1, Parts 1, 2, and 3. 88th Congress, 1st Session, Washington, D. C., Government Printing Office, 1963.

5. U. S. Congress, House Select Committee on Government Research, Report on H. R. 504, "Documentation and Dissemination of Research and Development Results," 88th Congress, 2nd Session, Washington, D. C., Government Printing Office, November 1964.

6. Hoshovsky, A. G., Survey of Federal Agencies Involved in Handling Scientific and Technical Information, Washington, D. C., Office of Aerospace Research, U. S. Air Force, March 1965.

7. Kruzas, Anthony T., "Special Libraries and Information Centers: A Statistical Report on Special Library Resources in the United States," Detroit, Gale Research Co., 1963.

8. Kruzas, Anthony T., "Special Libraries and Information Centers: A Statistical Report on Special Library Resources in the United States," Detroit, Gale Research Co., 1965.

9. Librarian of Congress, *Annual Report of the Librarian of Congress for FY 64*, Washington, D. C., Government Printing Office, 1965.

10. National Referral Center for Science and Technology, Library of Congress, *A Directory of Information Resources in the United States*, Washington, D. C., Government Printing Office, 1964.

11. National Science Foundation, *Specialized Science Information Services in the United States*, NSF 61-68, Washington, D. C., Government Printing Office, November 1961.

12. Office of the Federal Register, The National Archives of the United States, *United States Government Organization Manual 1964–1965*, Washington, D. C., Government Printing Office, June 1964.

13. Steckler, Phyllis B., *The Bowker Annual of Library and Book Trade Information*, New York, R. R. Bowker Co., 1965.

14. Stevens, M. E., *Automatic Indexing: A State-of-the-Art Report*, National Bureau of Standards Monograph 91, March 1965.

15. U. S. Senate, Committee on Government Operations, Subcommittee on Reorganizations, *Summary of Activities toward Interagency Coordination*, 89th Congress, 1st Session, Report 369, June 1965.

Chapter Four

Document Users

The purpose of a document system for science and technology is to serve the information needs of scientists, practitioners, engineers, students, and managers. It follows that an "ideal" system is one that effectively serves the needs of each individual member of these communities efficiently. Information specialists recognize the importance of understanding these information needs and expend effort toward accumulating data about them. Their studies are commonly referred to as "user studies" and the populations studied as "users."

This chapter describes the results of an analysis of user studies. A detailed description of the individual findings of these studies is beyond the scope of this discussion. References are given, however, to support the conclusions expressed. The objectives of the analysis were to:

1. Examine the adequacy of existing studies that describe the users of document systems.

2. Determine any patterns or conclusions that have significance for the planning of future document-handling and information system modifications.

APPROACH

A bibliography of all those documents that describe user needs was compiled and each document was examined for its contribution to an understanding of the user population. Only those documents that describe studies and supply findings based on objective data were analyzed in detail. An analysis was made of the characteristics of each study and the results compiled to determine:

1. Quality of the studies.
2. Extent of user coverage by discipline, activity, type of agency, etc.

3. Contributions of the studies to an understanding of the needs of user populations.

4. Requirements for future studies.

In addition, an analysis was made of each study to determine if there are recognizable patterns of information use common to members of the scientific and technical community taken as a whole.

INTERPRETATION OF FINDINGS

Characteristics of User Studies

Approximately 450 publications were identified which in some manner discussed the information needs of members of the community of scientists and technologists. The overwhelming majority of the documents consisted of journal articles expressing the author's opinions of what a particular group of users needed, or outlining his preferred approaches or innovations designed to satisfy some group of users. A second group of documents were reviews of opinions of user needs, critical reviews of studies based on survey and other data, or pleas for more and better user studies. Only the 58 that met the criterion of being based on objective data are included within the user analysis. (Several other studies appeared to meet this criterion but published findings were unavailable.)

Quality of Studies Analyzed. The 58 studies selected for the analysis vary in quality. Taken as a group, however, most contribute substantially to an understanding of user behavior. The most comprehensive and best-designed studies were conducted most recently, indicating: (1) a growing understanding of the importance of this type of information for system planning; and (2) an upsurge of interest in the field of information science. Some of the studies which indicate an

improving trend in user research are the studies of the American Psychological Association [2–13], Menzell at Columbia University [48], George Washington University [29, 30], West at Lehigh University [68], and Auerbach Corporation [14, 15]. Almost without exception all studies utilized questionnaires and interviews similar to those commonly seen in survey research. Such an approach employs a set of questions designed to elicit responses which can be categorized and quantified. Since the method depends on a subject's recall of his past behavior, the validity of the method often is questioned on the grounds that a person's recall of his past behavior frequently is inaccurate.

A few of the studies employed a form of time-motion study techniques, requiring that each person record his information-seeking activities for some specified period. In some cases investigators took samples of user behavior as recalled over short periods of time.

User studies, when viewed collectively, contain many limitations in methodology and analysis which prevent one from making generalizations for the design of a national document-handling system, although they do give some guidance for more limited goals. Examples of these limitations include:

1. Most studies were designed to investigate a particular user population and little or no attention was given to their relationships to other user studies. Although it is quite appropriate to design a study to accomplish certain specific objectives (e.g., improving the service of a particular agency), such an approach often limits its usefulness to the population investigated.

2. Many studies used population samples that did not assure representative samples of the groups being investigated.

3. Some investigators failed to report sufficient details to allow a comparison of populations. These studies included populations described generally as "scientists," "engineers," or "scientists and engineers," often including administrative and library service personnel. Often no attempt was made to present the data by discipline, position, or nature of work.

4. Little attention was given to validating the questionnaire prior to its use as a measuring device. This resulted in overlapping response categories, frequent "other" or "blanks" responses.

Table 4-1   General Categories of User Studies Analyzed

Category	U. S.	Foreign	Total
Scientists, mixed disciplines	20	13	33
Engineers, mixed types	2	1	3
Scientists and engineers, mixed	12	1	13
Population undefined	7	2	9
Total	41	17	58

5. Response categories seldom coincided from study to study, making cross comparisons impossible.

6. Questions and responses usually were designed for a high level of abstraction, thus prohibiting specific description of actual behavior under differing conditions.

7. Most experimental designs did not provide for a systematic control of variables.

8. Few efforts were made to distinguish between what a person did as opposed to what he said he did, or to distinguish between uses, needs, and wants.

Problems associated with the interpretation and usefulness of past user studies are discussed in detail in a recent study by the Auerbach Corporation [15]. This report, which reaches conclusions similar to those of this analyst, states:

"With such varying and vague methods of measurement, each study can be criticized not only on the basis of the internal data it developed, but also for the lack of any valid way to relate data between different studies. With different, ill-defined, or non-existent units in each study, no method to correlate, or cross tabulate data, can be developed. This has been a major stumbling block in the formulation of a methodology capable of prescribing diverse user data for broad system design applications. . . ."

Populations Covered by User Studies. The analyzed user studies varied widely in the nature of the populations sampled. Table 4-1 is a tabulation of the studies by gross categories.

Approximately 30 per cent of the studies were conducted in foreign countries. The significance of the findings from these studies for the design of an information system within the United States is difficult to calculate because of intercultural

differences. Nevertheless it is believed that there are many common practices between information users in this country and in Western Europe. Thus European studies may well supplement studies in this country.

The majority of American user studies are concentrated in the "scientists" category. Reference to Table 4-2 will show, however, that except for psychologists only six studies have "pure" populations in the sense that they are limited to a single discipline. Of these six studies, only chemists show more than one

study. Thus it becomes evident that only the "scientists" category provides an extensive data base for analysis.

A look at these data indicates further difficulties in analysis. The "scientists" category includes both the research scientist and the applied scientist. These two fields, in turn, include various population samples within the several disciplines, and sample users in academic institutions, industrial communities, and government establishments. Since the user studies themselves indicate that many information needs would

Table 4-2   Frequency of Disciplines Sampled

	U. S.		Foreign		Total	
Discipline	*Mixed*	*Single*	*Mixed*	*Single*	*Mixed*	*Single*
Engineers						
General	6	1	2	0	8	1
Aeronautical and astronautical	0	0	0	0	0	0
Mechanical	0	0	0	0	0	0
Civil	0	0	0	0	0	0
Electrical	2	1	0	1	2	2
Chemical	2	0	0	0	2	0
Scientists						
General	2	0	2	0	4	0
Physical scientists and mathematicians						
General	2	0	0	2	2	2
Chemists	5	3	4	0	9	3
Earth scientists	2	0	1	0	3	0
Mathematicians	4	0	1	0	5	0
Metallurgists	4	0	1	0	5	0
Physicists	5	0	4	3	9	3
Life scientists						
Agricultural	2	0	0	0	2	0
Biological scientists	4	0	3	2	7	2
Medical scientists	2	1	0	0	2	1
Psychologists	2	11	2	0	4	11
Social scientists						
General	1	0	0	0	1	0
Anthropologists	1	0	0	0	1	0
Economists	0	0	0	0	0	0
Sociologists	0	0	0	0	0	0
Populations undefined in report	7	0	2	0	9	0
Totals	53*	17	22*	8	75*	25

* The number of disciplines exceed the number of user studies since frequently more than one discipline is included in the population sampled. "Mixed discipline" refers to studies that contain both engineers and scientists, either as general groupings or as specific disciplines. Thus a study that includes electrical engineers and mathematicians would be considered mixed, whereas a study including engineers or scientists only would be considered "single disciplines." The "general" categories refer to populations which are only broadly defined as engineers or scientists without giving specific disciplines.

vary from user to user under these various conditions, insufficient data exist either for identifying areas of common use or for generalizing as to the nature of the subpopulations.

One must conclude from an examination of the numbers, quality, and population coverage of completed user studies that the need of the user is still not well enough known to permit one to completely formulate a design for an information system that will serve him. Even in the field of psychology, where perhaps more data have been collected about the generation, processing, and dissemination of scientific and technical information than in any other discipline, much collection and data analysis must still be done.

The foregoing cautions are not meant to imply that user studies are of insignificant value in understanding the information needs of scientists, engineers, and technicians. Such studies are essential if the information specialist is to respond to the users' needs. It is implied, however, that careful planning and attention must be given to this area to ensure that future studies provide valid data and cover the user populations systematically.

It seems probable that certain user needs are common to all users of scientific and technical information. Since this possibility exists, and since one would prefer to have an information system that incorporates as many common features as possible, future studies should be designed with common data elements to facilitate comparisons across populations. This approach would require, however, that more attention be given to planning and coordinating research studies, perhaps through some centralized agency.

Implications of User Studies

The findings from the user studies are presented below; each is followed by a statement of its implication for system design.

1. *Principle of Least Effort.* People in general expend as little energy as possible in pursuit of their particular goals. We would not expect people to depart significantly from this behavior pattern when seeking scientific and technical information [33, 38, 46, 52, 53].

SYSTEM IMPLICATION. The system should be easy to use. It should optimize providing the right number of documents in the right form to the right person at the right time with the least effort on the part of the user.

2. *Resistance to Change.* Except in cases in which a man is highly motivated, changes in his behavior occur rather slowly [25, 38, 46, 48].

SYSTEM IMPLICATION. Changes in the system which directly affect the user should be evolutionary—not revolutionary, unless a critical need is perceived by the user or the system change is clearly easier to use.

3. *Quantity of Information Consumed.* There is a wide range among users in the quantity of information needed or consumed. This varies both between and within disciplines. This variability is related to such factors as individual motivation and capacity, nature of tasks, etc. [2, 13, 14, 17, 19, 27, 39, 41, 56, 57, 60].

SYSTEM IMPLICATION. The system should be designed so that the range of its services meets the needs of the most, as well as the least, motivated and productive members of the community.

4. *Research Scientists Prefer to Do Their Own Searches.* Most research scientists presently prefer to do at least part of their own searches and request or require hard copy. Since this appears to be related to their own need for assurance that an adequate search has been accomplished, they will most likely continue this practice in the future [14, 18, 23, 24, 32, 42, 54, 56].

SYSTEM IMPLICATION. The system should be designed to facilitate efficient searching by the scientist and to provide hard copy of all needed documents, both foreign and domestic, within any reasonable specified time.

5. *Professional and Trade Publications.* Most scientists, engineers, and technicians read professional and trade publications within both their own and related fields. Many of these are personal subscriptions particularly through membership in their professional societies, but more often the publications are furnished by the employing agency. These publications play an important part in keeping the professional worker abreast of current research and development and frequently stimulate him to new ideas and research. Most often journal articles are read only

because they are immediately available in a field of interest. Research scientists consider this the most important single source of information, although oral communication is not significantly less important than journal articles as an information source [1, 8, 9, 11, 19, 20, 24, 27, 31, 34, 48, 54, 56, 57, 60, 62].

SYSTEM IMPLICATION. Provisions should be made for the scientist and practitioner to have easy access to current professional and trade publications in their own and related fields.

6. *Information Lag.* About 20 per cent of scientists and practitioners admit to information gaps or duplication of work caused by the lack or inability to locate information in informal and formal publications [2, 5, 8, 9, 14, 16, 32, 47, 54, 59, 64, 68].

SYSTEM IMPLICATION. The system should make provisions for disseminating information about current research projects and unpublished reports, and reduce the time lag in formal publications.

7. *Users' Needs Vary.* Information requirements vary with the individual scientist, practitioner, and engineer as to his role, discipline, project, and environment [2, 12, 13, 14, 17, 19, 25, 39, 41, 46, 56, 57, 60, 63, 67].

SYSTEM IMPLICATION. The system should be capable of supporting a variety of different user configurations.

8. *Quality of Information.* The quantity of information available in many fields is exceeding the capacity of the individual to consume it. There is an expressed need for better rather than more information [12, 28, 54, 63].

SYSTEM IMPLICATION. The system should provide for an improvement in the quality of documentation produced, the condensing of information, and the purging or retiring of files and document stores of unused materials.

9. *Age of Journal Articles.* The frequency with which an article from a serial publication is used is inversely related in a linear fashion to the age of the article. Approximately 95 per cent of all journals consulted are less than twenty years old, and approximately 50 per cent are less than five years old [12, 28, 40, 57, 62, 66, 69].

SYSTEM IMPLICATION. The system should provide for storing documents infrequently used because of age to facilitate the distribution of more used documents and to better preserve the old.

10. *Awareness of Information Services.* Many users are unaware of information sources, how to utilize them, or what services are available to aid them with their problems [45, 46, 54, 61, 62].

SYSTEM IMPLICATION. The system should be designed and operated so that its retail services and responsibilities can be clearly understood by the scientific and technical community. It should provide for the educating and training of users and prospective users (students) in its services.

11. *Quality of Services.* The user often is disappointed with the quality of service rendered by libraries, information agencies, and their associated personnel. Collections are sometimes inadequate [8, 14, 23, 25, 42, 45, 47, 51, 56, 61, 62].

SYSTEM IMPLICATION. (*a*) The system should provide a mechanism for obtaining competent qualified personnel. This should include periodic review of position descriptions, specification of training requirements, review of manning levels, and sponsoring of training program development, both within the system and in the academic curriculum. (*b*) The system should provide for quality assurance programs designed to measure the efficiency of its services.

12. *User Studies.* Research programs to determine user needs have been hampered in the past by lack of funds, lack of coordinated planning, lack of quality, and lack of sufficient recognition of their value. Programs for the systematic study of user patterns in present information agencies are almost nonexistent [15, 21, 22, 25, 47, 48].

SYSTEM IMPLICATION. The system should provide for a broad program of research that includes particular attention to determining user needs and user satisfaction. Such a program should strive for improving techniques for measuring user behavior as well as the behavior itself.

13. *Foreign Publications.* Users frequently find difficulty in obtaining foreign documents and

translations of these foreign publications [2, 12, 47].

SYSTEM IMPLICATION. The system should provide for easy access to all important foreign publications, preferably with English translations.

14. *Oral Communication.* Oral communication plays an important role in the dissemination of scientific and technical information [6, 9, 14, 27, 32, 34, 35, 45, 46, 60, 62].

SYSTEM IMPLICATION. The system should provide for facilitating the dissemination of scientific and technical information through oral communication media.

Discussion of Findings

Systems for generating, indexing, and disseminating scientific and technical documents have existed in the United States for decades. The degree to which they have effectively served the community of scientists and engineers has been and still remains in the realm of speculation. This seems to stem primarily from the lack of good information about the needs and behavior of the persons making up the scientific and technical communities. It follows that without such information it is impossible to measure the degree of success existing systems might have obtained.

Rubenstein [55], voicing the need for more and better user studies, quotes Mrs. Helen L. Brownson, Program Director for Documentation Research, Office of Science Information Service, National Science Foundation, as stating:

". . . [I]t goes without saying that the information needs of the scientific community should determine the character of new information services and techniques. Although there is a good deal of intuitive and subjective knowledge about the various ways in which scientists communicate the results of their own work to others and learn about the work of others, there is very little precise objective knowledge of the inadequacies in the present flow of scientific information and of the cost to scientists and to society of those inadequacies. A deeper understanding of the role of the mechanics of communication within the sciences and of the information problems and needs of scientists would be of assistance to scientific societies and other organizations involved in planning and maintaining publication programs and scientific and technical information services. Such understanding is also needed for the design of information-handling systems and procedures that will provide the sort of help scientists can use to best advantage."

Often such criticism is directed toward those who, even with good intentions, seem more inclined to *acquire* a new system or technique rather than to *build* or *design* a new system or technique to serve the needs of the user.

It is easy to criticize, particularly when viewing a problem in retrospect. Criticism, however, is one of the elements of scientific progress. The determination of user needs presents a problem with no easy solution. The Auerbach study [15] pinpointed, in a sympathetic tone, one of the most difficult problems to solve when it concluded:

"The most serious criticism that can be brought against previous user studies (and the most difficult problem to overcome) was the criticism of the vague and varying ways in which the information used, or preferred, were defined. No measurably significant unit of information was provided in any study; and when some defined parameters were employed to examine certain aspects of the information patterns of a user, the variables not considered usually outweighed any measurable variations in the hypotheses to be tested. For example, if a precise measure of time were developed, the unit of information was not clearly determined or the function served considered. And such results, which accurately show that 11.9% of a physicist's reading time was devoted to the *Physical Review* and only 3% to the *Scientific American,* seem significant of very little, in spite of the mathematical model developed to prove the statistics validity of a random alarm method. And, when the information used was somewhat defined, the purposes served, or the requirements for the information, were not established. And again, results which gave vague 'use ratings' for Density and Solar Radiation, or 'desire ratings' for loose-leaf manuals or accession lists determine little about general system requirements. Similar conclusions may also be made about most known studies conducted to date."

Most criticisms leveled at past studies are directed toward the methodology and not toward the usefulness of such studies. Herner [36]

correctly attempted to put the problem in truer perspective when he wrote:

"As is true of most utilitarian items, it is very difficult to design effective information systems in the abstract. Before entering into the engineering and design phases of a system, it is necessary to know just what the system is supposed to do and for whom. This information can only be obtained by studying the habits and requirements of the potential user.

"There have been innumerable user studies performed over the past decade or more. These studies, which have utilized a wide variety of analytical methods, have been reviewed in papers by Egan and Henkle, Shaw, and Tornudd. Unfortunately, these reviews and most recent discussions of user requirements have been more concerned with method than with applicable results. In their preoccupation with *how* past studies were done, the reviewers and discussants have overlooked the fact that most of them were done by working librarians and information specialists for specific practical purposes connected with the improvement of existing information programs. While admittedly imperfect in conception and execution, the majority of these studies have produced results, in the sense that they have furnished operators of information programs insight as to how these programs are used or are likely to be used. A striking characteristic of these results is that despite the fact that they have been derived by a variety of means they have corroborated one another in a number of important respects."

Studies are now underway, many sponsored by the National Science Foundation [50], which promise to substantially advance knowledge in both the methodology needed to conduct user studies and the information needs of various user communities.

User needs, however, do not remain static. In addition to an initial effort to determine user requirements for system modifications through questions, observations, and experimentations, there is a need for a dynamic feedback loop in all information agencies serving users of documentation. This feedback loop must facilitate intelligent planning and budgeting for most of the agencies' functions; as, for example, which documents are rarely used and should be stored for better preservation? Which documents are in great demand and should be purchased or duplicated in quantity? What kinds of new services or innovations should be planned? And, how should old services be improved?

Libraries give considerable attention to the role of providing documents for users. Professional staff members continuously scrutinize subject areas for completeness of coverage, particularly in subject areas of prime interest, and purchase as many documents as funds permit. Unfortunately, less attention is given to a systematic recording and analysis of the user patterns which emerge from day-to-day operations. Proper data collection and analysis functions should be a part of the regular operations of libraries and other document distribution systems and information centers. In many cases, such information would be available at little additional cost, since many organizations presently keep other kinds of related data. Doyle [26] has paid particular attention to this problem in one of his recent publications.

Oral and other informal forms of communication play a vital but vaguely understood role in the work of scientists, practitioners, and engineers. Some of these needs will never be completely satisfied by other communication media or even any one method of informal exchange. Menzel [47] found cases where needed experimental techniques or equipments dictated that unusual extrapolation, requiring extensive informal search, be made from other undocumented experimentation. Menzel also found studies which indicate that the exchange of informal information is not always efficient, that persons selected for contacting by the researcher seeking information may not be the best source for information, and that personal sources of information may arise "accidentally." Newspapers, newsletters, information exchanges, and other such media have been suggested as means for improving the flow of current or unpublished research information, but these suggestions were based more on opinion than experimentation.

Nondocument communication often is required even when the results of studies appear in the literature. This need for additional communication results from the lack of sufficient detail in the published articles to permit the investigator to replicate an experiment. Questions immediately arise as to how one might correct this problem. Should we have more detail published with an article? Would it be more

efficient and economical to have a depository for supplying supplemental data and information? Is this problem really a critical one? Answers to such questions are obviously necessary before corrective action can be taken.

These, then, are some of the problems and hopeful indications for the future. Where do we go from here?

The most important lesson to be learned from an analysis of past user studies is that there is a need for wider recognition of and support for research. One cannot hope to put the "house of information science in order" without better information about the process of scientific and technical communication and what is needed to facilitate it. Such a conclusion leads to the question of what form such a research program should take. Aside from the fact that it must be broad, coordinated, and well planned, the most important single step might be to foster a recognition of the importance of information communication research through the encouragement and formal recognition of an already emerging field of information science dedicated to the study of all aspects of the information field.

RECOMMENDATIONS

Research

There is not sufficient recognition of the value of user studies to the design of experimentation leading to development of improved information systems. This lack of recognition is demonstrated by the limited number of studies conducted, the small amount of funds available for user studies and experimentation, and the lack of a coordinated research program.

Recommendation. That research in the information sciences be recognized by national policy makers as critical to the future development of a national information system(s) and to the progress of science and technology in the United States.

The following actions are essential to the implementation of an effective research program:

1. The centralized agency responsible for developing a national information system(s) should be assigned the responsibility for planning, encouraging, coordinating, and conducting research in user needs, including experimentation with new methods for better serving user

needs, as an important part of its total research program.

2. Provide appropriate funding to ensure an adequate research program.

Quality Assurance

Most federal information services do not perform quality assurance studies to determine the adequacy of their services to the customer, or the degree to which the costs of these services are justified by beneficial results obtained.

Recommendation. That systematic data be collected from the users of the federal libraries, information centers, and other information-handling agencies to determine the quality of service, to identify losses caused by deficiencies, and to define requirements for improvements.

National System(s) Design

The present analysis of user studies resulted in identifying fifteen implications for system design. Each of the implications were considered in the development of the recommended and alternate system concepts described in Chapters 7 through 10.

Recommendation. Implications for system design described earlier in this chapter under "Implications of User Studies" should be considered in the design of any national or federal system(s).

REFERENCES°

1. Ackoff, Russell L., and Michael H. Halbert, "An Operations Research Study of Scientific Activity of Chemistry" (mimeo), Cleveland, Ohio, Case Institute of Technology, Operations Research Group, 1958.

2. American Psychological Association, "Archival Journal Articles: Their Authors and the Processes Involved in Their Production" (revised December 1963), APA-PSIEP #7, *Project on Scientific Information Exchange in Psychology*, Washington, D. C., American Psychological Association, August 1963, p. 153.

3. American Psychological Association, "A Comparison of Scientific Information—Exchange Activities at Their Levels of Psychological Meetings," APA-PSIEP #8, *Project on Scientific Information Exchange in Psychology*, Washington, D. C., American Psychological Association, December 1963, p. 187.

4. American Psychological Association, "Convention Attendants and Their Use of the Convention as a Source of Scientific Information," APA-PSIEP #4, *Project on*

° Reference numbers in parentheses indicate a reference other than a user study.

Scientific Information Exchange in Psychology, Washington, D. C., American Psychological Association, August 1963, p. 75.

5. American Psychological Association, "Convention Participants and the Dissemination of Information at Scientific Meetings," APA-PSIEP #5, *Project on Scientific Information Exchange in Psychology,* Washington, D. C., American Psychological Association, August 1963, p. 105.

6. American Psychological Association, "The Discovery and Dissemination of Scientific Information among Psychologists in Two Research Environments," APA-PSIEP #11, *Project on Scientific Information Exchange in Psychology,* Washington, D. C., American Psychological Association, September 1964, p. 47.

7. American Psychological Association, "A General Study of the Annual Convention of the American Psychological Association," APA-PSIEP #3, *Project on Scientific Information Exchange in Psychology,* Washington, D. C., American Psychological Association, August 1963, p. 39.

8. American Psychological Association, "An Informal Study of the Preparation of Chapters for the Annual Review of Psychology," APA-PSIEP #2, *Project on Scientific Information Exchange in Psychology,* Washington, D. C., American Psychological Association, August 1963, p. 23.

9. American Psychological Association, "A Preliminary Study of Information Exchange Activities of Foreign Psychologists and a Comparison of Such Activities with Those Occurring in the United States," APA-PSIEP #10, *Project on Scientific Information Exchange in Psychology,* Washington, D. C., American Psychological Association, June 1964.

10. American Psychological Association, "The Role of the Technical Report in the Dissemination of Scientific Information," APA-PSIEP #13, *Project on Scientific Information Exchange in Psychology,* Washington, D. C., American Psychological Association, April 1965.

11. American Psychological Association, "Scientific Activity and Information Problems of Selected Psychologists: A Preliminary Survey," APA-PSIEP #1, *Project on Scientific Information Exchange in Psychology,* Washington, D. C., American Psychological Association, August 1963, p. 11.

12. American Psychological Association, "The Use of Scientific Journals by Psychologists and the Readership of Current Journal Articles," APA-PSIEP #9, *Project on Scientific Information Exchange in Psychology,* Washington, D. C., American Psychological Association, December 1963, p. 213.

13. American Psychological Association, "Publication Fate of Formal Presentations at the 1957 Convention of the American Psychological Association," APA-PSIEP #6, *Project on Scientific Information Exchange in Psychology,* Washington, D. C., American Psychological Association, August 1963, p. 135.

14. Auerbach Corporation, *Department of Defense User Needs Study, Phase I,* Vols. I and II, Philadelphia, May 1965.

(15.) Auerbach Corporation, "Review of Methodologies for Studying User Needs for Scientific and Technical Information," Philadelphia, January 6, 1965. Includes 676-item bibliography.

16. Barnes, R. C. M., "Some Recent Investigations into Information Use at A.E.R.E., Harwell," in *Looking Forward in Documentation, Papers and Discussion,* ASLIB 38th Annual Conference, 1964.

17. Bernal, J. D., "Preliminary Analysis of Pilot Questionnaire on the Use of Scientific Literature," The Royal Society Scientific Information Conference, June 21–July 2, 1948, London, The Royal Society, 1948, pp. 589–637.

(18.) Bourne, Charles P., et al., *Requirements, Criteria, and Measurements of Performance of Information Storage and Retrieval Systems,* AD 270942, Menlo Park, Calif., Stanford Research Institute, December 1961.

19. Bureau of Social Science Research, Inc., *A Survey of Users of the American Society for Metals—Western Reserve University Searching Service,* Washington, D. C., July 1962.

20. Cole, P. F., "The Analysis of Reference Question Records as a Guide to the Information Requirements of Scientists," *Journal of Documentation,* Vol. 14, No. 4, December 1958, pp. 197–206.

21. Columbia University, "Review of Studies in the Flow of Information Among Scientists," Vol. I, New York, Bureau of Applied Social Research, Columbia University, January 1960.

22. Columbia University, "Review of Studies in the Flow of Information Among Scientists," Vol. II, New York, Bureau of Applied Social Research, Columbia University, January 1960.

23. Cuadra, C. A., and E. M. Wallace, "Library Services Support Study, Part I, Summary Report on Technical Services Support Study" (unpublished report), Santa Monica, Calif., System Development Corp., February 1, 1964.

24. Department of Defense, *Detailed Answer to Questions Relating to Chemical Information and Data System (CIDS)* (informal report), December 1964.

25. Division of Medical Sciences, National Academy of Sciences, National Research Council in cooperation with Federation of American Societies for Experimental Biology and Institute for Advancement of Medical Communication, "Communication Problems in Biomedical Research: Report of a Study," reprinted from *Federation Proceedings,* Vol. 23, No. 5, September–October 1964.

(26.) Doyle, L. B., "Perpetual User Studies, A Prerequisite for Management of Information on a National Scale," Santa Monica, Calif., System Development Corp., June 1965.

27. Fishenden, R. M., "Methods by Which Research Workers Find Information," *Proceedings of the International Conference on Scientific Information,* Washington, D. C., National Academy of Sciences, 1959, pp. 163–179.

28. Fussler, H. H., and J. L. Simon, *Patterns in the Use of Books in Large Research Libraries,* Chicago, University of Chicago, 1961.

29. George Washington University, *Informal Communication among Bioscientists: Biological Sciences Com-*

munication Project, Part I, Washington, D. C., George Washington University, December 1963.

30. George Washington University, *Informal Communication among Bioscientists: Biological Sciences Communication Project, Part II*, Washington, D. C., George Washington University, June 1, 1964.

31. Gerard, R. W., *Mirrors to Physiology*, Washington, D. C., American Physiological Society, 1958.

32. Glass, Bently, and Sharon Norwood, "How Scientists Actually Learn of Work Important to Them," in *Proceedings of the International Conference on Scientific Information*, Washington, D. C., National Academy of Sciences, 1959, pp. 195–197.

(33.) Guthrie, E. R., "Conditioning: A Theory of Learning in Terms of Stimulus Response and Association," in *The Psychology of Learning*, pp. 37–45, 51–54, Part II of the *Forty-First Yearbook of the National Society for the Study of Education*, ed. Nakow B. Henry, 2 vols., Chicago, University of Chicago Press, 1942.

34. Herner, Saul, "The Information-Gathering Habits of American Medical Scientists," in *Proceedings of the International Conference on Scientific Information*, Washington, D. C., National Academy of Science, 1959, pp. 267–276.

35. Herner, Saul, "Information-Gathering Habits of Workers in Pure and Applied Science," *Industrial and Engineering Chemistry*, Vol. 46, 1954, pp. 288–236.

(36.) Herner, Saul, "The Relationship of Information-Use Studies and the Design of Information Storage and Retrieval Systems," AD 213 781, Washington, D. C., Herner and Co., 1958.

37. Hersey, David F., and Monroe E. Freeman, "User Responses in the Evaluation of a Flexible Indexing and Retrieval System," in Part I of *Short Papers of the ADI Annual Meeting*, Washington, D. C., American Documentation Institute, 1963, pp. 117–118.

(38.) Hilgard, Ernest R., *Theories of Learning*, New York, Appleton-Century-Crofts, 1956, pp. 53–57.

39. Hogg, I. H., and Roland Smith, "A Survey of the Use of Literature and Information in the Research and Development Branch" (mimeo), Risley, Warrington, Lancashire, England, Industrial Group Headquarters, 1959.

40. Kessler, M. M., "Technical Information Flow Patterns," AD 261 303, Lincoln Laboratories, 1961.

41. Levy, N. P., "A Survey on the Information Practices of Engineers at Western Electric," *American Documentation*, Vol. 15, No. 2, April 1964, pp. 86–88.

42. Maizell, Robert E., "Information Gathering Patterns and Creativity," *American Documentation*, Vol. 11, No. 1, January 1960, pp. 9–17.

43. Martyn, John, and Margaret Slater, "Characteristics of Users and Non-Users of Scientific Information," in *Looking Forward in Documentation: Papers and Discussion*, ASLIB 38th Annual Conference, 1964.

44. Martyn, John, "Literature Searching by Research Scientists," ASLIB Research Department, 1964.

45. Materials Advisory Board, Division of Engineering and Industrial Research, National Research Council,

"Dissemination of Information on Materials: An Analysis of a Survey of Materials Information Users to Determine Effectiveness of Information Dissemination," prepared for the National Academy of Sciences, National Research Council, Washington, D. C., 1964.

46. McLaughlin, Curtis P., et al., *Technology Transfer and the Flow of Technical Information in a Large Industrial Corporation*, Vols. I and II, Cambridge, Mass., Harvard University, March 1965.

47. Menzel, Herbert, "The Flow of Information among Scientists—Problems, Opportunities, and Research Question" (mimeo), New York, Columbia University, Bureau of Applied Social Research, 1958.

48. Menzel, Herbert, "The Information Needs of Current Scientific Research," *Library Quarterly*, Vol. XXXIV, No. 1, January 1964.

(49.) Mooers, Calvin N., "Information Retrieval Selection Study," Part II, Chicago, Zator Co., August 1959, p. 34.

(50.) National Science Foundation, *Current Research and Development in Scientific Documentation*, No. 13, Washington, D. C., November 1964.

51. Panning, I. J., et al., *Survey and Analysis of Specialized Science Information Services in the United States*, AD 285 108, Columbus, Ohio, Battelle Memorial Institute, September 1962.

(52.) Parsons, H. M., "Avoidance Conditioning of Four Human Operant Responses by Induced Muscular Tension," Ph.D. dissertation, University of California at Los Angeles, 1963, pp. 22–24, 38y.

53. Resnick, A., "The Information Explosion and the User's Need for Hard Copy," in *Proceedings of the American Documentation Institute Annual Meeting*, Vol. 1, 1964, pp. 315–317.

54. Resnick, A., and C. B. Hensley, "The Use of Diary and Interview Techniques in Evaluating a System for Disseminating Technical Information," Yorktown Heights, N. Y., IBM Advanced Systems Development Division, December 1961.

(55.) Rubenstein, Albert H., "Timing and Form of Researchers Needs for Technical Information," *Journal of Chemical Documents*, Vol. 2, January 1962, pp. 28–31.

56. Scott, Christopher, "The Use of Technical Literature by Industrial Technologists," in *Proceedings of IRE International Conference on Scientific Information*, Washington, D. C., November 16–21, 1958. Washington, D. C., National Academy of Sciences, National Research Council, Vol. I, 1959, pp. 245–266.

57. Shaw, Ralph R., "Pilot Study on the Use of Scientific Literature by Scientists" (mimeo), under grant from the National Science Foundation (Studies 1 and 2), 1956.

(58.) Taube, M., "An Evaluation of Use Studies of Scientific Information," Bethesda, Md., Documentation Inc., December 1958.

59. Tornudd, Elin, "Study on the Use of Scientific Literature and Reference Services by Scandinavian Scientists and Engineers Engaged in Research and Development," in *Proceedings of the International Conference on Scientific Information*, Washington, D. C., November 16–21,

1958. Washington, D. C., National Academy of Sciences, National Research Council, Vol. I, 1959, pp. 9–65.

60. Tornudd, Elin, "Professional Reading Habits of Scientists Engaged in Research as Revealed by an Analysis of 130 Questionnaires," unpublished master's dissertation, Carnegie Library School, Carnegie Institute of Technology, 1953.

61. U. S. Atomic Energy Commission, *Report on Survey of Users U. S. AEC Headquarters Library,* Washington, D. C., June 1964.

62. U. S. Department of Agriculture, *Report of Task Force ABLE, Agricultural Biological Literature Exploitation,* Washington, D. C., March 1965.

(**63.**) U. S. Department of Commerce, *Scientific and Technological Communication in the Government,* Washington, D. C., Government Printing Office, 1962 (Crawford Report, part of HR-1946) AD 295 545.

64. University of Denver, "The Commercial Application of Missile/Space Technology," Parts 1 and 2, Denver Research Institute, University of Denver, September 1963.

65. University of Chicago, "A Survey of Research Potential and Training in the Mathematical Sciences," Part I, Chicago, University of Chicago, 1957.

66. Urquhart, D. J., "Study on the Use of Scientific Literature and Reference Services by Scandinavian Scientists and Engineers Engaged in Research and Development," in *Proceedings of the International Conference on Scientific Information,* 1958, pp. 9–65.

67. Voigt, Melvin J., "Scientists' Approaches to Information," *ACRL* Monograph, No. 24, Chicago, American Library Association, 1961.

68. West, F. J., *Studies in the Methodology of Measuring Information Requirements and Use Patterns, Report No. 1: Questionnaire,* Bethlehem, Pa., Center for the Information Sciences, Lehigh University, May 1965.

69. Wilson, C. W. J., "Use of Periodicals in the Royal Aircraft Establishment Library, 1956–57" (mimeo), London, Ministry of Supply, 1957.

PART TWO

*The Problem and
Basic Propositions*

Chapter Five

The National
Document-Handling Problem

"From a library podium this evening I propose to touch on but three facets of this multiplex phenomenon: 1) the driving federal emphasis on scientific and particularly industrial research; 2) the global scope of contemporary university involvement in behalf of the national effort, together with changing emphases in social science research; and 3) the emerging recognition at the federal level of the importance of humanistic research.

"In discussing these aspects of the new search for knowledge, I will suggest that consistently and shortsightedly we have failed to undergird this major social effort with proper library support for the inquiring mind, that unless we soon alter public policy we will only compound an already crippling deficit of reference and research library resources and services, and finally that the federal government has both a fundamental stake in and a direct responsibility for the present frustrating state of library affairs. At this point, I conclude, the effective resolution of the library and information problems faced by research can come only through the proper development of a wise and forceful national policy in generous support of overall library service to research and inquiry" [1].

From the Inaugural Address of
Robert G. Vosper as President of
the American Library Association, 1965

There are still some who argue that there is no real S&T information and documentation problem. After having reviewed the area in detail we can only conclude that such assertions either are made from a narrow consideration of the many facts involved or are made regarding some very limited aspect of the problem.

Those who contend that there is no real problem tend to be composed of the elite scientists. In their heads, their filing cabinets, their personal collections of the important journals in their field, but also in their correspondence, visits to colleagues' laboratories, small special symposia, etc., they have at their immediate command the essential S&T information and documentation that they need. But they are only a small part of the many involved, as demonstrated by this recent statement of the problem by a university administrator:

"Perhaps we have become the prisoners of our own propaganda. It is easy to become mesmerized by Sunday-supplement versions of the 'knowledge explosion.' True, there is a vast expansion in the output of research. Vast quantities of new information and new knowledge are available. We know more than ever before about everything—lasers, plasma physics, kinship patterns of the Mexican family, reading handicaps of slum children, the movement of dollars in our economy, and the flow of waters underground. The new knowledge is both abundant and unavailable. It is 'locked up' in the minds of specialists. And it is locked up in libraries that no longer serve as adequate instruments for making knowledge freely available. The contemporary library is an anachronism; we are far short of a workable technology that will package and disseminate new knowledge cheaply and quickly" [2].

No doubt this comment by a university president reflects the traditional faculty grumbling and budgetary pressure to which the administrators of higher education must react, but these difficulties are also voiced by some within the

library community. In a penetrating article William Dix [3], of the Princeton University Library, writes:

"Among the new problems which size poses, the most obvious is sheer mass, the bulk of the collections themselves. What is one to do with all these books? Consider for a moment the implications. The usual rule of thumb for estimating space requirements is that 15 volumes, arranged in the conventional fashion on standard shelving, require one square foot of floor space, allowing only for the standard access aisles. Thus a collection of two million volumes requires some 133,333 square feet, or more than three and one-half acres. Since at least as much more space is required for readers, staff, and all the other essentials, not to mention the nonbook material, such as the more than 20,000 current journals which a library of this sort will receive, manuscripts, government documents, etc., etc., a library of two million volumes in one location requires a building with net floor space of at least seven acres. . . .

"Repeated tests have indicated that the [Farmington] Plan has indeed enriched the national resources by bringing into the country useful books which would otherwise have been missed—but the secondary hope of the founders of the Farmington Plan has not been achieved. There was at least some anticipation that if librarians and faculty members could be assured that each field was being covered systematically on a worldwide basis somewhere in the country, the growth of individual, duplicative collections might be slowed down somewhat. This effect has not been noticeable. Individual libraries continue to grow at the same inexorable rate."

In this chapter the problem is considered from a broad point of view; in Chapter 6 the basic propositions and detailed requirements of the system design are presented. A full appreciation of the S&T information and documentation problem can be gained from a careful perusal of this entire book, but a summary statement will give the reader a feeling of the problem.

NEED FOR THE ADOPTION OF A FUNDAMENTAL STATEMENT OF POLICY

It is stated as a fundamental proposition that the federal government has the responsibility to assure that there exists within the United States at least one accessible copy of each significant publication of the worldwide scientific and technical literature. (This proposition is presented and discussed in detail in Chapter 6.) This basic proposition has not previously been explicitly accepted as a responsibility of the federal government, but it seems apparent that such a proposition is fundamental in our increasingly complex and sophisticated technical society. For our society to retain its leadership in science and technology, it is necessary that the government make available within the United States the basic documentation and information underlying science and technology. While this is true of our industrial technology generally, it is even more true of our defense technology. The unusual and frequently unanticipated needs for information about foreign developments, geography, cultures, and potentials become of great importance in times of national emergency. This proposition regarding S&T information and documentation is a keystone to continued excellence in both the civilian and defense sectors, but it has not been formally adopted as a matter of policy. As a result, many of the information services of the government are not prepared to take steps to implement such a broad and expanded conception of their mission, nor would they be prepared to do so readily if the policy were formally adopted.

THERE ARE INCREASING NUMBERS OF USERS AND USER REQUIREMENTS

Data in the tables of Appendix 2 spell out the rapidly increasing number of users of S&T information and documents. It can be said that there will be about a 50 per cent increase in the number of scientists and technologists in the next five years, and estimates show a continual growth. In 1960 there were 2,370,000 scientists, engineers, and technicians in the United States; it is estimated there will be 4 million by 1970, at which time they will represent 4.7 per cent of the total labor force. By the very nature of their work, those engaged in science and technology require scientific and technical documents and information. Their requirements differ substantially, depending on the kind of work they are doing. Scientists and scholars require one kind of service, engineers another kind, and managers of technical efforts a third kind. There is considerable evidence that the present S&T information and documentation

system of libraries and information centers is not adequately meeting even current needs, and that it will be increasingly difficult to cope with a large increase in user requirements.

NUMBER OF DOCUMENTS IS INCREASING

Most of us know that the sheer number of journals, reports, books, and pamphlets is increasing. Individually, we are inundated by too much material. But how many of us stop to think that the number of publications doubles about every fifteen years? One estimate places the number of technical documents published in 1961 at 658,000 and the number to be published in 1970 at 1,143,000. In 1964 the Library of Congress had over 43 million items in its collection. This collection grew over 180 per cent in the last 26 years—no wonder new buildings are required! As the sheer number of documents increases, it becomes more and more difficult to cope with the acquiring, cataloging, indexing, announcing, circulation, and storing activities that must go on in any large research library. Libraries try to solve some of these problems by becoming more specialized, by restricting their clientele, or by just not keeping up. Clearly, a rationalized system for dealing with the increasing number of documents is needed.

PRESENT SYSTEM IS IN DIFFICULTY

In spite of the efforts of librarians and administrators to improve the services of libraries, there are many indications that the present system is having a more and more difficult time in rendering quality services. It is hard to give exact figures to support this statement, but there are many separate pieces of information which lead to this conclusion. Examples are:

1. At the 1965 session of Congress the Library of Congress helped sponsor a special appropriation of $5 million, part of which will finance an accelerated cataloging effort. Library of Congress catalog cards are used throughout the libraries of the nation, but their publication lag has been such that members of the Association of Research Libraries were able to get Library of Congress cataloging copy when they needed it for only 50 to 55 per cent of their current acquisitions.

2. Some libraries have large backlogs of documents and books which they cannot process into their collections. As an extreme example it is reported that one major library has 250,000 serial issues which are simply placed in storage because they cannot be processed fast enough.

3. Many new information exchange mechanisms are coming into use because the traditional means of communications are inadequate. The large number of trips from center to center, the informal publications, the extensive use of very early preprints, and the restricted symposia are all evidences that older and more public methods of communication are being supplemented.

4. Although they want to give service to all legitimate users, many of the nation's libraries are adopting restrictive policies regarding the services they render. Increasingly, major university libraries are curtailing their services to geographically related industrial organizations beause they lack adequate library resources.

5. User studies show a significant dissatisfaction with the present system and, at the same time, a serious lack of information about how to use the system. The user, as customer, is turning to other sources or is not using the system to the extent he should.

6. The number of people trained and attracted to librarianship is much less than the demand, and the number of new people entering the field represents a growth which is lower than the rate of growth of the general professional work force.

7. The budgetary situation for most private research libraries is critical. Major public libraries are curtailing services and stinting on staff because they cannot raise the money to maintain their usual services. Large private foundations and philanthropists are no longer supporting library operations, and municipal funds are in short supply.

8. In an uncoordinated fashion many parts of the S&T information and documentation system are depending on federal support. Direct subsidies, page charges, special grants, overhead allowances, special working agreements, and contracts all signal the dependence of the traditional system on the federal government.

NEW TECHNOLOGIES NOT APPLIED

It is something of a paradox that libraries have been very slow to adopt modern technology and computer techniques. There are a few

exceptions, but most libraries use virtually the same manual techniques today that they used 50 years ago. There are three basic causes for this situation. Most librarians and the traditions of librarianship are grounded in the humanities rather than in technology. As a result, many policy-makers in libraries tend to be unsure of the potentials of modern technology. As Dix [4] says, "Although most libraries are so under-staffed that technological unemployment because of automation is hardly likely to present difficulty, automation does present a problem to the librarian in that he has been until now usually ill-equipped by training to cope with its theory and technology in the more advanced stages, and during the next few decades he will have to adapt his systems to a major revolution." Another cause is the relative poverty of libraries. Usually, libraries have barely been able to fund their current operations, let alone experiment with new techniques. The third cause is that automated techniques are not yet developed for easy adaptation to many libraries. The development cost to adapt automation and advanced technology to document and information center problems is quite high. So far the federal government's efforts in this direction have been very modest, but if we are to cope with increasing numbers of users and increasing numbers of documents, new techniques need to be developed and applied. Demonstration projects need support and general packages of software need development so that they can be readily adapted to many libraries. Without government support for the introduction of modern technology, it appears that the document system will become less and less able to cope with the demands being made by users and with the number of documents to be handled. (See Appendix 1 for a discussion of the capabilities of technology for assisting in the S&T information and documentation areas.)

LONG-RANGE PLANNING NEEDED

The present system (described in detail in Chapters 2 and 3) is composed of many independent units: within the Government, at universities, in professional societies, as private efforts, and in industry. Each of these units goes its separate way in terms of its local plans and resources. Each perceives its individual problems, but may or may not be aware of the larger national problem (including problems of overlapping collections, duplicate cataloging, and inadequate service to some user communities.) There is no national long-range plan or planning body to bring about any cohesion in these separate efforts. There is a need for the development of national policy regarding S&T information and documentation problems. The progressive assessment of the problems and the direction in which solutions should evolve need continuous attention. In the past, ad hoc study groups or individual government professionals have developed plans or suggested solutions to the problems, but these efforts have not led to any consistent action. Often partial solutions represent the success of a particular user group, such as medicine's success in achieving government establishment of the National Library of Medicine, and the rendering of MEDLARS services to the medical profession. The lack of any plan and the promotion of various partial efforts has resulted in the situation where the Government has no consistent position toward either its own agencies or toward the support of external S&T information and documentation activities. As the pressures of increasing user populations, increasing numbers of documents, and increasing potential of advanced technology continue to mount, we see both a slow reduction in the quality of previous services and also efforts which find only partial solutions to problems. Long-range plans are clearly needed [5].

REFERENCES

1. Vosper, Robert G. Libraries and the Inquiring Minds. *ALA Bulletin,* **59,** 709–717 (1965).

2. Enarson, H. Our Emerging Educational Establishment. *Science,* **151,** 1068–1072, Copyright 1966 by The American Association for the Advancement of Science.

3. Dix, W. S. New Challenges to University Libraries. *University: A Princeton Quarterly,* Fall, 1965, No. 26, 3–16, Copyright 1965 by Princeton University.

4. *Ibid.*

5. In September 1966 President Johnson appointed a National Advisory Commission on Libraries "To evaluate policies, programs, and practices of public agencies and private organizations . . . and to recommend actions which might be taken by public and private groups to ensure an effective, efficient library system for the nation."

Chapter Six

Basic Propositions and System Requirements

BASIC PROPOSITIONS REGARDING DOCUMENT-HANDLING SYSTEMS

In the design of any system it is of fundamental importance to state clearly the basic propositions or assumptions that form the foundation on which the design rests. Discussed below is a set of basic propositions which has guided the system concepts presented in this book.

The federal government has the responsibility to ensure that there exists within the United States at least one accessible copy of each significant publication of the worldwide scientific and technical literature.

This statement is fundamental to the entire system conception, yet it contains several ideas that need elaboration or qualification.

The phrase "each significant publication" implies several problems. How do we determine what is significant? This must be based on human judgment and implies that a document or a good abstract must be available from which the judgment can be made. If a document (significant or not) is not in the United States, then the judgment must be made by someone in a foreign country; presumably the foreign country of the document's origin contains experts best able to judge the quality of the publication. But are they best able to judge its significance as far as the United States is concerned? Before 1963 how sure would we have been of the significance of a description of the geography or geology of the caves of Cuba? Judgments of significance cannot be made in terms of current perception of possible mission relevance since this is subject to periodic change. Rather, significance needs to be judged in terms of the soundness or workmanlike character of the work reported. In the long run the system should aspire to having each published document available in the United States and evaluated by appropriate American specialists. As a minimum effort we would want to include all published serials. Documents from established monograph services and books from established publishers should be included. Occasional reports and pamphlets would be the last to be included. How soon this goal can be achieved is largely a matter of how important it is relative to competing goals and the willingness of Congress to make funds available. (The United States government may be closer to this goal than many realize. The holdings of the intelligence agencies are vast. While beyond the scope of this book, the extent to which the unclassified intelligence community holdings can be made available more rapidly to the civilian community should be investigated.)

The phrase "the federal government has the responsibility to ensure" has vast implications. For one thing, it implies that a system in the federal establishment will know what is available in the United States—not only in government depositories, but in private and university libraries. In other words, there must be a national union listing and an indexing of document holdings of major libraries. This is a vast undertaking and implies a degree of government responsibility and awareness which has not been explicitly accepted in the past.

"One accessible copy" also needs explanation. It implies that there must be at least one copy of each document which can be reached in an effective manner by some yet-to-be-defined class

of users. The idea of "accessibility" does not mean that there exists one copy which can be obtained in an emergency or under a court order; rather, it implies that a copy or a reproduction will be available in reasonable time to any qualified user.

What is meant by "scientific and technical literature"? There is no disagreement about including the basic sciences—astronomy, mathematics, physics, chemistry, biology—but what about the behavioral and social sciences? The system should include these areas because of their increasing national importance and their rapid advances. In other words, psychology, sociology, cultural anthropology, political science, and economics fall within our definition of science and technology. "Technology" also needs definition. How far do we go in areas such as industrial engineering, manufacturing technology, and management engineering? The system should include these areas. Again, achievements will be measured by the success of those responsible for obtaining the funds and operating the system, but the goal is to cover science and technology as broadly defined.

The federal government has the responsibility to see that there is appropriate acquiring, announcing, processing, and making accessible this significant worldwide scientific and technical literature.

To some extent this proposition is an elaboration of the previous proposition. It spells out the things that have to be done and asserts the Federal Government's responsibility to see that they are done. The word "appropriate" modifies all of the gerunds following it, since each implied action has some limitation—acquiring is limited as discussed previously and, similarly, for each action. But how much announcing—to each citizen, to each interested citizen, to each qualified user? These are details which will evolve as the system develops and which will change as the system changes. For the time being, "appropriate" will be defined by the actions taken in meeting the requirements of the first proposition.

The word "processing" needs definition. By processing we mean the internal operating processes that must take place in a library or center when it receives a document and prepares for its storage and circulation—such things as accounting, descriptive cataloging, and classifying

are included. The processes of translating, indexing, and abstracting are also included unless the context indicates otherwise. In an automated system, processing would also include whatever preparation in digital form is required to enter the document into the system. Processing would also frequently include some form of copying for microreproduction. Processing implies many professional and clerical operations and judgments.

The federal government has the responsibility to ensure that the worldwide scientific and technical literature is accessible to qualified individuals within the United States.

How do we interpret "to ensure that the worldwide scientific and technical literature is accessible to qualified individuals"? First, it seems that there needs to be some restriction on who should have the right to documents at government expense. Presumably the government has no obligation to make documents available free to every citizen. But how do we establish criteria as to who is "qualified"—what attributes must a person have to be qualified and who will judge? Our feeling is that the criteria should be as broad as possible and that any except the grossest screening may well be more expensive and cumbersome than it is worth.

This brings us to the question of the meaning of "ensuring the accessibility." This does not mean the free accessibility. The user should be willing to show that he is qualified to receive the document by expressing a willingness to pay a reasonable fee for the document. The fee should be as modest as possible to cover only a fraction of the overall average cost of obtaining, processing, and copying documents, even though the cost of processing particular documents may be quite high. If the fee involved can be kept small enough to be met by serious users, the whole question of who is qualified probably does not need to be considered (except for matters of military classification).

There is another point regarding accessibility that has to do with when and where a document is accessible. It is believed that the "where" part of the question may become unimportant if a user is ensured of receiving, within five working days of his request, a copy of the desired document. (While five working days falls short of the ideal, it appears that it cannot be readily bettered if the document must be obtained away

from the requester's work location and is transmitted by routine mail or delivery services.) At times this will be too slow. The federal government should have a responsibility for ensuring faster service if the user is willing to pay a price which is appropriate for such faster service. It is felt that faster than five-day regular service is not now feasible, although ultimately a faster time is desirable.

Any system(s) must take account of primary publications (e.g., books, serials, pamphlets, reports) and secondary publications (e.g., indexes and abstracts) and their processing.

Information centers are a permanent part of any national system(s) for handling scientific and technical information.

A critical part of the scientific and technical information system is in the nondocument areas, such as oral communications and conferences.

This proposition is included because nonformal means of communication are very important to the working scientist and engineers. Meetings, symposia, etc., have as their formal products published proceedings or reports which enter the document system and are handled like any other document. But because a national information system should have as a goal the promotion of the expeditious exchange of scientific information, it should support visits from laboratory to laboratory, informal newsletters, and small restricted meetings at the most productive level.

Any comprehensive federal system(s) must be the responsibility of the executive branch of the government.

Under our system of government it is axiomatic that the management and operation of any major operational activity fall under the purview of the executive branch of government. In the next section there are listed a number of functions which must be discharged by some agency. It seems apparent that such activities properly belong with the executive.

Although the system(s) established for the federal government will be inclusive of all the significant scientific and technical literature, nevertheless, there will be important portions of the national information system(s) (publishers, abstracting and indexing activities, research li-

braries, etc.) independent of the federal government. The impact of the federal portion, in terms of subsidy, cooperative services, and leadership, will have an important influence on the nonfederal portion, and this relationship must be continuously explored and defined, with the government taking such actions as are necessary to maintain a viable system.

The document-handling system(s) will service a wide variety of users, including, among others, the following:

1. Scientists, technical personnel, scholars, and students working in academic settings.

2. Scientists and technical personnel working privately, in industry, and in the government.

3. Administrators, managers, and legislators.

This statement is intended to emphasize the idea that the users to be served by a national system form a heterogeneous group, each having a need for somewhat different services. Frequently, past systems have concentrated on one or another of the user groups without showing much concern for filling the needs of the wide variety of users. Here it is explicitly recognized that a national document system(s) must render services to all the users listed above.

Recognition of the wide variety of users brings into focus the "wholesaler-retailer" concept. It is sometimes said that the national system should ensure that regional or local libraries have ready access to documents from a central system (the wholesaler concept). The local libraries would, in turn, be the focus of interaction with the individual user (the retail concept). Although this would no doubt be the typical form of operation, it is nevertheless true that often our present national libraries and centers serve individuals in the same manner as local libraries. It thus seems apparent that a mixed mode of operation is in effect and will probably continue.

This basic premise does not mean to imply that the national system would directly service those students or scholars who are now adequately served by our fine research libraries. At the same time, it does emphasize that a national system would have responsibility to see that all classes of users are served at costs which are reasonable to the user. Clearly, complex relationships between government services and other services are implied and will need to be worked out as the system evolves.

The introduction of advanced technology into the national document-handling system is required. Ultimately, the growth in number of documents and their representations will be so great that problems of costs, storage space, preservation of documents, indexing, etc., will become so large that many of the present manual systems will become inadequate.

Questions of cost/effectiveness in introducing new technologies into the document-handling system need to be considered in terms of the services rendered, not by comparison to the costs of manual systems which do not effectively perform all of the required functions.

Any systems proposed must be evolutionary in character in the sense that they will start with the present systems (libraries, information exchanges, etc.) and evolve to forms that will be consistent with an overall plan. There must be flexibility for new organizational and administrative arrangements in terms of broad, long-range plans.

The systems developed for the scientific and technical literature need not necessarily be compatible with systems used for other parts of the world literature, such as law, the arts, and humanities. For instance, the indexing, cataloging, processing, and storage systems for scientific and technical literature may be different from those for other literature.

Classification and indexing schemes adopted for the United States national systems should be as compatible with international procedures and standards as is feasible.

STATEMENT OF SYSTEM REQUIREMENTS

The basic propositions previously presented form a foundation on which system designs should be based; this section adds more detailed and more specific requirements. The following set of requirements for a national document-handling system was derived from the results of our analyses of user studies, previously proposed plans, the current system, the life cycle of documents in the scientific and technical document system, and statistical summaries. Additionally, the requirements were added to or modified as a result of our discussions with a number of well-informed people in this area. As presented,

they represent our judgment regarding the various problem areas that must be dealt with in any satisfactory system design.

These requirements were used as the basis for the evaluation of all the system concepts set forth in the next three chapters. The results of this evaluation are presented in Chapter 11.

The requirements are organized into the following eight groups:

1. Administrative and Organizational Requirements
2. User-Oriented Requirements
3. Internal System Operations Requirements
4. Requirements Regarding the Production and Representation of Documents
5. Requirements Regarding Dissemination and Special Services
6. Requirements for System Evolution
7. Requirements for Education and Training
8. Research and Development Requirements

Administrative and Organizational Requirements

This group of requirements defines the need for administrative and organizational changes and some of the functions which should be satisfied.

A central administrative and policy-setting organization is required to coordinate and implement overall policy concerning the federal government's role with respect to the national system for scientific and technical document handling.

There is a requirement to establish federal policy and recommendations concerning legislative bases for document and information services in the several agencies. This is required in order to develop more effectively any national system. Proper coordination with Congress will be necessary. In order to implement this requirement the following steps must be taken:

1. A review of existing legislation.
2. A review of proposed legislation affecting documents and information services and the proposal of appropriate legislation to make the legal basis for document and information services consistent and coherent with respect to a national information system.

Policies are required to allow budget estimates for and actual costs of document and information handling services to be readily identified. This implies the following:

1. Comparable cost data must be acquired and analyzed.

2. The central organization should review with each agency its budgetary requirements in terms of document and information handling services.

3. A policy is required which provides that the central organization be involved in the actual budget review of all agencies relative to document and information handling services with the Bureau of the Budget.

Overall planning and coordination is necessary to achieve long-range goals for document and information handling services. Included in this requirement is the need to provide for coordination of the development of certain facilities (e.g., central computer stores or microform reproduction and storage centers) and the development of plans to coordinate the concept of regional services (e.g., agency and GPO depositories). Also included is the need for policies to coordinate switching (i.e., referral) means for the document and information handling systems with centers of information about current research and development efforts.

There is a requirement for detailed and consistent records and procedures oriented toward document and information handling and related services.

User-Oriented Requirements

These requirements specify the kinds of users to be served and the needs of these users:

The system must remain continuously responsive to the needs of its users. The staff of the system should view the users as constituting a group of customers, the satisfaction of whose needs is the basis for the establishment and continued existence of the system, and for the creation and maintenance of any particular service.

The system should have the capacity to handle an increasing number of users.

The system must provide for serving a wide range of users: for example, scientists, technical personnel, scholars, and students working in academic settings; scientists and technical personnel working privately, in industry, and in the government; administrators, managers, and legislators. The system should provide for a wide range of services to these users.

The system should operate in such a manner that all classes of users (e.g., engineers, researchers, practitioners, information technologists, and librarians) may use it in fulfilling their appropriate needs.

The system should be easy to use; it should provide the appropriate documents with the least effort on the part of the user; for example, scientists, engineers, and practitioners should have easy personal access to current professional and trade journals in their own and related fields.

The system should provide efficient methods for conducting searches, processing requests, and disseminating documents and information.

The system should be capable of fast response. An interim goal for the speed of response should be to guarantee that a request for a document should be filled within a maximum of five working days, and that a bibliographic request should be filled within a maximum of three working days. Shorter times than these should be the long-range goal. In addition, the system should be capable of providing faster responses in special circumstances.

Users should be able to influence the system through the establishment of appropriate feedback mechanisms.

A referral system is needed that will accomplish the following:

1. Inform users about current research and development efforts pertinent to their interests.
2. Guide users to the collection, storage, distribution or other activity of the S&T document and information handling system that is most appropriate to their needs.

Internal System Operations Requirements

This set of requirements is concerned with the operation of the system as a system. The requirements deal with documents and their processing and control:

The system should contain at least one reproducible copy of every significant foreign and domestic document and at the same time minimize unnecessary duplication of acquisition.

The system should provide for complete coverage of science and technology assuring that

no significant gaps exist. This implies the following:

1. Recurrent review and assessment of the current status of collections with respect to scientific and technological coverage.
2. The assignment of responsibility should be clear and coordinated.

At least one copy of each document entering the system should always be readily locatable thereafter. This implies the following:

1. Maintenance of current inventories of libraries, document and information centers, and the like, both for the purpose of proper internal administration and for the purpose of ensuring continuing accessibility.
2. Knowledge of the principal subject content sufficient to locate desired documents in the system.
3. The system should minimize redundant control files. A long-range goal is centralized control files that are so easily accessible that only minimal local files are necessary.

The system should employ efficient management techniques for document and information handling. This includes the use of automated equipment and techniques where appropriate.

There is a requirement to have decentralized local access points to documents and information in order to meet the needs of a geographically dispersed user population.

After acquisition the system should provide for the long-term preservation and retention of its document holdings. Periodic review of holdings should allow for purging from active files based on document usage. This requirement influences policy with regard to the loan, reproduction, and distribution of documents to qualified requesters.

Criteria, processes, and techniques should be developed for minimizing unnecessary redundancy in the system. This would include consideration of the following:

1. Overlap in collections.
2. Duplication of indexes, abstracts, and translations of the same item.
3. Duplication of loan, reproduction, and reference services.
4. Ongoing studies and reviews of duplicative services.

With respect to processing and manipulation of documents, there is a requirement to develop standards and ensure compatibility of the various products.

1. Standards for document reproduction and specification of techniques for reproduction.
2. Compatibility of products such as indexes, catalogs, and thesauri so that the tools used by the various agencies are readily convertible.
3. Both hardware and software aspects of machine system applications need to be reviewed and criteria and standards for their applications specified.

Standard methods for processing and servicing requests for documents need to be developed.

The system should minimize redundant keyboarding. Control information should be created early in the document cycle and accompany the items through the cycle, for exploitation with minimum manual labor.

Requirements Regarding Production And Representation of Documents

These requirements are concerned with the number of documents, their quality, restrictions regarding their use, and related matters:

The system should have the capacity to handle a 5 to 6 per cent annual increase in significant documents. An increase in translation capability will also have to be provided.

The system should encourage the improvement of document quality and the reduction of document volume by efficient use of such techniques as critical review, technical evaluation, purging, retiring of unused or infrequently used materials, and bibliographic control of collections. This requirement implies the following:

1. Improved acquisition policies including the coordination of acquisitions among the several agencies within the system.
2. The development of methods for screening documents by critical review.
3. There is a need for providing for the archival function, i.e., the function of ensuring the permanent retention of at least one accessible copy of each document entering the system.
4. There is a requirement for the development of explicit policies on the purging of docu-

ments from working collections. These policies will depend on the means by which the archival function is provided. Guidelines will be needed for purging as a function of document usage, document age, etc.

5. The system must minimize redundant analysis of content for bibliographic identification. The system must provide minimal criteria, procedures, and codes necessary to ensure consistency in the rating, tagging, and identification of each item it is to handle.

Policies are required to insure minimum time lag between completion of research and development work and announcement and publication of results.

Policies are required concerning federal support for professional societies related to their effective functioning as a part of any national scientific and technical document-handling system, particularly their activities in abstracting, indexing, and dissemination.

Requirements Regarding Dissemination and Special Services

These requirements specify the kinds of dissemination that should be made and define various user services:

A requirement exists to provide efficient and economic dissemination techniques. Dissemination techniques should be continually re-evaluated. This includes:

1. Providing for appropriate channels and mechanisms for storing and disseminating the documents.
2. Responsibility for the capability of the system to provide a hard copy and/or microform copy of each document.
3. Provision for efficient and timely distribution of documents.
4. Establishing criteria and guidelines concerning application of active dissemination techniques.

There is a requirement to minimize constraints on the dissemination of scientific and technical information imposed by proprietary and security restrictions or by discrimination against potential users who are not members of a given document "community." To implement this requirement the system should:

1. Establish a policy which requires the continuous review and justification of practices with respect to security classifications of scientific and technical reports.
2. Cause more vigorous applications of the time-phased downgrading principle where it does not now operate.
3. Require that Federal policies with respect to reporting results of government-sponsored S&T activities be effectively implemented.

Policies should be established which minimize the cost to users of large dissemination activities (e.g., the Clearinghouse for Federal Scientific and Technical Information).

More efficient acquisition and dissemination of foreign source materials and their translations should be effected.

The system should provide for the dissemination of scientific and technical information through oral and other informal communication media.

A number of information analysis centers have evolved as part of the present de facto system. Appropriately, these information analysis centers differ in structure, organization, and services. The system should provide for the review of the basis for the existing activities and determine criteria for establishing information analysis centers applicable to the entire national system.

Requirements For System Evolution

These requirements define the factors which lead to modifications in the system:

Changes should be evolved in such a way as to minimize the disruption in present services.

The system should provide for the coordination of a user-oriented quality assurance program designed to measure and improve the efficiency of services.

The system should provide for continual review of its operations in order to be capable of modifying them appropriately and promptly.

The system should be so designed as to provide for efficient and timely modification brought on by changing requirements.

The system should be responsive to changes required as a result of user needs evaluation,

development of new techniques, and the application of research findings.

Requirements for Education and Training

These are requirements to educate and train both those who use the system and those who operate it:

Users and potential users (e.g., students) should be made aware of the available services; educational and training programs concerning the use of the system should be provided.

There is a national requirement to ensure that sufficient numbers of adequately trained personnel are available to operate the system. This includes categories such as librarians, information technologists and scientists, and clerical personnel. This implies that the system:

1. Give examples and suggestions for curricula in colleges and specialized schools.
2. Give examples and curricula for in-service and on-the-job education and training.
3. Provide support and subsidies to appropriate educational institutions.
4. Help specify performance standards for various tasks to be performed.

There is a requirement that the system be designed so as to minimize the amount of training required for its operations.

Research and Development Requirements

There is a requirement for a coordinated program of research and development in the information sciences and the information technol-

ogies. The emphasis here is on the need for coordination to establish a balanced program that will give appropriate weight to all aspects of the necessary research and development. Among the areas of most pressing current needs for research are:

User Studies. Research is needed to determine both the recognized and the unrecognized needs of users and to devise means of making the information systems more responsive.

Document Representations. Studies are needed of how documents can be condensed and represented by both manual and automated means, to serve more effectively in providing current awareness and in aiding retrospective searches.

Evaluation Tools and Techniques. Tools and techniques are needed for assessing the adequacy of information systems and their continuing ability to serve their users.

Communication of Information. Research is needed to determine the most appropriate means for the system to facilitate information transfer through informal and oral means as well as through formal documents. Research is needed to clarify the role of documentation and other media of information transfer in the growth of science and technology.

Equipment for Information Handling. There is a requirement for research and development directed toward the provision of automated equipment aids for the storage, manipulation, and transmission of information to users.

PART THREE

Alternative Approaches to the Problem

Chapter Seven

Selected Plans for National Document Systems

During the last few years a number of plans have been developed for a national information system for science and technology. The plans have suggested organizations with varying degrees of formality and of reliance on automated assistance. The developers of the plans have included professional librarians, computer experts, and men of high standing in science, business, and government who could bring fresh viewpoints and valuable administrative experience to bear on the information problem.

The primary purpose of reviewing these plans for a national information system was to identify major features seen as important for such a system by a number of information experts. (Some of these features are reflected in the presentation of system requirements in Chapter 6.) Like many other aspects of the field of information retrieval, the idea of a national information system utilizing the tools and techniques of automation may be said to have begun with Vannevar Bush's famous article, "As We May Think" (*Atlantic Monthly*, July 1945). But the idea really caught fire only in the late 1950s, perhaps sparked by the publication in 1958 of the PSAC (Baker) Report on "Improving the Availability of Scientific and Technical Information in the United States." All told, over twenty plans have been published discussing—at widely varying levels of detail—the need for a national system, what its nature might be, and the difficulties of establishing it.

We have selected fifteen of the plans for review here, primarily those that are best known. A secondary consideration was to select a wide range of proposed organizations, from a single central information agency, covering all of science and technology, to a decentralized, widely dispersed system of loosely associated information centers.

The latter arrangement should, of course, be recognized as the existing "system." This "system" consists of the federal, state, local, private, academic, and industrial libraries and information centers of the United States, together with the set of cooperative agreements on matters such as acquisitions, loans, and exchange through which they seek to carry out their responsibilities. This de facto system does exist, and will continue to exist relatively unchanged, unless a conscious effort is made to change it. The alternative to formally establishing a national information system for science and technology is not the absence of any such system, but rather the continuance of the informal, very loosely organized present system.

In this chapter we review the selected plans of national information systems on two levels of detail. First, we give a summary of common features of the plans, plus comments on what we consider to be some significant gaps. Second, we present organizational and technical aspects of the plans in the form of charts to facilitate comparisons among the plans, and we have included diagrams of the organizational structures of those plans for which it was feasible to do so. In addition, we present a summary of the Soviet Union's information agency, the "All-Union Institute of Scientific and Technical Information," known as VINITI. And we conclude with comments on selected discussions of a national information system that did not fit readily

into the format we employed in reviewing the plans.

OUTLINE OF THE PLANS

The plans may be divided into two categories, those which dealt with a limited subset of the total national scientific and technical information problem with a moderate degree of detail, and those which treated the broad problem in very general terms. Whether specific or broad, the plans generally envisioned a decentralized system of information services centers and a central capping agency with varying degrees of authority.

Two features important to such plans—a discussion of necessary legislative action and a time-phased implementation schedule—appeared only in the Crawford Plan. Discussions of other features follow, under the headings: Organizational Aspects; Scope of the Plans; Users; Costs; and Topics for Further Research.

Organizational Aspects

The majority of the plans concentrated on the organizational aspects of the national information problem and gave relatively little attention to its technical aspects. Almost all the plans held that there should be a central organization to administer the national information system, and that the processing and dissemination activities should be decentralized.

Explicitly or implicitly the central organization was seen to residue in the executive branch with varying degrees of control and authority. Some plans envisioned only a coordinating and advisory central organization, while other plans proposed an autonomous organization with a full range of fiscal, administrative, and operational powers. The majority of the plans provided general guidelines outlining the responsibilities of the proposed central organization, but no plan specifically defined its internal organizational structure or spelled out its functional responsibilities in adequate detail. A few of the plans specified the rank or position of the central organization within the Federal structure.

The majority of the plans considered the national information problem from a federal viewpoint, but some attention was given to the prob-

lems of the interface between federal and non-federal activities. The plans paid varying degrees of attention to the existing principal federal S&T information-handling activities. Generally, the maintenance of the existing system was implied with certain recommended modifications, the most common of which were increased coordination and the development of standardized procedures. Some of the problems stemming from the fact that the Library of Congress is in the legislative branch were addressed in the Crawford Plan.

Only a few of the plans considered the role of the more than 900 existing regional government document depositories or the activities of the many smaller government organizations that engage in information-handling activities. Some of the plans dealt with the role of the professional societies in abstracting, indexing, and dissemination. Most agreed that the federal government should refrain from interfering with this phase of their activities and, furthermore, that some measure of federal support was required in order to aid in the maintenance and expansion of these activities.

Scope of the Plans

Most of the plans assumed that the information to be dealt with was already in hand. They concerned themselves with the problems of storing, processing (e.g., indexing, abstracting, translating), and disseminating the information. Nowhere was any real attention given to the problem of purging. Except in the Weinberg Report, little attention was given to the acquisition problem in either its collection or its evaluation aspects.

The collection problem can be conveniently discussed under two headings, domestic and foreign. Only one plan dealt explicitly with the problems of acquiring foreign literature. Saliently lacking was any discussion of the large roles currently played by the State Department and by the intelligence community in acquiring foreign literature, and how their efforts might be integrated with a national information system. With regard to domestic literature, the Weinberg Report alone recommended an *evaluative* selection of technical reports for input to the system. Even this recommendation was

confined to the evaluation of technical reports; and it was implied that in the case of journal articles and books, the existing selection processes preceding publication operate satisfactorily.

Most plans recognized the problem of informal communication, though they declined to incorporate a means for dealing with such communication as part of a national information system. This was one of the areas recommended for further study by the federal government.

With respect to equipment problems, the plans tended to offer general statements about the desirability of employing computers and microform-storage techniques, together with cautions about the danger of placing too much reliance on the potential of computers for solving all information-handling problems.

Users

The problem of identifying the needs of the users of the proposed system was generally overlooked in the plans. Most of the plans grouped their users into gross categories, e.g., government, university, private industry, scientist, technologist, student. Some of the plans recommended further studies of the users of existing systems, though there was no emphasis on studies aimed at unearthing and defining the *unrecognized* needs of users of scientific and technical literature. None of the plans included in its scheme a mechanism for on-going collection and exploitation of statistics and other data on users of the proposed system.

In general, the plans emphasized the "wholesaler-to-retailer" problem; i.e., the problem of getting documents from a central store (or from the appropriate one of several major stores) to a local information service point, such as a university or company library. It seemed to be assumed that the "retailer-to-consumer" problem was either nonexistent or, at least, easily solvable. The majority of the reports paid no attention to the educational problems involved in the development of any national information system. Some plans commented on the desirability of developing academic curricula for "information scientists" or of increasing the emphasis, in the training of librarians, on the handling of scientific and technical information. Only the Warren

and Weinberg Reports regarded the education of users of the system as a major problem. The Weinberg Report included a recommendation that training in the use of information systems be incorporated in the basic curricula for scientists and engineers, along with a recommendation for better training in writing as a means toward improving the generation of scientific and technical information.

Costs

The majority of the plans dealt only in general terms, if at all, with the budgeting and costing aspects of their proposed "systems." Those plans that did present costing figures gave only very gross estimates of required federal expenditures (the Crawford Report was the most detailed in this respect). Every plan required the expenditure of federal funds in one form or another (e.g., direct funds to finance the central agency, plus grants-in-aid). One proposal claimed that its system would eventually be self-supporting.

Topics for Further Research

Most of the plans identified areas requiring further research and investigation. The most frequent recommendation was to develop "standards" of one kind or another (e.g., standards for indexing, abstracting, communications, hardware, cataloging). A notable feature of these recommendations was that the plans called for *what* was to be standardized, but made no recommendations about *how* this was to be accomplished. The next most frequently mentioned areas for additional research were those of developing educational curricula and of studying the needs for better equipment and facilities. Other important topics proposed for research and investigation included:

1. Informal communications.
2. User needs and characteristics.
3. Inventories of libraries and other information resources.
4. Improvement of publications and technical writing.
5. Copyright and patent problems.
6. Classified and proprietary information.

CHARTS ON NATIONAL INFORMATION SYSTEM PLANS

The preceding paragraphs have presented a summary of organizational and technical aspects of the selected plans for a national information system. We present a set of tables dealing with details of the plans at the end of this chapter (placed there, for convenience, after the following discussions of VINITI and of three important expositions of the need for a national information system). The set begins with tables detailing organizational aspects. Next are tables detailing technical aspects of the plans. Following next is a table detailing some of the technical recommendations of the plans. Concluding the chapter are organization diagrams for some of the plans.

VINITI,* THE ALL-UNION INSTITUTE OF SCIENTIFIC AND TECHNICAL INFORMATION

Should VINITI Be a Model for a U. S. National Information System?

The problems stemming from the growth of S&T information and documents are by no means restricted to the United States. Within recent years France, Great Britain, Japan, and West Germany, for example, have announced plans or undertaken steps for establishing concerted national attacks on the problems of S&T information. Among the various foreign efforts, however, the Soviet Union's attempts to cope with these problems have been given the greatest amount of attention in this country, chiefly in respect to VINITI, the All-Union Institute of Scientific and Technical Information, which dates from 1952. Since VINITI has received so much attention, it is appropriate to discuss it here at some length in order to dispel certain widely held erroneous notions.

There is a widespread impression in the United States that VINITI constitutes the entire Soviet S&T information system, that it is a completely centralized organization, and that it is

* VINITI is an acronym derived from the English transliteration of the Russian name for the Institute, *Vsesoyuznyy Institut Nauchnoy i Tekhnicheskoy Informatsii.*

an ideal answer to S&T information problems. None of these beliefs is correct. Because of them, however, the All-Union Institute has frequently been offered as a justification for a comparable United States effort to establish a national information system, as a model for such a United States system, and as an argument by analogy for making a United States system a centralized one.

Confronting this argument, the Baker Report commented: "Available evidence indicates that the Institute operates effectively in meeting the needs of Russian science. But it must not be overlooked that in planning the establishment and operations of the Institute, the Russians could not call upon the services of scientific information organizations such as we find already in existence in the private enterprise structure of our country, and which have been in operation many years. The solution the Russians have developed for meeting their own problems in our judgment *would not* [the Report's italics] be equally effective in meeting ours."

Without commenting in turn upon the Baker Report's statement, we present a brief outline of VINITI, summarizing some of its features under the same headings of organizational and technical aspects which we used to discuss the various proposals for a United States system.

Summary of Approach

VINITI collects scientific and technical information from over 90 countries in more than 60 languages. Some 12,000 foreign and 2500 domestic Soviet serials are subscribed to. In addition, patents, monographs, books, proceedings, etc., are covered. Incoming information is routed to language and/or subject specialists, translated and/or abstracted, and the abstracts are published in one or more issues of an appropriate *Referativny Zhurnal*, RZh (Abstract Journal). As of 1963, RZhs were published monthly or biweekly in 23 series covering broad subject areas, with 120 subseries covering subdivisions of these broad areas, plus thirty monthly or bimonthly series covering cross-disciplinary areas of specialization.

In addition to the basic RZhs, VINITI also publishes a large number of series of *Ekspress Informatsiya* (Express Information). These in-

clude especially important results that merit very rapid dissemination. A third series, called *Itogi Nauki* (Scientific Results), presents summaries and retrospective state-of-the-art studies. And, not content with these abstracting and reviewing activities, VINITI also publishes the equivalent of Library of Congress catalog cards for scientific and technical documents.

A separate VINITI responsibility is research and development in the area of automated equipment and techniques for handling information.

Major Entities: Funding, Staffing, and Function

VINITI is administered jointly by the Academy of Sciences of the USSR and the State Committee for the Coordination of Scientific Research (formerly known as the State Scientific-Technical Committee). This split would appear to have resulted more from historical reasons than from logical determination of a position for VINITI. Internally, VINITI has three major subdivisions, headed by a Deputy Director for Foreign Relations, a Deputy Director for Information Processing, and a Deputy Director for Research. VINITI is largely centralized, with a full-time staff of about 2200 (as of 1963) located in Moscow. However, some 20,000 outside scientists and technicians assist by acting as part-time abstractors.

The RZhs are sold by susbcription, but it is not known whether the proceeds from the sales cover the production costs.

Subsidiary Entities Funding, Staffing, and Function

Contrary to the widespread notion that the Soviet S&T information system consists solely of the centralized VINITI, the Pucinski Committee's report points out that the "network consists of 84 national-level organizations; these include ten specialized information institutes (e.g., the All-Union Scientific-Research Institute of Technical-Economic Information of Radioelectronics), 94 regional bureaus of technical information at the sovnarkhozes (economic units based on regional administration), over 4000 bureaus of technical information at research insti-

tutes and production facilities, and more than 16,000 technical libraries."

To the same point, Boris M. Tareev of VINITI writes: "In addition to the information activities of [VINITI], considerable work is also done in other organizations. The Book Chamber prepares a bibliographic listing of all the books published in the USSR, and issues a weekly bibliography *Knizhnaya Letopis'* (Book Index). The papers from many Soviet journals and publications of Soviet scientific research institutes are listed in the weekly *Letopis' Zhurnal'nykh Statei* (Index of Periodical Articles). Book reviews and critical reviews are listed in the quarterly *Letopisi Retsensii* (Review Index). The descriptions of bibliographic guides which have been issued in separate editions or have been published in journals and books are listed in the annual *Bibliografiya Sovetskoi Bibliografii* (Bibliography of Soviet Bibliographies). Books published abroad are listed (and often reviewed) in the monthly *Novye Knigi za Rubezhom* (New Books Abroad) which is published in two series by the Foreign Literature Publishing House. Information on new inventions for which authors' certificates have been issued in the USSR are reported in *Byulleten' Izobretenii* (Bulletin of Inventions) published by the Committee for Inventions and Discoveries. Annotated bibliographies of scientific literature by subject field are issued from time to time by the Academy of Sciences of the USSR and by some of the larger libraries. The USSR Academy of Sciences publishes lists of publications by notable scientists of the USSR. Many institutions of higher learning issue lists of literature recommended for their students and research workers. Many ministries, agencies, sovnarkhozes (regional economic councils) and the larger industrial enterprises compile specialized bibliographic bulletins in different, relatively narrow, subject fields of technology to inform the workers in industry of published reports on new and significant developments."*

It thus appears that VINITI itself serves primarily the functions of acquisition, processing (translating and abstracting, in part through its

---

* Tareev, Boris M., "Methods of Disseminating Scientific Information, and Science Information Activities in the USSR," *American Documentation*, July 1962, p. 340.

outside part-time employees), and dissemination via its journals and special reports. Information storage and retrieval appear to be carried out primarily within other components of the Soviet information system.

Estimated Annual Costs

No cost figures appear to be available for VINITI or other components of the Soviet information system.

System Inputs: Document Types, Orientation, Sources, and Pre-Input Processing

As of 1963, VINITI subscribed to about 12,000 foreign and 2500 domestic Russian scientific journals. It also receives books, conference proceedings, patents, standards, and monographs. Its RZhs cover a variety of fields that appear to have been determined pragmatically rather than by any "logical" categorization of knowledge. For example, among the basic subject-area series of RZhs, the Pucinski Committee's report lists such epistemologically disparate areas as air transportation, biology, geology, light industry, mathematics, physics and water transportation. Nevertheless, Tareev* reports that VINITI's RZhs do "not cover several important fields of science and technology, such as medicine (where a similar journal is published by the Academy of Medical Sciences of the USSR), building and construction, farming, and others."

System Users: Institutions and Organizations, Individuals, and Types of Requests

VINITI's users include both institutions and individuals. The broad subject-area RZhs are generally subscribed to by institutions; the more specialized RZhs, which are smaller and hence less expensive, are subscribed to by individuals. VINITI also sells photocopies and microfilm copies of papers referenced in the RZhs, translations of such papers, and bibliographic cards (i.e., catalog cards). Bibliographic searches are also made on request, but the Pucinski Committee's report suggests that VINITI is trying

* *Op cit.*, p. 341.

to shift the burden of such searches to other organizations, such as the libraries to which it sells catalog cards.

Hardware Orientation

As of 1963, VINITI made little use of automated equipment or techniques, though, of course, its printing activities entailed machinery. Its Research Division is concerned with developing equipment for large-scale, long-term machine storage and retrieval of information.

Types of Internal Processing and System Outputs

VINITI prepares bibliographic citations for incoming material, translates material when necessary, abstracts material in-house or sends it out to its part-time abstractors, and publishes the abstracts in its various series of RZhs and in its *Ekspress Informatsiya* and *Itogi Nauki* series. Apparently, dissemination is entirely by subscription or direct purchase; i.e., the available published literature in VINITI does not suggest that any special alerting function or active dissemination is carried out.

Troubles in the USSR's S&T Information System

Contrary to the notion that VINITI constitutes a model information system, the Soviets themselves have criticized it. For example, at a conference in Moscow on April 10, 1964, sponsored by the State Committee for the Coordination of Scientific Research, numerous troubles with the Soviet information system were discussed. In a paper presented to this conference, with the lengthy title of "Results of a Check of the Fulfillment of the Resolution of the Council of Ministers of the USSR 'About Measures for the Improvement of the Organization of Scientific and Technical Information in this Country'," V. S. Malov made such statements as:

"Serious inadequacies in the work of information have been revealed."

"In the institutes of scientific and technical information, publishing activity is hypertrophied, to the detriment of other forms of information work."

"The institutes continue to publish periodicals that duplicate other scientific and technical journals."

"In connection with the tendency to publish more, workers of GOSINTI [the State Scientific Research Institute of Scientific and Technical Information] expended much energy on the search for subscribers for their publications; the Institute sent numerous representatives to the Union Republics."

"Publishing activity of institutes of scientific and technical information costs the State very dearly. Enterprises pay for their publications at a price exceeding by 3–5 times the nominal values established for State publishing houses."

"Periods of issue of VINITI's publications are impermissibly long. Abstracts are published on the average 7–8 months after publication of the article abroad; not infrequently these periods are extended to a year and more."

"In the Central Institute of Scientific and Technical Information of the Food Industry, preparation of surveys takes up to 9 months or more."

"In collections of the Institute of Technical Information of the Ukrainian SSR, materials are placed after lapses of up to two years after publication."

"Acquisition and use of foreign scientific and technical literature is unsatisfactorily organized; actions of institutions and departments are inadequately coordinated. Therefore, the same periodicals are subscribed to by numerous organizations. Thus, the American 'Journal of the Iron and Steel Institute' is ordered in 120 copies. These journals are used poorly. During a check on the use of foreign journals in the libraries of a number of scientific research institutes in Moscow, it was found in many cases that whole sets of foreign journals lie without being disturbed, or are used by readers only once or twice in several years. At the same time, due to unwise expenditure of foreign exchange allocations, many journals do not generally enter the Soviet Union, as a consequence of which abstract information published by VINITI turns out to be incomplete."

Malov had much more to say along the same lines, but what we have quoted should suffice to give the flavor of his criticisms—and to pro-

vide the reader with an all-too-familiar echo of S&T information-handling problems in the United States.

OTHER CONTRIBUTIONS TO PLANNING FOR AN S&T INFORMATION SYSTEM

The discussions reviewed below did not lend themselves to being analyzed in the same manner as the selected plans for a national information system. Yet they are significant contributions to overall planning efforts for any system addressing itself to the problems of S&T information and document handling and, as such, deserve the special attention accorded them here. (Other pertinent references are provided in the Selected Bibliography at the back of the book.)

The Humphrey Report

U. S. Congress. Senate Committee on Government Operations. "Summary of Activities Toward Interagency Coordination." Senate Document 369, 89th Congress, 1st Session. Washington, D. C., Government Printing Office, 1965.

The report was issued over the signature of Vice President Hubert H. Humphrey, the then Chairman of the Subcommittee on Reorganization and International Organizations. Among the studies reviewed in this report is one entitled "Interagency Coordination of Scientific and Technical Information." Its objective was "to help assure maximum efficiency of Federal programs in storage, retrieval, review, and dissemination of scientific and technical information." After a review and summary of past activities in this area, the study concludes by presenting views and suggestions for the future. The recommendations are:

1. Control of physical items.
   (a) A mechanized inventory of scientific journals and other publications should be issued serially.
   (b) A cooperative cataloging system should be developed leading toward a mechanized national union catalog as well as specialized catalogs.
   (c) An effective coordinated acquisitions program is needed.

(d) An effective transmission network for facsimile and microform is needed.
2. Control of description of information contents of items. Standards are needed for:
   (a) General characterization of the contents of a book or article.
   (b) Identification of specific data, ideas, etc.
3. Coordinated provisions of local access.

Other subjects stressed by the study include the need for Federal unity, information as a resource, high-speed transmission, and nonprinted media.

The Pucinski Report

"Hearings before the Ad Hoc Subcommittee on a National Research Data Processing and Information Retrieval Center of the Committee on Education and Labor, House of Representatives, 88th Congress, 1st Session, on H. R. 1946," Appendix to Vol 1, Parts 1, 2, 3. Washington, D. C., Government Printing Office, 1963.

These hearings were held to determine if the National Defense Education Act should be amended to permit the Office of Science Information Service to establish a National Research Data Processing and Information Retrieval Center. The subcommittee was chaired by Representative Roman C. Pucinski. The subcommittee heard many witnesses from various Government agencies, private industry, scientific societies, and universities.

In his opening remarks Pucinski set the stage for the significance of these hearings when he said, "This Nation spends billions of dollars annually in scientific research both through activities of the Federal Government and in the private sector of our economy. There can be no question that some adequate method must be determined to coordinate the knowledge gained from this massive research and make it readily available to all of our scientists . . . . This whole matter of properly coordinating and making available to scientists scientific research . . . is rapidly becoming one of the most important problems to confront this nation."

In addition to the testimony of the witnesses, the report (and its associated appendix) provide a fine compilation of factual data, studies, expert opinion, and reports relevant to national S&T document- and information-handling problems and activities.

Licklider Panel Report

Report by an Office of Science and Technology (OST) Panel on Scientific and Technical Communications to Dr. Donald F. Hornig, President's Science Advisor, February 8, 1965. (The Panel was chaired by Dr. J. C. R. Licklider.)

The purpose of the report was to assess the situation in, and the trend of, scientific and technical communication. The results are the following:

1. OST support is needed to meld public and private efforts in information handling.
2. Fair progress is being made by Federal agencies to handle federally generated information.
3. COSATI is doing a good job.
4. The Government is only partially successful in its efforts to integrate private and public services.
5. Demands for a unified system are increasing.
6. The field is not yet well enough defined to attempt to design a national system.
7. A coherent plan and strong leadership are needed.

The recommendations were:
1. OST should strengthen its leadership.
2. Follow-on panels should be established to study the problems.
3. Journals, monographs and books have not been given enough attention. The library system should be developed.
4. "Conspicuous portals" should be available for users of the system.
5. There is a need for more interaction between users and system designers.
6. Technical writing should be improved.
7. Experiments (pilot type) should be run.

Other topics discussed were:
1. Specialized technical information centers.
2. Centralization and distribution.
3. The "real" needs of users.
4. Effective use of computers.

5. National and local libraries.

6. Informal communications.

7. Review articles and monographs.

8. Government subsidy and the publishing industry.

9. Security and proprietary considerations.

Three appendices discuss:

1. Proposed explorations and experiments in S&T communications.

2. Two suggestions concerning government subsidy of the publishing industry.

3. The concept of "national library."

Table 7-1a   Organizational Aspects of Stanford, Crawford, and Cahn Plans

PLAN	SUMMARY OF APPROACH & CONTENT
STANFORD (SRI) "A DRAFT PROGRAM FOR A NATIONAL TECHNICAL INFORMATION CENTER" STANFORD RESEARCH INSTITUTE JANUARY 1958	A VERY BROAD AND NONSPECIFIC PROPOSAL. PLACES HEAVY RELIANCE ON COMPUTER AND ASSOCIATED HARDWARE USAGE. HEAVY EMPHASIS ON NEED FOR FURTHER R&D. SPECIFIES NEED FOR CENTRALIZATION OF ALL SYSTEM ASPECTS WITH THE EXCEPTION OF DECENTRALIZED TECHNICAL CENTERS.
CRAWFORD "SCIENTIFIC AND TECHNOLOGICAL COMMUNICATION IN THE GOVERNMENT: TASK FORCE REPORT TO THE PRESIDENT'S SPECIAL ASSISTANT FOR SCIENCE AND TECHNOLOGY" JAMES H. CRAWFORD, JR., CHAIRMAN, ET AL. APRIL 1962 SPONSOR: JEROME B. WIESNER OFFICE OF SCIENCE AND TECHNOLOGY	THIS REPORT OFFERS SWEEPING REORGANIZATION AND REORIENTATION OF THE FEDERAL SIDE OF THE INFORMATION HOUSE. SWEEPING LEGISLATIVE CHANGES ARE PROPOSED WHICH WOULD, FOR EXAMPLE, REMOVE THE SCIENCE AND TECHNOLOGY DIVISION FROM LC, REMOVE RESPONSIBILITY FOR THE CLEARINGHOUSE FROM COMMERCE, TRANSFER THE SIE TO THE PROPOSED "CLEARINGHOUSE" ORGANIZATION. USER EMPHASIS IS ON MANAGEMENT BUT DOES NOT EXCLUDE THE SCIENTIFIC AND TECHNICAL USERS. INFORMATION TO BE PROCESSED INCLUDES THE CONTENT OF R&D PROJECTS (PRESENT AND PROPOSED) AND INFORMATION ABOUT R&D PROJECTS (EQUIPMENT, PERSONNEL, COSTS, FACILITIES, ETC.). THE PRIVATE SECTOR OF THE INFORMATION HOUSE IS NOT SPECIFICALLY CONSIDERED BY THE TASK GROUP (BY DIRECTION). HEAVY EMPHASIS IS PLACED ON LEADERSHIP, POLICY FORMATION, AND SUPPORT FROM THE EXECUTIVE BRANCH (SPECIFICALLY THE PRESIDENT). THE REPORT IS <u>ORGANIZATIONALLY</u> ORIENTED AND DOES NOT ADDRESS THE TECHNICAL PROBLEMS TO ANY GREAT DEGREE.
CAHN "'B.I.T.S.' – BUREAU OF INFORMATION FOR TECHNOLOGY AND SCIENCE PROPOSED AS 'KEY STATION' OF FEDERAL 'NETWORK' OF INFORMATION SERVICES TO U.S. FREE ENTERPRISE SYSTEM" JULIUS N. CAHN, DIRECTOR, SCIENTIFIC RESEARCH PROJECT, SUBCOMMITTEE ON REORGANIZATION AND INTERNATIONAL ORGANIZATIONS, COMMITTEE ON GOVERNMENT OPERATIONS, U.S. SENATE 17 JANUARY 1962	OUTLINES A "NETWORK" CENTERED AROUND THE "B.I.T.S." IN THE DEPARTMENT OF COMMERCE. B.I.T.S. WOULD BE THE NATIONAL COLLECTION, STORAGE, DISSEMINATION, AND REFERRAL CENTER. VOLUNTARY COOPERATION WOULD LEAD TO MACHINE SYSTEM COMPATIBILITY AND INTEGRATED DISSEMINATION AMONG EXISTING FEDERAL LIBRARIES AND INFORMATION CENTERS, TOGETHER WITH ANY PRIVATE ORGANIZATIONS THAT WISHED TO JOIN THE NETWORK. THE FIELD OFFICES OF THE DEPARTMENT OF COMMERCE WOULD BE MAJOR DISSEMINATION POINTS TO THE PUBLIC.

LEGEND:

FCST = FEDERAL COUNCIL FOR SCIENCE AND TECHNOLOGY
LC = LIBRARY OF CONGRESS
NS = NOT SPECIFIED
NTIC = NATIONAL TECHNICAL INFORMATION CENTER
OST = OFFICE OF SCIENCE AND TECHNOLOGY
PSAC = PRESIDENT'S SCIENCE ADVISORY COMMITTEE
SIE = SCIENCE INFORMATION EXCHANGE

Table 7-1a　*(Continued)*

MAJOR ENTITY(IES)			
NAME(S)	SOURCE OF FUNDING	STAFF	FUNCTIONAL RESPONSIBILITIES
A CONSTITUTED FEDERAL AGENCY	FEDERAL	SMALL	POLICY (OVERALL) CONTRACTUAL (NTIC & R&D) ADMINISTRATIVE (OVERALL) COORDINATION REVIEW & CONCURRENCE (ALL FEDERAL PROJECTS) ENCOURAGEMENT (PRIVATE PROJECTS)
OST (PSAC & FCST)	FEDERAL	COMMITTEE TYPE	FEDERAL POLICY DIRECTION AND REVIEW OF PLANS, PROVIDE FOR IN- TERFACE WITH PRIVATE
NATIONAL TECHNICAL RESOURCES BOARD	FEDERAL	RESOURCES	MAINTAINING TECHNICAL RESOURCES INVENTORY COORDINATING BUREAU OF TECHNICAL RESOURCES CLEARINGHOUSE SERVICE AND BUREAU OF TECHNICAL RESOURCES ANALYSES ACTIVITIES
B.I.T.S. — BUREAU OF INFORMATION FOR SCIENCE AND TECH- NOLOGY (COMMERCE DEPARTMENT)	FEDERAL, PLUS MODEST FEES FOR PRIVATE USERS	NS	NATIONAL COLLECTION, STORAGE, DISSEMINATION AND REFERRAL CENTER

Table 7-1b   Organizational Aspects of Stanford, Crawford, and Cahn Plans

PLAN	SUBSIDIARY ENTITY(IES)		
	NAME(S)	SOURCE OF FUNDING	STAFF
STANFORD (SRI) "A DRAFT PROGRAM FOR A NATIONAL TECHNICAL INFORMATION CENTER" STANFORD RESEARCH INSTITUTE JANUARY 1958	NATIONAL TECHNICAL INFORMATION CENTER (NTIC) (INTERIM)	FEDERAL & USER	LARGE TECHNICAL
CRAWFORD "SCIENTIFIC AND TECHNOLOGICAL COMMUNICATION IN THE GOVERNMENT:TASK FORCE REPORT TO THE PRESIDENT'S SPECIAL ASSISTANT FOR SCIENCE AND TECHNOLOGY" JAMES H. CRAWFORD, JR., CHAIRMAN, ET AL. APRIL 1962 SPONSOR: JEROME B. WIESNER OFFICE OF SCIENCE AND TECHNOLOGY	GOVERNMENT R&D AGENCIES (VIA A "HIGHLY PLACED OFFICE" IN EACH)	FEDERAL	NS
	BUREAU OF TECHNICAL RESOURCES CLEARINGHOUSE SERVICE (BTRCS)	FEDERAL	NS
	BUREAU OF TECHNICAL RESOURCES ANALYSIS (BTRA)	FEDERAL	NS
	NATIONAL SCIENCE FOUNDATION (NSF)	FEDERAL	NS
	5 CLEARINGHOUSES	FEDERAL	NS
CAHN "'B.I.T.S.' – BUREAU OF INFORMATION FOR TECHNOLOGY AND SCIENCE PROPOSED AS 'KEY STATION' OF FEDERAL 'NETWORK' OF INFORMATION SERVICES TO U.S. FREE ENTERPRISE SYSTEM" JULIUS N. CAHN, DIRECTOR, SCIENTIFIC RESEARCH PROJECT, SUBCOMMITTEE ON REORGANIZATION AND INTERNATIONAL ORGANIZATIONS, COMMITTEE ON GOVERNMENT OPERATIONS, U.S. SENATE 17 JANUARY 1962	EXISTING FEDERAL LIBRARIES AND INFORMATION CENTERS, PLUS COMMERCE FIELD OFFICES, PLUS VOLUNTARILY COOPERATING PRIVATE ORGANIZATIONS	NS	NS

LEGEND:

NA = NOT APPLICABLE

NS = NOT SPECIFIED

STINFO = SCIENTIFIC AND TECHNICAL INFORMATION

Table 7-1b *(Continued)*

FUNCTIONAL RESPONSIBILITIES	ESTIMATED ANNUAL COST	CENTRALIZED AND/OR DECENTRALIZED
COORDINATION COMMUNICATION CONTRACTUAL (SUPPORT SERVICES) TRANSLATING ABSTRACTING INDEXING DISSEMINATION	$50M IN FIRST YEAR; $100M ANNUALLY IN SUCCEEDING YEARS	CENTRALIZED POLICY & ADMIN-ISTRATION DECENTRALIZED CENTERS (UNCLEAR HOW)
COORDINATE THE DIRECTION & CONTROL OF STINFO PROVIDE FOR AGENCY'S COM-PATIBILITY IN FUNCTIONS AND OPERATIONS DIRECT CLEARINGHOUSES WHICH COLLECT INFORMATION ON THE R&D RESOURCES OF FUNDS, FACILITIES, MANPOWER, EQUIPMENT, ORGANIZATIONS, AND STINFO PROVIDE COORDINATED AN-ALYSIS OF R&D RESOURCES: 1) FUNDS, 2) ORGANIZATION & MANPOWER, 3) FACILITIES & EQUIPMENT, & 4) STINFO SUPPORT BASIC RESEARCH, SCIENTIFIC & TECHNICAL EDUCATION, RESEARCH FOR FACILITIES & EQUIPMENT, & STINFO RESEARCH SEE TECHNICAL ASPECTS	$60M	CENTRALIZED POLICY AND REVIEW FOR FEDERAL PARTI-CIPANTS, CENTRALIZED CLEARINGHOUSES FOR R&D STINFO LOOSELY CENTRALIZED AUTHORITY FOR FEDERAL AGENCY IN-HOUSE R&D ACTI-VITIES
NS	NS	DECENTRALIZED EXCEPT FOR B.I.T.S.

Table 7-2a   Organizational Aspects of Weinberg and Management Technology Plans

PLAN	SUMMARY OF APPROACH & CONTENT
WEINBERG "SCIENCE, GOVERNMENT, AND INFORMATION" ALVIN M. WEINBERG, CHAIRMAN, ET AL., PANEL ON SCIENCE INFORMATION, PRESIDENT'S SCIENCE ADVISORY COMMITTEE 10 JANUARY 1963	PRESENTS, RATHER THAN A SYSTEM PLAN, A LARGE NUMBER OF RECOMMENDATIONS TO THE TECHNICAL CO[MMUN]ITY AND TO GOVERNMENT AGENCIES, CONCERNING FUTURE ACTIONS TO IMPROVE THE COMMUNICATION OF S[CIEN]TIFIC AND TECHNICAL INFORMATION. IN THE WORDS OF THE REPORT, ITS "MAJOR FINDINGS AND RECOMM[ENDA]TIONS" ARE: "THE WORKING SCIENTIST MUST...SHARE MANY OF THE BURDENS THAT HAVE TRADITIONALL[Y] CARRIED BY THE PROFESSIONAL DOCUMENTALIST. THE TECHNICAL COMMUNITY GENERALLY MUST DEVOTE [A] LARGER SHARE THAN HERETOFORE OF ITS TIME AND RESOURCES TO THE DISCRIMINATING MANAGEMENT OF [THE] EVER-INCREASING TECHNICAL RECORD. DOING LESS WILL LEAD TO FRAGMENTED AND INEFFECTIVE SCIENC[E AND] TECHNOLOGY."
MANAGEMENT TECHNOLOGY "A NATIONAL SCIENTIFIC AND TECHNOLOGICAL INFORMATION SYSTEM" MANAGEMENT TECHNOLOGY, INC. APRIL 1963	PROPOSES THE CREATION (BY THE FEDERAL GOVERNMENT) OF A NATIONAL DOCUMENTATION CENTER (NDC) [AND A] NATIONAL INFORMATION CENTER (NIC). ALL EXISTING LIBRARIES AND DATA AND INFORMATION CENTERS W[OULD] BECOME TECHNICAL INFORMATION CENTERS FOR THE SYSTEM. EXISTING GOVERNMENT INFORMATION ACTI[VITIES] WOULD BECOME EITHER SPECIALIZED TECHNICAL DOCUMENT OR INFORMATION CENTERS IN THE SYSTEM (E[.G.,] AEC, NASA, NLM, ETC.). NIC'S AND NDC'S WOULD ALSO EXIST AT A REGIONAL LEVEL. BASICALLY, TH[E PRO]POSAL OFFERS AN ORGANIZATIONAL APPROACH TO THE SOLUTION OF THE NATION'S INFORMATION PROBLEM[. IT] ALSO RECOGNIZES THE NEED OF CONGRESS FOR AN ORGANIZED METHOD OF OBTAINING INFORMATION.

LEGEND:

AEC = ATOMIC ENERGY COMMISSION
CFSTI = CLEARINGHOUSE FOR FEDERAL SCIENTIFIC AND TECHNICAL INFORMATION
COSATI = COMMITTEE ON SCIENTIFIC AND TECHNICAL INFORMATION
DDC = DEFENSE DOCUMENTATION CENTER (DOD)
DTIE = DIVISION OF TECHNICAL INFORMATION EXTENSION (AEC)
FCST = FEDERAL COUNCIL FOR SCIENCE AND TECHNOLOGY
NA = NOT APPLICABLE
NASA = NATIONAL AERONAUTICS AND SPACE ADMINISTRATION
NIS = NATIONAL INFORMATION SYSTEM
NLM = NATIONAL LIBRARY OF MEDICINE
NS = NOT SPECIFIED
OST = OFFICE OF SCIENCE AND TECHNOLOGY
OSTI = OFFICE OF SCIENTIFIC AND TECHNICAL INFORMATION (NASA)
PSAC = PRESIDENT'S SCIENCE ADVISORY COMMITTEE
S&T = SCIENTIFIC AND TECHNICAL

Table 7-2a   (Continued)

MAJOR ENTITY(IES)			
NAME(S)	SOURCE OF FUNDING	STAFF	FUNCTIONAL RESPONSIBILITIES
(A) ADMINISTRATIVE PSAC	FEDERAL	NA	ATTEND TO BALANCE BE- TWEEN GOVERNMENT AND NON-GOVERNMENT SCIENCE INFORMATION ACTIVITIES
FCST	FEDERAL	NA	SURVEILLANCE OF GOVERN- MENT INFORMATION SYSTEMS
(B) TECHNICAL LARGE GOVERNMENT DEPOSITORIES, E.G., DDC, DTIE, OSTI	FEDERAL	NS	ACT AS WHOLESALERS TO SPECIALIZED INFORMATION CENTERS
GOVERNING COUNCIL (REPORTS TO OST)	SELF	REPRESEN- TATIVES OF ALL USERS	ESTABLISH & INSURE IM- PARTIAL SERVICE TO USERS
EXECUTIVE STAFF (REPORTS TO GOVERNING COUNCIL)	FEDERAL	UNSPECIFIED	IMPLEMENTATION & OPERA- TION OF NATIONAL INFOR- MATION SYSTEM CONDUCT OF R&D
NATIONAL DOCUMENT CENTER (NDC) (RUN BY CFSTI-COMMERCE) (TECHNICAL DIRECTION OF COSATI & FCST)	FEDERAL	UNSPECIFIED	ASSURE S&T DOCUMENTS CONFORM TO REQUIRE- MENTS OF NIS PROCESS & DISSEMINATE DOCUMENTS TO DESIGNATED USERS, INCLUDING UTILI- ZATION & VALUE INFORMA- TION PRIMARILY CONCERNED WITH DOCUMENT DISSEMI- NATION (ASSUMED)
NATIONAL INFORMATION CENTER (NIC) (RUN BY CFSTI-COMMERCE) (TECHNICAL DIRECTION OF COSATI & FCST)	FEDERAL	UNSPECIFIED	ASSURE S&T DOCUMENTS CONFORM TO REQUIREMENTS OF NIS PROCESS & DISSEMI- NATE DOCUMENTS TO DESIG- NATED USERS, INCLUDING UTILIZATION & VALUE IN- FORMATION PRIMARILY CON- CERNED WITH INFORMATION ABOUT DOCUMENTS & R&D PROJECTS (ASSUMED)

Table 7-2b   Organizational Aspects of Weinberg and Management Technology Plans

PLAN	SUBSIDIARY ENTITY(IES		
	NAME(S)	SOURCE OF FUNDING	STAFF
WEINBERG [1] "SCIENCE, GOVERNMENT, AND INFORMATION" ALVIN M. WEINBERG, CHAIRMAN, ET AL., PANEL ON SCIENCE INFORMATION, PRESIDENT'S SCIENCE ADVISORY COMMITTEE 10 JANUARY 1963	SPECIALIZED INFOR- MATION CENTERS, MISSION- OR DISCIPLINE- ORIENTED AS APPROPRI- ATE, LOCATED AT RE- SEARCH CENTERS.	PRIMARILY FEDERAL	NS
MANAGEMENT TECHNOLOGY "A NATIONAL SCIENTIFIC AND TECHNOLOGICAL INFORMATION SYSTEM" MANAGEMENT TECHNOLOGY, INC. APRIL 1963	TECHNICAL INFORMATION CENTERS (TIC) LIBRARIES, DATA CENTERS, INFORMATION CENTERS	FEDERAL BY CONTRACT	SCIENTISTS ENGINEERS INFORMATI SPECIALIS
	SPECIALIZED TECHNICAL INFORMATION CENTERS (STIC) AND SPECIALIZED TECHNICAL DOCUMENTATION CENTERS (STDC) E.G., AEC, NLM, NASA	ASSUMED TO BE FEDERAL- LY SUPPORTED, UNLESS IN- HOUSE GOVERN- MENT ACTIVITIES	EXISTING STAFFS
	REGIONAL OFFICES AND DEPOSITORIES OF THE NIC AND NDC	NS	NS

LEGEND:

NDC = NATIONAL DOCUMENTATION CENTER
NIC = NATIONAL INFORMATION CENTER
NS = NOT SPECIFIED
S&T = SCIENTIFIC AND TECHNICAL
SOTA = STATE-OF-THE-ART

Table 7-2b   (Continued)

FUNCTIONAL RESPONSIBILITIES	ESTIMATED ANNUAL COST	CENTRALIZED AND/OR DECENTRALIZED
ACT AS RETAILERS TO INDI-VIDUAL USERS, EVALUATE LITERATURE, PREPARE SOTA REVIEWS, DISSEMINATE ACTIVELY.	NS	DECENTRALIZED
REVIEW OF S&T DOCUMENTS ACT AS REFERRAL CENTERS CATALOG & PROCESS DOCU-MENTS INTO THEIR INVENTORY REVIEW & ANALYZE DOCUMENTS FOR COMPLIANCE DISSEMINATE DOCUMENTS & ABSTRACTS	NS	CENTRALIZED ORGANIZATION, POLICY, AND CONTROL DECENTRALIZED GEOGRAPH-ICALLY AND FOR DISSEMINA-TION
PREPARE STATE-OF-THE-ART COMPILATIONS BY THEIR DISCIPLINE, SEND TO NDC & NIC.		
NS		

¹ SOME OF THE MAJOR RECOMMENDATIONS IN THE WEINBERG REPORT WERE: THE "DELEGATED AGENCY" CONCEPT, EXEMPLIFIED BY AEC AND NASA, SHOULD BE ADOPTED ELSEWHERE. THE NATIONAL REFERRAL CENTER FOR SCIENCE AND TECHNOLOGY SHOULD BE THE NETWORK'S MAIN "SWITCHING POINT." THE SCIENCE INFORMATION EXCHANGE SHOULD BE STRENGTHENED AND FUNDED SEPARATELY. SPECIALIZED INFORMATION CENTERS SHOULD BE INCREASED IN NUMBER AND BE LOCATED AT RESEARCH CENTERS. GOVERNMENT AGENCIES SHOULD PLACE TECHNICAL INFORMATION ACTIVITIES IN THE RESEARCH AND DEVELOPMENT ARM. THE TECH-NICAL COMMUNITY SHOULD ACCORD INFORMATION SPECIALISTS ESTEEM COMPARABLE TO THAT ACCORDED RESEARCH SPECIALISTS. TECHNIQUES OF HANDLING INFORMATION SHOULD BE TAUGHT TO ALL SCIENTISTS AND ENGINEERS. FURTHER RESEARCH IN BOTH HARDWARE AND SOFTWARE FOR INFORMATION HANDLING, ESPECIALLY FOR VERY LARGE DOCUMENT COLLECTIONS, SHOULD BE SUPPORTED.

Table 7-3a   Organizational Aspects of Heller, Taube, and Kelley Plans

PLAN	SUMMARY OF APPROACH & CONTENT
HELLER A NATIONAL PLAN FOR SCIENCE ABSTRACTING AND INDEXING SERVICES" ROBERT HELLER & ASSOCIATES 15 MARCH 1963 SPONSOR: NATIONAL FEDERATION OF SCIENCE ABSTRACTING AND INDEXING SERVICES	THE HELLER STUDY ONLY ATTACKS THE NATIONAL A&I PROBLEMS. RECOGNITION IS GIVEN TO BOTH THE PROFE SIONAL AND PROJECT ORIENTED A&I SERVICES. A STRUCTURE IS PROPOSED (ORGANIZATION "X") TO IMPROVE QUANTITY AND QUALITY OF THE PROJECT-ORIENTED SERVICES. RECOGNITION IS THEREFORE GIVEN TO THE INC IN MULTI-DISCIPLINE INFORMATION REQUIREMENTS OF SCIENTISTS AND TECHNICIANS.
TAUBE "PROPOSAL FOR THE ESTABLISHMENT OF A GOVERNMENT CORPORATION TO CREATE AND PROVIDE SERVICES FROM AN INTEGRATED STORE OF SCIENTIFIC AND TECHNICAL INFORMATION" MORTIMER TAUBE, DOCUMENTATION INC. 30 JULY 1963	PROPOSES A SINGLE COLLECTING, PROCESSING, STORAGE, AND SERVICE CENTER FOR ALL SCIENTIFIC AND TEC NICAL REPORTS FROM DOD, AEC, AND NASA, PLUS THEIR CONTRACTORS AND THE INDUSTRIAL AND SCIENTIFIC COMMUNITIES IN GENERAL. THE CENTER WOULD BE OPERATED BY A PROPOSED NEW GOVERNMENT CORPORATIO ESTABLISHED FOR THE PURPOSE AND MODELLED AFTER, E.G., COMMUNICATIONS SATELLITE CORP. THE CENT WOULD INCLUDE STAFFING BY PERSONNEL OF DOD, AEC, AND NASA TO ENSURE THE BEST POSSIBLE SERVICE T THESE ORGANIZATIONS.
KELLEY "MEMORANDUM FOR DR. JEROME B. WIESNER, SUBJECT: GOVERNMENT SCIENCE PACKAGE" J. HILARY KELLEY, OFFICE OF SCIENCE AND TECHNOLOGY 23 NOVEMBER 1963	THE PROPOSAL EMPHASIZES REGIONAL DECENTRALIZATION OF A WIDE RANGE OF FEDERAL SERVICES, BOTH TEC NICAL AND NONTECHNICAL. THE "STRICTLY SCIENTIFIC AND TECHNICAL SERVICES ARE MORE THAN SUFFICIE TO SUPPORT SUCH A PACKAGE." THIS GOVERNMENT SCIENCE PACKAGE SHOULD BE AN IDENTIFIABLE ENTITY IF IS TO IMPROVE THE ENTROPY VALUE OF THE SERVICES. STRONG CONGRESSIONAL SUPPORT IS SEEN AS THE KE TO THE SUCCESS OF SUCH A PLAN.

LEGEND:

A&I = ABSTRACTING AND INDEXING
NFSAIS = NATIONAL FEDERATION OF SCIENCE ABSTRACTING AND INDEXING SERVICES
NS = NOT SPECIFIED

Table 7-3a   *(Continued)*

MAJOR ENTITY(IES)			
NAME(S)	SOURCE OF FUNDING	STAFF	FUNCTIONAL RESPONSIBILITIES
STEERING COMMITTEE	SOME FEDERAL VIA NSF	REPRESEN-TATIVES OF THE PROFESSIONAL SOCIETIES, NSF & SPONSORING GOVERNMENT & PRIVATE OR-GANIZATIONS	ORGANIZE "X." ESTABLISH POLICIES
ORGANIZATION "X"	FEDERAL SUPPORT FROM NSF, ETC.	SMALL & PROFESSIONAL	IMPROVE, PRODUCE & MARKET PROJECT-ORIENTED SERVICES (A&I) COORDINATE ACTIONS OF PROFESSIONAL-ORIENTED SERVICES (A&I)
NATIONAL FEDERATION OF SCIENCE ABSTRACTING AND INDEXING SERVICES	SELF	ITS OWN	EXPAND ACTIVITIES AND BROADEN MEMBERSHIP OF NFSAIS
A GOVERNMENT CORPO-RATION	NS	SEE COMMENTS	OPERATE THE INFORMATION CENTER; ESTABLISH POLICY AND GROUND RULES; EVALU-ATE QUALITY AND UTILIZATION OF CENTER'S OPERATIONS.
NS	NS	NS	NS

Table 7-3b   Organizational Aspects of Heller, Taube, and Kelley Plans

PLAN	SUBSIDIARY ENTITY(IE		
	NAME(S)	SOURCE OF FUNDING	STAFF
HELLER "A NATIONAL PLAN FOR SCIENCE ABSTRACTING AND INDEXING SERVICES" ROBERT HELLER & ASSOCIATES 15 MARCH 1963 SPONSOR NATIONAL FEDERATION OF SCIENCE ABSTRACTING AND INDEXING SERVICES	PROFESSIONAL-ORIENTED SERVICES OF NFSAIS	SELF	OWN ⟶
TAUBE [1] "PROPOSAL FOR THE ESTABLISHMENT OF A GOVERNMENT CORPORATION TO CREATE AND PROVIDE SERVICES FROM AN INTEGRATED STORE OF SCIENTIFIC AND TECHNICAL INFORMATION" MORTIMER TAUBE, DOCUMENTATION INC. 30 JULY 1963	NONE	NONE	NONE ⟶
KELLEY [2] "MEMORANDUM FOR DR. JEROME B. WIESNER, SUBJECT: GOVERNMENT SCIENCE PACKAGE" J. HILARY KELLEY, OFFICE OF SCIENCE AND TECHNOLOGY 23 NOVEMBER 1963	REGIONAL FEDERAL SERVICE CENTERS	FEDERAL	NS

LEGEND:
A&I = ABSTRACTING AND INDEXING
CFSTI = CLEARINGHOUSE FOR FEDERAL SCIENTIFIC AND TECHNICAL INFORMATION
DDC = DEFENSE DOCMENTATION CENTER
GPO = GOVERNMENT PRINTING OFFICE
MEDLARS = MEDICAL LITERATURE ANALYSIS AND RETRIEVAL SYSTEM (NATIONAL LIBRARY OF MEDICINE)
NAL = NATIONAL AGRICULTURAL LIBRARY
NFSAIS = NATIONAL FEDERATION OF SCIENCE ABSTRACTING AND INDEXING SERVICES
NIH = NATIONAL INSTITUTES OF HEALTH
NRCST = NATIONAL REFERRAL CENTER FOR SCIENCE AND TECHNOLOGY (LIBRARY OF CONGRESS)
NS = NOT SPECIFIED
PHS = PUBLIC HEALTH SERVICE
SIE = SCIENCE INFORMATION EXCHANGE
VA = VETERANS ADMINISTRATION

Table 7-3b (Continued)

FUNCTIONAL RESPONSIBILITIES	ESTIMATED ANNUAL COST	CENTRALIZED AND/OR DECENTRALIZED
PROVIDE NECESSARY SUPPORT TO ORGANIZATION "X" TO PRODUCE & MARKET PROJECT-ORIENTED A&I SERVICES	PREDICTED AS "LOW" FOR ORGANIZATION "X"	CENTRALIZATION OF POLICY, PRODUCTION, AND MARKETING OF A&I SERVICES AND MATERIALS FOR DECENTRALIZED PROJECT- AND PROFESSIONAL-ORIENTED A&I SERVICES
NONE	NS	ONE INTEGRATED, AUTOMATED, COMMON STORE OF INFORMATION
TO PROVIDE GOVERNMENT SERVICES LOCALLY. SEE COMMENTS.	$10M	GEOGRAPHICALLY DECENTRALIZED SERVICES

[1] THE CORPORATION WOULD HAVE A BOARD OF DIRECTORS MADE UP OF REPRESENTATIVES OF THE EXECUTIVE DEPARTMENTS SERVED PLUS A REPRESENTATIVE FROM THE GENERAL SCIENTIFIC AND INDUSTRIAL COMMUNITY. IN ADDITION TO THE CORPORATION'S OWN STAFF, PROVISION WOULD BE MADE FOR PERSONNEL FROM EACH AGENCY SERVED TO WORK ON-SITE AT THE INTEGRATED INFORMATION SERVICE CENTER TO ENSURE MAXIMUM PAY-OFF FOR EACH AGENCY'S OWN MISSION.

[2] AMONG THE MORE IMPORTANT OF THE SERVICES TO BE PROVIDED LOCALLY ARE: 1) COLLECTIONS OF CENSUS DATA, E.G., CENSUS OF MANUFACTURERS; 2) PATENTS; 3) REPLICAS OF CFSTI HOLDINGS; 4) GPO PRODUCTS; 5) NATIONAL STANDARD REFERENCE DATA SERVICE INFORMATION; 6) NASA AND AEC DOCUMENTS; 7) COPYRIGHT DATA; 8) MEDLARS, DRUG CLEARINGHOUSE, SIE, NAL, AND NRCST SERVICES; 9) DDC SERVICES; 10) SMALL BUSINESS ADMINISTRATION, LABOR DEPARTMENT, PHS, ARMY MAP, GEOLOGICAL SURVEY, REGULATORY AGENCY, VA, COMMERCE, AND NIH SERVICES; 11) INFORMATION ON GOVERNMENT CONTRACTS; AND 12) CAREER INFORMATION.

Table 7-4a   *Organizational Aspects of Simpson and Warren Plans*

PLAN	SUMMARY OF APPROACH & CONTENT
SIMPSON "A PENTAGON OF U.S. SCIENTIFIC AND TECHNICAL INFORMATION AND DATA SERVICES" G.S. SIMPSON, JR., BATTELLE MEMORIAL INSTITUTE 27 NOVEMBER 1963	THIS "PENTAGON" PLAN PRESENTS A VERY BROAD ORGANIZATIONAL SOLUTION TO THE NATIONAL INFORMATION PROBLEM. A REORIENTATION OF THE FUNCTIONS OF EXISTING AGENCIES (DOD, CFSTI, NASA, AEC, NBS, ETC IS PROPOSED THAT WOULD TAKE ADVANTAGE OF THEIR PRESENT INFORMATION PROCESSING CAPABILITIES. TI "SPLIT" OF DATA AND INFORMATION INTO CLASSIFIED AND UNCLASSIFIED GROUPINGS IS EMPHASIZED.
WARREN "MEMORANDUM FOR THE PRESIDENT ON A NATIONAL LIBRARY OF SCIENCE SYSTEM" STAFFORD L. WARREN, M.D., EXECUTIVE OFFICE OF THE PRESIDENT 17 FEBRUARY 1964	A NATIONAL LIBRARY OF SCIENCE SYSTEM IS PROPOSED WHICH WOULD COLLECT, PROCESS, AND DISSEMINAT INFORMATION CONCERNING THE OPEN PUBLISHED SCIENTIFIC LITERATURE (THE SCIENTIFIC JOURNALS) TO ALL CLASSES OF USERS. THE PROPOSED SYSTEM RELIES HEAVILY ON THREE FACTORS: THE DEVELOPMENT OF STANDARDS (FOR ABSTRACTING, INPUT FORMATS, INDEXING, ETC.); THE RELIANCE ON COMPUTERS AS THE CENTRAL PROCESSORS OF THE SYSTEM, AND AN INVENTORY AND SUBSEQUENT ALLOCATION OF RESPONSIBIL TO LIBRARIES IN THE SYSTEM (FOR JOURNAL CONTENT). THE SYSTEM REQUIRES THAT THE EXISTING AUTONO OPERATING LIBRARIES AND SPECIAL INFORMATION CENTERS (FEDERAL AND PRIVATE) ACT AS THE PRIME MOD COLLECTION, COMMUNICATION, AND DISSEMINATION. SEVEN MAJOR CENTERS ARE PROPOSED AT GEOGRAPHIC DECENTRALIZED POINTS. THE WASHINGTON REGION WOULD BE RUN OUT OF PHS–NLM–MEDLARS.

LEGEND:

CFSTI = CLEARINGHOUSE FOR FEDERAL SCIENTIFIC AND TECHNICAL INFORMATION

COSATI = COMMITTEE ON SCIENTIFIC AND TECHNICAL INFORMATION

FCST = FEDERAL COUNCIL FOR SCIENCE AND TECHNOLOGY

MEDLARS = MEDICAL LITERATURE ANALYSIS AND RETRIEVAL SYSTEM

NA = NOT APPLICABLE

NBS = NATIONAL BUREAU OF STANDARDS

NLM = NATIONAL LIBRARY OF MEDICINE

NS = NOT SPECIFIED

OSIS = OFFICE OF SCIENCE INFORMATION SERVICE

OST = OFFICE OF SCIENCE AND TECHNOLOGY

PUBLIC HEALTH SERVICE

Table 7-4a   (Continued)

MAJOR ENTITY(IES)			
NAME(S)	SOURCE OF FUNDING	STAFF	FUNCTIONAL RESPONSIBILITIES
OST, FCST, COSATI	FEDERAL	NA	COORDINATION
NSF (OSIS)	FEDERAL	NS	OVERALL RESEARCH SUPPORT
ADVISORY COMMITTEE ON OPERATIONŚ	FEDERAL	15	COORDINATION OF ASSIGN- MENTS REVIEW OF STANDARDS OVERALL POLICY
ADVISORY COUNCILS & STUDY SECTIONS	FEDERAL	UNSPECIFIED BUT VARYING WITH TIME	R&D EDUCATION & TRAINING PUBLICATIONS FACILITIES

Table 7-4b   Organizational Aspects of Simpson and Warren Plans

PLAN	SUBSIDIARY ENTITY(IES)		
	NAME(S)	SOURCE OF FUNDING	STAFF
SIMPSON "A PENTAGON OF U.S. SCIENTIFIC AND TECHNICAL INFORMATION AND DATA SERVICES" G.S. SIMPSON, JR., BATTELLE MEMORIAL INSTITUTE 27 NOVEMBER 1963	NATIONAL DEPOT OF CLASSIFIED SCIENTIFIC AND TECHNICAL INFORMATION (WITH REGIONAL OUTLETS)	DDC	NS
	NATIONAL DEPOT OF UNCLASSIFIED INDIGENOUS SCIENTIFIC AND TECHNICAL INFORMATION (WITH REGIONAL OUTLETS)	CFSTI OR ELSEWHERE IN COMMERCE DEPT.	NS
	NATIONAL DEPOT OF FOREIGN SCIENTIFIC AND TECHNICAL INFORMATION	NASA	MENTION OF NEED FOR SPECIAL SKILLS HERE
	NATIONAL CLASSIFIED DATA CENTER	TO BE CREATED WITHIN DOD OR NASA	NS
	NATIONAL UNCLASSIFIED DATA CENTER	NBS	NS
WARREN[1] "MEMORANDUM FOR THE PRESIDENT ON A NATIONAL LIBRARY OF SCIENCE SYSTEM" STAFFORD L. WARREN, M.D., EXECUTIVE OFFICE OF THE PRESIDENT 17 FEBRUARY 1964	7 REGIONAL CENTERS (INCLUDING WASHINGTON)	FEDERAL BY CONTRACT	LARGE PROFESSIONAL
	WASHINGTON CENTER (PHS–NLM–MEDLARS) OTHER MAJOR LIBRARIES	FEDERAL	LARGE PROFESSIONAL
	AUTONOMOUS OPERATING LIBRARIES & SPECIAL INFORMATION CENTERS	EXISTING	OWN

LEGEND:

CFSTI = CLEARINGHOUSE FOR FEDERAL SCIENTIFIC AND TECHNICAL INFORMATION
DDC = DEFENSE DOCUMENTATION CENTER
MEDLARS = MEDICAL LITERATURE ANALYSIS AND RETRIEVAL SYSTEM
NBS = NATIONAL BUREAU OF STANDARDS
NLM = NATIONAL LIBRARY OF MEDICINE
NS = NOT SPECIFIED
PHS = PUBLIC HEALTH SERVICE

Table 7-4b   *(Continued)*

FUNCTIONAL RESPONSIBILITIES	ESTIMATED ANNUAL COST	CENTRALIZED AND/OR DECENTRALIZED
EACH DEPOT WOULD CONDUCT ALL PHASES OF INFORMATION HANDLING, FROM COLLECTION TO DISSEMINATION.	NS	CENTRAL COORDINATION. CENTRAL HANDLING OF EACH OF THE FIVE CATEGORIES OF INFORMATION. DE-CENTRALIZED DISSEMINATION THROUGH REGIONAL OUTLETS.
ACQUISITION, ANALYSIS, CODING, STORAGE, RETRIEVAL, & DISSEMINATION	IST YEAR, $10M 2ND YEAR, $27.75M 3RD YEAR, $84.5M 4TH YEAR, $64.5M 5TH YEAR, $70.0M 6TH YEAR, $52.0M SEE COMMENTS.	CENTRALIZED CONTROL OF POLICY, STANDARDS, ETC. DECENTRALIZED GEOGRAPHICALLY
NLM IN-HOUSE RESEARCH FACILITY, OTHERWISE SAME AS OTHER REGIONAL CENTERS		
SAME AS REGIONAL CENTERS		

¹ THE FIRST THREE YEARS' BUDGETS REFLECT HEAVY EXPENDITURES IN RESEARCH AND DEVELOPMENT, CONSTRUCTION, AND EDUCATION AND TRAINING. THE FOURTH AND FIFTH YEARS' BUDGETS INCLUDE FUNDS FOR COMPLETING CONSTRUCTION OF FACILITIES. THE SIXTH YEAR'S BUDGET MAY BE TAKEN AS AN EXPECTED ANNUAL OPERATIONAL COST.

Table 7-5a Organizational Aspects of Jonker and Goldberg Plans

PLAN	SUMMARY OF APPROACH & CONTENT
JONKER "A MODEL INFORMATION RETRIEVAL NETWORK FOR GOVERNMENT, SCIENCE, AND INDUSTRY" FREDERICK JONKER, ET AL., JONKER BUSINESS MACHINES, INC. MAY 1964 SPONSOR: INFORMATION RESEARCH DIVISION AIR FORCE OFFICE OF SCIENTIFIC RESEARCH	ATTACKS THE INFORMATION PROBLEM FROM A MISSION AND DISCIPLINE CONCEPT. PROPOSES MISSION– DISCIPLINE–ORIENTED NETWORKS, EACH OPERATED INDEPENDENTLY BY A SUPPORT AND CONTROL CENTER. WORKS CAN INTERACT ON A REFERRAL BASIS THROUGH THE ESTABLISHMENT (BY THE FEDERAL GOVERNMEN A NATIONAL INFORMATION–RETRIEVAL NETWORK COORDINATION CENTER. ALL NETWORKS ARE ESTABLISHE DE FACTO, BY THE "LEADER" OF A PARTICULAR MISSION OR DISCIPLINE GROUP. THE PROPOSAL GOES INTO GREAT DETAIL CONCERNING THE TECHNICAL ASPECTS OF DEPTH INDEXING, USE PROFILES, SPECIALIZED EQUIPMENT, ETC. THE NETWORKS ARE ORGANIZED SIMILAR TO A LATTICE; AS SUCH, THE CRITICAL PATH FOR COMMUNICAT WITHIN THE NETWORK IS NOT UNIQUE AND DEPENDS ON INDIVIDUAL REQUIREMENTS.
GOLDBERG "ENGINEERING DATA AND INFORMATION SYSTEM (EDIS)" STANLEY A. GOLDBERG, ET AL., OFFICE OF THE DIRECTOR OF ARMY TECHNICAL INFORMATION JULY 1964 SPONSOR: OFFICE OF THE CHIEF OF RESEARCH AND DEVELOPMENT DEPARTMENT OF THE ARMY	THIS STUDY OUTLINES THE CONCEPT AND ACTION PLAN FOR AN ENGINEERING DATA AND INFORMATION SYST (EDIS). BASICALLY, IT PROPOSES THE DEVELOPMENT OF ENGINEERING–DISCIPLINE–ORIENTED SWITCHIN WORKS WHICH WOULD FUNCTION AS A MODIFIED REFERRAL CENTER, WITH A NUMBER OF DATA AND INFORM BANKS INTERCONNECTED THROUGH THE SWITCHING CENTER (WHICH ITSELF HAS A LIMITED DATA AND INFO BANK). PARTICIPANTS ARE ABLE TO SECURE ALL NECESSARY DATA AND INFORMATION WHILE MAINTAININ MAXIMUM AUTONOMY IN THEIR INTERNAL INFORMATION–HANDLING SYSTEMS.

LEGEND:
NS = NOT SPECIFIED

Table 7-5a   *(Continued)*

MAJOR ENTITY(IES)			
NAME(S)	SOURCE OF FUNDING	STAFF	FUNCTIONAL RESPONSIBILITIES
NATIONAL INFORMATION RETRIEVAL NETWORK COORDINATION CENTER	FEDERAL	UNSPECIFIED	SET STANDARDS PERFORM INTER—NETWORK SEARCHES CENTRAL DEPOSITORY FOR ENTIRE NETWORK'S INFOR—MATION CLEARINGHOUSE FOR DOCU—MENTS THAT HAVE TO BE ENTERED INTO MORE THAN ONE NETWORK
SUPPORT & CONTROL CENTERS	PROFESSIONAL OR GOVERNMENT OR—GANIZATION & FEDERAL GRANTS & LOANS	EXISTING	HUB OF EACH NETWORK MAJOR HARDWARE CENTER FOR THE NETWORK PRODUCTION ACTIVITIES SELECTIVE DISSEMINATION POLICY MAKING FINANCIAL & ADMINISTRA—TIVE CONTROL ACCEPTS INPUT FROM COM—MUNICATION CENTERS SERVES ENTIRE DISCIPLINE OR MISSION
SWITCHING CENTERS	FEDERAL	NS	MAINTAIN LIMITED STORAGE OF DATA AND INFORMATION (AS A RESULT OF DEMAND HISTORY) MAINTAIN INDEXES OF TOTAL NETWORK PROCESS REQUESTS FROM HOME BANKS IN NETWORK & FILL REQUEST DIRECTLY. IF "NO FIND," REQUEST IS REFERRED TO APPROPRIATE HOME BANK

Table 7-5b   Organizational Aspects of Jonker and Goldberg Plans

PLAN	SUBSIDIARY ENTITY(IE		
	NAME(S)	SOURCE OF FUNDING	STAFF
JONKER "A MODEL INFORMATION RETRIEVAL NETWORK FOR GOVERNMENT, SCIENCE, AND INDUSTRY" FREDERICK JONKER, ET AL., JONKER BUSINESS MACHINES, INC. MAY 1964 SPONSOR: INFORMATION RESEARCH DIVISION AIR FORCE OFFICE OF SCIENTIFIC RESEARCH	COMMUNICATION CENTERS	MAJOR LIBRARY OR PROFESSION-AL SOCIETY FEDERAL GRANTS & LOANS	EXISTING
	INFORMATION CENTERS	SMALL UNITS LIKE CORPORATE LIBRARIES & FED-ERAL GRANTS & LOANS	EXISTING
	USE UNITS & INDIVIDUALS		
GOLDBERG "ENGINEERING DATA AND INFORMATION SYSTEM (EDIS)" STANLEY A. GOLDBERG, ET AL., OFFICE OF THE DIRECTOR OF ARMY TECHNICAL INFORMATION JULY 1964 SPONSOR: OFFICE OF THE CHIEF OF RESEARCH AND DEVELOPMENT DEPARTMENT OF THE ARMY	"HOME" DATA AND INFOR-MATION BANKS	NS	NS

LEGEND

NS = NOT SPECIFIED

Table 7-5b *(Continued)*

FUNCTIONAL RESPONSIBILITIES	ESTIMATED ANNUAL COST	CENTRALIZED AND/OR DECENTRALIZED
SERVICES ENTIRE SUBDISCI- PLINE OR SUB-MISSION ACQUIRES INFORMATION TRAINS IN DEGREES HANDLES INQUIRIES COMMUNICATES WITH OTHER COMMUNICATION CENTERS MARKETS SERVICES	$7.5M PER NETWORK PER YEAR	CENTRALIZED COORDINATION, POLICY, STANDARDS, FINANCIAL, AND ADMINISTRATIVE CONTROL (SUPPORT & CONTROL CENTERS) DECENTRALIZED (GEOGRAPHICAL AND FUNCTIONAL) SERVICES BY DISCIPLINE AND/OR MISSION
INDEXES ORIGINAL MATERIAL FORMULATES REQUIREMENTS FOR SELECTIVE DISSEMINA- TION SENDS SEARCH REQUESTS		
BASIC SOURCES & USERS OF THE NETWORK (PAY FEES FOR USE)		
INDEX AND STORE LOCALLY GENERATED DATA AND INFOR- MATION. RESPOND TO LOCALLY INITIATED QUERIES. PASS "NO FINDS" TO SWITCHING CENTER. HANDLE REFERRALS FROM SWITCHING CENTER AND NOTIFY IT OF COMPLIANCE.	NS	NO CENTRALIZED CONTROL OF ALL NETWORKS DECENTRALIZED SYSTEM OPERATIONS BY DISCIPLINE INDIVIDUAL NETWORKS HAVE A CENTRALIZED COMMUNICATIONS NETWORK IN THE SWITCHING CENTER

Table 7-6a   Organizational Aspects of Mayo-Wells, Kelsey, and Hoshovsky-Album Plans

PLAN	SUMMARY OF APPROACH & CONTENT
MAYO-WELLS "ORGANIZATION OF A NATIONAL SCIENTIFIC AND TECHNICAL INFORMATION CENTER" WILFRID JAMES MAYO-WELLS, CONSULTANT 7 OCTOBER 1964	PROPOSES A NATIONAL INFORMATION ANALYSIS CENTER THAT WOULD PUBLISH ABSTRACTS, STATE-OF-THE REPORTS, BIBLIOGRAPHIES, ETC., AND WOULD FURNISH CONSULTANT SERVICES. ULTIMATELY, NIAC WOU DEPEND ON THE DEVELOPMENT OF "CONCEPTUAL LATTICES FOR CONVERGENT RETRIEVAL."
KELSEY "A NATIONAL DRUG INFORMATION CLEARINGHOUSE" F. ELLIS KELSEY, PUBLIC HEALTH SERVICE 8 DECEMBER 1964	DEALS PRIMARILY WITH INTERNAL INFORMATION SERVICES **FOR DHEW.** THE NEED FOR A NATIONAL DRUG IN MATION CLEARINGHOUSE (OTHER TYPES OF CLEARINGHOUSES ARE IMPLIED) IS DEFINED. EMPHASIS IS PL ON THE NEED FOR <u>CENTRALIZED</u> COLLECTION, PROCESSING, TRANSLATION, ABSTRACTING, ETC., AND FOR <u>DECENTRALIZED</u> DISSEMINATION. IT IS BASICALLY A PLAN TO INTEGRATE THE EXISTING SCIENTIFIC INFO TION ACTIVITIES WITHIN HEW, WITH EMPHASIS ON THE DRUG INFORMATION PROBLEM.
HOSHOVSKY-ALBUM "TOWARD A NATIONAL TECHNICAL INFORMATION SYSTEM" A. G. HOSHOVSKY AND H. H. ALBUM, OFFICE OF AEROSPACE RESEARCH, U.S. AIR FORCE JANUARY 1965	THIS PROPOSAL IS BASED ON THE PREMISE THAT A NATIONAL INFORMATION SYSTEM CANNOT BE SUCCESS IF IT REQUIRES ANY ADMINISTRATION OR ORGANIZATIONAL UPHEAVAL OF THE EXISTING FEDERAL STRUCTUR HENCE, A NATIONAL TECHNICAL INFORMATION AGENCY IS PROPOSED WHICH WOULD ACT AS A COLLECTION F REFERRAL CENTER, AND CLEARINGHOUSE FOR ALL INFORMATION PROVIDED TO IT BY EXISTING FEDERAL AN PRIVATE LIBRARIES, ABSTRACTING AND INDEXING SERVICES, AND SPECIALIZED INFORMATION CENTERS (I. THE NTIA IS THE PRIME MODE IN A SWITCHING NETWORK). THE PROPOSAL RECOGNIZES THAT SYSTEMS AR EVOLVED WITHOUT PRICE PLANNING AND, HENCE, IT ONLY SPELLS OUT THE NECESSARY STEPS TO BE TAK BEFORE THE CONCRETE ANALYSIS AND DESIGN OF A NATIONAL INFORMATION SYSTEM ARE UNDERTAKEN.

LEGEND:

DHEW = DEPARTMENT OF HEALTH, EDUCATION, AND WELFARE
NAS = NATIONAL ACADEMY OF SCIENCES
NIAC = NATIONAL INFORMATION ANALYSIS CENTER
NS = NOT SPECIFIED
NTIA = NATIONAL TECHNICAL INFORMATION AGENCY

Table 7-6a *(Continued)*

MAJOR ENTITY(IES)			
NAME(S)	SOURCE OF FUNDING	STAFF	FUNCTIONAL RESPONSIBILITIES
NATIONAL INFORMATION ANALYSIS CENTER	EVENTUALLY SELF-SUPPORTING THROUGH FEES FOR SERVICES & SPONSORSHIP BY INDUSTRY	NS	NATIONAL COLLECTION, STORAGE, ANALYSIS, DISSEMINATION, AND RETRIEVAL CENTER
ADVISORY COMMITTEE FOR SCIENCE COMMUNICATIONS (HEW ONLY)	FEDERAL (HEW)	SUBSTANTIAL, BOTH TECHNICAL AND SUPPORT	IDENTIFY PRESENT AND FUTURE SCIENCE INFORMATION NEEDS, THE TECHNICAL MEANS TO SATISFY THEM, AND ASSOCIATED COSTS. RECOMMEND WAYS TO OVERCOME INSTITUTIONAL OBSTACLES. ANALYZE USER NEEDS. SET UP MODEL SYSTEMS. EXERCISE OVERALL CONTROL OF INFORMATION IN HEW, INCLUDING THE PROPOSED DRUG INFORMATION CLEARINGHOUSE.
NATIONAL R&D INFORMATION POLICY COUNCIL (UNDER NAS)	FEDERAL	SMALL GOVERNMENT & NON-GOVERNMENT	ESTABLISH STANDARDS PROVIDE FOR COMPATIBILITY BETWEEN PUBLIC & PRIVATE SECTORS PROVIDE FOR NECESSARY FEDERAL REORGANIZATION
NATIONAL TECHNICAL INFORMATION AGENCY (NTIA)	FEDERAL (DIRECT & CONTRACTUAL) WOULD RECEIVE INCOME FOR WORK DONE FOR PRIVATE CONCERNS	UNSPECIFIED TECHNICAL	ACT AS CENTRAL ACQUISITION & SWITCHING GROUP COLLECTION POINT CLEARINGHOUSE REFERRAL CENTER SUPPLIER (PRIMARILY WHOLESALE)

Table 7-6b Organizational Aspects of Mayo-Wells, Kelsey, and Hoshovsky-Album Plans

PLAN	SUBSIDIARY ENTITY(IE		
	NAME(S)	SOURCE OF FUNDING	STAFF
MAYO–WELLS "ORGANIZATION OF A NATIONAL SCIENTIFIC AND TECHNICAL INFORMATION CENTER" WILFRID JAMES MAYO–WELLS, CONSULTANT 7 OCTOBER 1964	NONE	NONE	NONE
KELSEY "A NATIONAL DRUG INFORMATION CLEARINGHOUSE" F. ELLIS KELSEY, PUBLIC HEALTH SERVICE 8 DECEMBER 1964	NATIONAL DRUG INFORMA—TION CLEARINGHOUSE(S)	FEDERAL (HEW)	SPECIALL TRAINED TECHNICA STAFF
HOSHOVSKY–ALBUM "TOWARD A NATIONAL TECHNICAL INFORMATION SYSTEM" A. G. HOSHOVSKY AND H. H. ALBUM, OFFICE OF AEROSPACE RESEARCH, U.S. AIR FORCE JANUARY 1965	EXISTING FEDERAL & PRIVATE SERVICE GROUPS (LIBRARIES, A&I SERVICES, SPECIALIZED INFORMATION CENTERS)	EXISTING	EXISTING

LEGEND:

A&I = ABSTRACTING AND INDEXING

NS = NOT SPECIFIED

NTIA = NATIONAL TECHNICAL INFORMATION AGENCY

Table 7-6b   *(Continued)*

FUNCTIONAL RESPONSIBILITIES	ESTIMATED ANNUAL COST	CENTRALIZED AND/OR DECENTRALIZED
NONE	NS	ONE INTEGRATED, ULTIMATELY AUTOMATED, COMMON STORE OF INFORMATION
USUAL CLEARINGHOUSE FUNCTIONS	NS	CENTRALIZED CONTROL, COLLECTION, AND PROCESSING; DECENTRALIZED DISSEMINATION
PERFORM "NORMAL" FUNCTIONS SUPPLY NTIA WITH SOURCE INFORMATION & SUPPORT SERVICES (AND VICE VERSA)	NS	CENTRALIZED POLICY, CENTRALIZED COLLECTION AND CLEARINGHOUSE, DECENTRALIZED SERVICES AND INFORMATION DISSEMINATION

Table 7-7a   Technical Aspects of Stanford and Crawford Plans

PLAN		TYPE OF DOCUMENTS	SYSTEM MISSION OR DISCIP ORIENTATION
STANFORD (SRI) "A DRAFT PROGRAM FOR A NATIONAL TECHNICAL INFORMATION CENTER" STANFORD RESEARCH INSTITUTE JANUARY 1958		JOURNALS, ARTICLES, BOOKS, DOCUMENTS; FOREIGN AND DOMESTIC; CLASSIFIED AND UNCLASSIFIED	INTERIM: PHYSICAL AI BIOLOGICAL SCIENCES ENGINEERING, AND ME EXPAND TO INCLUDE A SCIENCE AND TECHNOL
CRAWFORD "SCIENTIFIC AND TECHNOLOGICAL COMMUNICATION IN GOVERNMENT: TASK FORCE REPORT TO THE PRESIDENT'S SPECIAL ASSISTANT FOR SCIENCE AND TECHNOLOGY" JAMES H. CRAWFORD, JR., CHAIRMAN, ET AL. APRIL 1962 SPONSOR: JEROME B. WIESNER, OFFICE OF SCIENCE AND TECHNOLOGY	CLEARINGHOUSE I "CURRENTLY PLANNED AND ACTIVE R&D EFFORTS"	SUPPORTING FUNDS, ORGANIZATION AND MANPOWER, FACILITIES AND EQUIPMENT, AND THE SCOPE, PROGRESS, AND RESULTS. (CLASSIFIED, PROPRIETARY, OPEN)	DEPENDS ON R&D PROJ COVERAGE
	CLEARINGHOUSE II "RESULTS OF COMPLETED R&D EFFORTS"	DOCUMENTS REPORTING RESULTS OF R&D EFFORTS (CLASSIFIED, PROPRIETARY, OPEN)	SAME AS ABOVE
	CLEARINGHOUSE III "REFERRAL SERVICE TO R&D EFFORTS OF FEDERAL ENTITIES"	INFORMATION CONCERNING THE CONTENT AND RETRIEVAL CAPABILITIES OF THE LIBRARIES, COLLECTIONS, ETC., OF FEDERAL ENTITIES	SAME AS ABOVE
	CLEARINGHOUSE IV "COORDINATING ACCESS TO SPECIALIZED INFORMATION CENTERS AND SERVICES"	INFORMATION CONCERNING THE SCOPE OF AVAILABLE INFORMATION AT SPECIALIZED INFORMATION CENTERS AND SERVICES	NA
	CLEARINGHOUSE V "FORMAL SCIENTIFIC AND TECHNICAL MEETINGS"	PLANS, SCHEDULES, AND CONTENT OF FEDERALLY SUPPORTED MEETINGS	NA

LEGEND:

NA = NOT APPLICABLE
NS = NOT SPECIFIED

Table 7-7a *(Continued)*

SOURCES OF DOCUMENTS	PRE-INPUT PROCESSING REQUIRED	SYSTEM USERS		TYPES OF REQUESTS
		INSTITUTIONS AND ORGANIZATIONS	INDIVIDUALS	
PUBLISHED LITERA-TURE	ABSTRACTING AND TRANSLATING	GOVERNMENT, INDUSTRY, AND ACADEMIC WORLD	SCIENTISTS, TECH-NICIANS	NS
FEDERAL AGENCIES (FOR IN-HOUSE R&D AND SUPPORTED R&D)	ORGANIZING THE IN-FORMATION(ASSUMED)	FEDERAL AND NON-GOVERNMENT ORGAN-IZATIONS(VOLUNTARY)	NS	NS
SAME AS ABOVE	NS	SAME AS ABOVE EX-CEPT WHERE THEY RECEIVE ANNOUNCE-MENTS VIA AUTOMA-TIC DISTRIBUTION	NS	COPY OF DOCUMENTS ANNOUNCED
SAME AS ABOVE	NS	FEDERAL AND NON-GOVERNMENT ORGAN-IZATIONS(VOLUNTARY)	NS	FOR REFERRAL BY CLEARINGHOUSE III AND FOR A SEARCH AT THE DESIGNATED FEDERAL AGENCY
FEDERALLY SUP-PORTED SPECIALIZED INFORMATION CEN-TERS AND SERVICES	NS	SAME AS ABOVE	NS	FOR REFERRAL AND COORDINATION OF USE
SPONSORING FEDERAL ENTITY	NS	SAME AS ABOVE	NS	NS

Table 7-7b   *Technical Aspects of Stanford and Crawford Plans*

PLAN		HARDWARE ORIENTATION
STANFORD (SRI) "A DRAFT PROGRAM FOR A NATIONAL TECHNICAL INFORMATION CENTER" STANFORD RESEARCH INSTITUTE JANUARY 1958		HEAVY
CRAWFORD "SCIENTIFIC AND TECHNOLOGICAL COMMUNICATION IN GOVERNMENT: TASK FORCE REPORT TO THE PRESIDENT'S SPECIAL ASSISTANT FOR SCIENCE AND TECHNOLOGY" JAMES H. CRAWFORD, JR., CHAIRMAN, ET AL. APRIL 1962 SPONSOR: JEROME B. WIESNER, OFFICE OF SCIENCE AND TECHNOLOGY	CLEARINGHOUSE I "CURRENTLY PLANNED AND ACTIVE R&D EFFORTS"	NO BASIS TO JUDGE
	CLEARINGHOUSE II "RESULTS OF COMPLETED R&D EFFORTS"	NO BASIS TO JUDGE
	CLEARINGHOUSE III "REFERRAL SERVICE TO R&D EFFORTS OF FEDERAL ENTITIES"	NO BASIS TO JUDGE
	CLEARINGHOUSE IV "COORDINATING ACCESS TO SPECIALIZED INFORMATION CENTERS AND SERVICES"	NO BASIS TO JUDGE
	CLEARINGHOUSE V "FORMAL SCIENTIFIC AND TECHNICAL MEETINGS"	NO BASIS TO JUDGE

LEGEND:

NS = NOT SPECIFIED

W&R = WHOLESALE AND RETAIL

Table 7-7b *(Continued)*

TYPES OF INTERNAL PROCESSING	SYSTEM OUTPUTS	
	TYPES	DISSEMINATION
NS	NS	W&R
NS	NS	W&R
NS	ANNOUNCEMENTS OF DOCUMENTS AVAIL- ABLE AND HARDCOPY	W&R
RETROSPECTIVE SEARCH AND RE- TRIEVAL	REFERRAL LIST	W&R
NS	IDENTIFICATION OF SUCH CENTERS AND SERVICES	W&R
NS	PRE-MEETING AND POST-MEETING IN- FORMATION, INCLUD- ING CONTENT OF PRESENTATIONS	W&R

Table 7-8a Technical Aspects of Cahn, Weinberg, Management Technology and Heller Plans

PLAN	TYPE OF DOCUMENTS	SYSTEM MISSION OR DISCIP ORIENTATION
CAHN "'B.I.T.S.' – BUREAU OF INFORMATION FOR TECHNOLOGY AND SCIENCE PROPOSED AS 'KEY STATION' OF FEDERAL 'NETWORK' OF INFORMATION SERVICES TO U.S. FREE ENTERPRISE SYSTEM" JULIUS N. CAHN, DIRECTOR, SCIENTIFIC RESEARCH PROJECT, SUBCOMMITTEE ON REORGANIZATION AND INTERNATIONAL ORGANIZATIONS, COMMITTEE ON GOVERNMENT OPERATIONS, U.S. SENATE 17 JANUARY 1962	ALL	BOTH
WEINBERG "SCIENCE, GOVERNMENT, AND INFORMATION" ALVIN M. WEINBERG, CHAIRMAN, ET AL., PANEL ON SCIENCE INFORMATION, PRESIDENT'S SCIENCE ADVISORY COMMITTEE 10 JANUARY 1963	ALL	BOTH
MANAGEMENT TECHNOLOGY "A NATIONAL SCIENTIFIC AND TECHNOLOGICAL INFORMATION SYSTEM" MANAGEMENT TECHNOLOGY INC. APRIL 1963	WORLD WIDE SCIENTIFIC AND TECHNICAL DOCUMENTATION (CLASSIFIED AND UNCLASSIFIED) FEDERALLY SUPPORTED R&D PROJECT INFORMATION (CURRENT AND PROPOSED)	BOTH, WITH HEAVY EM SIS ON MISSION ORIEN
HELLER "A NATIONAL PLAN FOR SCIENCE ABSTRACTING AND INDEXING SERVICES" ROBERT HELLER & ASSOCIATES 15 MARCH 1963 SPONSOR: NATIONAL FEDERATION OF SCIENCE ABSTRACTING AND INDEXING SERVICES	WORLD WIDE SCIENTIFIC AND TECHNICAL LITERATURE FROM PUBLISHED JOURNALS AND REPORTS AND PRIMARY AND AUTHOR ABSTRACTS	EMPHASIS IS ON MISS (PROJECT) TYPE ORIEN TION, BUT DISCIPLINE FESSIONAL) IS ALSO C SIDERED.

LEGEND:

NS = NOT SPECIFIED

Table 7-8a *(Continued)*

SOURCES OF DOCUMENTS	PRE-INPUT PROCESSING REQUIRED	SYSTEM USERS		TYPES OF REQUESTS
		INSTITUTIONS AND ORGANIZATIONS	INDIVIDUALS	
BOTH PRE- AND POST-PUBLICATION MATE-RIAL	NS	ALL-INCLUSIVE	ALL-INCLUSIVE	NS
ALL	TITLES MUST BE MADE MEANINGFUL. AUTHORS SHOULD PROVIDE ABSTRACTS. TECHNICAL REPORTS SHOULD BE REFERRED OR SCREENED BEFORE BEING ADMITTED TO THE INFORMATION SYSTEM, PREFERABLY BY RESIDENT REFEREES WHO ARE TECHNICAL EMPLOYEES OF THE CONTRACTORS GENERATING THE REPORTS.	ALL-INCLUSIVE	ALL-INCLUSIVE	NS
INDIVIDUAL SCIENTISTS AND ENGINEERS, FEDERAL RESEARCH AND DEVELOPMENT AGENCIES	TRANSLATION, INDEXING, ABSTRACTING, CATALOGING	GOVERNMENT (LEGISLATIVE, JUDICIAL AND EXECUTIVE) STATE AND LOCAL GOVERNMENT UNIVERSITIES AND SCHOOLS PRIVATE INDUSTRY PRIVATE INSTITUTIONS	MANAGERS SCIENTISTS ENGINEERS STUDENTS	FOR R&D SUMMARIES FOR DOCUMENTS FOR REFERRAL SERVICE ABSTRACTS
PUBLISHED JOURNALS AND REPORTS	ABSTRACTING, TRANSLATING	ALL-INCLUSIVE	ALL-INCLUSIVE	REQUESTS FOR ABSTRACTS, BIBLIOGRAPHIES, AND HARDCOPY

Table 7-8b *Technical Aspects of Cahn, Weinberg, Management Technology, and Heller Plans*

PLAN	HARDWARE ORIENTATION
CAHN "'B.I.T.S.' — BUREAU OF INFORMATION FOR TECHNOLOGY AND SCIENCE PROPOSED AS 'KEY STATION' OF FEDERAL 'NETWORK' OF INFORMATION SERVICES TO U.S. FREE ENTERPRISE SYSTEM" JULIUS N. CAHN, DIRECTOR, SCIENTIFIC RESEARCH PROJECT, SUBCOMMITTEE ON REORGANIZATION AND INTERNATIONAL ORGANIZATIONS, COMMITTEE ON GOVERNMENT OPERATIONS, U.S. SENATE 17 JANUARY 1962	NA
WEINBERG [1] "SCIENCE, GOVERNMENT, AND INFORMATION" ALVIN M. WEINBERG, CHAIRMAN, ET AL., PANEL ON SCIENCE INFORMATION, PRESIDENT'S SCIENCE ADVISORY COMMITTEE 10 JANUARY 1963	NA
MANAGEMENT TECHNOLOGY [2] "A NATIONAL SCIENTIFIC AND TECHNOLOGICAL INFORMATION SYSTEM" MANAGEMENT TECHNOLOGY INC. APRIL 1963	SOME EMPHASIS ON COMPUTER AUTOMATION
HELLER "A NATIONAL PLAN FOR SCIENCE ABSTRACTING AND INDEXING SERVICES" ROBERT HELLER & ASSOCIATES 15 MARCH 1963 SPONSOR: NATIONAL FEDERATION OF SCIENCE ABSTRACTING AND INDEXING SERVICES	MINIMAL EMPHASIS

LEGEND:

AUTODIN = AUTOMATIC DIGITAL COMMUNICATIONS NETWORK (DOD)

CFSTI = CLEARINGHOUSE FOR FEDERAL SCIENTIFIC AND TECHNICAL INFORMATION

COSATI = COMMITTEE ON SCIENTIFIC AND TECHNICAL INFORMATION

DDC = DEFENSE DOCUMENTATION CENTER

FCST = FEDERAL COUNCIL FOR SCIENCE AND TECHNOLOGY

NA = NOT APPLICABLE

NS = NOT SPECIFIED

STI = SCIENTIFIC AND TECHNICAL INFORMATION

W&R = WHOLESALE AND RETAIL

Table 7-8b   (Continued)

| TYPES OF INTERNAL PROCESSING | SYSTEM OUTPUTS | |
	TYPES	DISSEMINATION
NS	NS	W&R
CITATION INDEXING SINGLED OUT FOR SPECIAL COMMENDA-TION. RAPID SWITCH-ING (I.E., USER REFERRAL) HELD TO BE VERY IMPORTANT.	NS	W&R
STATE-OF-THE-ART COMPILATIONS BY TECHNICAL DISCI-PLINES PRIORITY AND SELEC-TION CRITERIA FOR DISTRIBUTION CATALOGING INTO IN-VENTORY REVIEW AND ANALYZE DOCUMENTS TO AS-SURE COMPLIANCE WITH PROCESSING REQUIREMENTS REVIEW "USE AND VALUE OF STI" STATEMENTS IN ABSTRACTS	DOCUMENTS ABSTRACTS REFERRALS RESEARCH AND DEVELOPMENT INFORMATION	W&R
INDEXING BY SUBJECT AND AUTHOR	ABSTRACTS, BIBLI-OGRAPHIES, HARD-COPY (INCLUDING TRANSLATIONS), CITATIONS	W&R

[1] AMONG THE MORE IMPORTANT TECHNICAL RECOMMENDATIONS OF THE WEINBERG REPORT WERE: SCIENTISTS AND ENGINEERS SHOULD BE TAUGHT TO WRITE BETTER ENGLISH, AND SHOULD BE TRAINED IN THE PREPARATION AND USE OF THE LITERATURE. PREPARATION OF "SURVEYING AND SUMMARIZING BOOKS" SHOULD BE SUPPORTED BY THE GOVERNMENT. AN "AD HOC GROUP" OF COSATI SHOULD EXAMINE SECURITY PROBLEMS. FCST SHOULD EXAMINE THE PROBLEMS OF PROPRIETARY INFORMATION.

[2] PROPOSES THAT THE DDC OPERATIONAL DOCUMENT SYSTEM BE EXPANDED SO THAT IT WILL BECOME THE BASIS FOR NATIONAL DOCUMENTATION CENTER AND NATIONAL INFORMA-TION CENTER OPERATIONS. THIS ADDITIONAL DESIGN EFFORT IS TO BE ACCOMPLISHED BY CFSTI. PROPOSES USE OF AUTODIN FOR COMMUNICATION.

Table 7-9a   Technical Aspects of Taube, Kelley, Simpson and Warren Plans

PLAN	SYSTEM INPU	
	TYPE OF DOCUMENTS	MISSION OR DISCIPLIN ORIENTATION
TAUBE "PROPOSAL FOR THE ESTABLISHMENT OF A GOVERNMENT CORPORATION TO CREATE AND PROVIDE SERVICES FROM AN INTEGRATED STORE OF SCIENTIFIC AND TECHNICAL INFORMATION" MORTIMER TAUBE, DOCUMENTATION INC. 30 JULY 1963	TECHNICAL REPORTS FROM GOVERNMENT–SUPPORTED RESEARCH AND DEVELOPMENT	NS
KELLEY "MEMORANDUM FOR DR. JEROME B. WIESNER, SUBJECT: GOVERNMENT SCIENCE PACKAGE" J. HILARY KELLEY, OFFICE OF SCIENCE AND TECHNOLOGY 23 NOVEMBER 1963	ALL CURRENTLY AVAILABLE FEDERAL AND PRIVATE DOCU–MENTATION, BOTH TECHNICAL AND NON–TECHNICAL, BOTH CLASSIFIED AND UNCLASSIFIED	AGENCY OR FUNCTIONAL ORIENTATION
SIMPSON "A PENTAGON OF U.S. SCIENTIFIC AND TECHNICAL INFORMATION AND DATA SERVICES" G. S. SIMPSON, JR., BATTELLE MEMORIAL INSTITUTE 27 NOVEMBER 1963	TECHNICAL REPORTS, DOCUMENTS, JOURNAL ARTICLES, RESEARCH PAPERS, DATA, AND DRAWINGS. NO BOOKS, ENTIRE JOURNALS, LETTERS, PATENTS, PROGRESS REPORTS, OR CONTRACT DOCU–MENTS	ORIENTED BY PARAMETERS O CLASSIFIED–UNCLASSIFIED; DOMESTIC–FOREIGN; DATA–DOCUMENTS
WARREN "MEMORANDUM FOR THE PRESIDENT ON A NATIONAL LIBRARY OF SCIENCE SYSTEM" STAFFORD L. WARREN, M.D., EXECUTIVE OFFICE OF THE PRESIDENT 17 FEBRUARY 1964	SCIENTIFIC JOURNALS ONLY	BOTH, DEPENDING ON "ASSIG MENT OF JOURNAL RESPONSI–BILITY"

LEGEND:

NS = NOT SPECIFIED

Table 7-9a   *(Continued)*

SOURCES OF DOCUMENTS	PRE-INPUT PROCESSING REQUIRED	SYSTEM USERS		TYPES OF REQUESTS
		INSTITUTIONS AND ORGANIZATIONS	INDIVIDUALS	
GOVERNMENT CON-TRACTORS	NS	PARTICIPATING GOV-ERNMENT AGENCIES AND INTERESTED IN-DUSTRIAL ORGANIZA-TIONS	GENERAL SCIENTIFIC COMMUNITY	NS
EXISTING SYSTEMS' SOURCES	NS	EMPHASIS ON GENER-AL PUBLIC RATHER THAN ON ANY "SPECIAL PUBLICS"	ALL CITIZENS	NS
FROM ALL RESEARCH, DEVELOPMENT, TEST, AND EVALUATION OPERATIONS EXCEPT THOSE WHICH ARE EITHER PROPRIETARY OR COPYRIGHT AND WHICH HAVE NO GOV-ERNMENT SUPPORT	NS	LIBRARIES, INFOR-MATION CENTERS, PRIVATE INDUSTRY, UNIVERSITIES	SCIENTISTS, ENGI-NEERS, MANAGERS	NS
OPEN PUBLISHED SCIENTIFIC JOURNAL LITERATURE	SUMMARIZING ABSTRACTING CITATIONAL TRANSLATIONS(SOME)	GOVERNMENT UNIVERSITIES PRIVATE INDUSTRY	SCIENTISTS TECHNOLOGISTS STUDENTS	FOR "SYSTEM TAPES," HARDCOPY (MICROFORM), AND SEARCH REQUESTS

Table 7-9b   Technical Aspects of Taube, Kelley, Simpson and Warren Plans

PLAN	HARDWARE ORIENTATION
TAUBE "PROPOSAL FOR THE ESTABLISHMENT OF A GOVERNMENT CORPORATION TO CREATE AND PROVIDE SERVICES FROM AN INTEGRATED STORE OF SCIENTIFIC AND TECHNICAL INFORMATION" MORTIMER TAUBE, DOCUMENTATION INC. 30 JULY 1963	HEAVY
KELLEY "MEMORANDUM FOR DR. JEROME B. WIESNER, SUBJECT: GOVERNMENT SCIENCE PACKAGE" J. HILARY KELLEY, OFFICE OF SCIENCE AND TECHNOLOGY 23 NOVEMBER 1963	STRESSES THAT EACH REGIONAL CENTER SHOULD USE ADP AND EAM AND ASSOCIATED SOFTWARE
SIMPSON [1] "A PENTAGON OF U.S. SCIENTIFIC AND TECHNICAL INFORMATION AND DATA SERVICES" G. S. SIMPSON, JR., BATTELLE MEMORIAL INSTITUTE 27 NOVEMBER 1963	TO USE EXISTING OPERATING SYSTEM CAPABILITIES
WARREN [2] "MEMORANDUM FOR THE PRESIDENT ON A NATIONAL LIBRARY OF SCIENCE SYSTEM" STAFFORD L. WARREN, M.D., EXECUTIVE OFFICE OF THE PRESIDENT 17 FEBRUARY 1964	HEAVY (SPECIAL EMPHASIS ON COMPUTERS AND TAPE COMPATIBILITY) MICROFORM

LEGEND:

ADP = AUTOMATIC DATA PROCESSING

EAM = ELECTRONIC ACCOUNTING MACHINERY

NS = NOT SPECIFIED

W&R = WHOLESALE AND RETAIL

Table 7-9b   *(Continued)*

TYPES OF INTERNAL PROCESSING	SYSTEM OUTPUTS	
	TYPES	DISSEMINATION
NS	NS	PRIMARILY WHOLE-SALE
NOT SPECIFIED, BUT STRESSES USE OF EXISTING SYSTEMS	EXISTING, PLUS ADDED NONTECHNICAL SERVICES	RETAIL (SELF-SERVICE)
ALL CENTERS AND DEPOTS ARE TO USE: COMPATIBLE INVERTED COORDINATE INDEXING; STANDARD ABSTRACT FORMATS, COMPATIBLE ACCESSION NUMBERING, UNIFIED MACRO- AND MICRO-THESAURI	NS	W&R
COMPUTERIZED INDEXING AND PROCESSING OF SEARCH REQUESTS. STORAGE IN MICROFORM FOR SOURCE MATERIALS	SEARCHABLE TAPES BIBLIOGRAPHIES AND ABSTRACTS HARDCOPY (MICROFORM)	W&R

[1] STRESSES UNIFIED SECURITY CONTROL AND CLASSIFICATION-DECLASSIFICATION SYSTEM. STRESSES THAT NEED-TO-KNOW IS INDEPENDENT OF THE PRODUCING AGENCY. STATES THAT INFORMATION-PROCESSING TECHNIQUES FOR REPRODUCTION AND DISSEMINATION FOR UNCLASSIFIED INFORMATION SHOULD BE INDEPENDENT OF THOSE FOR CLASSIFIED INFORMATION.

[2] EMPHASIS ON STANDARDS (FOR TAPES, FORMAT, INDEXING METHODOLOGY, ETC.)

Table 7-10a   Technical Aspects of Jonker, Goldberg, Mayo-Wells, Kelsey, and Hoshovsky-Album Plans

PLAN	TYPE OF DOCUMENTS	SYSTEM IN MISSION OR DISCIPLI ORIENTATION
JONKER "A MODEL INFORMATION RETRIEVAL NETWORK FOR GOVERNMENT, SCIENCE, AND INDUSTRY" FREDERICK JONKER, ET AL., JONKER BUSINESS MACHINES, INC. MAY 1964 SPONSOR: INFORMATION RESEARCH DIVISION AIR FORCE OFFICE OF SCIENTIFIC RESEARCH	INITIALLY: WORLD-WIDE SCIENTIFIC AND TECHNICAL INFORMATION (CLASSIFIED AND UNCLASSIFIED), AND RESEARCH AND DEVELOPMENT PROJECT INFORMATION. LATER: INFORMAL AND UNPUBLISHED INFORMATION, DATA, AND PRODUCT DESCRIPTIONS.	BOTH TYPES OF INFORMAT RETRIEVAL NETWORKS AR DISCUSSED
GOLDBERG "ENGINEERING DATA AND INFORMATION SYSTEM (EDIS)" STANLEY A. GOLDBERG, ET AL., OFFICE OF THE DIRECTOR OF ARMY TECHNICAL INFORMATION JULY 1964 SPONSOR: OFFICE OF THE CHIEF OF RESEARCH AND DEVELOPMENT DEPARTMENT OF THE ARMY	ALL ENGINEERING DATA AND INFORMATION FOR RESEARCH, DEVELOPMENT, TESTING, AND EVALUATION	ENGINEERING DISCIPLINES (E.G., MECHANICAL, CHEMICAL, ELECTRICAL)
MAYO-WELLS "ORGANIZATION OF A NATIONAL SCIENTIFIC AND TECHNICAL INFORMATION CENTER" WILFRID JAMES MAYO-WELLS, CONSULTANT 7 OCTOBER 1964	"ALL INFORMATION ON SCIENCE AND TECHNOLOGY THAT DEFINES THE STATE-OF-THE-ART, SPECIFIES ADVANCES IN THE ART, AND PROMISES ADVANCES IN THE ART."	BOTH
KELSEY "A NATIONAL DRUG INFORMATION CLEARINGHOUSE" F. ELLIS KELSEY, PUBLIC HEALTH SERVICE 8 DECEMBER 1964	NS	DISCIPLINE-ORIENTED CL INGHOUSES TO SERVE MIS ORIENTED INFORMATION C TERS
HOSHOVSKY-ALBUM "TOWARD A NATIONAL TECHNICAL INFORMATION SYSTEM" A. G. HOSHOVSKY AND H. H. ALBUM, OFFICE OF AEROSPACE RESEARCH, U. S. AIR FORCE JANUARY 1965	RECORDED SCIENTIFIC KNOWLEDGE. INFORMATION CONCERNING ACTIVE RESEARCH AND DEVELOPMENT EFFORTS FOREIGN AND DOMESTIC	EMPHASIS ON MISSION (C DISCIPLINARY) BUT SOME DISCIPLINARY

LEGEND:

NS = NOT SPECIFIED

Table 7-10a   *(Continued)*

		SYSTEM USERS		
SOURCES OF DOCUMENTS	PRE-INPUT PROCESSING REQUIRED	INSTITUTIONS AND ORGANIZATIONS	INDIVIDUALS	TYPES OF REQUESTS
ALL SCIENTIFIC, TECHNICAL, AND RE-SEARCH AND DEVEL-OPMENT ORGANIZA-TIONS AND INDIVID-UALS PUBLISHERS	ALMOST NONE	ALL-INCLUSIVE WITHIN A NETWORK, SUBJECT TO SECURITY AND PROPRIETARY CLEARANCES. CONCEPT OF "USE UNITS" IS DEVELOPED, TO INCLUDE BOTH ORGANIZATIONS AND INDIVIDUALS.		BIBLIOGRAPHIC AND SUBJECT SEARCHES HARDCOPY
HOME DATA AND IN-FORMATION BANKS	INDEXING	GOVERNMENT, IN-DUSTRY (CONTRAC-TORS AND VENDORS)	FROM BENCH-LEVEL SCIENTISTS AND ENGI-NEERS TO TOP-LEVEL MANAGEMENT	FOR EITHER DOCU-MENTS OR DATA
NS	NONE	ALL-INCLUSIVE	ALL-INCLUSIVE	NS
NS	NS	HEW ORGANIZATIONS, OTHER FEDERAL GOV-ERNMENT ENTITIES, STATE AND LOCAL GOVERNMENTS, UNI-VERSITIES, PROFES-SIONAL SOCIETIES, INDUSTRY, AND IN-TERNATIONAL ORGAN-IZATIONS	RESEARCH WORKERS AND ADMINISTRATORS, REGULATORY AGENCY PERSONNEL, PHYSI-CIANS AND OTHER HEALTH-CARE PER-SONNEL	NS
GOVERNMENT, PRIVATE, AND FOREIGN	TRANSLATING, AB-STRACTING	ALL-INCLUSIVE	ENGINEERS, SCIEN-TISTS, GOVERNMENT AND NON-GOVERNMENT MANAGERS	FOR REFERRAL, HARDCOPY, BIBLI-OGRAPHIES, AB-STRACTS

Table 7-10b   Technical Aspects of Jonker, Goldberg, Mayo-Wells, Kelsey, and Hoshovsky-Album

	HARDWARE ORIENTATION
JONKER[1] "A MODEL INFORMATION RETRIEVAL NETWORK FOR GOVERNMENT, SCIENCE, AND INDUSTRY" FREDERICK JONKER, ET AL., JONKER BUSINESS MACHINES, INC. MAY 1964 SPONSOR: INFORMATION RESEARCH DIVISION AIR FORCE OFFICE OF SCIENTIFIC RESEARCH	MODEST USE OF COMPUTERS AND COMMUNICATIONS HARDWARE AT SUPPORT AND CONTROL CENTERS ALSO 16MM MICROFILM
GOLDBERG[2] "ENGINEERING DATA AND INFORMATION SYSTEM (EDIS)" STANLEY A. GOLDBERG, ET AL., OFFICE OF THE DIRECTOR OF ARMY TECHNICAL INFORMATION JULY 1964 SPONSOR: OFFICE OF THE CHIEF OF RESEARCH AND DEVELOPMENT DEPARTMENT OF THE ARMY	COMPUTERS THOUGHT TO BE ADVANTAGEOUS RELIANCE ON EXISTING EQUIPMENT
MAYO-WELLS "ORGANIZATION OF A NATIONAL SCIENTIFIC AND TECHNICAL INFORMATION CENTER" WILFRID JAMES MAYO-WELLS, CONSULTANT 7 OCTOBER 1964	EMPHASIZES SOFTWARE AND THEORY DEVELOPMENT
KELSEY[3] "A NATIONAL DRUG INFORMATION CLEARINGHOUSE" F. ELLIS KELSEY, PUBLIC HEALTH SERVICE 8 DECEMBER 1964	EMPHASIZES USE OF MODERN HARDWARE OF ALL TYPES
HOSHOVSKY-ALBUM[4] "TOWARD A NATIONAL TECHNICAL INFORMATION SYSTEM" A. G. HOSHOVSKY AND H. H. ALBUM, OFFICE OF AEROSPACE RESEARCH, U. S. AIR FORCE JANUARY 1965	EMPHASIZES USE OF ADP IN THE NATIONAL TECHNICAL INFORMATION AGENCY

LEGEND:
ADP = AUTOMATIC DATA PROCESSING
DDC = DEFENSE DOCUMENTATION CENTER
NS = NOT SPECIFIED
W&R = WHOLESALE AND RETAIL

Table 7-10b   (Continued)

TYPES OF INTERNAL PROCESSING	SYSTEM OUTPUTS	
	TYPES	DISSEMINATION
SUBJECT SEARCH SELECTIVE DISSEMINATION PROCESSING BIBLIOGRAPHIES INDEXING ABSTRACTING TRANSLATING (ASSUMED)	16MM MICROFILM INDEXES TO USERS HARDCOPY BIBLIOGRAPHIES ABSTRACTS	W&R. USER PROFILES ARE TO BE EMPLOYED.
INDEXING, REFERRAL, AND STORAGE OF DATA AND DOCUMENTS	DATA AND HARDCOPY DOCUMENTS	WHOLESALE AND RETAIL FROM SWITCHING CENTER. RETAIL FROM HOME BANKS.
CATALOGING, ABSTRACTING, AND ANALYSIS	DATA, DOCUMENTS, ANNUAL REVIEWS OF STATE-OF-THE-ART, PERIODIC NEWSLETTERS	W&R
ALL KINDS, INCLUDING RETROSPECTIVE SEARCH	NS	SOME WHOLESALE, BUT MOSTLY RETAIL THROUGH DECENTRALIZED DISSEMINATION
INDEXING, SEARCHING	NOTIFICATION OF DDC AVAILABILITY, HARDCOPY, MICROFORM, ABSTRACTS, BIBLIOGRAPHIC IDENTIFICATION	W&R

[1] WEEKLY ISSUANCE OF DOCUMENTS RECEIVED BY SELECTIVE DISSEMINATION
QUARTERLY ISSUANCE OF TITLE LISTS WITH TERM ABSTRACTS
COORDINATED INDEX

[2] SUGGESTS DEVELOPMENT OF A COMMON LANGUAGE FOR COMMUNICATIONS INTERFACES

[3] MENTIONS NEED FOR STANDARD VOCABULARY

[4] CALLS FOR DEVELOPMENT OF STANDARDS

Table 7-11   Technical Recommendations in National Information System Plans

RECOMMENDATION	STANFORD (SRI)	CRAWFORD	CAHN	WEINBERG	MANAGEMENT TECHNOLOGY	HELLER
DEVELOP STANDARDS		■			■	
DEVELOP EDUCATIONAL CURRICULA	■		■	■	■	
STUDY REQUIREMENTS FOR EQUIPMENT AND FACILITIES, AND FOR IMPROVING MACHINE CAPABILITIES	■	■	■	■	■	
STUDY USER NEEDS AND CHARACTERISTICS	■				■	
DEVELOP SUBJECT–FIELD THESAURI			■		■	
INCREASE USE OF AUTHOR–WRITTEN ABSTRACTS			■		■	
DEVELOP USER STATISTICS (NATURE, FREQUENCY, AND NUMBER OF INQUIRIES)	■				■	
EXPAND RESEARCH IN INFORMATION SCIENCE		■			■	
IMPROVE EXISTING PUBLICATIONS			■			■
STUDY DISSEMINATION TECHNIQUES FOR BOTH DOCUMENT AND NONDOCUMENT INFORMATION			■			
IMPROVE COMMUNICATIONS TECHNOLOGY		■				
IMPROVE TECHNICAL WRITING		■	■			
INCREASE USE OF TECHNICAL EVALUATION OF INFORMATION		■	■			
ASSESS DISTRIBUTION OF SOURCES OF TECHNICAL INFORMATION BY COUNTRY AND BY LANGUAGE	■					
ASSESS VOLUME OF TECHNICAL PUBLICATIONS IN VARIOUS SUBJECT–FIELD CATEGORIES	■					
CONDUCT RESEARCH TO IMPROVE FRUITFULNESS OF PROFESSIONAL SOCIETY MEETINGS		■				
CONSIDER QUESTION OF WHAT KINDS OF INFORMATION THE SYSTEM SHOULD PROCESS						
DEVELOP COMPATIBLE INVERTED–COORDINATE INDEXING TECHNIQUES						
DEVELOP MORE POWERFUL THEORIES FOR STORING AND RETRIEVING INFORMATION						
DEVELOP STANDARDIZED ABSTRACT FORMATS						
INCREASE USE OF ENCYCLOPEDIC FUNCTION, E.G., SURVEY ARTICLES, TEXTS, COMPILATIONS			■			
INVENTORY ABSTRACTING AND INDEXING SERVICES	■					
INVENTORY MAJOR LIBRARIES AND PROFESSIONAL SOCIETIES						
STUDY COPYRIGHT PROBLEMS						
STUDY INFORMAL COMMUNICATIONS		■				
STUDY PROBLEMS OF CLASSIFIED AND PROPRIETARY INFORMATION			■			
STUDY PROBLEMS OF ORGANIZING AND CODIFYING KNOWLEDGE INTO SUBJECT FIELDS			■			
TRAIN USERS IN HOW TO USE INFORMATION RESOURCES			■			

Table 7-11   (Continued)

PLAN

TAUBE	KELLEY	SIMPSON	WARREN	JONKER	GOLDBERG	MAYO-WELLS	KELSEY	HOSHOVSKY-ALBUM
		■	■		■	■	■	
		■	■					
		■						
				■		■		
	■	■		■		■		
							■	
						■		
■				■				
							■	
					■	■		
						■		
			■					
	■							
					■			
	■							
		■						
				■				

CAUTIONARY NOTE: WE HAVE NOT ATTEMPTED TO MAKE THE ABOVE LIST AN EXHAUSTIVE COMPILATION OF THE RECOMMENDATIONS SET FORTH IN THE PLANS REVIEWED, NOR HAVE WE REFRAINED FROM GENERALIZING CERTAIN SPECIFIC RECOMMENDATIONS IN ORDER TO MERGE THEM WITH RECOMMENDATIONS FROM OTHER PLANS. THUS, THE LIST SHOULD NOT BE CONSIDERED AS REFLECTING ANYTHING OTHER THAN OUR INTERPRETATION OF THE MORE SIGNIFICANT TECHNICAL RECOMMENDATIONS IN THE PLANS FOR A NATIONAL INFORMATION SYSTEM.

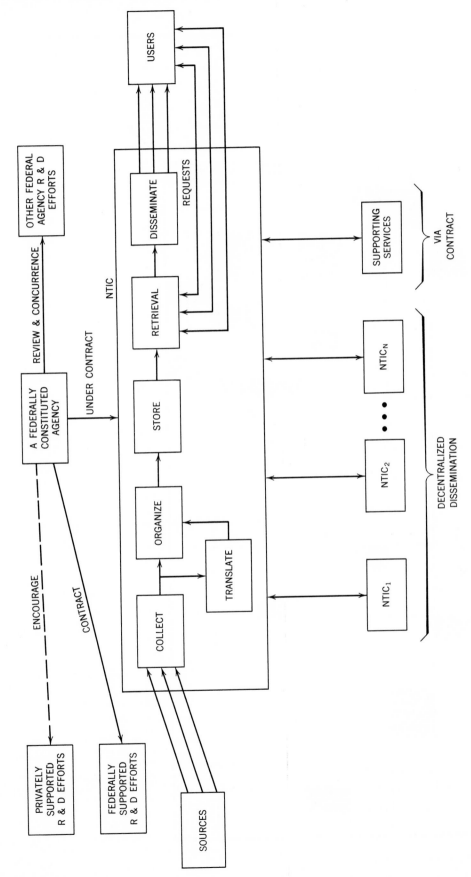

Fig. 7-1 Stanford Research (SRI).

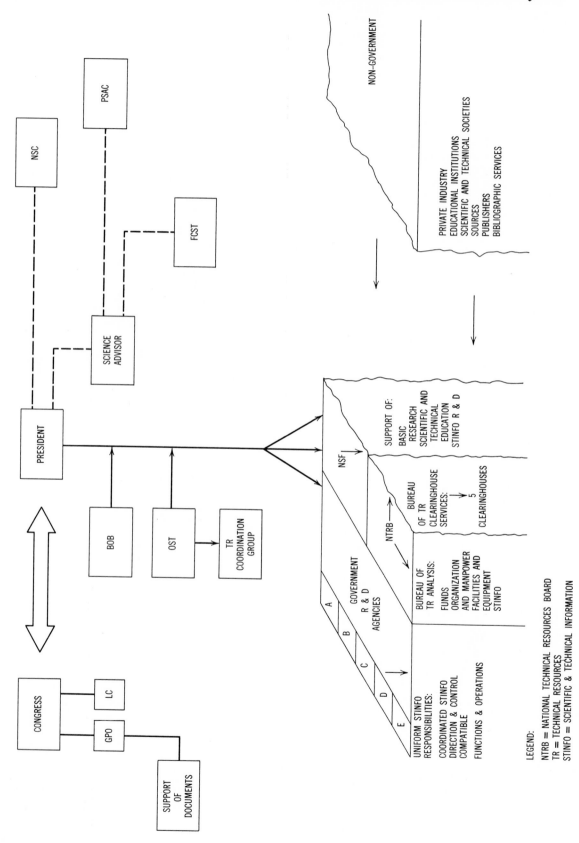

Fig. 7-2 Crawford.

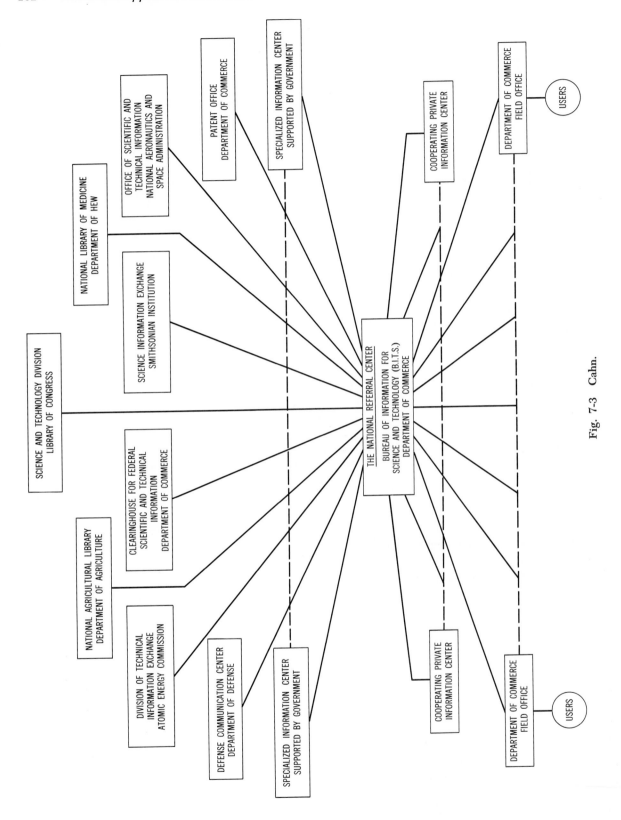

Fig. 7-3   Cahn.

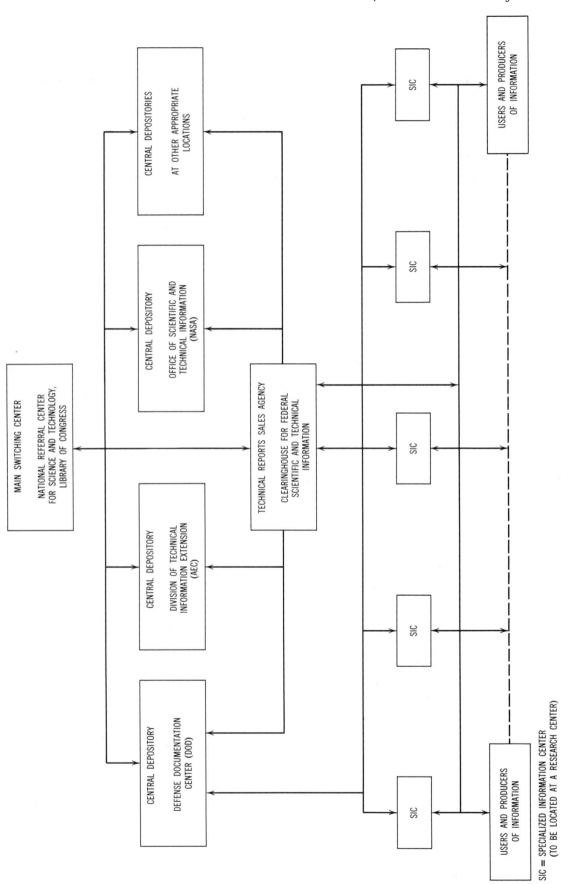

SIC = SPECIALIZED INFORMATION CENTER
(TO BE LOCATED AT A RESEARCH CENTER)

Fig. 7-4 Weinberg.

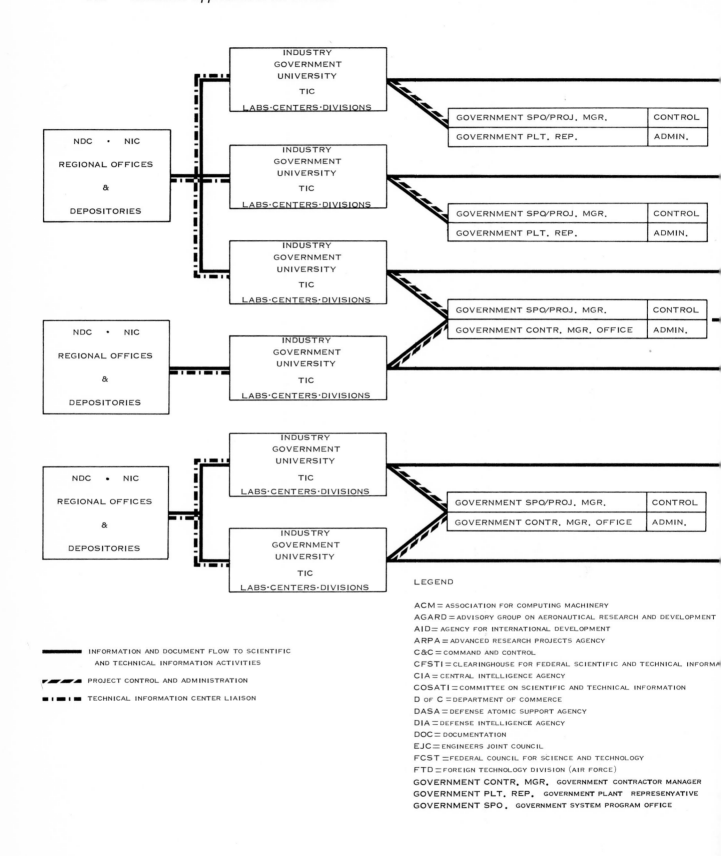

Fig. 7-5 Management technology.

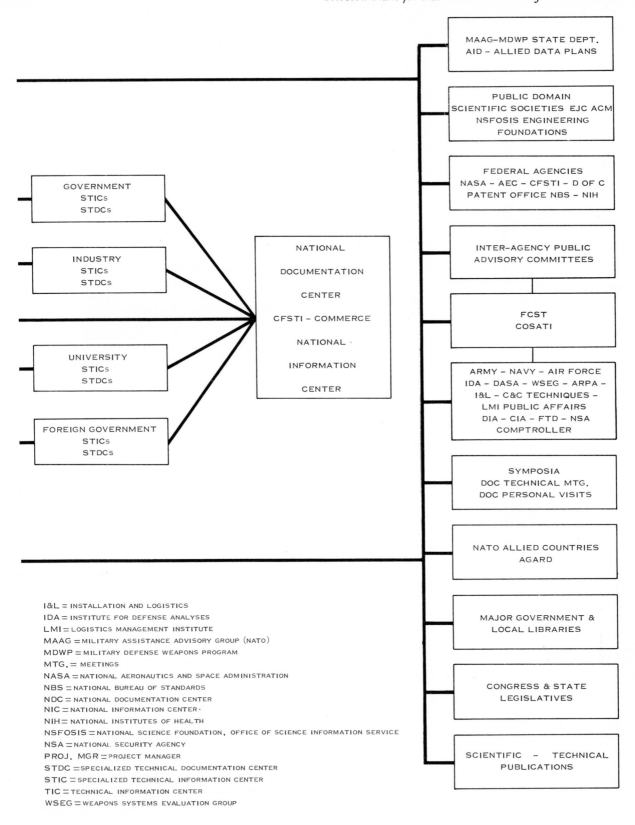

I&L = INSTALLATION AND LOGISTICS
IDA = INSTITUTE FOR DEFENSE ANALYSES
LMI = LOGISTICS MANAGEMENT INSTITUTE
MAAG = MILITARY ASSISTANCE ADVISORY GROUP (NATO)
MDWP = MILITARY DEFENSE WEAPONS PROGRAM
MTG. = MEETINGS
NASA = NATIONAL AERONAUTICS AND SPACE ADMINISTRATION
NBS = NATIONAL BUREAU OF STANDARDS
NDC = NATIONAL DOCUMENTATION CENTER
NIC = NATIONAL INFORMATION CENTER·
NIH = NATIONAL INSTITUTES OF HEALTH
NSFOSIS = NATIONAL SCIENCE FOUNDATION, OFFICE OF SCIENCE INFORMATION SERVICE
NSA = NATIONAL SECURITY AGENCY
PROJ. MGR = PROJECT MANAGER
STDC = SPECIALIZED TECHNICAL DOCUMENTATION CENTER
STIC = SPECIALIZED TECHNICAL INFORMATION CENTER
TIC = TECHNICAL INFORMATION CENTER
WSEG = WEAPONS SYSTEMS EVALUATION GROUP

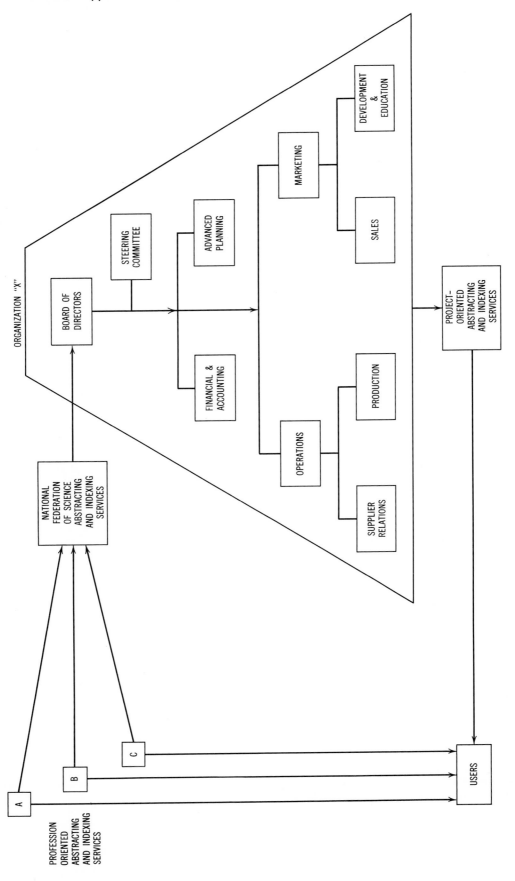

Fig. 7-6 Heller.

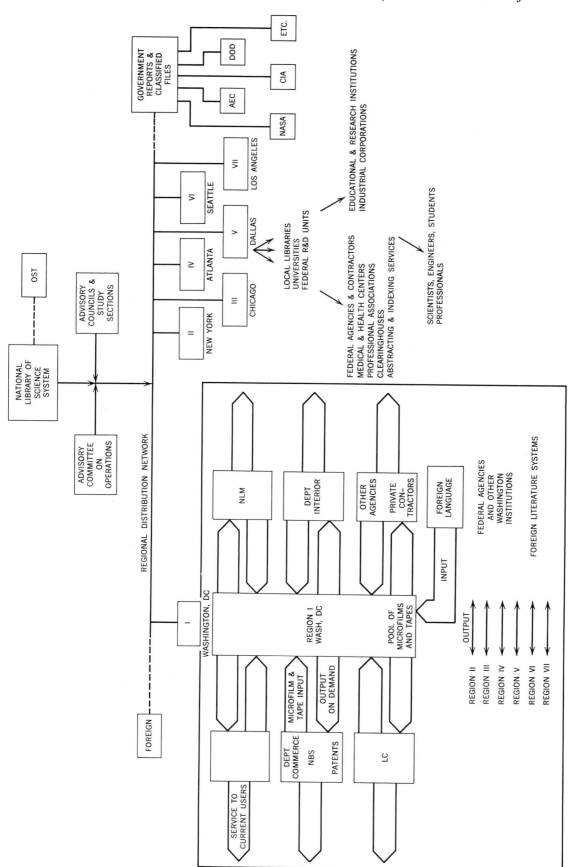

Fig. 7-7 Warren.

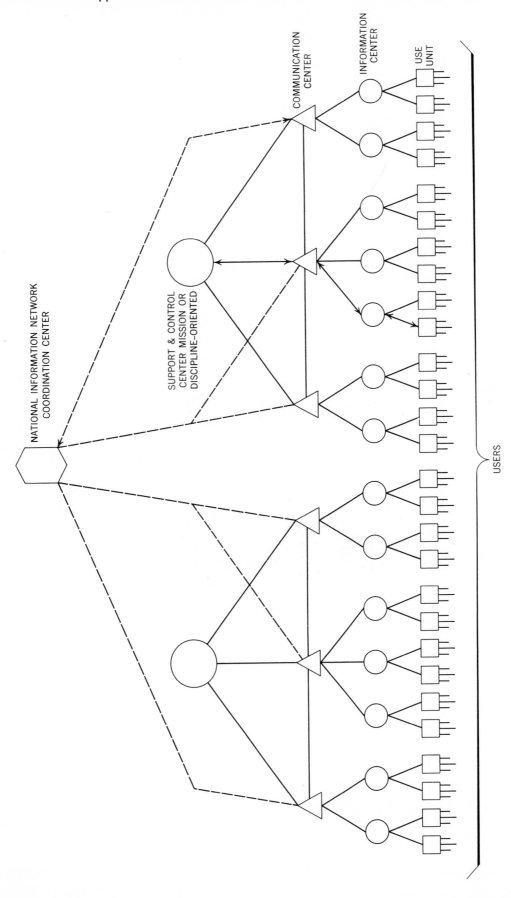

Fig. 7-8   Jonker.

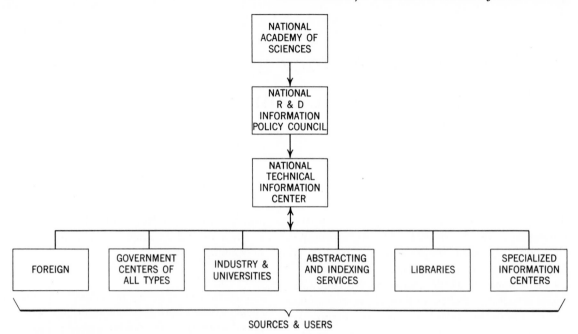

Fig. 7-9   Hoshovsky-Album.

The Capping Agency and Responsible Agent Concepts

This and the next two chapters present the recommended system concept and several alternative concepts. Each major design is considered in detail relative to its operating characteristics, the functions it would perform, its organizational structure, and feasibility of its implementation. Once the idea has been developed, the arguments in favor of and opposed to the particular design are given. In Chapter 11, after all the alternatives have been considered individually, evaluative comparisons are made. These comparisons show the relative strength and weakness of each of the different concepts.

The number of basically different approaches that can be taken to the S&T document and information problem is fairly limited. We consider four quite different approaches (although there are three variations to one idea). One formulation emphasizes the need for an integrative and planning activity relative to national and federal policy, another emphasizes the idea of establishing responsibilities for the several federal departments and agencies, a different conception involves the centralization into one large federal or private organization of all operating responsibility, while another features the slow evolution of the existing system. All of these can be given various interpretations and emphasis and can also be considered in several combinations.

A CAPPING AGENCY

Several considerations presented in Chapter 6, where the requirements for a national system were stated, lead to the recommendation that a capping agency be established. Here the nature and functions of the agency are presented. The agency's name, organization, placement, and costs are considered. Finally, the arguments in favor of and opposed to such an agency are presented.

Functions

The functions to be performed by the new agency, called here the "Scientific and Technical Information Bureau," are presented below.

It is hard to overemphasize the importance of these functions. They represent activities that must be performed someplace in the executive branch of the government if we are to have an integrated and planned national S&T document system. Our original report did not make this point strongly enough and some seemed to believe that our emphasis was on a capping agency per se. It is true we judge that it was unlikely any of the existing agencies would—without very significant changes—be able to perform these functions adequately and our reasons are given later. But we wish to say again that the critical point is that the functions discussed below must be performed with authority by some part of the executive branch.

Formulate Policy Regarding the Areas of Responsibility for National S&T Information and Documentation Activities. There are now several national libraries, and it is argued that several other national systems should be established. The Bureau should determine the S&T information and documentation areas to be covered by the several departments and agencies. It should define the responsibility of the departments and agencies relative to a broad range of activities, as implied by the additional functions enumerated below.

Formulate Policy Regarding Nongovernment Libraries. The Bureau should establish federal pol-

icy with respect to support and cooperation with nongovernment libraries. As the federal S&T information and documentation program becomes elaborated and standardized, it will have a significant effect on nongovernment libraries. Problems of the nature of support to be given such libraries need to be considered. Some federal agencies may delegate part of their responsibilities to libraries or organizations outside the government. To the extent that major university libraries or private libraries support or back up federal interests, they should be supported by federal funds. At present there is no comprehensive national policy defining the expectations or relations between the federal government and the private S&T information and documentation sector.

Formulate Policy Regarding Information Centers. There are some 300 major science and technology information centers throughout the country. Some of these are supported by the federal government, some are in private industry, and some are in universities. The services they render differ widely, ranging from centers which make simple referral, to centers which supply facts regarding physical phenomena, to centers which undertake detailed analyses with associated conclusions. User knowledge regarding these centers varies from complete unfamiliarity to that developed through intimate use. Consistent federal policy needs to be formulated regarding support and sponsorship of information centers.

Formulate Policy for Depositories of Government Documents. At the present time there are more than 1200 libraries throughout the country which are depositories of government documents. The extent of their receipts and holdings differs considerably. Some receive all "official" GPO-published documents, others receive documents from specific government departments, others are depositories for the government-supported "report" literature. Generally, these libraries do not receive support for the costs of personnel or space associated with handling government documents. Policy regarding distribution, processing, and support for these depositories needs to be developed.

Formulate Policy for Support of Nongovernment Publications. At the present time there are many

practices being followed with respect to nongovernment scientific and technical publications. In the primary publication field there is some direct subvention; there is often payment of page charges through research contracts, and at times journals published by professional societies refuse direct payment of page charges on the ground that it gives authors of government-supported research an advantage over other researchers. Similarly, in the secondary publications area, some abstracting publications receive a very substantial subsidy while other abstracting services receive none, or have yet to obtain any. Policy and funding patterns in this area need rationalization.

Formulate Policy Regarding Nondocumentary Communications. Many studies show that a primary method of communication among scientists consists of both formal and informal nondocumentary methods of letters, visits, small meetings, symposia, and national meetings. Federal policy relative to such activities varies. Sometimes travel is supported directly or through contract, sometimes symposia are supported, sometimes national meetings are supported through the mechanism of substantial registration fees which are paid by those working under government contract. This whole area needs extensive study, policy development, and implementation.

Collect Statistical Information. The study team's data collection activities revealed that effective management is being inhibited by lack of reliable statistics in the S&T area. Although this book contains a large amount of statistical information, it is often far short of that required for maintaining a well-rationalized system. Figures on size of collections, use statistics, and budgets are often not comparable from activity to activity. It is well known that the Department of Labor and the Office of Education were faced with these problems in their fields and have made progress in developing sound data bases. An effort needs to be made throughout the S&T information and document area to develop reliable statistical information.

Establish Standards. The Bureau should develop minimal standards for information handling to be followed by all federal organizations having S&T information and document responsibilities. These standards should include both perfor-

mance standards and technical standards. Performance standards are concerned with such matters as completeness of coverage, speed of service, nature and quality of services to users, etc. Technical standards deal with a number of detailed problems such as cataloging standards, methods of classification, bibliographic standards, standards relative to the use of microstorage, and standards to be used in the application of automation techniques.

Recommend Information Science Research. The National Science Foundation now has an important responsibility for both information science research and various science information activities. The establishment of the Bureau would change this situation relative to the science information area. However, it is anticipated that basic information science research would remain a responsibility of NSF and enjoy the same status as any other major area of scientific research. The Bureau should make recommendations regarding needed areas of research support.

Promote the Development of Information Technology. There needs to be broad guidance and encouragement in the development of advanced technology in the S&T area. The requirements listed in Chapter 6 spell out this need. With several notable exceptions, libraries have been slow to adopt new technology. The Bureau should actively support the application of advanced technology and automation techniques to government libraries and other information centers. Networks should be developed to rapidly retrieve information and documents and to transmit such material to users throughout the country. The effecting of proper coordination and active promotion should be a high-priority activity of the Bureau.

Formulate Policy for the Training of Librarians and Information Technologists. There is currently a shortage of information technologists and librarians trained in science and technology, and the situation will not improve under the current level of interest and support. Federal policy regarding the support of training of librarians and information technologists needs to be stated and funds need to be made available for this purpose. Such responsibility should be discharged by the Bureau.

Formulate Policy Regarding Foreign Documents. There are many more foreign than domestic serials and documents, although 60 per cent of all S&T documents are published in English. There are two major problems in this area: (a) in the acquiring of the documents and (b) in their translation.

Acquiring documents involves the State Department, the Smithsonian Institution, the Library of Congress, the National Library of Medicine, the National Agricultural Library, and various intelligence activities. Some feeling for the magnitude of the problem can be gathered from the fact that the Smithsonian Institution, as the major government agent for foreign exchange, handles over a million tons of exchange documents annually. Because many agencies are involved in acquisition there is a considerable amount of duplicate acquisition. Even so, there are many gaps in our coverage of foreign literature.

Translation also presents a problem—Americans are notoriously weak in languages other than English, and the development of services to assure awareness and to facilitate abstracting needs attention. Extensive study and policy formulation is required.

Publicize Information about Information Services. Many scientists and engineers are uninformed regarding services which are now available. The Defense Documentation Center, the Clearinghouse for Federal Scientific and Technical Information, the National Referral Center for Science and Technology, and other information centers are often unknown to working professionals. The Bureau should be responsible for publicizing sources of information and services and help in training users to effectively use the available services.

Formulate Copyright and Patent Policy. The Copyright Office is in the Library of Congress. In addition to published material, software (computer programs, manuals, training programs) is now under the jurisdiction of the Copyright Office and is becoming an important proprietary commodity. As documents reporting the details of software developments and the knowledge they contain become more valuable, problems of protection of proprietary rights will become more acute. Already cheap and efficient copying techniques are raising copyright problems and, as large computer net-

works are developed to transmit data stores and documents, the problem will become urgent. A centralized policy agency in the executive branch is needed to consider these problems, and the Bureau should serve this function.

Perform Budget Review and Funding Control. S&T information and documentation represents a major federal direct expenditure of about $200 million annually. (This figure is probably much too low; some estimates show the figure to be about $400 million.) In addition to normal department review by the Bureau of the Budget there should be an across-the-board review and funding control by the Information Bureau for the S&T information and documentation area. The Bureau should determine that each activity is discharging its established responsibilities and is requesting sufficient funds to do so, and the Bureau should have funds of its own which it can transfer to various departments for special development activities. The Bureau should also have responsibility for defending before Congress the total government program in the S&T information and documentation area. No doubt the several agencies will still need to defend their individual programs, but the Congress should have one central contact point for the national program.

Formulate Policy for Legislative Relations and Legal Matters. As the agency responsible for the national S&T information and documentation program, the Bureau should review all administration-developed legislative proposals in this area. It should generate proposals where national policies are concerned.

Develop Long-Range Plans. Chapter 7 details fifteen plans that have been developed since 1958 to deal with the problem of handling scientific and technical information. While many of these plans are excellent in conception, they are single planning attempts and do not represent a continuing planning effort. The development of technology and the growing requirement for service indicate the need for a continuing planning activity in the S&T information and documentation area.

Organization

As indicated later in considering the placement of the Bureau, it should probably be estab-

lished as an independent agency. A suggested organization is presented in Table 8-1.

Office of the Director. The organization of the Bureau has been developed in terms of the functions which need to be discharged. Two advisory groups are indicated. It is believed that a group such as the present COSATI organization should be retained. This would provide a communication link between the director and the chief scientific and technical information officer of each of the departments and agencies. Similarly, a nonfederal advisory group is indicated to represent the nongovernment library and information science community. Two groups are suggested rather than a single one because it is believed that the problems and concerns of the two communities are somewhat different as they relate to the Bureau's functions. The director would have line responsibility for the operation of the Bureau and would see that it performs the functions discussed above.

Office of Information Services. The primary function of this office is the supplying of information about the Bureau and services available in the S&T information and documentation area. The range of services available and the many places at which they can be obtained do not seem to be as well known among system users as is desirable. Since the Bureau and the concepts it will develop will be new and not well understood, an extensive educational program will be needed within both the federal government and the nonfederal community.

Systems Office. The Systems Office is primarily concerned with defining policy and establishing responsibilities relative to the federal scientific and technical information and document system. Its orientation is focused within the government. This office's functions are concerned with establishing policy, giving guidance to other government departments, and agencies, and reviewing budgets for S&T activities.

External Policies and Support Office. This office is concerned with S&T problems which are primarily external to the federal government. This office would be concerned with government interaction with nonfederal libraries, with publishers of primary and secondary documents, and with other functions listed on the organization chart. Foreign acquisition, exchange, and translation policy would fall into this office. We have

Table 8-1   The Capping Agency

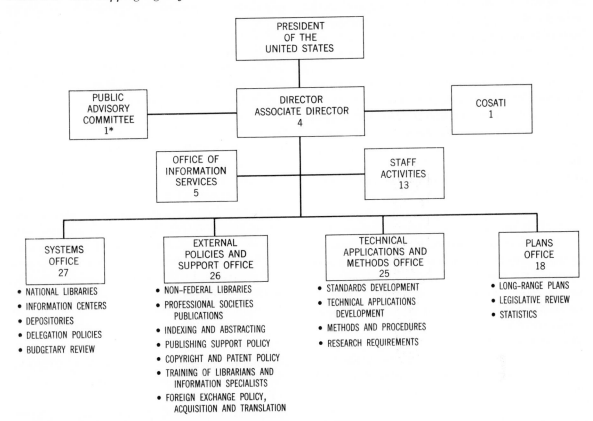

*NUMBERS REPRESENT APPROXIMATE SIZE OF THE PROFESSIONAL STAFF FOR EACH UNIT.

also placed problems in the area of indexing and abstracting in this office, since most of these services originate outside of the federal government. At the same time, indexing and abstracting services form an integral part of any formal document system, and it might be argued that actions involving them might have considerable impact on the activities of the Systems Office. However, this argument can be made about almost any function since all activities should support system operation; and it does not seem to contradict this placement in the External Policies and Support Office.

Technical Applications and Methods Office. The activities of this office are defined by the functions indicated on the organization chart. It should be stressed that the development of standards is most important to a well-functioning system. Likewise, this office will need to take the national lead in both developing and promoting new technology as it applies to the S&T information and documentation area. By and large, librarians are not trained in the technical disciplines and have tended to be slow in pushing for the application of modern technology

partially because of their lack of technical orientation. But a more important reason for this slow application of modern technology is that these techniques have not been well adapted to use in libraries. For example, computers have been vigorously applied to problems of scientific computation and commercial record-keeping, but the necessary funding and technical development have not been forthcoming to make them easily applied to document handling. This office should support through funding and leadership the development of document handling technology.

Plans Office. The Plans Office performs a function which has long been needed. The collection of statistics in the S&T information and documentation area is assigned to this office, since a collection of sound statistics is fundamental to good planning. The legislative review function is likewise here, since proposals for legislation should result from planning activities.

Name of the Capping Agency

The name of the capping agency should indicate its stature and function. Unfortunately,

within the Executive Office of the President and in the independent offices and establishments area there does not seem to be any consistent nomenclature regarding names. There are bureaus, offices, councils, commissions, administrations, and agencies.

Although the choice is not clear-cut we tend to favor "Scientific and Technical Information Bureau." "Bureau" brings to mind the Bureau of the Budget, which has many of the same functions relative to federal budget activities that this new Bureau would have with respect to federal scientific and technical information activities.

Placement

There are a number of possible placements for the Bureau. Although many different placements might be considered, those which seem most feasible are presented below. Our recommendation is that the Bureau be organizationally a part of the independent offices and establishments and be given the executive and directive authority of the President for discharging the duties and functions detailed above. As a rough analogy, the authority of the Bureau can be thought of as similar to that of the Civil Service Commission relative to federal personnel policies and practices; namely, it would set policies and monitor other organizations but not perform the actual operations. It would be preferable to place the Bureau in the Executive Office of the President since such placement would emphasize the directive and review authority of the Bureau relative to the departments and independent agencies. However, the Bureau's size (approximately 120 professionals and 130 other people) and detailed technical work probably argue against this. Except for the CIA, which is a special case, the Bureau of the Budget, with about 475 people, is the largest organization in the Executive Office. All of the other offices are considerably smaller; the Office of Science and Technology, for example, has fewer than 25 professionals. That an organization in the independent offices and establishments can exercise the requisite authority required by the Bureau can be illustrated by the United States Civil Service Commission. The Civil Service Commission operates under several acts of Congress dating back to 1883, but it also derives considerable authority from executive orders and the Reorganization Act of 1949. Its functions relative to personnel matters are multitudinous and authoritative relative to other departments and agencies. A somewhat comparable authority needs to be vested in the Bureau. In view of the statutory status of scientific and technical information activities in the several departments and agencies, a careful job of drafting appropriate legislation needs to be undertaken. (See Appendix 3 for a summary of current statutory laws in this area.)

Bureau of the Budget. It has been suggested that the Bureau might well be a part of the Bureau of the Budget. The BOB does have budget review authority and also has considerable management authority relative to the departments and agencies. The Bureau needs to exercise both of these in the S&T information area. Nevertheless, it is believed such a placement would not be wise. In the first place the Bureau needs to exert considerable technical supervision, which requires very specialized manpower quite different from that in the BOB. Furthermore, it is desired to make the S&T area stand out as an independent area; just as personnel activities or budget activities are independently supervised, so should S&T activities be independent. Finally, to do an adequate job the Bureau needs about 250 people; it seems unlikely that the BOB, in its present form, could expand that much for a single, nonbudgetary functional area.

General Services Administration. It has also been suggested that the Bureau might be a part of the General Services Administration (GSA). There are several points in favor of such a placement. GSA has as its mission the servicing of other departments and agencies, and this is also one of the Bureau's functions. Also, GSA has responsibility for the establishment and operations of the Federal Telecommunications System and for many administrative and coordinating activities relative to automatic data processing equipment and software (see BOB Circular No. A-71, dated March 6, 1965). Certainly, telecommunications and automation equipment will be most important to the Bureau's work. Finally, the National Archives and Records Service is a part of GSA. The National Archives and Records Service includes the keeping of historical documents, the maintenance of regional government records centers, and the operation of the various Presidential Libraries. Arguments against such a placement center around a prevalent

attitude that GSA is concerned with rather mundane nontechnical areas like motor pools and janitorial service, and that to be successful the Bureau must be perceived as a technically oriented organization. Furthermore, many of the Bureau's activities are oriented toward non-federal aspects of the S&T information and documentation area, and GSA is less responsible here than toward government services. Finally, the S&T information and document area needs the status and prominence an independent organization would give it.

National Science Foundation. It has been suggested that the Bureau be placed with the National Science Foundation which now has a sizable program in the Office of Science Information Service (OSIS) and in its other divisions. Would it not be sensible to expand NSF to include the functions listed for the Bureau? There is much to be said for this suggestion. The NSF has the nucleus of the necessary staff, and for a number of years has been concerned with research and development in this area. The NSF's close association with the scientific community would be a distinct asset. The major, and seemingly overriding, argument against such a placement is the fact that traditionally NSF has deliberately stayed away from either operating responsibility or overall policy direction relative to other departments or agencies. If NSF's general role in the government were to change in the direction of operations or policy setting, then the Bureau's placement with NSF would be reasonable, but present practices argue against this.

Staffing the Bureau

Presented below is a breakdown of the staffing of the Bureau. Clearly, such a statement of personnel requirements must be only approximate, but there is a need for understanding the general size and character of the organization. The figures indicate that we are talking about an organization of about 120 professional people or a total of about 250 people, when clerical, stenographic, and other support personnel are included. A first-order detailing of the professional staff requirements of the Bureau is shown in Table 8-2a, b, and c. In evaluating these personnel requirements it is important to remember the functions to be served by each unit of the Bureau.

Table 8-2a   Professional Staffing of the Bureau

Director's Office	2	Senior science administrators
	2	Technical assistants
	2	Staff assistants
Total	6	
Information Service Office	2	Librarians
	1	Information technologist
	2	Public relations specialists
Total	5	
Staff Activities	3	Administrative specialists
	2	Legal counsel
	2	Personnel administrators
	2	Publications specialists
	3	Budget and accounts specialists
	1	Facilities engineer
Total	13	
Systems Office	3	Senior librarians
	9	Librarians
	10	Information technologists
	5	Budget specialists
Total	27	
External Policies and Support Office	3	Senior librarians
	3	Librarians
	3	Publications specialists
	3	Legal specialists
	3	Training specialists
	4	Professional societies experts
	2	Foreign publications specialists
	5	Information technologists
Total	26	
Technical Applications and Methods Office	4	Information systems scientists
	2	Electronics engineers
	1	Optical engineer
	1	Photo chemist
	4	Computer systems specialists
	5	Programmer analysts
	2	Methods analysts
	2	Information systems researchers
	4	Experimental librarians
Total	25	
Plans Office	2	Senior information planners
	3	Information planners
	3	Legal counsel
	3	Senior statisticians
	7	Statisticians
Total	18	

Table 8-2b   Total Professional Staff

Director's Office	6
Information Service Office	5
Staff Activities	13
Systems Office	27
External Policies and Support Office	26
Technical Applications and Methods Office	25
Plans Office	18
Total	120

A further picture of the kind of organization envisaged can be gained from a consideration of the skills involved:

Table 8-2c   Bureau Professional Personnel by Skill

	Number
Librarians	24
Information technologists and scientists	20
Computer systems specialists	4
Programmer analysts	5
Electronics engineers	2
Methods analysts	2
Information systems researchers	2
Statisticians	10
Budget and accounting specialists	8
Legal counsel	8
Planners	5
Publications specialists	2
Foreign publications specialists	4
Professional societies specialists	2
Training specialists	3
Senior science administrators	2
Other technical and administrative personnel	17
Total	120

If these functions are to be done well, sufficient manpower must be put against the job. In determining the amount of personnel required, each function was considered, and the number and type of personnel needed to discharge that function was estimated. Although the number of personnel may seem large, it is believed that any significant reduction would result in an inadequate performance of some of the functional responsibilities of the Bureau.

Costs and Services

This section attempts to make some estimates of the costs associated with the Bureau and considers those funds and services which are required but outside the normal budget of other agencies.

Costs of the Bureau. The previous section considers the probable level of manning of the Bureau. It is estimated that approximately 120 professional people would be involved. Their support in terms of clerical assistance, stenographers, reproduction services, ADP equipment operators, etc., would probably be about 130, for a total of 250 people. If we assume the average professional salary to be $12,500 per year,

and the average support salary to be $5000 per year, and add 100 per cent for overhead—building space, equipment, fringe benefits, external administrative support, etc.—then the annual cost of the Bureau is about $4.2 million per year. We should always be careful to include overhead costs in such calculations since they are significant in assessing overall costs.

External Support. As has been mentioned previously, the federal government is involved in supporting primary publications and secondary publications. It is almost impossible to assess accurately the extent of the support since so much of it occurs indirectly through page charges and overhead. However, NSF, through the Office of Science Information Service, has directly supported for limited time periods some 33 established publications. The NSF has also been instrumental in starting new journals, and between 1959 and 1963 granted $305,000 for this purpose, and also granted $2 million in support of monographs, handbooks, and catalogs from 1952–1964. Likewise, NSF and other parts of the government give support to abstracting and indexing services. In FY 64 NSF made grants of $564,000 to this purpose, and very recently an agreement was reached with *Chemical Abstracts* to give $5 million support (from several government sources) over 24 months for the development of an expanded, semiautomated indexing system.

It is not clear that this is an area the Bureau should control directly. Perhaps NSF support of primary and secondary publications is comparable to NSF support of new laboratories or various science departments. On the other hand, the policy toward and support of primary and secondary sources will become more and more important and difficult as the sheer volume of publication expands. Likewise, as automation is introduced into library and information centers, there will be a need for close coordination regarding the format and early representation of documents in digital form. Thus primary and secondary publications problems become central to the efficient operation of the activities under the Bureau's cognizance. It seems from such considerations that the federal government's support of primary and secondary publications should be directly undertaken by the Bureau, and soon this would amount to several million dollars annually.

Special Information Services. In addition to regular library and information center services, the federal government operates several specialized services, such as the Science Information Exchange, the National Referral Center for Science and Technology, the Clearinghouse for Federal Scientific and Technical Information (CFSTI), and the Defense Documentation Center (DDC). Each of these represents a special funding or coordination picture.

The Science Information Exchange (SIE) is operated by the Smithsonian Institution but is funded by the National Science Foundation. Its annual cost is just over $2 million. The SIE is a marginal member of the information services and, although it is not a document or content information center, it is able to supply information regarding the subject matter, investigators' names and institutions, and funding for many of the current unclassified research and development projects being funded by the government. Although SIE may not be a typical information center, its output is useful to government administrators and to scientists interested in the location or subject matter of particular areas of study —which is certainly an information service. To broaden SIE's coverage and to help in assuring inputs to it, the Bureau could help strengthen SIE. SIE funding seems peculiarly placed since it comes directly in the NSF budget but the operation is elsewhere. It is believed that the budget item should appear in the operating agency's budget; but the Bureau should help defend the budget and coordinate it with the scientific and technical information budgets of the other agencies or departments.

The National Referral Center is a somewhat similar case. The Referral Center is operated by the Library of Congress, but its annual cost of about $400,000 is funded by the National Science Foundation. The National Referral Center is an unusual information service, since it does not supply content information but refers users to sources which can supply the content information they need. In other words, the National Referral Center tells you where to go to find out the answer to your query. It is believed that the National Referral Center should be removed from the Library of Congress and assigned to an agency in the executive branch. This seems essential if the executive branch is going to exercise responsibility in the S&T information and documentation area. It would seem

that a case can be made for combining the Referral Center with SIE. Both agencies supply information about where something is going on or where information can be found. A more intimate tie between the two could enhance the total capability by the use of common data base handling procedures. As in the case of SIE, the budget of the Referral Center should be a part of the agency responsible for operating the Center.

The Defense Documentation Center and the Clearinghouse for Federal Scientific and Technical Information serve similar functions, in the sense that both supply copies of reports prepared by the government or under government contract. The FY 64 budget for DDC was $6 million and that for CFSTI was $4.5 million for FY 65 (although about 25 per cent was collected from fees). DDC primarily serves the Department of Defense technical community, both that part within the Department and that part with defense contractors. The Clearinghouse serves the public generally (although charging a fee for its services). The expanded Clearinghouse is quite new, seems to be progressive in its application of technology, and has achieved good working relationships with DDC. Thus no budgetary or organizational changes seem indicated at this time, but the budgets of both organizations should be reviewed by the Bureau as a part of its responsibility for rationalizing the government S&T information and documentation activities.

Technical Developments Sponsored by the Bureau. Elsewhere in this book there is a consideration of the application of advanced technology and automation to the S&T information and documentation area. It seems clear that, even with the presently available equipment and state of software development, quite considerable advances in handling documents can be made. In a few years this capability will be much greater and mandatory for the volume of material being produced (see Appendix 2). It seems apparent that the Bureau should aggressively initiate programs to assure the application of advanced technology in this area. Money should not be the primary limitation; rather the supply of qualified people to undertake such work and the development of proven techniques should be limiting factors. The Bureau should encourage government agencies to move in this direction as rapidly as efficiencies can be demonstrated

and should be prepared to give support to efforts in the private sector—university research libraries, public libraries, and professional society information services. The size of support required is considerable. The committee studying the automation of the Library of Congress estimated that between $50 million and $70 million would be required to automate the Library of Congress, although this did not include storage of all documents in digital form. DDC and MEDLARS are examples of partially automated systems as far as bibliographic and circulation control are concerned. It is estimated that the Bureau annually should be able to support at least $25 million worth of technical developments and installations within the federal government, plus another $25 million outside the government.

The Extent to which the Capping Agency Concept Satisfies the Design Requirements

The idea of a capping agency requires that there be other organizations which carry out the actual operations in the S&T information and documentation area. Thus the fulfillment of all of the design requirements depends on both the capping agency concept and the responsible agent concept. In Chapter 11 we will examine the extent to which the Bureau in conjunction with the responsible agent concept meets the design requirements. In that chapter we conclude that this concept merits recommendation over all the other concepts considered.

Considerations in Favor of a Capping Agency

When considering a solution to any difficult problem, the course of action is not always completely clear and there are arguments which favor and which oppose any suggested solution. The arguments in favor of a capping agency are:

The Problem Is Becoming Critical and Requires Executive Action. There are a number of factors which show that the S&T information and documentation problem is critical and that the situation may actually be degenerating. As is discussed in the requirements, Chapter 6, the sheer volume of material doubles about every 15 years. The 1963 and 1964 annual reports of the Librarian of Congress show that in 1938 the Library of Congress had 8,731,139 items, whereas in 1964 the comparable figure had grown to 24,555,825 (and, in addition, 18,970,817 manuscripts). This is an increase of more than 180 per cent in 26 years in all fields combined; the S&T literature is growing even faster. Libraries and information centers are now a major investment, and much larger investments will be required in the near future. The growth of new forms, such as informal information exchanges, extensive traveling to laboratories, informal newsletters, etc., can be used as an argument to indicate that the traditional system is not adequately serving its purpose. The existence of large backlogs of uncataloged books and unprocessed serials in major libraries is well known. During the 1965 session of Congress the Library of Congress, with the active sponsorship of the Association of Research Libraries, requested a special appropriation of $5 million, a part of which will be used to cope with the backlog problem. All of these considerations argue for strong executive action now.

S&T Information and Document Activities Are Now a Major Uncoordinated Expenditure. Although estimates are uncertain, there are figures to show that the direct annual federal expenditures in this area are currently at least $200 million and probably much higher. It is believed that these figures are considerably below actual federal outlays, for there are many "hidden" costs, such as page charges, library support out of overhead charges on government contracts, and general university support. The total of such expenditures is large, but perhaps the major problem is that they are uncoordinated. In spite of efforts by COSATI and the Bureau of the Budget this area remains a problem. More than in almost any other area, S&T information and documentation problems pervade all government departments and agencies. Some agencies have pursued progressive programs, while others have been slow to show concern regarding the problem; some have clearly identified budget items for S&T information and documentation, whereas others include their activities under headings which make identification of expenditures difficult. Clearly, greater executive coordination is needed.

Previous Studies Recommend a Capping Agency. The situation described above has been widely recognized. Chapter 7 shows that many previous groups have recognized the problem

and have made similar recommendations, although usually without adequate detailing of the concept.

There Is Lack of a General Policy. At present there is a lack of any general policy position by the federal government. Each of the various departments and agencies follows the policies that seem most appropriate to its particular needs. Although there is some merit to this procedure, it also results in inefficiencies. For example, it is reported that there is as much as 60 per cent overlap in the holdings between several of the major government libraries, yet no one knows for sure what the situation really is, nor is there a mechanism for finding out. Similarly, it is reported that there are significant gaps in the serial literature coverage. Agreements regarding coverage are made which may close these gaps for a while, but as new personnel or budget constraints appear, each agency follows its own course, frequently without co-ordination with affected organizations in other agencies.

There Is a Problem of Overlapping Programs. As mentioned above, there are problems of overlap. The collections of the Library of Congress, the National Agricultural Library, and the National Library of Medicine overlap to a great extent—probably there is greater than 50 per cent overlap between any pair. This results in unnecessary acquisition costs, unnecessary processing costs, and unnecessary storage costs. It is estimated that there are over 300 major library collections in federal agencies, yet there is almost no knowledge regarding the extent to which they are unique or the extent to which they make use of already existing resources. The Bureau is needed to gather statistics regarding the situation and to arrive at an optimization of the proper degree of redundancy in collections.

Potentially serious problems exist in agencies whose missions come close together. The DOD and NASA have similar missions, when viewed technically, and the technical reports and information of one should be of assistance to the other. It appears that recent agreements between DOD and NASA go far toward solving the document exchange problems between these agencies, but only experience will indicate how the agreement will be implemented. The Bureau should maintain cognizance in such areas.

Current Funding Patterns Are Confused. The situation regarding the funding of SIE and the National Referral Center has been discussed previously. There seems to be little logical reason for NSF to be responsible for this funding, and misunderstandings are quite possible. The operating organizations may perceive that they have a continuing commitment from NSF to fund these activities without NSF's having such a perception. Similar funding problems have existed with regard to report depositories. In the past private libraries felt they had a government commitment to continue support costs of depositories, but found after two years that further funds were unavailable. Another example is that many federal and private libraries depend on the Library of Congress as a catalog source, yet funding and other factors have kept the Library of Congress from keeping up to date with its cataloging. Thus not only the Library of Congress but also private libraries and other government libraries are affected because of funding problems of the Library of Congress. The Bureau could rationalize present funding practices.

There Is a Precedent for Such a Solution. The creation of the Bureau would follow a well-established precedent for handling problems which cut across many government departments and agencies. Just as the Civil Service Commission concerns itself with personnel problems, and the Bureau of the Budget with fiscal problems (which are the responsibility of the executive but have an impact on all parts of the executive branch), in a similar manner the Bureau would concern itself with the S&T information and documentation problem. The organizational placement of the Bureau has been discussed previously and shown to be quite feasible.

A Focal Point for Congressional Interaction Would Be Established. At present there is no focal point for Congressional interaction. This is a two-way problem. In budgetary hearings Congress must deal with each agency independently, and no unified picture is obtained. When proposals for new legislation are made, Congress must hear from many different parts of the executive branch since there is no single focal point. Similarly, the several departments and agencies make proposals to Congress which, while appropriate to their area, do not necessarily reflect the coordinated position of the ex-

ecutive. The Bureau, acting as a coordination point, would be helpful to both the Congress and the executive branch.

The Library of Congress Problem Would Be Ameliorated. As has been implied before, there are certain problems which arise from the placement of the Library of Congress in the legislative branch of government. The Library of Congress is the world's largest library, reporting for 1964 a collection of 43,526,642 items, including 18,970,817 manuscripts. In addition to its vast holdings, the Library of Congress has intimate ties with the library community at large, both because of its historical place in the American library community and because of its role as the nation's cataloger. But this great library has a limited role relative to the public-at-large and to the needs of the executive branch. The Library's main function is to serve Congress—not to be the policy-setting and supervising body for the administrative arm of the government. With the present somewhat unorganized and widely diverse S&T information and document situation in the executive branch, there is no obvious leader within the federal government. The establishment of the Bureau would correct this situation by clearly marking a focal point for government S&T information and document interaction, and would serve to define the policy and responsibility of the federal government in this area.

The Evolutionary Approach Is Emulated. There have been proposals to centralize all S&T information and document functions in one large operating agency or to give the Library of Congress total responsibility in this area. Such approaches would be truly revolutionary and require great changes in the responsibility for and operation of the present system. On the other hand, the establishment of the Bureau promotes an evolutionary approach in which present operations and establishments would largely continue their present work which would be improved by the coordination and encouragement of the Bureau. See, later in this chapter, a description of the responsible agent concept to gain a fuller appreciation of the constructive nature of the idea of marrying the capping agency and responsible agent ideas, as contrasted with more radical solutions, such as the new operating agency concepts described in Chapter 9.

Considerations Opposed to a Capping Agency

There are several arguments which can be marshalled to indicate that the establishment of the Bureau is unnecessary and would be unwise. These are:

COSATI Achieves Adequate Coordination. The Crawford report of 1962 recommended, among other actions, the formation of a coordinating agent among the departments and agencies. The Federal Council for Science and Technology established the Committee on Scientific and Technical Information (COSATI). COSATI has been in existence for about three years, and already better coordination is being achieved, as exemplified by the recent agreement on microfiche standards and the establishment of a number of study panels. With a permanent executive secretary and the backing of the Office of Science and Technology, a beginning has been made in solving the coordination and policy-setting problems. (See Chapter 10 for a fuller discussion of the ability of COSATI to adequately fill the required role.)

The Establishment of the Bureau Interferes with Legitimate Departmental Functions. Each department and agency has a set of defined areas of responsibility. In discharging its responsibility each needs to have control over the resources needed to accomplish its mission. Funds, personnel, and information are all resources essential to any agency, and each agency should have the greatest freedom possible in their use, if it is to be held responsible for effective performance. Under general authoritative direction from the Executive Office of the President the several departments and agencies are able to discharge their S&T information and documentation responsibilities. If there are clear problems to be solved, one or the other of the agencies should be assigned responsibility for their solution. The way to get things done is to assign general responsibility to responsible organizations and let them deal with the problem. Each department has its unique requirements which it can best determine how to discharge. This does not require the establishment of a large capping agency.

The Bureau Does Not Solve the Problem. Although a number of the functions defined would

be the responsibility of the Bureau, they are of the general nature of coordination or policy setting. What is really needed is definitive action regarding the problem. If the President were to issue a policy statement, the departments and agencies would then have enough general guidance to proceed with getting the actual job done. What is needed are funds and people to work at real problems, not just another coordinating group.

The Bureau Represents an Unnecessary Budgetary Drain. As has been shown, the Bureau will require $4 to $5 million a year simply for its internal operations. This much money would support several major libraries or the introduction of new techniques in present libraries. Such sums, if available, should be spent on actual operations rather than on supervisory functions.

The Bureau Will Inhibit Innovations. The solution to the many S&T information and documentation problems requires many approaches. Some libraries require extensive automation while others can operate effectively with manual systems. For some problems better libraries are the answer; for others, information centers are indicated; for still others, informal exchange between scientists is effective. A large, high-level bureaucracy will tend to see only one solution to many problems, or one favored technical approach, when in fact a diversity of approaches is needed. Although the Bureau's direction may make things neater, it will have the much worse effect of promoting unnecessary uniformity.

The Bureau May Alienate the Technical Community. The establishment of the Bureau as a separate policy and planning organization, unrelated to the immediate generators and users of S&T information, may alienate the technical community. The best information systems are those in which scientists and engineers are personally involved rather than those operated by information specialists.

THE CONCEPT OF A SYSTEM OF RESPONSIBLE AGENTS

Definition of the Responsible Agent System

In this section we describe our recommended concept for a national information system for science and technology, which we call the responsible agent system. By the phrase "responsible agent system" we mean a system concept in which a competent authority establishes a particular organization as the agent having the primary responsibility for assuring the satisfactory performance of all tasks necessary to provide information services in a particular limited subset of the broad spectrum of science and technology.

This definition contains a number of terms requiring clarification. First, the phrase "competent authority" may be interpreted in this section as referring to the capping agency, the Scientific and Technical Information Bureau. In other circumstances, it might appropriately be used to refer to an organization such as the Federal Council for Science and Technology, or to an individual such as the President's Science Advisor. Within the executive branch the ultimate competent authority is, of course, the President himself.

Second, the word "organization" is employed to refer to an administrative unit of the federal government, including but not necessarily confined to cabinet departments and independent agencies reporting directly to the President.

Third, the phrase, "assuring the satisfactory performance of all tasks necessary," is intended to exclude the notion that the organization would necessarily perform all the tasks itself. As we shall discuss in some detail later, the concept of the responsible agent system does *not* imply that the agent must perform the tasks directly, but only that the agent must assume and carry out the duty of *assuring the performance* of the tasks. The tasks themselves may be performed internally within the organization designated as the responsible agent, or elsewhere in the government, or in the nonfederal sector.

Fourth, the notion of a "limited subset of science and technology" obviously offers difficulties. Indeed, it must be recognized explicitly that the fixing of firm boundaries for any subset of the spectrum of science and technology is, in practice, simply impossible. Nevertheless, it turns out to be feasible to develop a subdivision of the spectrum that serves well both the goal of establishing reasonably logical boundaries for subsets of science and technology, and also the goal of fashioning a reasonable correspondence between these subsets and the interests of certain major federal organizations.

Such a subdivision is proposed herein; together with establishment of responsibilities for the organizations, it constitutes our recommended responsible agent system. The existing *de facto* national information system consists of similar correspondences—whether formally, pragmatically, or even accidentally determined—between subsets of the spectrum of science and technology on the one hand, and organizations on the other. Any discussion of formally establishing an information system for science and technology must consider the possibility of formalizing, and hopefully rationalizing, this existing *de facto* system. We believe that the responsible agent system will provide such a rationalization.

The responsible agent (RA) system has been developed out of careful consideration by the System Development Corporation and others of the "delegated agent" concept. The RA system concept differs little, in fact, from certain interpretations of the delegated agent concept. Unfortunately, a number of other interpretations of the delegated agent concept are also current. It has become clear that a distinctive name is necessary for the sake of unambiguous exposition of the RA system.

Since the RA system is related to the delegated agent concept, it will be helpful to trace next some of the history of the latter concept.

Origins of the Responsible Agent System in the Delegated Agent Concept

The delegated agent concept may be said to have begun with the Weinberg report,* in the sense that this report recognized the special nature of the information activities being carried on by the Atomic Energy Commission (AEC) and the National Aeronautics and Space Administration (NASA), and referred to the activities of these agencies as being those of "delegated agents" in their respective fields. The term "delegated agent" is defined only implicitly in the Weinberg report, but is explored in greater

_____

* "Science, Government, and Information," subtitled "The Responsibilities of the Technical Community and the Government in the Transfer of Information," a report of the President's Science Advisory Committee, The White House, January 10, 1963. (This is known as the Weinberg report because Dr. Alvin M. Weinberg chaired the PSAC Panel on Science Information which produced the Report.)

detail in a later study by the Suttle Task Force, to be discussed below.

The Weinberg Report

INTRODUCTION OF THE DELEGATED AGENT CONCEPT. The Weinberg report develops the delegated agent concept by referring to the "AEC and NASA; these agencies are delegated agents in atomic energy and space technology. They interpret their responsibilities very broadly; AEC's DTIE [Division of Technical Information Extension] therefore tries to keep track of all information on atomic energy whether it is generated within the Atomic Energy Commission or elsewhere. Its abstract journal and technical reviews cover both the Government and the non-Government literature, and it runs a full-fledged atomic energy information service, not merely a technical reports depository; in addition, it encourages non-Government communication in atomic energy. At the other extreme is DOD [Department of Defense] whose central information system, ASTIA [the Armed Services Technical Information Agency, which is now DDC, the Defense Documentation Center], handles only DOD reports."

The Weinberg report then poses the question, "Should agencies other than AEC and NASA become delegated agents for dissemination of documents in their respective fields; i.e., should they collect and disseminate in their central depositories *all* the information relevant to their missions, whether or not it stems from work they support?"

Without answering the question, the report goes on to mention one major advantage of and one caution for the delegated agent concept: "One obvious advantage of a single agency's becoming the delegated agent for a particular field is the great convenience to the users; a space scientist or information center need look only at the tools supported by NASA, since NASA, by melding its own announcement service with that of the non-Government Institute of Aeronautical Sciences, covers all space literature. On the other hand, where the agency's mission confines it to only a small segment of the field, it would be unnatural and unwise for the agency to preempt the entire field."

Continuing this line of argument, the report observes that "obviously DOD, because of its size and diversity of interests, cannot become a delegated agency for all technology. Yet we

believe that DOD could and should become a delegated agent in each of certain mission-oriented areas—for example, in undersea warfare, in radar, in civilian defense. In these areas DOD ought to supply the same kinds of bibliographic tools and services as AEC does in atomic energy, or as NASA does in space. It should actively encourage non-Government information activities, and it should interweave its own services with those of the non-Government agencies. On the other hand, where the area is very broad and not clearly mission oriented, as, say, chemistry or physics, then DOD obviously cannot serve as a delegated agent—even though the headings 'chemistry' and 'physics' should continue to appear in the ASTIA announcement bulletin."

RECOMMENDED EXTENSION OF THE DELEGATED AGENT CONCEPT. The Weinberg panel made only one other specific recommendation for extending the delegated agent concept beyond AEC and NASA. This recommendation was that the National Institutes of Health (NIH) "might identify special areas that are particularly germane to the work of its separate institutes, and that each institute consider establishing what would amount to a very elaborate specialized information center with services available to the entire biomedical community. The whole complex of NIH information centers might be serviced by the National Library of Medicine and, particularly, by the Medlars system. The focal point of responsibility within NIH would be expected to eliminate overlaps and omissions in this complex."

This recommendation is particularly interesting, for it goes to an opposite extreme from the very broad and massive collections in the delegated agent information stores of AEC and NASA, by recommending that each institute establish "a very elaborate specialized" information center and that these various information centers be coordinated at NIH level and serviced by the National Library of Medicine. In making this recommendation the Weinberg panel clearly envisioned the possibility that delegated agents might well assume responsibility for very small and highly specialized subject fields.

FEDERAL AND NONFEDERAL COOPERATION. Furthermore, the Weinberg panel clearly envisioned federal and nonfederal cooperation in the delegated agent concept. The report states, "in becoming a delegated agent for a given field, an agency must assume many responsibilities beyond merely collecting, announcing, and abstracting relevant material. The agency must help establish and support specialized information centers in the field; it must support worthy publishing ventures that would otherwise not receive support; and it must generally take active leadership in encouraging better communications in the field both within and without the Government." In support of these comments the report observes that "communication is an essential part of research; if an agency sponsors research in support of the agency mission, it ought also to allocate resources to support the communication necessary for effective conduct of that research."

To bring about this cooperative federal and nonfederal system within the delegated agent concept, the Weinberg panel envisioned action by both the operating agencies of government and the National Science Foundation (NSF): "The agencies would support mission-oriented information activities; NSF would do the same for the discipline-oriented activities. For example, if the American Institute of Physics wished to experiment with a central depository, and if it needed Government support, it would go to NSF; if the American Nuclear Society needed similar support, it would go to AEC. A specialized information center in crystallography would be the responsibility of NSF, in viruses, of NIH."

PROBLEMS OF OVERLAP AND OMISSION. In making these recommendations, the Weinberg panel also anticipated one of the major problems arising in the delegated agent concept. The report points out that "the separation between mission and discipline is not sharp, and some overlap between NSF and other agencies is to be expected. The FCST's [Federal Council for Science and Technology] Committee on Information [now, COSATI] would have to be sensitive to just such overlapping or omissions and would help keep the whole arrangement sensible and effective."

THREE IMPORTANT CAUTIONS. Finally, the Weinberg report makes three comments that would be important in implementing any delegated agent system, or similar system. First, "The user

sensitivity of the better technical society information systems is a precious thing; we should not lightly replace such systems with ad hoc systems conjured up by Government bureaucrats. . . . We point out that *support* of an activity by Government does not necessarily mean domination by Government. We envisage that much of what an agency spends for information handling would be spent by contract to non-Government institutions."

Second, whether or not the federal agency concerned is a delegated agent, the report insists that "the focal point of responsibility [for information activities] in each agency be part of the agency's research and development management. Much of the user insensitivity of Government information systems results, we believe, from their being part of administration rather than of research."

Third, as both an argument for, and a caution concerning, the delegated agent concept, the report observes that "by delegating responsibility for mission-oriented information handling to mission-oriented agencies, the Government will be represented by agency technical men who are usually members of the technical community that centers around the agency's mission. They would be expected to speak both languages, the technical community's and the documentalist's; when they sponsor information activities they could be expected to temper any expansionistic predilections of the Government with an understanding of what the field really needs."

SUMMARY OF THE WEINBERG REPORT. To summarize the Weinberg report, we note that it identifies the information activities of AEC and NASA as being those of a new pattern, which it calls the "delegated agent" concept. The report recommends the extension of this concept to the information activities of other agencies of the government and makes a very strong recommendation concerning government information activities: "Each Federal agency concerned with science and technology must accept its responsibility for information activities in fields that are relevant to its mission. Each agency must devote an appreciable fraction of its talent and other resources to support of information activities."

However, the Weinberg report fails to go so far as to recommend what we are proposing in this report—the assumption by the federal government of responsibility for assuring the provision of information services in the entire spectrum of science and technology, and the implementation of that assumption of responsibility through a system of responsible agents. The report does, indeed, observe, "Obviously the Government is responsible for disseminating and retrieving its own report literature. One question that needs clarification is how much further does the Government's responsibility go—how should it deal with information, other than its own reports, that is relevant to its mission?" But the Weinberg report does not answer this question.

The Suttle Report. The Weinberg report was, it may be recalled, a report of the President's Science Advisory Committee. It was referred to the Federal Council for Science and Technology (FCST) for further study of its implications for the various federal agencies. As a part of this review FCST referred the Weinberg report to COSATI (Committee on Scientific and Technical Information, at that time known as COSI, the Committee on Scientific Information) and COSATI in turn established a task force headed by A. D. Suttle, Jr., to explore the delegated agent concept in detail. The Suttle task force's report was not published but is discussed here because it was important in the development of the responsible agent concept.

The Suttle report re-poses the basic question of the Weinberg report regarding the delegated agent concept: namely, whether other federal agencies than AEC and NASA should follow the example of these two and become "delegated agents for dissemination of documents in their respective fields." The Suttle report's answer to this question is "a qualified 'yes'."

CHARACTERISTICS OF THE AEC-NASA DELEGATED AGENT PATTERN. The Suttle report explains its "qualified 'yes'" in part by attempting to identify the historical reasons for the development of AEC and NASA as delegated agents for information in their respective fields. The report cites four characteristics common to both AEC and NASA that help to explain how their information activities developed in the delegated agent pattern.

First, explosive growth. The report notes that "each of these agencies . . . was established to serve as a focal point for the administration of an enormous Federally sponsored program in

areas of science and technology whose bases were rather small before Federal stimulation. The explosive growth in scientific and technical information which ensued constituted an overwhelming burden for the non-Governmental information system and services which existed in this field, and the direct participation of the Federal agencies in the transfer of information became a patent and obvious necessity."

Second, security considerations. "The nature, goals, and results of the R&D effort frequently involved considerations of national security, proprietary interest, industrial security, etc., so that the responsibility for the selection of documents to be released and the timing of the announcement, abstracting and release of these documents was a non-delegatable responsibility of the agency. . . ."

Third, concern with technology as opposed to science. The report observes that both AEC and NASA are "heavily oriented to technological development work, carried out through the instrumentality of research or development contracts, executed in industrial more frequently than academic environments, dedicated more to applied than to theoretical science, with the results of the research and development summarized more frequently in technical reports than in scientific and technical papers for the open literature."

Fourth, orientation toward products rather than documents. "The work of these two agencies is, to a very high degree, engineering in character and the engineering community appropriately emphasizes products rather than papers as the goal of a research or development effort. Extremely useful and practical devices may be fabricated without the collection and the exacting preparation of data necessary for publication in traditional scientific journals." The information system of a delegated agent must include "those technical reports describing advances which are, for a variety of reasons, inappropriate for publication in the open literature."

CRITERIA FOR DELEGATED AGENTS. On the basis of these four characteristics of the AEC and NASA information activities, the Suttle report proposes five criteria by which to judge whether a federal agency might appropriately become a delegated agent:

1. "Sharply targeted and well defined technical goals" for the mission of the agency.

2. "Sudden infusion of massive government support, dwarfing both the previous size of the field and the information system used for information transfer within that field."

3. "Heavy reliance upon report rather than the open literature for the announcement of the results of research and development."

4. "Research and development carried out through highly organized, interdependent, and centrally coordinated team efforts."

5. "Research and development programs the results of which are important to the overall objectives of the agency even when, for varying reasons, such results would be unacceptable for publication in traditional scientific journals."

The report states, "It would seem clear that whenever a majority of these criteria are met, the modus operandi of AEC and NASA would seem an appropriate device for maintaining a system of information services for the area in question."

CONTRAINDICATIONS FOR THE DELEGATED AGENT CONCEPT. Having set forth these criteria, the Suttle task force further clarified its "qualified 'yes'" by saying, "Implicit in the above discussion is the consensus of the Task Force that the AEC-NASA modus operandi should not be adopted by all Federal agencies and would indeed not be appropriate as a system of information services for many of them. . . . The informational needs of a very large segment of the scientific community have [long] been met . . . by a complex of information services under both public and private auspices. . . . Most of these systems have a long history of satisfactory performance, are intimately connected to the learned societies which have been organized to advance the field, and have evolved highly responsible mechanisms for maintaining the excellence of the contents of the system. Indeed the AEC and NASA have accepted the preferences of biomedical and other scientists to operate, at least in part, through private systems of information services. It may well turn out that both directly operated and indirectly supported systems of information services will be appropriate for a number of Federal Agencies, and are found currently in existence in Federal Agencies. The Task Force feels that it would be a mistake to recommend the extension of the *Delegated Agent* 'style' to such situations."

The Suttle task force thus revealed that it was using the term "delegated agent" in a very narrow sense. The task force apparently regarded the delegated agent concept as implying a system that would be wholly operated by the government and would necessarily act to the detriment of any possible private competing systems in the same general subject field.

Such a narrow definition is somewhat surprising since the Suttle report points out that AEC and NASA are themselves exceptions to this definition. It is still more surprising in view of the care with which the Weinberg report emphasizes—in its interpretation of the delegated agent concept—the importance of the private sector's information activities and the desirability of the government's cooperating with them, supporting them, and even enhancing their roles.

In recommending a responsible agent system, we share the Weinberg and Suttle reports' views on the importance of the private sector and on the feasibility of federal-private cooperation. We see no incompatibility between a system of responsible agents in the government and continued information activities in the private sector. Instead, we view cooperation between the federal and private sectors as indispensable for satisfactory information services.

PROBLEMS OF THE DELEGATED AGENT CONCEPT. The Suttle report goes on to discuss other difficulties in implementing a broad delegated agent concept within the government. The primary problems are those of delimiting reasonably narrow subject areas within the broad spectrum of science and technology, and of matching these delimited subject areas with the interests of one or more government agencies. There is a further problem when there are competing interests among the agencies: the problem of deciding which agency should be the delegated agent for that subject area.

AN ENDORSEMENT. It is important to note that despite its reservations, the Suttle report does state that it "endorses the general principle that the Federal agencies should assume responsibility for guaranteeing the viability of science information services by indirect support through grants, contracts, and other mechanisms in those areas of science and technology in which the Federal agencies have a direct interest, and in

which an AEC-NASA style of operation is inappropriate or not feasible."

Tasks in the Responsible Agent System

Earlier in this chapter we discussed the origin of the delegated agent concept in the Weinberg report and its further exploration in the Suttle report. Both reports, it must be emphasized, dealt with the delegated agent concept in connection with existing areas of scientific and technical interest on the part of agencies of the federal government.

A broader matter is now at issue: should the federal government assume responsibility for assuring that information services will be provided for the entire spectrum of science and technology? We believe that the formal acceptance by the government of this responsibility is vital for ensuring the continued growth of science and technology in the United States.

In this broader framework, federal agencies would undertake to be responsible agents (RAs) for dealing with subsets of the spectrum of science and technology. In some cases an agency might not have had a major prior interest in a portion of its subset of science and technology. Such a portion would be added to the agency's responsibility as a part of the task of assuring complete coverage of science and technology, in the sense of there being RAs somewhere within the federal government for all portions of the spectrum of science and technology.

Some agencies would thus undertake responsibilities for information services in portions of science and technology in which they had not previously had a major interest. But in most cases the responsibilities to be undertaken would be merely formalizations of existing responsibilities, within the new framework of overall federal responsibility for assuring the satisfactory performance of S&T information services. In other words, in most cases the agency's previous interest would not be changed; and in no case would the change be other than that of an expansion of responsibility by some relatively small degree.

It is clear that the RA system concept would, in many cases, involve expansion of the information activities of various federal agencies, in that the RAs would undertake responsibility for a greater variety of information services (e.g., collecting, abstracting, translating, disseminating) than was previously the case. On the other hand,

it is in nowise implied that an RA must perform these services itself. As we have said before and shall say again, the RA system concept is simply that of establishing responsibilities, not that of requiring federal performance of all the multitudinous subtasks involved in the information service.

Levels of Responsibility. The concept of the responsible agent system is based upon a competent authority's establishing various federal organizations as the agents responsible for assuring the satisfactory performance of all tasks necessary in providing information services to limited subsets of the spectrum of science and technology. It is important to recognize that there are necessarily several levels of responsibility.

The first level of responsibility in the responsible agent system concept belongs to the executive branch of the federal government, since the basis of the concept is that the government would assure the performance of information services covering the entire spectrum of science and technology. To do this, executive branch agencies must have first-level responsibility for assuring the performance of the tasks necessary for providing these information services. The first-level responsibilities must be assumed by the heads of cabinet departments or of independent agencies who report directly to the President. This is a vital point, and it must always be clearly understood that the ultimate responsibility for assuring information services within each subject area belongs to the cabinet officer or agency head concerned.

These cabinet officers and agency heads would, of course, assign their responsibility in turn to the head of some subordinate organization within their departments or agencies. These second-level assignments would naturally be the prerogative of the cabinet officer or agency head, although in practice it could be expected that the assignments would be worked out in cooperation with the capping agency. Suggestions are made later in this section concerning possible assignments of second-level responsibilities, but these are to be understood as being only suggestions; for the assignment must be made by the cabinet officer or agency head concerned. Wherever possible it should, however, be standard policy to place the second-level responsibility in the research and development arm of the department or agency. This would be in keeping with one of the strongest recommendations made in the Weinberg report.

The second-level agent would, in turn, assign third-level and lower-level responsibilities for dealing with specific tasks necessary in providing the information services. It is to be emphasized here that some of these functions would be performed within the federal structure, both inside and outside the federal agency that is the responsible agent concerned, and that other functions would be performed in the nonfederal sector, as determined to be appropriate by the second-level agent in coordination with the capping agency.

A note on terminology: In the remainder of this section, whenever we use the term "responsible agent" without any modifier, we shall always be referring to a *first-level* responsible agent. References to lower-level RAs will always specify the level.

Discussion of Specific Information-Services Tasks. It may be helpful at this point to emphasize the multifaceted nature of the federal and nonfederal cooperative system we envision, by discussing a number of the individual tasks necessary in providing satisfactory information services within a given subset of the spectrum of science and technology.

PUBLISHING (PRIMARY PUBLICATION). The responsible agent would be concerned with assuring that reports of federally performed research and development are published and reach the information system. The RA would also be responsible for assuring that the reports of research and development sponsored by the government reach the system. The RA would be responsible for supporting the publication of primary journals in pertinent fields, and for encouraging and supporting the writing and publishing of review articles and books, in close cooperation with nonfederal publishing enterprises.

ACQUISITION. The RA must assure the establishment of mechanisms for actively seeking documents and other forms of information transfer. There must be a continual review of potentially pertinent literature, such as that of related S&T areas. There must be frequent contact with informed persons who can suggest otherwise overlooked documents. The RA would have the responsibility of making its interests known as

widely as possible and encouraging the submission of possibly pertinent documents.

To fulfill the responsibility at the national level for satisfactory coverage of its subject area, the RA must assure that suitable mechanisms and procedures are established for purchasing documents, for exchanging documents, for subscribing to journals, and for continually reviewing the status of subscriptions to assure that all copies of journals are received, that new journals are noticed, and that subscriptions to them are added to the system.

We believe that the long-range goal of the RA should be to work toward assuring exhaustive collection of significant documents within its assigned area. However, we recognize that this is a long-term goal and that initially it would be necessary to have less than exhaustive collection. In this circumstance, evaluative acquisition of information is important. Hence the RA must assure the establishment of mechanisms for the evaluation of the documents that are received.

TRANSLATION. When the RA system acquires a document in a foreign language, it would be necessary either to translate the whole document or to prepare an adequate condensed representation of the document in English. Decisions on whether to translate the whole document, or to prepare a condensed representation in English, would need to be made as a part of the evaluation process. The responsible agent must assure that there exists a capability for providing a translation of the document to qualified requesters and at reasonable cost. An important function would be coordination, through the capping agency, to avoid unnecessary duplication of translation efforts. The RA must also be responsible for assuring the accessibility of the document in its original language for those users who wish to refer to the original.

PROCESSING AND REPRESENTING DOCUMENTS. When the RA system acquires a document, initial processing must take place. This would include classification and/or indexing of the document, depending upon the needs and preference of the users. (In this context we mean by classification the assignment of the document to one or more predetermined subject categories; by indexing, we mean the assignment of index terms or descriptors to the document.)

The RA must ensure that abstracts, reviews, citation indexes, permuted title indexes, and other forms of condensed representations of the acquired documents would be prepared. The services to be performed in this area would again depend upon the needs and preferences of the users of information in the RA's portion of science and technology.

ANNOUNCEMENT (SECONDARY PUBLICATION). The announcement of system acquisitions could be handled in two basic ways: through general announcements, and through mission- or discipline-oriented announcements. By general announcements, we mean such devices as the bulletins of abstracts published by the Defense Documentation Center and the Clearinghouse for Federal Scientific and Technical Information, the Government Printing Office's *Selected List of Government Publications,* and the Patent Office *Gazette.* These publications are characterized either by their containing announcements in a number of subject areas or by their being aimed at a very broad and general public having a great variety of interests. By mission- and discipline-oriented announcements, we mean such activities as those represented by *Biological Abstracts, Chemical Abstracts, Index Medicus, Mathematical Reviews,* and *Scientific* and *Technical Aerospace Reports.*

It would be expected, for example, that the lower-level RA for announcement in the field of chemistry would be the Chemical Abstracts Service, and in the field of mathematics, the American Mathematical Society. These examples again point out the intricate interdependence of the federal and nonfederal sectors envisioned in the RA system.

In announcements in both the general and the mission- and discipline-oriented areas, the RAs would be concerned with ensuring full coverage of all primary publications within the subject areas. Although the RAs and the capping agency together must concern themselves with *unnecessary* overlap, it is important that doubtful cases be resolved in the direction of too broad rather than too narrow coverage. In addition, the RAs and the capping agency must jointly remain constantly alert to shifting areas of emphasis on the part of their users. They must respond to these shifts and to the development of new areas of interest, especially in interdisciplinary areas that are growing in importance,

and in areas of specialization or new development that represent rapidly expanding S&T interest and activity. Another facet of announcement activities is that the RAs should, where appropriate, provide support to existing nonfederal secondary publication services in addition to those that have lower-level responsibilities in the RA system.

ACTIVE DISSEMINATION. By active dissemination, in contrast to announcement, we mean individually personalized dissemination services. These are performed at present by certain libraries and information centers, where people perform the function of screening incoming journals and reports for articles of interest to the local user community. Active dissemination is also represented by the growing use of "selective dissemination" systems based on computer programs that match characteristics of incoming documents to the interest areas of users.

Automated techniques offer the potential for a major expansion in the scope of active dissemination services and in the number of users that can be served. Active dissemination will become an increasingly important information service, and the RAs should assure that it is available to qualified users at reasonable fees.

STORAGE AND RETRIEVAL. The RAs must be concerned not only with centralized storage of documents and other information materials, but also with the needs for at least partially decentralized storage. One such need arises from the geographical dispersion of the user community. There is need, we feel, for decentralized, duplicate storage of, at least, basic items of reference nature and other similar materials. A rule-of-thumb with regard to locally held materials might be to make them available if they were requested so frequently that it would be cheaper to supply local copies than to pay for the communication costs associated with remote use of central copies. Such a rule would, for example, imply that in general newer materials should be more widely held than older materials. Actual decision rules should be based on experience. The decentralized collections should both utilize and serve the existing university, industrial, societal, private, and nonfederal government libraries and information centers.

The RAs must be continually concerned with maintaining accessibility to the collections on the part of the users. This means not only "passive" accessibility, in the sense of allowing users to make use of the collection, but also "active" accessibility in the sense of providing such aids as selective bibliographies, organized so as to facilitate their use by the particular user community concerned. In the area of passive accessibility, the RA must see to it that equipment and techniques for long-distance rapid access are made available. The goal should be to work toward the capability of browsing from any point in the United States. Clearly, this would also be a concern of the capping agency.

Another aspect of storage and retrieval is the set of problems implied by the term "the purging problem." User studies have shown that the vast majority of requests for S&T documents consist of requests for documents published within the preceding twenty years. These studies allow us to conclude that most primary publications may be purged within a maximum of twenty years. By "purging" we do *not* necessarily mean destruction. Purging includes the notion of retirement of a document, for example, to an archive or to microform storage with perhaps only shallower indexing available.

The retirement of certain copies of documents to low-level-access stores might well take place much sooner than twenty years. One appealing suggestion is that libraries might continue their present practice of subscribing to professional journals but simply discard the copies of the journals after, say, two or five years. Thereafter, requests for copies of the journal, or an article in it, would be filled from the central store. The users, being guaranteed access to the article on request through the central store, could be expected not to object to the destruction of the local copy, or to its retirement to a lower level of access.

It may, admittedly, be reasonable to destroy some documents; but despite the appeal of destruction as a means of handling storage problems, we feel that recognition should be made of the importance—at least for future historians of science and technology—that most publications be retained in at least some low-level access, microform-storage medium. It should, therefore, be a function of the responsible agent to ensure that at least one copy of every significant document be kept for archival purposes.

INFORMAL COMMUNICATIONS. It is well known that a great deal of the communication of scientific and technical information, particularly the communication of the most recent developments, occurs through nonformal document media, for example, through letters, informal memoranda, conferences, and symposia. It would be the responsibility of the RA to facilitate these informal means of communication within its subject area, by such methods as the support of conferences.

The recommendation of greatest immediate importance for informal communications is probably that of assuring adequate handling of conference and symposium papers. At present the information system's coverage of conference proceedings is markedly inferior to its coverage of the regular journal publications, as has been shown by recent studies (e.g., Hanson and Janes, 1961). The RA must assure that the proceedings of S&T conferences and symposia would be acquired by the information system and that their contents would be treated in the same fashion as those of other documents in the system. Also important would be the assurance of more adequate provisions for recording, transcribing, and selectively editing and publishing the informal discussions at conferences, such as those following the presentation of papers.

It should also be a concern of the RA and the capping agency to consider means of making conferences more productive. One suggestion—a practice that has been gaining in popularity in recent years—is that of encouraging publication and distribution, in advance of a conference, of the formal papers to be presented there, so that at the conference itself the participants can spend their time in discussing with the speaker a paper that they have previously had time to read and consider.

Another aspect of the informal communications area is the need for the RA to facilitate the circulation of appropriate informal memoranda and to assure that copies are selectively acquired by the system and treated thereafter like other documents reaching the system.

INFORMATION TO, FROM, AND ABOUT USERS. One of the most important responsibilities of the RA would be the establishment of continuing efforts to inform users about the services that the information- and document-handling system can provide them. Studies have shown that scientists and technologists are sometimes unaware of the existence of information- and document-handling activities that are available to them. In the face of too frequent ignorance of the existence of such activities, it is safe to infer that there is even more frequent ignorance of the total scope and variety of the services that these activities offer their users. As the RA system expanded and improved its services, the need for user awareness of the services would increase.

Another important responsibility of the RA would be to assure the provision of mechanisms for obtaining information from the users about their experience with and views of the services that the system is performing for them. These mechanisms should be designed to involve the user in the system to such an extent that he would probe the full range of possibilities for exploiting the system to satisfy his information needs, and would be motivated to suggest innovations and improvements in the system's services. The efforts exerted to make the user aware of the services available to him could well include efforts to encourage him to offer such suggestions.

In addition to inviting suggestions from the users, the RA should establish means for collecting and evaluating data on the interactions of the users and the system. These should include not merely statistics on the number of documents circulated or on the number of user requests, but also information about what it was the user was really seeking, which sometimes needs to be distinguished from the question that he presented to the system after his own analysis of the way to approach his real information need. Probably most of us have had the experience of needing some item of information, deciding on some likely reference source for it, asking a librarian for that reference source only to find it unavailable, and not till then telling the librarian what we really wanted to know—whereupon it turned out to be readily available from some other source. The use of automated equipment and techniques will facilitate the collection of information about these distinctions between the question asked and the question intended. It should be noted also that provision for feedback is already an important part of at least one automated technique for active dissemination.

RESEARCH AND DEVELOPMENT SUPPORT. Research in the information-handling area would be primarily a function of the capping agency and NSF, as discussed earlier in this chapter. However, more direct involvement in research by an RA could well be desirable in certain circumstances. The development of individual systems would be a matter to be worked out in each case by the responsible agent concerned, in cooperation with the capping agency.

Performance of Specific Information-Services Tasks. We re-emphasize here that in each of the above ten areas there are appropriate places for performance of functions directly by the responsible agent, for performance of functions by other federal agencies, and for performance of functions by various portions of the non-federal sector of our society.

We also point out that each one of the relatively well-distinguished functions that we have been discussing here might be spread among several agencies. For example, the Weinberg report suggested that within the National Institutes of Health (NIH) there might be an "elaborate specialized information center with services available to the entire biomedical community" established at *each* of the separate Institutes, and that "the whole complex of NIH information centers might be serviced by the National Library of Medicine and, particularly, by the Medlars System." Here we have an example in which the first-level of responsibility would be that of the Secretary of Health, Education, and Welfare. He could make a lower-level assignment of responsibility to an organizational unit of each Institute, which would operate or contract for the specialized information center proposed. (We use this example because it it one that was originally proposed by the Weinberg report; we are not attempting to suggest that this particular set of subassignments of responsibility would necessarily be an appropriate one.)

As another example, it would seem likely that the existing announcement bulletins of the Defense Documentation Center and the Clearinghouse for Federal Scientific and Technical Information (CFSTI) would continue to be used and would, indeed, be expanded in the RA system we are proposing. It might be desirable that CFSTI's bulletin be the basic general-purpose announcement bulletin in scientific and technical areas for the government, and that individual

RAs supplement it with their own more specialized announcement services.

An example of the latter might be a service maintained by the RA for chemistry through a contract (i.e., a subassignment) with the Chemical Abstracts Service. Thus *Chemical Abstracts* would be the primary source of announcements to chemists, but a selection of announcements about chemical articles of more general interest would appear in the CFSTI bulletin. Again, chemical patents would be included in both the Patent Office *Gazette* and in *Chemical Abstracts*, as worked out cooperatively by the RA for patents and the RA for chemistry, in conjunction with the capping agency.

What we have attempted to show by these examples is that we envision the responsible agent system as a multifaceted system in which the various functions would be carried on by a number of different organizations, both federal and non-federal, under the general supervision and with the support of the first-level responsible agent, the head of a cabinet department or independent agency.

Arguments for and against the Responsible Agent System Concept

The responsible agent system concept must be weighed against essentially two competing concepts: (1) the concept of strengthening the existing system, and (2) the concept of some form of centralized system. The first concept, that of making no changes other than perhaps strengthening some of the existing coordinative mechanisms, is dealt with in Chapter 10; the second is dealt with in Chapter 9.

Advantages of the Responsible Agent System Concept. Several of the important advantages of the RA system concept may be grouped together in what we call the "natural habitat effect." By this effect we refer to the potentials in the RA system for closer contact between the user of the information and the services being provided to him and for enlisting the user's direct participation in the services. In detail, these arguments are the following.

A closer relationship between the users of the service and the organization providing the services should result in better access by the users to the services. This argument says that if the services are close to the users in either a geo-

graphical or an organizational sense, or both, then the users will find it easier to take advantage of the services.

A closer relationship between the users and the services should result in fuller exploitation of the resources and personnel of the information service. It can be expected that the information services will be more efficient if they are close to the users. For example, the average workload on the document collection can be expected to be higher, and the collection, being more readily accessible to the users, will be more conducive to browsing.

The system should be better able to tailor its functions and services to the users' needs if there is a close relationship between the users and the services. This argument is based on the expectation that a system whose staff and administration are close to a major group of users will be able to tailor its functions and services more closely to the expressed—and even to the unexpressed—needs of that major group of users. If this group includes personnel working in a particular scientific or technical field, then the tailoring of the system's functions and services can be expected to benefit other workers in the field as well.

The system will be better able to draw upon and involve the users as participants in the system operation. This argument is based upon the expectation that through organizational, geographical, and/or professional closeness between the system and a major group of its users, the staff of the system should be able to use the user group as an intermittent source of guidance and information. For example, a staff member of the system, upon receiving a request for which he needed technical assistance, might turn to a nearby researcher for help.

Participation by the users in system operation should result in services more appropriate to the needs of the users. Such increased appropriateness of the services would obviously stem from the ability to draw upon the researchers as one of the information sources of the system. But another effect needs to be recognized here which is also an expectable result of involving the users in the activities and operations of the information system: namely, that such involvement can be expected to result in suggestions from the users about ways of more closely tailoring the system's services to the needs of the users.

Each portion of the information system will be serving a major agency interested in the subject area of that portion, and can thereby expect better support from the agency itself. An agency's own involvement in the scientific or technical subject area for which it is the RA can be expected to heighten the interest on the part of the agency staff and administration in ensuring that the information system is as satisfactory for their needs as possible. This in turn will result in better information services to the other users of the information system outside that agency.

The foregoing six arguments are those which we view as constituting the "natural habitat effect." There are other advantages of the RA system concept, such as the following three that relate to consequences of having smaller collections than would be the case in a centralized system.

In a diversified RA system, there will be the potential for greater flexibility than would be the case in a centralized agency. A centralized agency can be expected to tend toward standardization in a variety of ways, including the forms of service to its users. In contrast, the decentralized RA system should result in diversified services to the users, with services being tailored to the needs of users in the various subject areas. Additionally, in a decentralized system it would be easier to conduct more varied experimentation with respect to services, equipment, and techniques.

It will be possible to have more precise vocabularies for indexing purposes, thus facilitating search and retrieval within the subject area. Since the document collections in the RA system will be individually smaller, it will be feasible—in terms of the state-of-the-art at any given time in machine-searching equipment and techniques—to provide more detailed sets of index terms for documents and/or greater depth of subject classification. In either case, search and retrieval of the document collection should be facilitated. This greater depth and precision of indexing will also facilitate the provision of an active dissemination service to the users of the system. (This argument has a counterpart in an argument *for* a centralized system, based upon the danger of increasing difficulties in communication across subject-area boundaries as individual subject-area vocabularies are developed and refined.)

Automation, particularly in the sense of machine storage and searching, is more feasible for smaller collections. This is especially true of existing techniques for storage and search, all of which rely essentially upon sequential searching techniques. If and when powerful associative searching techniques become feasible, this argument may have less weight.

Finally, two advantages of the RA system concept may be characterized as primarily administrative.

The RA system concept will provide clear-cut responsibility for coverages and services within limited subject areas. The agent having the responsibility for assuring information services within a given subject area will be spotlighted. Any inadequacies in coverage or in the provision of services can be attributed to a specific organization, and, indeed, to a specific individual. Thus, users of the system will be able to make their criticisms and desires known more directly to those responsible for providing the services.

A deliberately constituted responsible agent system can be readily evolved from the *de facto* existing system. The responsible agent system really amounts to little more than a formalization of existing responsibilities for subject-area coverage by Federal agencies. Such modifications as are envisioned are largely those of extending responsibility, not so much into new subject areas as in the direction of assuring the performance of all the information services necessary within subject areas already of interest to an agency. In addition, the RA system concept implies the formalization, through the medium of the capping agency, of various administrative and supportive operations now carried on in divers places or not at all. The RA system concept will also facilitate the retention of such desirable features of the present system as the voluntary assistance in abstracting and reviewing currently provided by scientists and technologists as a service to their professions through their professional societies. In short, the essence of this argument is that the RA system concept's evolutionary approach is the one best suited to making optimal use of the facilities, resources, personnel, and experience of the existing system while simultaneously providing specific mechanisms for improvement.

Disadvantages of the Responsible Agent System Concept. Opposed to the foregoing potential advantages of the responsible agent system concept are a number of arguments about possible disadvantages, which we discuss next.

Information services will have lower status in a mission- or discipline-oriented environment than in the information-science orientation of a centralized information system. Consequently, information technologists will lack prestige, and the development of information science as a distinct discipline will be impeded. This argument can be rephrased as implying that, for example, librarians and library science will have more status among other librarians than they will among research scientists. This is a widely held view within the research community, where anyone who is not a researcher, including librarians, tends to be looked down upon, and where often any discipline other than that which is the immediate concern of the researchers is also viewed condescendingly.

Since information stores will be, in general, smaller under the decentralized RA system concept, certain equipment and techniques of automation may become less efficient than they would be in a single, large centralized store. We have discussed earlier the possible advantages of decentralized stores with respect to automation. However, an argument can be made that possibly certain equipment would reach maximum efficiency only when used in connection with a very large store. No specific present equipment would appear to be of this nature; but since hardly any equipment has been developed specifically for the purpose of serving a huge store, it is impossible to say what operational efficiencies might result through the use of such equipment. Thus at present this is a hypothetical argument.

Lower practical limits to the size of document-store operations exist, and constitute a potential cause of inefficiency in the RA system concept. There is clearly a lower limit to the size of information stores for which it is financially feasible to maintain highly qualified professional staffs and automated equipment for their use. Subassignments of responsibility should not be so detailed as to result in too small document stores. This is a potential problem to which the RAs and the capping agency would have to give consideration in making the subassignments.

Overlap and duplication in storage and services are more likely in the RA system concept

than in a centralized store. Some overlap and duplication are inevitable no matter what degree of centralization of the basic document store may be envisioned; for both individuals and local information-service points will undoubtedly want their own retention copies of some documents in even an "ideal" system. Whether such overlap would be sufficient to constitute a serious problem would depend on many factors and would, in any case, be a continuing responsibility of the capping agency. Similar arguments could be adduced and answered with respect to other information functions besides storage and search.

Management costs will be higher in the RA system concept than in a centralized system. This is an argument in the abstract, since what is being contrasted is the management cost in an ideal centralized service with management costs in an ideal responsible agent system concept. Presumably, there would be higher management costs in the ideal decentralized system than in the ideal centralized system. However, in practice, questions of efficiency depend very heavily indeed upon individual persons and organizations.

Vocabularies will be proliferated, making interdisciplinary communication difficult. This argument has already been mentioned under the discussion of advantages of the RA system, where it was pointed out that specialized vocabularies will make deeper indexing feasible. Nevertheless, there is a clear danger of increasing difficulties of interdisciplinary communication as specialized vocabularies grow in size and the degree of specialization. Attention to this problem will be a continuing responsibility, not only of the capping agency but of the scientific and technical community as a whole.

The referral problem will be greater in the RA system concept than in a centralized system. The referral problem is that of directing a user to the appropriate point, within an information-service system, where his request can be filled. There is no doubt that the organizational and geographical dispersion envisioned in the RA system concept will result in some users' having to pass through more referral stages than they would in a centralized system. It is also likely that a greater number of partially duplicative referral mechanisms will have to be included in the responsible agent system.

Costs will be higher for acquisition and pro-

cessing in the RA system than in a centralized system. This argument clearly holds true for the problem of acquiring documents, because of the inevitable duplication in holdings within the RA system—in particular, the duplication in the frontiers between subject areas. This same overlap would probably give rise to higher costs in processing.

Active dissemination of information will be more costly in the RA system concept. The basis for this argument is that in many cases two or more RAs will need to maintain profiles on a given user. On the other hand, it seems likely that each of the two or more profiles would be smaller, and hence simpler to use and maintain. Additionally, the profiles might be more detailed, with at least the potential for providing better dissemination service to each user.

There will be potential conflict among the responsible agents over matters such as the areas of responsibility and allocation of funds. Such conflict exists in the present system. The RA system concept would bring these conflicts out into the open, and thus potentially aid in rationalizing them. However, the RA system concept does not go so far in the direction of precluding such conflicts as does the concept of a single centralized service.

There will be potential difficulties with respect to standards, personnel policies, management and accounting policies, etc. Again, these difficulties and differences exist at present. The RA system concept offers the potential of rationalizing them to some extent, although not to so great an extent as does the concept of a single centralized agency.

It may be difficult to ensure full coverage within the subject areas of responsibility in all cases. The argument here is that budgetary and other pressures may operate in somewhat the same fashion as they do at present: viz., the agent, whether *de facto* or assigned, might decide unilaterally to limit or to drop coverage of some particular subarea of his responsibility. The capping agency would need to establish mechanisms to guard against this.

The Recommended Adoption of the Responsible Agent System Concept

In reviewing the advantages and disadvantages of the RA system concept, we conclude that the advantages far outweigh the disadvantages.

Perhaps strongest of all is the fact that an RA system could be formally evolved from the existing *de facto* system much more readily than could a centralized system. Running a strong second in our opinion are the arguments based on the natural habitat effect, for there are many benefits to be derived from keeping the operations of the information-transfer system as close as possible to the producers and users of the information. Against these two strong groups of arguments for the RA system concept are opposed a number of disadvantages that seem to us either to be minor or else to be primarily problems that will inevitably be continuing concerns in any system, whether formal or *de facto*, centralized or decentralized. As such, they are easily outweighed by the arguments for the RA system concept.

We recommend, therefore, that the federal government formally adopt the concept of a system of responsible agents to assure the provision of information services for science and technology. The formal adoption of this concept would take place through legislative and executive action, and some of the steps are outlined later in this chapter.

The chain of reasoning that leads to this recommendation may be summarized as follows:

1. Our society is, and will become increasingly, dependent on science and technology to maintain present socioeconomic levels and on advances in science and technology to raise those levels.

2. In order that advances in science and technology may be achieved efficiently, information about previous and current research and development must be widely available.

3. The federal government shares vitally in our society's responsibility to ensure that advances in science and technology continue.

4. Almost all portions of the spectrum of science and technology have already become the concern, to some degree, of at least one federal agency.

5. To assume its proper share of the responsibility for ensuring the continued advance of science and technology, the federal government should formally accept responsibility for assuring that information about previous and current research and development in all portions of the spectrum of science and technology be widely available.

6. From the standpoints of technical desirability and of administrative practicality, the best way for the federal government to implement this responsibility is to adopt the responsible agent system concept.

IMPLEMENTATION OF THE CAPPING AGENCY/RESPONSIBLE AGENT SYSTEM

Earlier in this chapter we described the multifaceted system of various levels of responsibility for information services that we envision as constituting the responsible agent system. Now we turn to the details of how such a system could be established in conjunction with a capping agency. We shall be discussing primarily the first-level responsibilities, those to be undertaken by cabinet departments and independent agencies. We also offer suggestions as to possibly appropriate assignments of second-level and lower-level responsibilities; but these will be only suggestions, for these lower-level assignments will be the prerogative of the responsible agents.

Subjects and Agencies

We have already mentioned two of the principal problems in implementing an RA system: the problem of deciding on appropriate subdivisions of science and technology, and that of establishing these subdivisions as the ones in which various government agencies will undertake responsibilities for assuring the satisfactory performance of information services. Neither of these problems, we feel, is so difficult as, for example, the Suttle report views it. Two tacitly assumed factors may have led to the impression of difficulties in these respects. First, it must be pointed out that the subdivisions for an RA system need not necessarily follow some idealized, logical scheme of subdividing all knowledge—a scheme such as, for example, Melvil Dewey intended his decimal classification to constitute. (If it was not clear at the time Dewey proposed his classification, it has certainly become clear since then that a completely logical and permanently fixed set of subdivisions of all knowledge is both epistemologically and pragmatically impossible.) Instead, we can—and, indeed, must—deal with a pragmatically determined, and reasonably well agreed upon, set of subdivisions reflecting the subject specializations of scientists and technologists and the interests and missions of federal agencies. We

must also be willing and ready to change the subdivisions in accord with the needs of the users at some future time.

Second, to view the problem of establishing federal agencies as RAs as a major difficulty is to introduce what we think is an unreasonable and unjustified presumption that the agencies will quarrel over the designations or will refuse to cooperate in providing and using the services of the system. As just one example, the broad-gauged approach of the Department of Defense to matters of indirect concern to the actual defense of the nation such as support of basic research, finding new jobs for defense workers no longer required, etc., augurs well for a similarly enlightened approach to a matter of more direct concern—the S&T document-handling system—on the part of federal agencies.

Proposed Schema of S&T Categories and Responsible Agents

An outline of current relationships among some of the most important national goals, related S&T subject categories, and existing responsibilities and interests of federal agencies is exhibited in Table 8-3 which is organized by goals and categories. Table 8-4 presents the same relationships, organized by agency. The suggested S&T subject categories are heuristically defined by exemplary subheadings in Table 8-5. The departments and agencies shown in column 3 of Table 8-3 are "existing responsible agents" in the sense that they are already carrying out essentially all the duties of assuring the satisfactory performance of information services in their subject areas. AEC and NASA are, as noted earlier, "delegated agents" and hence are responsible agents. The others have, through designation or through response to recognized needs, undertaken efforts comparable to those we propose for responsible agents.

The responsibilities shown in these tables are for the conduct of federal research and development in the respective areas, or for support of such R&D to whatever extent the federal government has undertaken it. With certain exceptions closely related to the national security, the federal government has not undertaken to control R&D in any area of science or technology. Nor is such control envisioned in the RA system concept. We reiterate that this concept deals only with the problems of assuring satisfactory performance of information services in S&T subject

areas, and that the concept envisions accomplishing this goal through voluntary cooperation and contractual arrangements.

In particular, the establishment of a federal agency as the RA for a scientific or technical subject category should be on the basis of the agency's concern with the category and willingness to undertake to assure the provision of information services for the category. The working out of the requisite set of agreements as to the undertaking of the first-level responsibilities will be a matter to be negotiated by the capping agency and the departments and agencies concerned. Pending the establishment of the capping agency, the Scientific and Technical Information Bureau, these negotiations could well be initiated by the Office of Science and Technology. While the RA system concept would be best implemented through the coordinating activities of the Bureau, some aspects of the concept may be implemented without the aegis of a capping agency, as is demonstrated by the existence of the present responsible agents. There is little doubt that the present system can be strengthened without the Bureau. There is equally little doubt that the job would not be done as well or as completely without the Bureau.

Suggestions Concerning Lower-Level Responsibilities in the RA System. A few comments may be helpful concerning the potential responsible agents shown in the tables. The following discussion also includes suggestions about second-level and lower-level assignments of responsibility in the RA system.

For the category of Patents the existing responsible agent is the Department of Commerce. The obvious suggestion for the second-level assignment of responsibility for this category is the Patent Office. The Department of Commerce is also suggested as the potential responsible agent for four other categories: Atmospheric Sciences, General Science and Technology, Information Sciences, and Mathematics. The first of these categories is clearly pertinent to the mission of the Environmental Science Services Administration, and the last three are pertinent to the mission of the National Bureau of Standards. In the existing Commerce organization, both of these organizations are under the Assistant Secretary of Commerce for Science and Technology. Also under this Assistant Secretary is the Clear-

Table 8-3   *S&T Information Services Responsibilities by Goal and Category*

Representative National Goals (1)	Exemplary Related S&T Categories (2)	Existing Responsible Agent (3)	Potential Responsible Agent(s) (4)
Improved scope and quality of education	Education and training	Dept. of Health, Education, and Welfare (HEW)	
Improved scope and quality of medical care	Medical sciences	Dept. of HEW	
	Food and drugs	Dept. of HEW	
	Chemistry		Dept. of Agriculture; Dept. of HEW
Exploration of space	Space sciences and technology	National Aeronautics and Space Administration (NASA)	
	Astronomy		NASA; National Science Foundation (NSF); Smithsonian Institution
Advances in nuclear science and technology	Nuclear engineering	Atomic Energy Commission	
	Physics		Atomic Energy Commission
Scientific research and development (5)	Aeronautics	NASA	
	General science and technology		Dept. of Commerce; NSF
	Mathematics		Dept. of Commerce; NSF
	Information sciences		Dept. of Commerce; NSF
	Atmospheric sciences		Dept. of Commerce; Dept. of Defense
	Earth sciences		Dept. of Interior; Dept. of Commerce; Dept. of Defense
	Oceanography		Dept. of Defense; Dept. of Commerce
Industrial growth	Patents	Dept. of Commerce	
	Mechanical, industrial, and marine engineering		Dept. of Defense; Dept. of Commerce
	Electronics engineering		Dept. of Defense; Dept. of Commerce
	Materials technology		Dept. of Defense; Dept. of Commerce
Optimal use of natural resources	Conservation and natural resources		Dept. of Interior; Dept. of Agriculture
	Energy resources and conversion		Dept. of Interior
Improved socioeconomic environment	Behavioral sciences		Dept. of HEW
	Architectural, civil, and regional engineering		Dept. of Housing and Urban Development (HUD); Dept. of HEW
	Social sciences		Dept. of HUD; Dept. of HEW
Improved agricultural system	Agriculture	Dept. of Agriculture	
	Biology		Dept. of Agriculture; Dept. of HEW; Smithsonian Institution
Maintenance of national security (6)	Military technology and science	Dept. of Defense	

(1) These goals are illustrative only, and their order is not intended as a suggestion of relative priority.
(2, 5, 6) The S&T categories listed in the second column are based on those in the COSATI subject category list. It will be obvious to the reader that the categories listed with each representative national goal are not intended to be an exhaustive list of categories pertinent to the goal. This is most saliently illustrated by the categories of "Scientific research and development" and "Maintenance of national security," both of which encompass essentially all of science and technology.
(3) The departments and independent agencies named in this column are those having the primary existing responsibility within the federal government, as determined by legislation and/or executive order, for a major part—not necessarily all—of the category.
(4) The listing of a department or independent agency in this column is intended merely to reflect the existence of significant current concern with the category on the part of the department or agency, such that it should be considered as a potential candidate for being responsible agent. The listing is, of course, not exhaustive. Where two or more potential responsible agents are listed, the one named first is viewed as the leading candidate.

Table 8-5 (Continued)

shielding and protection; radioactive wastes and fission products; radioactivity; reactor engineering and operation; reactor materials; reactor physics; SNAP (systems for nuclear auxiliary power) technology

23. *Oceanography.* Biological oceanography; chemical oceanography; dynamic oceanography; hydrography; physical oceanography; underwater sound

24. *Patents.*

25. *Physics.* Acoustics; crystallography; electricity and magnetism; field theory; fluid mechanics; high-vacuum physics; lasers and masers; optics; particle accelerators; particle physics; plasma physics; quantum theory; solid-state physics; solid mechanics; thermal physics; thermodynamics; wave propagation

26. *Social Sciences.* Anthropology; archeology; criminology; demography; economics; economic statistics; political science; sociology; vital statistics

27. *Space Sciences and Technology.* Astronautical engineering; astronautics; exobionics; propulsion and fields; spacecraft; spacecraft launch vehicles and ground support; spacecraft trajectories and re-entry

is suggested that the second-level assignment of responsibility for these areas within the Defense Department might well be made to the Director of Defense Research and Engineering. An interesting possibility for a third-level assignment of responsibility would be to assign Oceanography to the Navy and to assign the other categories to the Defense Documentation Center, whose responsibilities would be enlarged (along the lines proposed above for CFSTI) to make it more than primarily a document storage, announcement, and distribution center.

The Department of Health, Education, and Welfare is the responsible agent for the categories of Medical Sciences, Food and Drugs, and Education and Training; it is viewed as the potential RA for the Behavioral Sciences category. Some reasonable lower-level assignments of responsibility would be to assign the first and last of these categories to the National Library of Medicine, the second category to the Food and Drug Administration, and the third to the Office of Education.

The Department of the Interior is viewed as the potential responsible agent for the categories of Conservation and Natural Resources, Earth Sciences, and Energy Resources and Conversion. The Conservation and Natural Resources category appears most pertinent to the purviews of the Assistant Secretaries of the Interior for Mineral Resources and for Public Land Management; Earth Sciences, to the Assistant Secretary for Mineral Resources; and Energy Resources and Conversion, to the Assistant Secretaries for Mineral Resources and for Water and Power Development. Since the categories cut across Interior's internal organizational lines and there is no single focus for research and development,

we suggest that the second-level responsibility of handling information in these categories might be assigned to the Interior Department Library, which might then be appropriately designated as the National Natural Resources Library.

The Department of Agriculture is the responsible agent for the category of Agriculture, and is viewed as the leading candidate for RA for Biology and Chemistry. In keeping with the Weinberg report's recommendation that information services be part of the research and development arms of federal agencies, we suggest that the second-level responsible agent be the Director of Science and Education of the Department of Agriculture. The National Agricultural Library is an obvious candidate for third-level assignments of responsibility for several of the necessary information-services tasks, since it has strong collections in these categories and is already engaged in some of the other functions, such as announcement.

We have thus commented about six of the eight agencies that are existing or potential responsible agents. Not yet discussed are AEC and NASA. These agencies, it may be recalled, are those which gave rise to the delegated agent concept in the Weinberg report, the concept out of which has grown the responsible agent system concept. In our suggested schema, AEC and NASA would each retain its existing areas of subject responsibility: in the case of AEC, responsibility for Nuclear Engineering; and in the case of NASA, responsibility for Aeronautics and for Space Sciences and Technology. Additionally, each is viewed as the leading candidate for RA for a related category: Physics for AEC, Astronomy for NASA.

OTHER AFFECTED AGENCIES. Besides the responsible agents, whose proposed responsibilities have been discussed above, three other existing agencies of the federal government are seen as being affected by the proposed RA system. These agencies are the International Exchange Service and the Science Information Exchange, both in the Smithsonian Institution, and the National Referral Center for Science and Technology in the Library of Congress.

The International Exchange Service is part of the acquisition function for the existing information system for science and technology, in the area of foreign documents. It is proposed that the International Exchange Service be affiliated with the capping agency, the Scientific and Technical Information Bureau, through administrative transfer or through establishment of a long-term contractual relationship, in order to continue the existing IES activities in the area of foreign acquisition. The Bureau will necessarily concern itself with other aspects of the foreign acquisition problem, such as the necessary coordination with the Library of Congress, the State Department, and the intelligence community. Such coordination should be aimed at assuring the continuation and improvement of existing procedures through which the foreign S&T documents acquired via State Department and intelligence community activities are, after their use by these agencies, channeled into the overall document- and information-handling system.

The Science Information Exchange is also proposed for affiliation with the Bureau through either administrative transfer or establishment of a long-term contractual relationship. In either case the Exchange would carry on its existing activities.

It is proposed that the National Referral Center for Science and Technology be transferred to the Bureau. At the very least, the Bureau should establish a long-term contractual relation with the Referral Center. The existing activities of the Referral Center would be continued and strengthened, for the Center will be a vital part of the responsible agent system. As we have mentioned earlier, it will be important to provide for the referral function within the RA system. It might well turn out to be desirable to have the Referral Center supervise and/or coordinate the referral service throughout the capping agency/responsible agent system in order

to assure the most rapid and efficient possible switching of inquiries and requests to the appropriate place within the system for these inquiries and requests to be filled.

A fourth agency—which is discussed elsewhere in this report in connection with its relation to information systems for science and technology—is the Government Printing Office. In the capping agency/responsible agent system concept, no change in existing GPO responsibilities and activities is seen. It is expected that the RAs would simply modify their existing contractual relationships with the GPO as may seem appropriate to them in carrying out their assigned responsibilities.

Implementation Schedule for the Capping Agency/Responsible Agent System

In this section we present a brief outline of the steps that can be foreseen as necessary in establishing and developing the capping agency/responsible agent system in its initial phases, together with a proposed schedule to guide this plan of action. The plan is presented in outline form in Figure 8-1 along with a schedule, and is intended to suggest only some of the outstanding features of the implementation of the system. The schedule is tentative, and the dates appearing on the chart should be taken as sanguine estimates of the times necessary for the various phases.

Phase 1: Review and Establishment of the System. Phase 1 begins on September 1, 1965, with the submission of the System Development Corporation (SDC) report to the Committee on Scientific and Technical Information (COSATI), and is tentatively seen as ending on July 1, 1966. After the submission of the report by SDC, the COSATI Task Group on a National System(s) for Scientific and Technical Information will enter into a process of review, modification, and, hopefully, approval of the report and, in particular, of the recommended capping agency/responsible agent system. The report will then go to the full Committee (COSATI) for further review, modification, and approval. Assuming approval by COSATI, the report will then be referred, in turn, to the Federal Council for Science and Technology and, ultimately, to the President.

Meanwhile, in the expectation of approval

from these higher levels (and, of course, working in cooperation with them for ongoing guidance), the Office of Science and Technology will draft legislation and/or a reorganization plan needed for the establishment of the capping agency/responsible agent system. This legislation and/or plan will be developed in coordination with COSATI, the Bureau of the Budget, the Congress, and the agencies which are existing or potential responsible agents or which will otherwise be involved in the implementation of the capping agency/responsible agent system. For convenience, the existing and potential responsible agents and the other agencies involved are here jointly referred to as the "affected agencies."

As a part of the process of developing legislation, it will likely become clear that certain executive orders by the President will be appropriate in implementing portions of the capping agency/responsible agent system. Thus, the plan of action suggests the issuance of such executive orders in January 1966, the same month in which the proposed legislation will be submitted to Congress. The process of review, modification, and approval by Congress is seen as occurring during the late winter and spring of 1966. Assuming Congressional approval by June, it will be possible to establish the Scientific and Technical Information Bureau and for the President to appoint its Director by July 1966.

Phase 2: Development of the System. With the appointment of the director of the Bureau, Phase 2 of the implementation of the capping agency/responsible agent system will begin. As soon as the director has been appointed, he can begin to recruit his initial staff. The development of the Bureau's staff will be a continuing activity throughout the balance of Phase 2.

At the same time, the Bureau and the affected agencies will cooperatively begin to implement the necessary changes, both those that have been prescribed by the legislation and those that follow from the executive orders. Among the affected agencies are the International Exchange Service and the Science Information Exchange of the Smithsonian Institution, and the National Referral Center for Science and Technology of the Library of Congress. It is proposed that these activities come under the control of the Bureau. Whether this step will be taken through

administrative transferral or through the formalization of long-term contractual relationships between the Bureau, the Smithsonian Institution, and the Library of Congress, is a matter that should be determined in the course of the development of the legislation establishing the Bureau.

Simultaneously with these actions concerning the Smithsonian and the Library of Congress, the Bureau and the responsible agents will be working together on the implementation of the responsible agent concept. With the advice of the Bureau, the responsible agents will be making their second-level and lower-level assignments of responsibility to the federal and the nonfederal sectors of our society.

Also during the fall and winter of 1966–1967, the Bureau will be initiating its activities in such areas as policy formation, budget review and funding control, support of publications, establishment of standards, specification and collection of statistics, coordination of research and development, and support of training of librarians and information technologists. These activities of the Bureau will involve continuing interaction with the nonfederal sector. By the spring of 1967, the combination of responsible agent operations and Bureau operations should be functioning as a capping agency/responsible agent system at an intermediate level of activity. By July 1967 the system should be clearly nearing full-scale operation.

Phase 3: The Operational System. Sometime after July 1967 the capping agency/responsible agent system will reach the level of full-scale operations. At the present time there is little that can usefully be said about schedules in this phase of the development of the system. For details as to the kind of functions that will be conducted, the reader is referred to the description of the functions of the Bureau and to the description of the detailed functions of the responsible agents presented earlier in this chapter. However, it should be emphasized once again that in the capping agency/responsible agent system there must be continual management review of the system operations on all levels, seeking ways to improve the system, maintaining alertness to newly developing needs of the users, and continuing in efforts to recognize and fulfill those needs, through activities in the federal and nonfederal sectors.

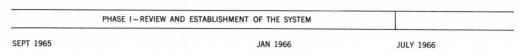

PHASE I—REVIEW AND ESTABLISHMENT OF THE SYSTEM

SEPT 1965   JAN 1966   JULY 1966

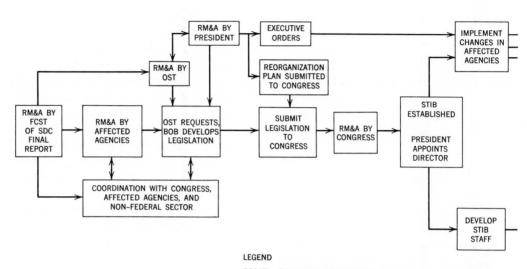

LEGEND

COSATI = COMMITTEE ON SCIENTIFIC AND TECHNICAL INFORMATION
IES = INTERNATIONAL EXCHANGE SERVICE
LC = LIBRARY OF CONGRESS
NRCST = NATIONAL REFERRAL CENTER FOR SCIENCE AND TECHNOLOGY
OST = OFFICE OF SCIENCE AND TECHNOLOGY

Fig. 8-1   Implementation of the capping agency/responsible agent system.

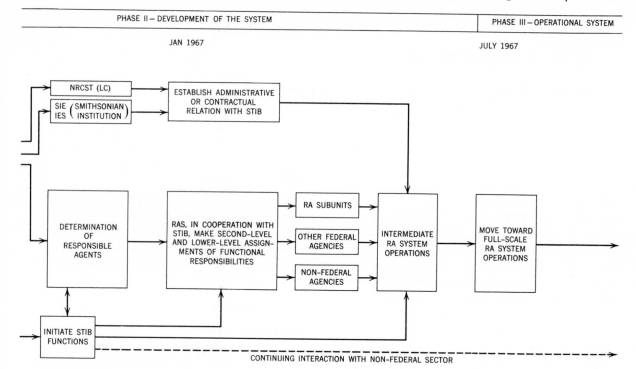

RA = RESPONSIBLE AGENT
RM&A = REVIEW, MODIFICATION, AND APPROVAL
SIE = SCIENCE INFORMATION EXCHANGE
STIB = SCIENTIFIC AND TECHNICAL INFORMATION BUREAU (THE CAPPING AGENCY)

Fig. 8-1   (Continued)

Chapter Nine

The Concept of New Operating Agencies

THE NEW OPERATING AGENCY CONCEPT

Several system design concepts were considered by the study group in arriving at a recommended solution to the scientific and technical information and documentation problem. Although none of these proved as attractive as the recommended solution, they have sufficient merit to justify advancing them as possible alternative solutions. One such alternative is the new operating agency concept. This alternative may seem drastic to some unfamiliar with the problems now facing the libraries and other document handling facilities serving the scientific and technical community. Others may agree to the urgency of the problem but disagree in some respects as to the technical feasibility or to the particular approach offered here. The new operating agency is offered as a concept which promises to meet head-on the challenge that will face us in the twenty-first century.

The concept encompasses the idea that it is possible to maintain and operate a centralized facility where all documents are stored, either in microform or hard copy, and reproduced and distributed upon request to qualified agencies within the federal government and the nonfederal sector. A document-processing center, operating as one element of the new operating agency, would be responsible for acquiring, indexing, and abstracting at least one reproducible copy of all significant documents, either directly or through agreements with other federal or nonfederal agencies, and announcing its holdings to the using communities. The concept calls for an evolutionary development of the centralized facility, starting with the present federal library facilities and transitioning into a completely centralized capability.

The new operating agency should be an inde-pendent agency within the executive branch. An appropriate name might be the National Scientific and Technical Information Agency (hereafter referred to as the Agency). The functions of the Agency and its organization, scope of activities, and costs are considered below.

Primary Mission

The primary mission of the Agency would be to provide scientific and technical information and document services to other federal agencies, and to the nonfederal sector. The Agency would amalgamate, coordinate, and provide, through an operating network, all federal document handling services. In addition, it would have the responsibility for offering its services and coordinating its programs with the nonfederal sector. Those services now provided by the several governmental agencies would become the sole responsibility of the Agency.

Services provided to government agencies by the Agency would be similar to those provided today. However, the nature of the facilities providing the services and the methods of operations will be changed. Each government department or agency would have one or more service centers located within it. Each center would provide for three basic types of services: (1) a reference service, (2) an information service, and (3) a document requesting service.

The Reference Service would provide reference materials such as an unabridged dictionary; encyclopedias; handbooks of specific interest to that location; document and book indices; current newspapers, magazines, trade and professional journals; and locally produced reports This service would also maintain some documents for purposes other than scientific and technical work, such as legal documents, management reference materials, etc.

The Information Service would provide the same services as now provided by information centers. Since the success of an information center depends in great part on its close association with the user, each location would reflect the specific needs of the agency being served. It would provide answers to specific questions, compile and condense data sources into useful documents, announce its specialized holdings, and conduct literature searches to identify theoretical areas for new research or technical application. Sensitivity to the user should be the prime consideration of those operating the service.

The Document Service would provide to the requester in hard copy or microform any useful scientific or technical document, including serials, published by other federal agencies, the nonfederal sector, or foreign countries. Service personnel working within the document service would request and obtain such documents from a central library maintained by the Agency.

Qualified users within the nonfederal sector would have access to documents held by the Agency. "Qualified" users in the nonfederal sector refers to wholesale outlets such as industrial document services, private and public libraries, state and local governments, and information centers.

Distinguishing Features

In addition to the method of providing services to accomplish its mission as described, there are several additional features which distinguish the Agency from the other concepts presented in this report.

Authority and Responsibility. The Agency authority and responsibility would extend to all functions related to the handling of S&T documentation, beginning with management functions such as the formulation of policy, supervision of personnel, planning of applied research and development, to the day-to-day operations associated with providing services to individuals within other Government organizations. In this role, it would have the authority and responsibility for creating new services and determining the funding requirements for its total operation.

Applied Research and Development. Since the Agency would be the sole user of products from an applied research and development program for S&T information- and document-handling in the federal government sector, all planning and execution of such programs would also become a centralized function within the Agency.

Federal Libraries. Under the new operating agency concept, S&T documents within libraries of the federal agencies would gradually disappear, being retired to historical archives. A complete store of documents would be maintained at a new central library, easily accessible to numerous service centers by rapid request and supply methods.

Functions

The functions of the Agency would be the same in the following areas as those for the capping agency as described in Chapter 8:

Formulate policy for:
    Nonfederal libraries,
    Information centers,
    Depositories of government documents,
    Support of nongovernment publications,
    Nondocumentary communications,
    Training librarians and information
      technologists,
    Foreign documents,
    Copyright, and
    Legislative relations and legal matters.
Collect statistical information.
Establish standards.
Promote the development of information technology.
Publicize information about information services.
Develop long-range plans.

However, in the following respects the functions of the Agency would differ from those of the capping agency:

Formulation of Policy. The Agency should determine, through coordination with representatives of other federal agencies and representatives of the nonfederal sector, all policy regarding the acquisition, announcing, storage, and dissemination of S&T documentation for federal use and dissemination. This should include the dissemination of information through appropriate

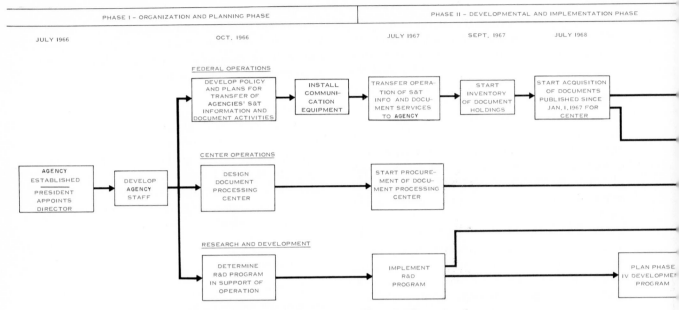

Fig. 9-1   National Scientific and Technical Information Agency.

information centers in support of federal operations.*

Operating Functions. The Agency should be an *operating* agency. It should provide for the acquisition of at least one reproducible copy of all S&T documents useful for scholarly and technical work, provide for the announcing of all holdings, provide storage of documentation in hard copy and/or microform, and provide services in the form of document distribution and the operation of information centers to all qualified users. The Agency would operate most of the present document services for the federal agencies. Source of documents to support these services would come, at first, from the present collections of federal departments and agencies, and later from both these collections and from a centralized facility developed by the Agency. Documents of more recent origin would be acquired, processed and stored in the new centralized facility. As the frequency of document requests declined for older documents, the libraries of Federal departments and agencies would become historical archives, and the new

* It is not imperative that the Agency assume the responsibility for policy functions. For example, a strengthened Committee on Scientific and Technical Information might assume these responsibilities, leaving the Agency the role of developing and operating a service.

centralized facility would operate as the principal source of S&T documents.

Recommend Science Research. Same as for the capping agency and, in addition, the Agency should conduct applied research and development and make recommendations to NSF regarding needed areas of broader research support.

Perform Budget Review and Funding Control. Same as for the capping agency and, in addition, the Agency should determine the requirement for its services and request, in a single appropriation, funds for providing these. The Agency should also have the responsibility for defending before Congress the total government program in the S&T information and documentation area.

Scheme of Operations

General Considerations. The Agency will act as a service organization to all federal departments and agencies and qualified members of the nonfederal sector. It will establish service centers in direct support of other federal agencies where personnel utilizing the service will have complete access to any useful unclassified scientific and technical document located either at the Agency depository or any one of a number of archival storage locations. In addition, reference services will be provided to the using agency (e.g., dictionaries, indices, local reports, legisla-

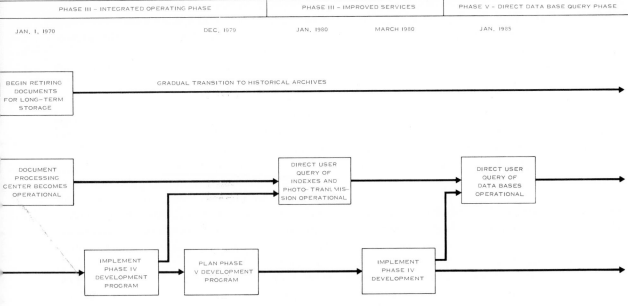

Fig. 9-1   (Continued)

tive reference materials, current magazines, trade and professional journals, etc.), and an information service appropriate to the location's need. The Agency will also provide for filling document requests from service points within the nonfederal sector (e.g., private and public libraries, industrial locations, and information centers).

The Agency will formulate and implement policy as described earlier. The authority and responsibility given to the Agency will permit it to effectively coordinate with other federal agencies and various nonfederal establishments toward specific goals required to evolve an effective system.

The formation and development of the Agency as an effective organization will require a series of implementation phases extending over a period of several years. (See Figure 9-1.) The specific responsibilities, scope of activities, and system configuration will change from phase to phase and often within each phase.

Phase 1: Organization and Planning. Phase 1 will begin with the creation by law and funding of the Agency. The initial funding will be for the creation of a headquarters with appropriate personnel to undertake planning and organizing functions. During this phase, policy will be formulated and plans written to specify such things as the Agency's relationship to the private sector,

programs to be undertaken in applied research and development, phasing schedules and system designs for implementing future system configurations, equipment and personnel requirements, and future budget requirements. Particular attention will be given to the design requirements and schedules for implementing Phase 2.

Phase 2: Developmental and Implementation. Phase 2 consists of a developmental subphase and a first-operating subphase in addition to normal administrative functions and further policy and plans development in support of the Agency's overall operation.

DEVELOPMENT SUBPHASE. The principal goal of the developmental subphase during Phase 2 is to obtain appropriate space for housing a state-of-the-art automated document processing, storage, and dissemination center for unclassified scientific and technical documentation and to develop, purchase, and install equipment. The center will not provide operating services during this period. It must be capable of housing a reproducible copy of all significant documentation for at least the first fifteen years of operation. "Document" is used here to mean a book, report, serial, reprint, or preprint.

The facilities developed during this period will reflect the greatest degree of automation consistent with the state-of-the-art and costs. However, concentration should be focused on

internal automation of document handling, such as indexing, abstracting, storing, retrieving, duplicating, mailing, etc. Equipment and associated programs for conducting limited bibliographic searches should be developed during this period. Communications and associated communications equipment will be provided for receiving document and/or search requests and for transmitting bibliographic listings and short abstracts. Electronic transmission of photo-images will not be required for the initial operating center.

OPERATIONAL SUBPHASE. This subphase has to do with the transfer of document handling services from the various other federal departments and agencies to the directorate of operations of the Agency. This transfer will occur at the beginning of FY 1968. At that time all personnel and facilities involved with unclassified document handling (excluding publishing and general library functions) will be transferred to the administrative and operating control of the Agency, with the exception of the Library of Congress and the Defense Documentation Center. The Agency will operate the various department and agency libraries, reference services, and information centers during Phase 2 much as they are operated today. Since the transfer of responsibility requires little or no relocation of personnel, no disruption of normal service is contemplated.

Once the Agency has assumed responsibility for operating these facilities, it will conduct an inventory of all transferred documents and establish a source reference catalogue. Excessive overlap in holdings will be eliminated.

One copy of each document published after January 1, 1967, will be acquired in either hard copy or microform for later use in the document processing center. This collection will provide a three-year inventory of documents to the Center when it becomes operational in January 1970. Studies indicate that scientists and technicians are mostly concerned with more recent publications, although the frequency of use by age of a document varies with some fields. Thus, one would expect that the Center would be supplying the majority of documents to requesters by the end of 1970, with the less frequently used documents being supplied by the Agency's department and agency libraries.

Temporary communications will be installed at each department and agency location to speed service requests until the Phase 3 communication net is available.

Phase 2 should begin on July 1, 1967, and end on January 1, 1970.

Phase 3: Integrated Operating. Phase 3 begins January 1, 1970, with the opening of the central Document Processing Center. This central facility will have the capability to acquire all scientific and technical documents published after that date, to process them from control, announcement, and retrieval, and to reproduce from hard copy and/or microform for dissemination to users within both the federal and nonfederal sectors. The Center will have communication terminals for receiving and processing requests, and transmitting bibliographic listings and short abstracts.

The Center will maintain a central index of its holdings and an index of holdings of each of the locations within the Agency system (e.g., National Agricultural Library, National Library of Medicine, and Army libraries). An index of new acquisitions will be published monthly and a cumulative index at least annually. A limited automatic search capability by subject area should be available early in Phase 3.

The above Center capabilities, added to nonfederal libraries and the Agency's library holdings at various geographical locations throughout other federal agencies, would permit the Agency to service requests either through a central request point or from any one of its associated locations. As shown in Figure 9-2, the system would operate in the following manner. A user would request documents from a service center. If a document was published after January 1, 1967, the request would be directed to and filled by the central Document Processing Center. If the document request is for a document published before that date, it will be forwarded by the Center to the appropriate agency library or a cooperating nonfederal library for action. Since the Agency will maintain an inventory of all documents at its various locations and will publish the location holding each document, service centers will have the capability to request documents directly from another service center rather than through the central Processing Center. During Phase 3, documents will be

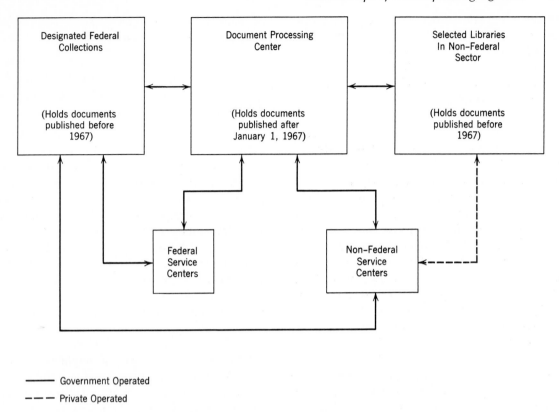

Fig. 9-2   Phase 3 operating network as of 1970.

transmitted by mail, since photo-transmission capability is not planned.

The number of requests which will be filled directly from the Central Processing Center will increase as its inventory accumulates. This will result from the fact that the frequency of document-use is inversely related to the age of the document and the more recent documents will be held at the Center. With this shifting load, department and agency libraries will revert primarily to service centers as described earlier in this report. Documents at those locations will be systematically retired to a few major archival depositories where they can be preserved better. Access to documents within these depositories will be maintained by a small staff. Personnel no longer required at these locations will be transferred to other duties within the Agency.

During Phase 3 a research and development program will strive for advancing the state-of-the-art toward the goal of improving document processing methods, developing an efficient photo-transmission system, and developing methods and equipment for storing and retriev-

ing information from large data bases. This phase will end by approximately 1980.

Phase 4: Improved Service. Phase 4 will overlap Phase 3. It is anticipated that many new innovations and improvements will be available during the operation of the Phase 3 system. Phase 4 introduces two principal extensions of service capability—the direct remote entry through a switching network to subject indices at the Center, and the rapid transmission of documents by photo-transmission techniques. Both services will be provided through a network of communications which will use satellite transmission to regional centers and coaxial cable relay to service centers. Service centers will possess the capability for copying these photo-transmissions at a rapid rate, thus requiring that the central Document Processing Center transmit from some form of either micro or computer-processed images. This phase will end by approximately the year 1985.

Phase 5: Direct Data Base Query. Phase 5 will permit the user to make direct request for

specific information from computers within the Document Processing Center. Information will be stored not as a document but as subject-related data. The user will be provided with consoles at service centers for directly querying the computer-based information.

DOCUMENT ACQUISITION. The Agency should have the responsibility for obtaining at least one reproducible copy of all significant S&T documents, both foreign and domestic, and should actively acquire at least one reproducible copy of all new publications. It should enter into agreements with foreign countries, either directly or through other agencies of the federal government or nonfederal sector, to obtain publications within those countries. Beginning January 1, 1970, all newly acquired documents and the acquired three-year backlog for 1967–69, would be housed at the Agency's new Document Processing Center.

DOCUMENT PROCESSING. The Agency should have the responsibility for the indexing and abstracting of all appropriate documents. This responsibility should be performed through the delegation of certain areas to the nonfederal sector, through contracts and subsidies, and through maintaining an indexing and abstracting service as a part of its own resources. It should produce a centralized index of all S&T documents held by the Agency and enter into cooperative arrangements for supplying cards for the larger Union Catalog. It should strive to standardize indexing and abstracting services, procedures, and formats.

FOREIGN TRANSLATIONS. The Agency should operate a foreign division whose responsibility is to acquire and translate, either directly or through agreements with the other government agencies, the private sector, and/or other countries, all significant scientific and technical foreign publications. This division should capitalize on favorable translation rates and excess foreign currency to obtain translations in other countries, and on translation capabilities in our own private sector. It should, however, maintain some in-house capability for assuring total coverage and a fast reaction-time for providing urgent translations. The system should be capable of providing hard copy or microform of either the original or an English translation.

DISSEMINATION. The Agency should provide essentially three types of services:

1. Appropriate federal information centers.
2. Document services for all federal agencies.
3. Documents to retail outlets in the nonfederal sector (e.g., libraries, information centers, etc.), for a fee.

The Agency should strive for acquiring economical techniques for filling document requests through electronic transmission where this is required. Publishing and mailing of hard copy and/or microform should be accomplished through facilities of the Agency at its centralized location, at various service centers, and/or through agreements with the Government Printing Office. The system should reimburse members of the private sector for publication rights as appropriate, through some agreeable formula.

Physical Facilities and Personnel

Additional facilities will be required to house the headquarters personnel and for the central document processing facility. Where possible, the Agency should utilize the present space and library inventories at the various federal departments and agencies for developing service centers and fulfilling requests for all documents until the Document Processing Center becomes operational in 1970. After the Center becomes operational, the federal department and agency libraries will supply only those documents published before 1967. Space for housing the Agency's services to new federal agencies should be determined through negotiations with the agencies being served. One would expect that as the Agency develops its programs of archival storage and elimination of multiple copies of materials, the requirements for space at the various agencies will decline.

The location of the central Document Processing Center should be determined by such factors as the availability of communications, the availability of postal services which can minimize the time required to reach the user, the availability of qualified personnel to man the Center, and costs.

New personnel should be selected, trained, assigned, and supervised by the Agency. Personnel now serving the various federal information and document services should be transferred to the new organization with minimum disruption of their present activities. The Agency should

undertake a program to define future personnel requirements and tasks required for its operation. It should initiate cooperative programs with educational institutions to assure the training of sufficient personnel with the appropriate knowledge and skills to fill future positions.

The Agency's Impact on Other Federal Organizations

Library of Congress. The Library of Congress would remain under the operating control of Congress and would continue to serve Congress and its public. However, the Agency would provide a service to the Library of Congress, as it would to any other Government agency, supplying services in the S&T field to its users. The Library of Congress, through the Agency, would have the availability of all significant S&T documentation. This would free it to concentrate on acquiring, announcing, and providing support related to non-scientific and non-technical documentation. The Agency would cooperate with the Library of Congress by furnishing it with index cards for inclusion in the National Union Catalog. The Library of Congress would be designated as one location for acquiring copies of documents published before 1967.

The Clearinghouse for Federal Scientific and Technical Information. The Agency should absorb the personnel and facilities of this organization. Collections of documents acquired by the Clearinghouse prior to 1967 would comprise one source of documents published before that date. By the year 1985 all documents now housed in this facility will become a part of the historical archives.

The Science Information Exchange. This service is now funded by the Office of Science Information Service on an experimental basis and located in the Smithsonian Institution. Because it is closely related to the S&T information and documentation problem and since it needs continuity that can be given only through an operating sponsor, it should become the responsibility of the Agency for its operation and funding.

The National Referral Center for Science and Technology. The National Referral Center is now located in the Library of Congress and funded on an experimental basis by OSIS. Because its function is closely related to the mission of disseminating S&T information, the re-

sponsibility and funding of this service should become a part of the Agency.

Defense Documentation Center. The DDC would not become a part of the Agency. Its function would remain essentially the same as today. Unclassified documents released by DDC would become a part of the Agency collection, while classified documents would remain the responsibility of DDC.

The National Science Foundation (NSF). That portion of applied research and development now sponsored by NSF, related to the acquiring, announcing, storing, using, and disseminating of S&T information and documentation should become a part of the Agency. Since the Agency would become a focal point for the improvement of services in the S&T information and documentation area, it would be in the best position to determine applied research and development requirements needed to improve its services. The NSF would continue basic research and the Agency would maintain close coordination with NSF to insure a mutually beneficial program.

Omitting Certain Federal Agencies. There are considerations (e.g., the high frequency with which an agency handles security information, the low frequency of scientific and technical information used, and the unusual location of facilities) which may be so overriding as to suggest omitting some locations from the Agency's control and responsibility or contracting to that department or agency for conducting its own service. Examples of such departments or agencies are the judiciary, certain DOD areas, and AEC. Policy regarding such areas should be developed and appropriate relationships established.

Organization

The Agency should be established as an independent agency of the executive branch. A suggested organization is shown in Figure 9-3.

Office of the Director. The organizational framework for the Agency has been developed in terms of the functions which need to be performed. Since it is a service organization, the organizational structure reflects its operating character. The director, assisted by a deputy director would be responsible through his advisors, assistants, and four associate directors for the operation of the Agency.

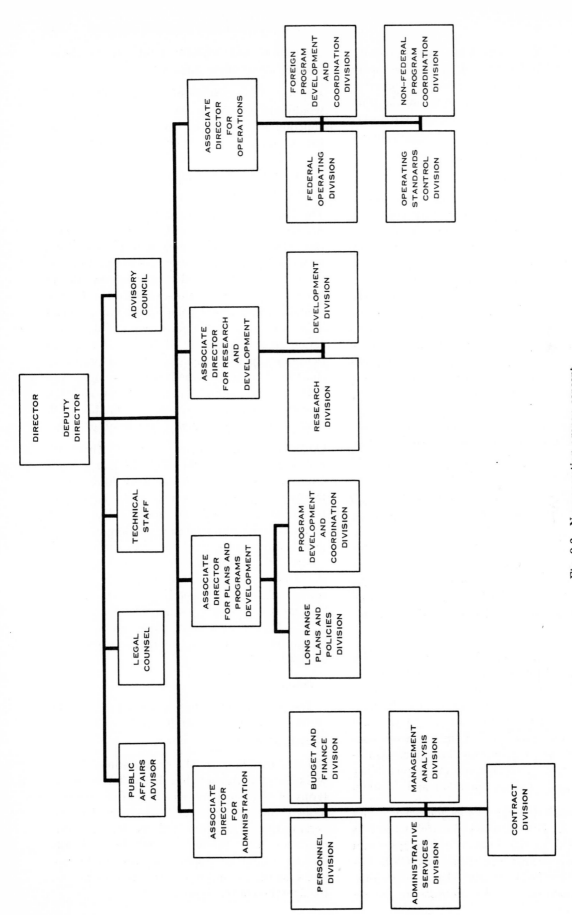

Fig. 9-3   New operating agency concept.

Directorates. The Agency would be comprised of four directorates, each headed by an associate director. The planning and execution, including administration, of all programs would rest with these directorates.

Divisions. Functions involved in the operation of the Agency and its associated administrative and technical support planning, would be performed by various divisions. Direct service support to the customer should rest with the four divisions, operating under the associate director of operations.

Personnel and Costs

Phase 1: It is anticipated that Phase 1 will require a headquarters staff of approximately 250 professional and 100 support personnel. If we assume the average professional salary to be $12,500 per year and the average support salary to be $5000 per year and add 100 per cent for overhead—building space, equipment, fringe benefits, etc.—then the annual cost for the initial headquarters personnel is about $7 million. Assuming that all personnel will not be available during the first few months, $6 million should be sufficient for personnel and other general costs during the first year, FY 1967.

Developmental studies and other contract work in direct support of developing plans for Phase 2 will require approximately $5 million in obligated funds the first year. Therefore, the total additional funds required to fund the Agency for FY 67, the first year, is approximately $11 million.

Phase 2: This phase includes two additional requirements not found in Phase 1. One is the operating of present services taken over from the various departments and agencies, the second is development funds for the Document Processing Center.

The present estimated direct costs for federal scientific and technical information ranges from $200 million to $400 million per year, including initial publication and distribution costs. Extrapolating from these estimates, and excluding initial publication and distribution costs, we would expect an expenditure of approximately $200 million by the beginning of FY 68 for those services proposed for the Agency. This funding is now considered by many experts to be approximately two-thirds of that needed to provide adequate services.

Developmental cost associated with the establishment of the new Center is estimated at approximately $350 million, of which $150 million would be committed during the first year of Phase 2. When these two costs are added to the operating costs of the Agency headquarters, the expenditure for FY 68 would total approximately $457 million.

Additional cost for development activities associated with development of the Center is estimated to be $150 million in the FY 69. This is in addition to operating costs. Operating costs are expected to increase at a rate of approximately six per cent annually. The total anticipated cost for development and operations for FY 69, therefore, is approximately $476 million.

Phase 3: The remainder of the $50 million developmental costs for the Document Processing Center would be expended during FY 70, before the Center becomes operational. In addition to normal operating costs in previous years, the Center will require an initial personnel manning of 25 professionals and 100 supporting staff. Using cost rates as stated in Phase 1, this additional cost would be approximately $2.5 million. The total expenditures for FY 70 would total approximately $396 million.

Phase 4: Developmental costs would drop again in FY 71. At the completion of the Center development for Phase 3, development costs will be spread out over several years. Some increase, however, would continue due to anticipated increasing costs for operating the system. Projected cost for FY 71 and beyond is approximately $381 million with some anticipated percentage increase per year based on volume of load. A summary of the costs for FY 67 through FY 71 is shown in Table 9-1.

Table 9-1 Estimated Costs for the Agency, FY 67 through FY 71 (In Millions of dollars)

Year	Headquarters Operation	Operating System (Inc. Subsidies)	Development (Inc. Center)	Totals
FY 67	$6,000	—0—	$ 5,000	$ 11,000
FY 68	7,000	$300,000	150,000	457,000
FY 69	8,000	318,000	150,000	476,000
FY 70	8,000	338,000	50,000	396,000
FY 71	8,000	358,000	15,000	381,000

Advantages of The Agency

There are a number of advantages which will accrue from a centralized system such as the National Scientific and Technical Information Agency:

Centralized Management. Today there is no single point within government where sufficient responsibility, authority, and leadership can be exerted toward the goal of providing better S&T information and documentation service. This has led to a number of problems which could be eliminated through centralized management: (a) Steps for eliminating duplication of functions, removing gaps, providing new services, eliminating unneeded services, and determining the needs of the total community now rest on the "cooperative" efforts of the various agencies. (b) There is no present provision for determining uniform procedures for document handling between the federal government and the private sector. (c) There is no one agency responsible for processing requests from the private sector related to research, funding, standardization of procedures of mutual concern, or desired legislation.

The Agency should be of great assistance in correcting these deficiencies.

Financial Support. Financial support for S&T information and documentation activities of the federal and nonfederal sectors is now scattered among numerous organizations. This has resulted in overlap of expenditures, inequities in services rendered, confusion as to source of support for the private sector, nonstandardized cost estimates, etc., the Agency would offer a uniform determination of costs based on needs of the user, centralized budget preparation based on standardized budget estimates, and a single responsibility for budget preparation for presentation to Congress.

Quality of Service. Present services vary from agency to agency. Some agencies consider S&T information and document services as worthy of careful attention; others relegate this function to the insignificant. The Agency would set and maintain uniform quality standards for all agencies, thus guaranteeing equal S&T information and document coverage of every area of science and technology.

Planning for Automation. The quality of S&T information and document services has been de-graded due to the ever-increasing volume of documentation handling required. Automation of some functions is essential to improved services.

At present there is no agency to plan, fund, and standardize an effort toward an integrated system using automated aids. The Agency would provide this need.

Foreign Document Acquisition. The responsibility for gathering significant foreign publications is shared by several agencies. Insufficient attention is given to the problem of avoiding duplication of effort, defining areas of potential interest to all users, and eliminating gaps in our acquisition. The Agency through its Foreign Program Development and Coordination Division, would give specific attention to this problem.

Library of Congress. The fact that the Library of Congress has been operated traditionally by Congress rather than by the operating arm of the Government, presents many problems relative to its position in a national system(s). The Agency would avoid the disruption of the present status of the Library of Congress by omitting it from its operational control and providing it with expanded service capability. The expanded capability would be provided by giving the Library of Congress access to all significant S&T information and documents through a service which is provided and funded by the Agency. This would permit it to concentrate on non-scientific and non-technical documentation and its services to Congress and its public.

Improved Services. Services now provided by the various agencies are marginal in some areas, due to incompleteness of coverage, the inability of users to know what is available, and slow reaction-times. There is a need for complete coverage of all useful documents for scientific and technical work, better source materials as to what is available, a faster delivery of critically needed documentation, and a convenient method for obtaining documents within the system. The Agency would provide the mechanism for obtaining these goals.

Document Storage. Presently, each department and agency maintains a library for its own use with an ever-increasing quantity of documents. Each document is frequently stored in quantity, and document collections overlap those of other agencies. Requirements for future storage space,

utilizing the present method of operation, would become prohibitive for many agencies to operate and maintain. The Agency would greatly reduce the need for library and document storage space by providing a readily accessible central store, containing only a single reproducible copy of each document.

Disadvantages of The Agency

Disadvantages to Using Agency. There are a number of possible disadvantages to the agencies which would be served by the Agency. These are:

1. The control of the quality of information services would no longer be under the direct control of the using agency, as the only representation that the using agency would have consists of a representative on the Advisory Council of the Agency.

2. The personnel engaged in serving the S&T document needs of the using agency would be no longer a part of the using agency.

3. The using agency may not wish to have another agency so intimately close to its operation.

4. The Agency, having many requirements to fulfill for several agencies, may not be as responsive to the specialized needs of the using agencies, or may be slow to react.

5. The proposed system would necessitate that each agency have a separate system for the control of proprietary and classified information, unless the Agency also assumed the responsibility for classified material.

Attitudes. Even though the formation of the Agency would offer many advantages, the concept does involve some dramatic changes in authority, responsibility, personnel management, etc. These changes might be perceived by some as too drastic a solution.

Costs. The initial implementation costs of the Agency will be higher than that for some other concepts, for example the capping agency and responsible agent concepts. However, certain efficiencies would accrue through the Agency which would not result from either of the other two (e.g., reduced storage space, a more complete collection, improved announcing, reduced overlapping).

Personnel. A centralized operation, using advanced methods, would require highly technical personnel for its operation. Skills necessary for operating such a system are in short supply. In addition, problems associated with administering and supervising personnel assigned over large geographic areas could present a problem.

Budget Visibility. The costs associated with the total operation, when placed in a single budget, would have great visibility. Even though there are some advantages to a centralized budget, as already mentioned, the size of the budget would have increased visibility and might present a tempting target for the annual "budget cutting."

A GOVERNMENT-CHARTERED CORPORATION AS THE OPERATING AGENCY

The previous section has described in detail the concept of a new operating agency which would have responsibility for the centralized operation of a complete S&T information and documentation service. This Agency was described as a new agency in the executive branch of the federal government. An attractive alternative to this concept is a similar operating organization as a government-chartered private corporation. This corporation would perform all of the functions previously outlined for the Agency. One of the most powerful arguments in favor of this concept is that the S&T information and documentation problem is both a federal government activity and an activity in the nonfederal sector. Because of this, a solution based solely on federal action is bound to be less than satisfactory and a special corporation could help bridge the area between the nonfederal sector and the government.

There are a number of precedents for the formation of government-chartered corporations to deal with special problems where either a natural monopoly exists or where there is an unusual requirement for government and industry cooperation in the mutual rendering of a service. Over 30 such corporations are presently chartered and several of them have characteristics which would be desirable for an operating corporation in the S&T information and documentation area. Table 9-2 gives a summary of some of the important features of the Tennessee Valley Authority, the Virgin Islands Corporation, and the Communications Satellite Corporation as these characteristics may be related to a

Table 9-2 Government Corporation Features Appropriate for Use in an S&T Information and Documentation Corporation

The features included in this table have application in the organizational, operational, and coordination aspects of an S&T information and documentation corporation. The Tennessee Valley Authority, the Virgin Islands Corporation and the Communications Satellite Corporation are abbreviated as TVA, VIC and COMSAT.

Chartered Attribute	Origin	Chartered Attribute	Origin
1. Management and control of operations of a multiple-mission nature established in areas previously controlled by government agencies and private firms.	TVA	couragement and support of private sector activities.	VIC
2. A government corporation with joint federal-private direction exercising policy responsibilities.	VIC	8. A corporation empowered to issue stock. The stock issue made to private firms whose functions and products are related to the purpose of the corporation issuing the stock, and also to the general public.	COMSAT
3. Joint federal-private organization for the promotion of services and products.	VIC	9. Representation of major private research, operational and service organizations on the Board of Directors.	COMSAT
4. Both federal government and private review and control of activities of a special corporation.	COMSAT	10. A strong commitment to activity in new high-priority government and private technical activities.	COMSAT
5. A congressionally chartered corporation with authority to make charges for its services and products.	TVA, COMSAT	11. Orientation toward promotion of wide application and dissemination of federally developed innovations.	COMSAT
6. Mixed and integrated federal-private scientific research and development activities.	TVA	12. Authority to effect joint agreements with foreign governments and private organizations, subject to review by the federal government.	COMSAT
7. Strong integrated federal-private en-			

corporation involved in the S&T information and documentation field.

From an examination of this table and a consideration of the functions to be performed in the S&T information and documentation field, it is apparent that there is real precedent for the proposal being made here.

The Government-Chartered Scientific and Technical Information Corporation and a Control Commission

It is apparent that the government should not delegate to a private corporation its responsibility for formulating policy in the S&T information and documentation area. Because of this, an essential feature of the idea of forming a government corporation is the establishment of a regulatory commission within the independent offices and establishments portion of the executive branch of the federal government. Thus there would be formed a commission to be known

as the Scientific and Technical Information Commission. The Commission would have general powers in the S&T information and documentation area similar to those the Federal Communications Commission has in its area of responsibility. The Commission's basic purpose would be to establish government policy with regard to fundamental questions of scientific and technical information handling. It would deal with such broad questions as the extent to which the federal government feels it necessary, for federal purposes, to increase or decrease the coverage of information or documents held by the operating organization; the degree of subsidy appropriate from the government in view of the corporation's assistance in helping the government discharge its basic responsibilities; the amount of competition or overlapping in service to be allowed between the federal agencies and the operating corporation; and similar questions regarding government participation in the corporation. It would also be concerned with policy

questions relative to other portions of the non-federal sector.

The companion organization to the regulatory commission would be a private government-chartered corporation known as the Scientific and Technical Information Corporation. It would be a part of the private sector, chartered by Congress, with a defined mission and area of exclusive responsibility. Under one scheme it would be managed by a board of trustees to be named by the President, part of whom would serve on the board in addition to their normal government appointments and part of whom would come from the private sector concerned with S&T information and documentation operations. In this way the corporation would be responsible to both the needs of the federal government and to the needs and services of private organizations. Under the direction of the board of trustees, a management would be appointed which would have the authority and responsibilities normally associated with the management of any large private corporation.

The ownership of the Corporation would depend on its initial funding, and several possibilities for funding exist. Probably the simplest method of financing would be by a special government grant made through a specific Congressional appropriation. In this case the federal government would own the assets of the corporation. Another appealing method of financing would be through the sale of stock. Perhaps the government would buy one-half the stock and the remainder would be sold to the public (with restrictions similar to those in the case of COMSAT). In any case, the solution to the problems of initial funding would tend to determine the structure of the board of trustees, but it should not affect the direct line management relative to the operations of the Corporation.

Operations of the Corporation

The Corporation would be responsible for the operation previously outlined for the Agency. In all operational respects it would be similar to the Agency except that it would not be restricted by the various regulations and customs governing government agencies. Since the Corporation would not be financed directly by the federal budget as the Agency would, it would need to be supported through the sale of its services. Each government organization needing the Cor-

poration's services would contract with the Corporation for the services it needed. The organization would receive these services from the Corporation in the same sense that Government units now receive utility services from private corporations. Generally, government organizations would be prohibited from meeting their needs by setting up internal competing services. This would be necessary to assure that the Corporation would have a sufficient volume of business to justify the considerable expense involved in maintaining a large centralized service in the S&T information and documentation area.

Similarly, the Corporation would offer its services to subscribers in the nonfederal sector. These subscribers might include universities, industrial organizations, cities, or any other organization or individual having a need for S&T information and documentation services. Each of these users would be charged for services on a basis similar to that used for the federal government.

In addition to selling services, the Corporation would receive an annual subsidy from the federal government. This subsidy would be sufficient to make up any difference between the operating expenses and income derived from selling services. Since the federal government has a recognized responsibility for treating scientific information and documents as a national resource and would have delegated operational responsibility for fulfilling this need to the Corporation, the government would recognize the requirement to subsidize the Corporation for maintaining this special national resource. The size of this subsidy and the nature of the resource to be maintained would be one of the major concerns of the regulatory commission mentioned previously.

Implementation. An implementation plan for the government-chartered Corporation has not been worked out in any detail. It is felt that the implementation plan previously presented for the New Operating Agency could be followed, although it would probably take longer and be more difficult to establish the Corporation. Clearly, there would need to be detailed negotiations and agreements with many parts of the private document handling sector. Also the laws required to establish such a corporation are in a

controversial area of public policy since they would involve government participation in and subsidy of a private organization.

Arguments in Favor of the Corporation Concept

The arguments previously given for the New Operating Agency, also apply to the Corporation, but there are some additional considerations which favor the development of this new concept.

The Corporation Could Better Serve the Nonfederal Sector. The S&T information and documentation area is divided between the federal sector and a large nonfederal sector. This sector is very diverse, including universities, professional societies, public libraries, private corporations, publishers, state and local governments, etc. The federal government would have difficulty in adopting rules and regulations so that flexibility could be achieved in dealing with this diverse nonfederal area. A private corporation is inherently more flexible than a government organization and would be able to formulate modes of operation which would be adaptable to each of the organizations mentioned above. It seems highly probable that an independent private corporation would be able to effect a better resolution to the diverse problems in the S&T information and documentation area than would an organization within the government structure.

Capital Investment Would Be Better Managed and Efficiently Used. As described in connection with the Agency, there would ultimately be a very large centralized store of information and documents which would be based on a highly advanced automated system. This system would represent a large capital outlay. To help amortize such a capital investment, the number of users should be kept as large as possible. A private corporation servicing both the government and the nonfederal sector would be in a better position to amortize this investment than would an organization in the federal government and responsible for services largely to the federal government.

The Corporation Would Be More Flexible. The Corporation would have greater flexibility to meet the complex and changing needs of the services to be offered than would an agency lodged in the federal government. Inevitably, there are various regulations regarding forms, budgets, personnel, etc., which, although appropriate for the government as a whole, make it difficult to operate a new organization rendering a service both to the government and to the nonfederal sector. The unusual technical nature of the S&T information and document handling system and the difficult operational activities involved make it desirable that the operating organization have the greatest possible degree of flexibility. This can undoubtedly be achieved more easily in a private corporation than in a government agency.

Personnel Management Would Be Simplified. Past experience has shown that a private corporation can recruit the highly specialized technical personnel required to operate an automated system more easily than can the federal government. The successful design, development, and implementation of a highly automated system requires unusual degrees of flexibility in recruiting and managing personnel.

The Corporation Would Be Efficient. Because of the nature of its operations, the Corporation would have unusual motivation for efficiency. Because it would sell its services to the government and to nonfederal organizations, it would be under pressure to render these services in an efficient fashion. If it did not do so, its sales would suffer accordingly and the size of the subsidy required would cause critical scrutiny of the management of the organization. Management would thus be under pressure to operate efficiently.

Arguments Against the Corporation Concept

In addition to the arguments which are made against the New Operating Agency concept, there are several other arguments which can be made against the Corporation concept.

The Corporation's Activity Would Be Too Involved in Government Operations. There is really no precedent for a private corporation having the power of servicing federal activities to the extent proposed. S&T information and documentation comprise an area pervasive throughout the government organization and fundamental to the effective discharge of government responsibilities. It would be out of keeping with the concept of federal responsibility to place operating responsibility for such an

important area in an organization outside the federal government.

Federal Agencies Would Compete With the Corporation. Even though policies may be set which would inhibit federal organizations from rendering their own S&T information and documentation services, actual experiences would undoubtedly show that the several federal agencies would feel compelled to maintain their own services. Because of the importance of S&T information and documentation to the successful operation of an agency, it would soon become apparent to each agency that the successful performance of its duties required the maintenance of alternate services under camouflaged names or organizations. This would greatly reduce the supposed effectiveness of the Corporation.

Private Organizations Would Compete with the Corporation. It is possible that the private sector would not be as receptive to the supposed advantages of the Corporation as has been suggested. A private organization such as the Corporation could not speak with the real authority of a federal agency. It is probable that many private organizations would be less than completely cooperative with another private organization in the S&T information and documentation area because competitive issues would arise and in the end the authority of the government would need to be used for the benefit of a particular private organization. This would create inequities which would eventually raise serious doubt regarding the propriety of a private corporation maintaining a preferred position in the S&T information and documentation area.

The Corporation Is Counter to the Idea of "In-House" Services. The idea of the Corporation is opposed to the government efforts to perform as many services as possible "in-house." The increased civil service pay, the latitude in management and funding arrangements recently made in many government organizations reflect a desire to establish conditions for "in-house" competence. The establishment of the Corporation would be interpreted as contrary to this policy.

A NATIONAL LIBRARY ADMINISTRATION AS THE OPERATING AND RESPONSIBLE AGENCY

This chapter has so far presented two versions of a completely new operating agency. The plan described here is one of building an operating agency around an existing organization within the federal government. The Library of Congress is a logical organization around which to build an operating agency because of the breadth of its collections and because it has by far the largest cadre of personnel experienced in acquisition and cataloging and the building of systems for servicing a very wide variety of documents. As an operating agency it would assimilate, coordinate and have direct administrative control over the provision of all federal document-handling services in the areas of science and technology. Because the current operations and responsibilities of the Library of Congress, both in the federal and nonfederal sectors, go beyond the subject areas subsumed under science and technology, it has been thought useful to consider extension of its operating responsibilities ultimately to comprehend all federal document-handling services. Such an agency could be named the National Library Administration (NLA).

The nature and functions of such an operating agency are now presented. It is assumed that the organization would be established by law within the executive branch as one of the executive departments and independent agencies. Of the current Library of Congress operations, only the Legislative Reference Service would remain under the direct administrative control of Congress. An initial organization is presented, together with the requirements and estimates of costs for the transition from the present status to the consolidation of all the affected services under one administrative unit. The NLA is conceived as initially confining its responsibility primarily to science and technology, and evolving gradually into a complete service covering all document-handling responsibilities. The arguments for and against the formation of such an operating agency include the following points.

Functions

The functions to be performed by the National Library Administration would be similar to those for the capping agency, with the differences and equivalences indicated below.

Formulation of Policy. The NLA would formulate policy for all federal activities concerning the acquisition, announcement, storage and dissemination of scientific and technical information

and documentation. It would define the responsibility of the departments and agencies relative to the full range of document-handling activities and the establishment of specialized centers and libraries, national libraries, and services.

Policy Responsibility and Operations with Respect to Nonfederal Libraries and Centers. Same as for the capping organization.

Information Centers. Control and responsibility for operation of centers now under diverse federal agencies and departments or operated within the private sector under government contract would be transferred to the NLA. This would involve contracting with the operating agencies or setting up operations at various sites directly subordinate to the NLA administration.

Federal Depositories. Same as for the capping agency.

Government Publications. Cataloging and indexing functions now placed within the Government Printing Office, NASA, DOD, AEC, and so on, would be assigned to these agencies, but with administrative policy control remaining with the NLA. The GPO would be assigned primary responsibility for government printing and primary distribution of unclassified documents.

Support of Nongovernment Publications.

Nondocumentary Communications.

Statistical Information.

Establishment of Standards.

} Same as for the capping agency

Research and Development in Information Technology. The NLA would be responsible for establishment of policy and coordination of research and development for information technology within the diverse agencies, such as NSF, ONR, RADC, AFOSR, NBS, etc. The NLA would become a major contracting agency for advanced development in information technology, librarianship and associated work. It would provide for and coordinate Federal support for these activities.

Education and Training of Librarians, Information Scientists and Technologists, Technicians and Clerical Personnel.

Foreign Documents and Translations.

Information About Information Services.

Copyright and Patent Policy.

} Same as for the capping agency

Budget Review and Funding Control. The NLA would formulate the total budget to Congress for federal government programs in the area of scientific and technical documentation handling and service. For those areas of government document-handling not directly within the administrative control of the agency, budget review powers would be established. This would require close coordination with the Bureau of the Budget.

Legislative Relations and Legal Matters.

Long-Range Plans.

} Same as for the capping agency

Organization

The NLA should be established as an independent agency reporting organizationally as a part of the executive departments and independent agencies under the executive and directive authority of the President.

Organizational Structure. An organization chart for the initial organization of the NLA is given in Figure 9-4. The chart indicates that the NLA would acquire direct administrative control over federal libraries and would establish offices for national S&T services that would acquire the comparable organizations for nonlibrary functions, exclusive of those handling security classified materials.

Office of the Administrator and Librarian of Congress. The NLA would be a service organization whose structure would reflect its operational mission and responsibilities. As in the case of the capping agency concept, two advisory groups are indicated. There would be an

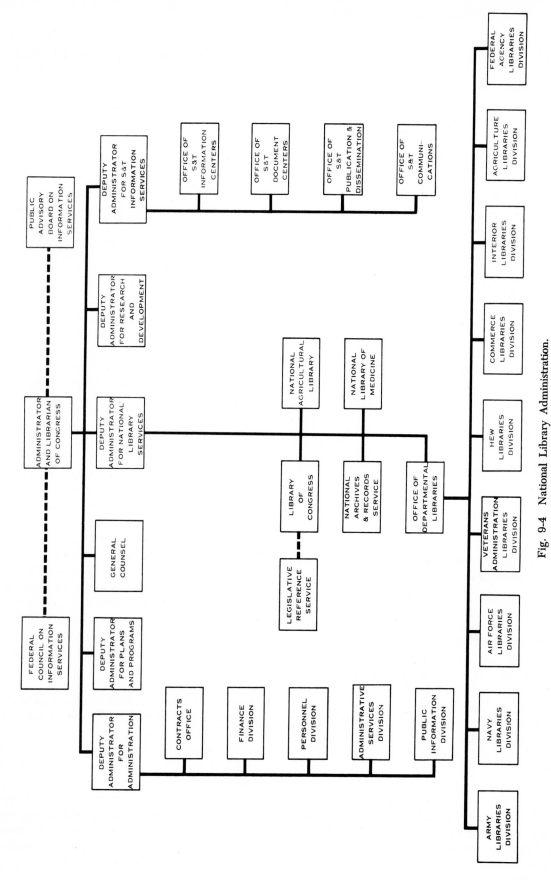

Fig. 9-4 National Library Administration.

243

advisory group comparable to the present COSATI organization, providing direct communications with the departments and agencies being served. Similarly an advisory group from the private sector would be constituted consisting of representatives from professional and industrial associations and the academic community to represent the nonfederal library and information technology interests.

Organization and Administration. The principal operational responsibilities, as indicated in Figure 9-4, would lie with a deputy administrator for National Library Services and a deputy administrator for S&T Information Services. In addition, there would be a deputy administrator for Administration, a deputy administrator for Plans and Programs, a general counsel, and a deputy administrator for Research and Development.

Deputy Administrator for Administration. This administrator would be responsible for a Contracts Office that would have cognizance over all contracts for the NLA. The organization would include the Finance Division, a Personnel Division, a Public Information Division, and an Administrative Services Division. These latter divisions would have responsibilities and functions comparable to those found in other large administrative structures within the federal system.

Deputy Administrator for Plans and Programs. This administrator would have the responsibilities for developing advanced plans and detailed designs for the modification of the national network and systems. He would have responsibility for compilation and normalization of statistical information gathered within the operation areas. He would have the responsibility for liaison with nonfederal libraries, professional society operations, indexing and abstracting services, publishing policies, and foreign exchanges. An additional responsibility would include developing programs of education and training for NLA personnel.

General Counsel. The general counsel would have the task of advising the administrator concerning the legal aspects of all functions and operations and would coordinate with the administrator for Plans and Programs with respect to legislative proposals at home and abroad. He would have the responsibility of assembling and analyzing the range of legislation for federal, state, municipal and foreign governments relevant to the NLA mission.

Deputy Administrator for Research and Development. This administrator would have responsibility for assessing the state of research and technology applicable to document and information handling, for developing programs to support research and development, and for contracting for same. He would also have the responsibility for liaison with the service organizations for the application of advanced technology to the functions and operations performed.

Deputy Administrator for National Library Services. This administrator would have under his cognizance the operations of the Library of Congress; the National Agricultural Library; the National Library of Medicine; the National Archives and Records Service, which would be transferred from the General Services Administration; and an Office of Departmental Libraries whose responsibilities would include the provision of library service within the departments and agencies.

Deputy Administrator for National Scientific and Technical (S&T) Information Services. This administrator would have under his cognizance an office of S&T Information Centers, an office of S&T Document Centers, an office of S&T Publications and Dissemination, and an office of S&T Communications. These offices would be responsible for operating or contracting for the operation of information centers, document centers, primary and secondary publications, support of communications, and meetings and other activities essential to science and technology.

Scheme of Operations

General Considerations. The NLA would act as a service organization for all federal agencies and qualified members of the nonfederal sector. It would operate library facilities within the federal government, excluding the judiciary. It would operate, delegate, or contract for the operation of information centers, document centers, and the various secondary indexing, abstracting, and other awareness services. It would coordinate the provision of support for conferences and other forms of interpersonal communication.

The NLA organization centered around the Library of Congress would operate as the main switching point for a decentralized network of libraries and centers; these satellite operations would be assigned responsibilities for processing and service in particular subject areas or format categories of documents. Through research, development, and implementation of advanced technology in the areas of computing, reprography, and communications, the network would be brought into a coordinated state of quick response to service demands.

The Legislative Reference Service would remain as an exclusive agency for the service of Congress and report administratively to Congress. Other services currently supplied to the Congress, its staff and constituents would be maintained, expanded and improved. The Congress would be able to draw upon the human and material resources of the entire system for service and support.

The NLA would provide for wholesaling of documents to its various government organizations, to libraries, and to other users in the non-federal sector. It would provide for the maintenance of at least one accessible reproducible copy, in full size or microform, of all significant documents in the scientific and technical areas.

The organization would provide for coordinated and compatible selection, acquisition, cataloging, indexing and other processing of documents within the system. It would provide for the building and maintenance of locating tools, such as union catalogs, union lists of serials, union lists of documents, such that every technical document of interest within the United States may be located and made accessible to users in the country. The NLA would coordinate and, where possible, centralize acquisitions functions, the establishment and maintenance of exchange agreements and cataloging and indexing for those organizations employing compatible practices. The development of a viable network would include the elimination of unnecessary duplication of efforts and redundancy in collections and announcing media.

Evolution of a National Network. Implementation of a plan for the creation of a National Library Administration as described herein would first require a drafting of appropriate legislation which would include revision of previous legislation, appropriate funding, and the assignment of responsibilities as indicated to the Library of Congress. This would include the provision of physical facilities in addition to those currently existing, and the transfer of personnel to the administration for building a headquarters operation (in addition to those staff members whose activities would be re-oriented within the Library of Congress).

It should be possible for the transfer of most library operations within the federal system to the NLA to be effective within one year of its creation. Within two years the various information centers, document centers, and other activities in the S&T information area would also have been brought under the NLA. The initial phase of acquisition of libraries and other functions would involve the transfer of budgets from the departments and agencies to the NLA, the assessment of the actual costs of operation in terms of departmental and agency budgets for overhead and other support operations not directly budgeted, and the establishment of general rules and regulations pertaining to the new organization. The personnel and facilities of existing organizations would be brought into the NLA intact without significant change in order to speed the creation of an effective national network.

In those instances where it would not be feasible at the time of the transfer to effectively absorb personnel, for example, from the DOD or AEC, arrangements would be made for delegation of functions and contractual support. The NLA would not acquire the operations involving the handling of security classified materials. Military and other personnel involved in sensitive areas relating to DOD, AEC, and NASA missions would not be transferred to the NLA. Considerable study and negotiation would be required for this transitional phase of operations.

Concurrent with the acquisition of relevant organizations would be the modification of current practices of administration processing, dissemination and service. It would be a prime responsibility of the deputy administrator for Plans and Programs to study and recommend the courses of action which could lead to coordinated operations and services. By the third year, effects of programs developed by the deputy administrator for Research and Development should also begin to have some effect upon actual operations. Among the changes which might be envisaged are creation of new national

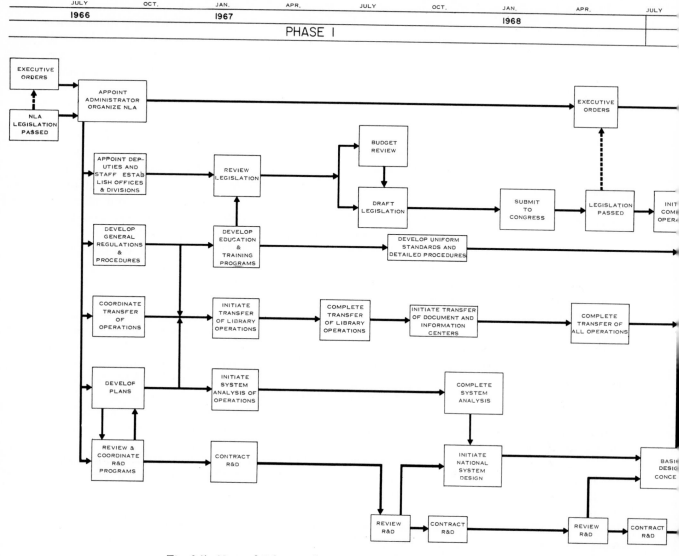

Fig. 9-5 National Library Administration implementation schedule.

libraries for specialized subject treatment, the development of microform service units strategically situated within the country for minimum response time and maximum service capability, and the consolidation of various library document and information center operations into fewer and more efficient operations.

A final phase, which could be foreseen at this time, is that of the development and comprehensive application of advanced technology to library and other document-handling functions. Through advances in the computer art, reprography and communication techniques, a first configuration of an integrated national network would be in operation within about five years after its establishment as a National Library Ad-

ministration. At this time the acquisition of all document-handling functions within the government would have been completed, exclusive of printing operations. The responsibility for printing and primary dissemination of government documents would remain with the Government Printing Office and such other institutions in the DOD, AEC, NASA, and other agencies as appropriate.

Implementation Schedule. Figure 9-5 presents a suggested implementation schedule for the period July 1966 to July 1970, indicating major milestones in the development of an integrated system. This development is divided into two phases of two years each. Phase 1, after enabling

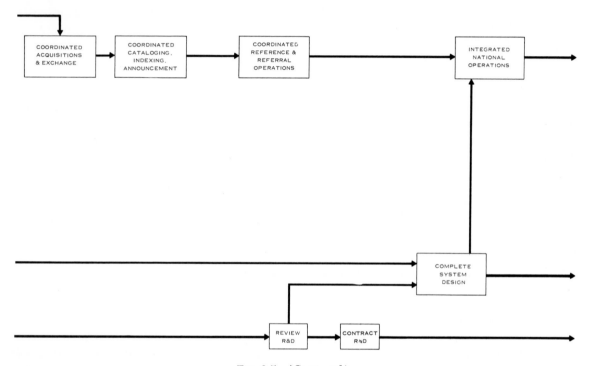

Fig. 9-5   (Continued)

legislation has been passed, would consist of organization, transfer of operations to the NLA, budget review, development of legislative proposals, planning and research. The major planning effort would comprise a system analysis of current operations and initiation of a system design effort.

The first product of the design effort would be a basic system concept or overall design whose details would be elaborated and scheduled for implementation at various times, as suggested in the figure, over the two years of Phase 2. By July 1970, the total design would have been completed and largely implemented. The following period, not shown, would constitute a third phase in which a new cycle of planning,

analysis, design, and implementation would be undertaken for further modification and improvement of the system.

Facilities and Equipment. Facilities and equipment for operations would be acquired through purchase, lease, and/or agreements with the agencies and departments serviced. Where possible the facilities would be transferred to the NLA.

Personnel. Personnel would be selected, trained, assigned and supervised by the NLA. The NLA would undertake programs to define future personnel requirements and position classifications in coordination with the Civil Service Commission. It would also coordinate with the Office

of Education for the development of education and training programs and support for academic institutions.

Budget. For the first year of its operation the NLA would require some $15 million in addition to funds transferred from the departments and agencies with the acquired operations. The third year would require support for some 12,000 personnel, new facilities, equipment, research, and development programs. In the third year, when the NLA would budget for the entire operation, it is estimated that the total budget would be of the order of $300 million, increasing to $400 million by the fifth year.

Placement of the National Library Administration

The NLA should be placed organizationally as a part of the executive departments and independent agencies and be given the executive and directive authority of the President for discharging the duties and functions detailed in the preceding sections.

Advantages of the National Library Administration as the Operating and Responsible Agency

The NLA would provide a single point of responsibility, leadership, and operational authority for a coherent and consistent organizational structure that could implement a national program and plan for a national network or system responsive to the current and future needs of the scientific and technical community. Furthermore, because it would be organized around the Library of Congress, the NLA could draw upon the most comprehensive collection and the largest cadre of trained librarians and subject and language specialists available within the federal government.

The NLA would provide for centralized planning, development, and implementation of advanced technology to document collection, representation, storage, retrieval, and use. Particularly for the development of compatible systems, an operating agency is probably the only type of entity which could effectively bring diverse practices into a compatible state.

The NLA would provide for uniform and compatible development in document-handling procedures for both the government and private sector. This development would be enhanced because of the unique status of the Library of Congress with respect to library operations throughout the country.

The NLA would provide a single point of contact for nongovernment agencies, foreign countries, libraries, professional organizations, publishers, and the like.

The NLA would provide for coordinated acquisitions of foreign documents and an effective coordination of exchange agreements toward complete coverage and reduction of duplicated efforts.

The NLA would establish an organization which would operate as a comprehensive source and service for access to all unclassified scientific and technical documentation.

The NLA would provide for appropriate study efforts and operational changes responsive to user requirements for documents and information.

The NLA would provide for potential overall cost reduction through rationalization, coordination, and advanced planning responsive to the requirements of a burgeoning technology. It would provide for uniform recording, analyses, and standards and, therefore, for a system-related budget.

The NLA's centralized authority and operation would provide a much higher likelihood of real cooperation and effective coordination between functions and operations now located in distinct administrative hierarchies.

The NLA would provide for minimization of unnecessary duplication of functions, operations, and services, and for the elimination of gaps in coverage and in service.

Disadvantages of the National Library Administration as the Operating and Responsible Agency

The concept is a radical departure from the past and involves a complete reorganization of information operations within the federal system, the withdrawal of the Library of Congress from the direct administrative control of Congress, and an unprecedented centralization of authority in this area of operations. Because the concept is so radical, it raises difficulties of implementation and of obtaining legislative approval.

The transition period for establishing and implementing the program outlined offers many difficulties. No newly established organizational

structure is wholly satisfactory because of the requirement of acquiring the operations "as they are" without change. This would hamper further development to more functional arrangements.

The initial implementation costs are likely to be very high. The costs of service and the budgets accompanying them would have visibility even at present levels of spending that might preclude appropriate levels of support being approved by Congress.

There is a serious question whether creating a National Library Administration around the Library of Congress would lead to improved services for the users of scientific and technical documents. This purely administrative solution does not really address the question of how the Library and its dependencies could be brought to any rapid, effective change in practices and procedures.

The tendency to standardize procedures of document description, handling, and operational services could very well have a baleful effect on the utility of the services performed by such entities as the National Library of Medicine, the National Agricultural Library, and other specialized services and centers. It may very well be that a variety of practices should be encouraged in view of the lack of optimum systems or techniques of operation at the present state of the art. With the implementation of advanced technologies and use of computers and mechanized communications networks, the tendency to create uniform practice in a centralized organization could lead to a monolithic, but relatively unresponsive system, which could not be readily altered to meet the changing directions of research and development.

There is very likely to be great resistance to effective establishment of any such structure in that the using agencies will fear that they will not be as well served as they are when they have control over the operations concerned. The operational consequences within the DOD, AEC, and other organizations having security and proprietary concerns will hamper or prevent complete implementation of any such program. Many operations handle a mixture of classified or restricted and unclassified and unrestricted documents. These agencies will resist any weakening of their cognizance or control over documentation functions essential to execution of their assigned missions.

Chapter Ten

Strengthening the Present System

One of the alternative organizational approaches to the national document and information handling problem is to leave the present organizational structure much as it is but strengthen the coordinating and policy-making resources of appropriate existing federal organizations. In this section we examine the opportunities for, and the advantages and disadvantages of, strengthening the present system.

The organizational approach proposed in this section interferes least with those organizations effectively pursuing a course toward improved services. At the same time, this approach provides for evolutionary changes in those services of the present system less able, by virtue of economics or inadequate management support, to render adequate services. Such organizations should be provided with guidance and support from an overall policy-setting body. After recognizing where the principal weaknesses of the present system exist, appropriate authority can take needed action.

In order to assess the impact of the concept proposed in this section, we will first summarize the organizational and functional relationships of the present system. A detailed description of this system is presented in Chapters 2 and 3.

A CHARACTERIZATION OF THE PRESENT SYSTEM

To refer to the present conglomeration of federal and nonfederal S&T document- and information-handling activities as a "system" does not do justice to the accepted meaning of the word "system." The present system was never designed as a system, thus it lacks coordination of activities as well as common goals. Some successful attempts have been made to overcome

these weaknesses, but so far they have barely scratched the surface of the problem. Common goals and coordination of activities should be inherent in any real system. Attempting to impose these features on a system which has developed for a considerable period of time in many directions and with diverse and oftentimes conflicting goals is not an easy task.

The integrative and coordinating organization for the Federal sector is the Committee on Scientific and Technical Information (COSATI), a committee of the Federal Council for Science and Technology (FCST). COSATI has been able to recognize and study the problems in this area but, since it lacks authority to directly implement policy, reliance for across-the-board federal action has been placed on the cooperation of the federal agencies under coordination by the Office of Science and Technology (OST). Figure 2-1 represents the Federal *structure* for S&T document and information handling activities, but should *not* be taken to represent any clearly defined lines of interagency authority. With a few exceptions such lines do not now exist. We propose a means of strengthening the present federal system so that such lines of authority may be defined or strengthened.

A diagram, similar to Figure 2-1 for the nonfederal sector of S&T document and information handling activities is not feasible. Nor would such a diagram be meaningful because of the independent nature of the components which make up this sector (e.g., university libraries, professional societies, specialized information centers, and abstracting and indexing services).

It is possible, however, to discuss both federal and nonfederal S&T document and information activities as functional groups. Chapter 2 of this report discusses the following functional groups:

libraries; information analysis centers; publication, announcement and distribution organizations; document generators and users; and administrative policy and support organizations. In addition, Chapter 2 gives examples of organizations in both the federal and nonfederal sectors that are deeply involved in the S&T document and information handling system in these designated functional groups.

The following paragraphs present a concept within the framework of this present system which will permit some of the more significant drawbacks of the system to be ameliorated or eliminated. This concept makes no recommendations for altering any present activities *except* as necessary to provide management for necessary support in decision making. It is in the organization described for this concept that primary responsibility must be lodged for management and support of national S&T document and information activities.

STRENGTHENING THE PRESENT SYSTEM

The essence of strengthening the present system lies in strengthening the cooperative efforts between several federal organizations, each of which has a defined role in science and technology and an established interface with the scientific and technological community as a whole. These organizations are: the Office of Science and Technology (OST), the Federal Council for Science and Technology (FCST), National Academy of Sciences-National Research Council (NAS-NRC), and the National Science Foundation (NSF). The concept requires that these organizations recognize and accept both a responsibility for and leadership in developing policies and plans for a coordinated national scientific and technical document and information handling system. A major advantage of this approach is that it does not call for a large expenditure, but concentrates on defining and strengthening lines of direction and support within the framework of the present system. Additionally, this approach emulates an evolutionary approach to S&T document and information problems.

The role of each of these organizations will now be discussed. Figure 10-1 depicts the relationships that are inherent in this concept of strengthening the present system.

OST as the Focal Point

The Office of Science and Technology is best suited to assume overall cognizance of and policy development for a national system for S&T document and information handling. Its knowledge of federal government long-range planning for scientific and technological efforts and its organizational placement in the Executive Office of the President make it a rational choice for this responsibility. Its authority in this area is already established by Reorganization Plan No. 2 of March 27, 1962. The Plan states in part, that OST will ". . . *advise* and *assist* [italics added] the President as the President may request with respect to: . . . (3) Review, integration, and coordination of major Federal activities in science and technology, giving due consideration to the effects of such activities on nonfederal resources and institutions. (4) Assuring that good and close relations exist with the Nation's scientific and engineering communities so as to further in every appropriate way their participation in strengthening science and technology in the United States and the Free World. . . ." OST, by expanding existing relationships with FCST and NAS-NRC, would be afforded advice and support from both federal and nonfederal S&T document and information handling organizations. Thus policy development and direction of implementation would be performed in a coordinated manner. NSF would be the supporting organization performing a multitude of tasks delegated to it by OST. An additional staff of a few experts in S&T document and information handling would be needed by OST to efficiently perform the necessary liaison, to coordinate activities, and to formulate and direct the implementation of this policy.

The Roles of FCST and NAS-NRC

FCST is composed of senior federal departmental and agency representatives in science and technology and through its Committee on Scientific and Technical Information (COSATI) has available a supporting organization in the area of S&T document and information handling. COSATI, through FCST, is the established and appropriate organization to support OST's efforts in policy development as the recognized representative of federal opinion concerning S&T document and information handling.

COSATI would continue to exploit the skills

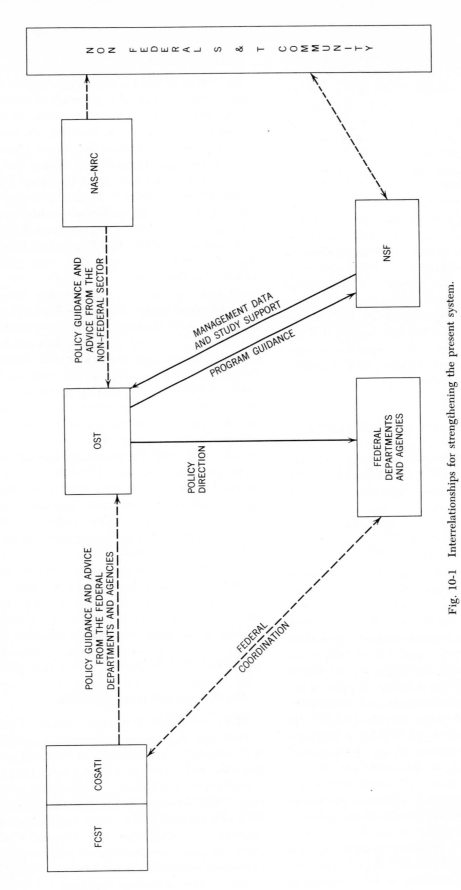

Fig. 10-1 Interrelationships for strengthening the present system.

252

of the personnel of the various agencies for support of study efforts. It is suggested that COSATI could be additionally supported by a small permanent staff to assist in its efforts in formulating policy recommendations, developing requests for action, and providing group responses to proposed policies for the federal sector.

OST would require inputs from the nonfederal sector to develop national policies for S&T document and information handling. It is suggested that NAS-NRC perform this function. NAS-NRC brings together the most competent scientists and engineers in the country to deal broadly with scientific problems. Its patterns of organization are kept flexible to permit each problem to be approached in a suitable manner. Work is carried on through permanent boards and institutes, committees, subcommittees and panels, as well as ad hoc groups for special purposes. Because the basis for this proposed advisory role to OST already exists, we recommend that NAS-NRC be the interface with OST for the nonfederal sector of S&T document and information handling activities. This could be accomplished by expanding the role of the NAS-NRC Office of Documentation of establishing a permanent group specifically for this purpose.

NSF's Role in Supporting OST

Sound long-range policies cannot be expected to emerge solely from pressures. Pressures must be evaluated and appropriate response formulated in terms of objective, timely, and comprehensive data and studies. OST must ensure that sufficient appropriate information is acquired to provide a sound basis for decision making. We have considered several organizations as candidates for the performance of this support function to OST, including the Bureau of the Budget, the Department of Commerce, the Smithsonian Institution, and the National Science Foundation. The National Science Foundation has been selected for three important reasons:

1. Its overall mission in science and science-education support.
2. It has an established mission to gather science management information in both the federal and nonfederal sectors.
3. NSF provides a vehicle for staff support for long-range planning for science.

These arguments in favor of selecting NSF as the supporting organization for OST far outweighed those in favor of any other alternative. Although NSF does not have an explicit mission in the realm of technology, its collection activities of science management information are commonly inclusive of technology. In contrast to other federal organizations being assigned these tasks, no change in mission would be involved in NSF's being assigned the responsibility for collecting and analyzing information and providing its findings to OST. The proposed mission of OST in S&T documentation and information would be supported by NSF as the focal point for acquiring information about S&T activities. NSF would be responsible for setting up and maintaining the system that provides this information to OST. However, in developing that system NSF should coordinate with COSATI to ensure that the federal aspects of the system are compatible with the requirements and capabilities of the individual departments and agencies. In the private sector, NSF is in a position to gather data on the status and plans of the activities supported through scholarly societies and academic institutions. The role of NSF as liaison with scholarly and commercial organizations in the field of scientific and technical documentation and information provides this opportunity.

NSF's staff would have to be increased as it acquired these additional functions. As additional requirements are placed on other government agencies and upon the private sector for increased efforts to develop new and expanded information services, an increase in personnel may be expected in those organizations.

ARGUMENTS FOR THE CONCEPT

Implementation of the Concept Would Cause a Minimal Disruption of the Present System

The concept requires no immediate changes in the service organizations of the present system. All system components with the exception of OST and NSF, would continue to perform their functions as they do now. No existing document or information handling activity would be required to "move" from its current organization, nor would normal agency and departmental functional responsibilities be altered. COSATI would continue to coordinate federal activities in its area of responsibility much as it has in

the past. Observation of events during the past five years leads to an extrapolation that the system will change in an evolutionary manner as it reacts to changing requirements, and that improperly functioning activities will be phased out and new activities created by the process of system maturation. The proposed strengthening of the present system would enhance this process.

Evidence is not persuasive that there are serious duplications and overlaps in the present system. Such features are not necessarily disadvantageous, except in an extreme degree. Furthermore, evidence to justify any drastic changes is less persuasive, and there is *no* foundation for a *particular* solution. A working relationship between OST, COSATI, NAS-NRC, and NSF, whereby the necessary information may be gathered, would produce the evidence to justify evolutionary system modifications. The critics of the current system seem unwilling to recognize that changes *are* taking place as a result of the efforts of COSATI and of other scientific and technical document-handling activities, both federal and nonfederal, to improve the quantity and quality of their services. A strengthening of these efforts cannot help but lead to an improved system.

Each Document-Handling Activity Would Continue to Give Services as It Sees Fit

Any major reorganization of federal S&T document and information handling services would require organizations to perform services which would not be primarily useful to their own staffs. Such a change would no doubt substantially modify the quantity and quality of their services. Related problems of budgeting and record maintenance would also become extremely difficult and cumbersome. Additionally, cross-agency services would represent an unprecedented method of operation for some agencies. Changing the services of the existing system would tend to confuse and complicate existing user patterns and activities and cause some S&T document-handling activities a good deal of difficulty in maintaining a continued level of service. Any *major* change would tend to reduce the control that individual S&T document- and information-handling activities now exercise over the determination of the "qualifications" of their

users. In several organizations, most notably the Department of Defense (DOD), the feeling exists that the determination of the qualifications for users of information should remain under their control. In conclusion, this concept of strengthening the present system would not require any major change in existing services.

The Concept Offers Increased Efficiencies at a Small Increase in Cost

The cost/effectiveness of any major organizational modification of the system would be difficult to determine. New and extensive funding would be better spent on strengthening the present system. There is evidence, e.g., previous proposals, studies, etc., to indicate that any form of major reorganization of existing scientific and technical document-handling activities would have a high cost associated with it.

Any major reorganization would entail a substantial initial implementation outlay and would increase the system's total annual operating expenses. The question is, "Would such an additional investment really have a demonstrable payoff in improved scientific and technical document handling and eliminate the redundancies and gaps that are purported to exist in the present system?" The results of any extensive change would only be moderate at best and not worth the necessary investment in dollars and personnel.

The concept of strengthening the present system does not call for any large expenditures, but concentrates on defining and strengthening lines of direction and support within the framework of the present system. When these organizational lines have been established, efficiencies in the coordinating and policy-making resources of the system would be realized at minimal cost.

Extensive Legislative Changes Are Not Necessary in Order to Implement This Concept

The bases for the legislative and executive controls necessary to implement this concept already exist. Reorganization Plan No. 2 of March 27, 1962, directs that the Office of Science and Technology will provide "proper coordination of Federal science and technology functions," and "review integration and coordination of federal activities in science and technology giving

due consideration to the efforts of such activities on nonfederal resources and institutions." Both P.L. 507, 81st Congress (1950) and Executive Order 10807 of March 17, 1959, (see Appendix 3 for a more detailed description) establish NSF as a focal point for the coordination of S&T document and information activities.

The Value of Innovation May Be Lost by Establishing a More Formal and Centralized Control Mechanism

The solution to the many S&T document and information handling problems requires many approaches. Some libraries require extensive automation while others can operate effectively with manual systems. For some problems, better libraries are the answer; for others, information centers are indicated; for still others, informal exchange between scientists is effective. A large, high-level bureaucracy might tend to see only a single solution to many problems, or one favored technical approach, when in fact a variety of approaches is needed. On the other hand, by clearly defining the roles of OST, COSATI, NAS-NRC, and NSF, the present system would be strengthened without inhibiting innovation.

ARGUMENTS AGAINST THE CONCEPT

Present System Does Not Adequately Serve All Users

Generally speaking, each of the present system's S&T information and document service units provides a specialized service to user groups within their own agencies. As a result, service units operated in this manner are unable to satisfy the broader information requirements of those requesters outside of a particular special interest group. Thus a large population of potential users are not being served at all; either their needs cannot be met by existing services or, as is often the case, they do not know where to find what they need. Furthermore, no vehicle is provided to tell them where to look, because there is only a partially coordinated referral function. We therefore have an existing situation where a small minority determines how the system will service users outside the special interest group. The proposed means of strengthening the present system would not adequately handle this problem.

Library of Congress Problem Would Not Be Solved

The Library of Congress, as an organization in the legislative branch, is not subject to the direct authority of any executive branch organization. The fact that the Library of Congress is in the legislative branch of the government whereas all other federal S&T activities are in the executive branch poses a serious problem concerning uniform policy development, coordination and implementation. The Library of Congress must be an integral part of any national scientific and technical document-handling system, but a strengthened present system does not provide for adequate means to cope with this problem.

Increasing Number of Documents Will Eventually Cause Great Difficulties for Existing System

Available statistical evidence (see Appendix 2) indicates that the volume of all types of scientific and technical documentation is increasing significantly each year. Not even a strengthened present system could adequately provide solutions to the problems of acquisition, storage, retrieval and dissemination of these masses of documentation.

The Concept Requires Establishment of an Unrealistic Administrative Network

The complexity of the present system as modified by the proposed strengthening would require a delicately interacting set of administrative procedures in order to make the concept workable. Much coordination and definition of these interrelationships would be necessary. In the final analysis, the entire concept would depend principally on the cooperative efforts of several disparate organizations, each of which is currently responsible to carry out a much more broadly defined mission. Effective and timely reaction to problems would be difficult to achieve if based primarily on cooperation.

Another danger in this concept is that its administration resides entirely in the Executive Office of the President. Each President uses these staff offices differently, which would tend to give a lesser degree of permanency to the concept than would be the case if it were administered by an Independent Agency or Department.

Attempts by OST to Assume Leadership for Science and Technology Might Be Resisted in the Nonfederal Sector

Even in the limited field of S&T documents and information, nonfederal elements might interpret any increased, though indirect, monitoring by OST as a threat to the freedom of action of private enterprise and the academic community. Attempts to derive consistent data from the nonfederal sector might be met with strong objections as wasteful of effort by creative people and of resource by private corporations.

Permanent Staff Support and Funding for COSATI May Be Difficult to Obtain

The proposed increase in activity and permanent staff for COSATI would require regular funding. Committees of the Federal Council for Science and Technology, such as COSATI, are not independently staffed and funded at the present time. Congress has expressed concern about expanding any interagency committee that does not directly report to it. COSATI is such a committee.

PART FOUR

*An Evaluation
and Prognosis*

Chapter Eleven

An Evaluation of Alternatives

In the system analysis of an area it is not enough to describe the present situation, state the problems, and devise several alternatives. We must make recommendations regarding the actions to be taken. But how can an evaluation of the alternatives be made? In system analyses involving large systems there are a number of factors that need to be considered; these include an evaluation of various technical solutions, implementation schedules, cost effectiveness, and assessment of the administrative and political feasibility of the alternatives. Sometimes evaluations are left to the overall, intuitive judgment of the evaluation team or the action agent, but a proper analysis requires an explicit statement of the basis on which final evaluations are based. It is always a difficult problem to devise a method of evaluation which will be readily accepted; this becomes more and more difficult as the system under consideration becomes larger and involves both technical and administrative aspects. Engineering methods, cost analysis techniques, psychometrics and other evaluative methods need to be employed.

In this study the evaluation of the various alternatives hinges on three factors. First is the extent to which the various basic propositions are accepted and the extent to which each alternative satisfies these propositions. Second are the detailed statements of system requirements and judgments regarding the way in which each of them is satisfied by each alternative. Finally, practical and political feasibility needs to be considered. A blending of these three factors can then lead to the recommendation of a preferred system concept. If there is not an explicit statement of the judgments made in arriving at a given recommendation, disagreement becomes a matter of overall and often vague feelings rather than a consideration of the specific points on which disagreement exists. No doubt some readers will feel that the recommended system configuration is not the one they would prefer. By definitely stating the basic assumptions and the system requirements, and also by giving the evaluations made in using them as points for evaluation, the reader can judge where he agrees or disagrees. Because it is easier to find difficulties with suggested solutions than it is to devise new solutions which come nearer to satisfying the system requirements, there is some obligation on the part of critics to suggest new alternatives which promise to encompass more nearly the system problems and general operating requirements.

This rather long preamble states the methodology and point of view used in arriving at evaluations of the various alternate system concepts. After the basic principles had been developed and accepted by the COSATI National Systems Task Group and after the system requirements had been stated, the several alternative system concepts were developed. Following this each member of the study team independently evaluated each of the alternatives for each of the system requirements. These ratings were then examined, and when there were differences the team members discussed the discrepancy and arrived at a common rating.

All of the system concepts considered were evaluated in light of the system requirements presented in Chapter 6. Tables 11-1 to 11-7 show how each of these alternative concepts was judged to satisfy each group of requirements. The following five-point scale was used:

Value
5 = Highly responsive to the requirement.
4 = Fairly responsive to the requirement.
3 = Somewhat deficient regarding the requirement.
2 = Very deficient regarding the requirement.
1 = Not responsive at all to the requirement.

Table 11-1 Administrative and Organizational Requirements

	Alternative Concepts				
Requirement	Bureau/ Responsible Agent	New Operating Agency	Government-Chartered Corporation	Library Adminis-tration	Strengthen the Present System
Central administrative and policy organization	5	5	5	5	4
Legislative policies	5	5	5	5	3
Budget and costs identifiable	4	5	5	5	3
Coordination of long-range plans	5	5	5	5	3
Detailed and consistent records and procedures	3	4	4	4	3

Table 11-2 User-Oriented Requirements

	Alternative Concepts				
Requirement	Bureau/ Responsible Agent	New Operating Agency	Government-Chartered Corporation	Library Adminis-tration	Strengthen the Present System
Responsive to user needs	5	3	3	3	4
Capacity to handle an increasing number of users	5	5	5	5	4
Wide range of users and services	4	5	5	4	3
Researchers and information technologists as users	5	4	4	4	3
Easy to use	5	4	4	4	3
Efficient methods	4	5	5	4	3
Fast response times	4	5	5	5	3
User feedback	4	3	3	3	2
Use of switching (i.e., referral) system	4	5	5	5	3

Table 11-3 Internal System Operations Requirements

	Alternative Concepts				
Requirement	Bureau/ Responsible Agent	New Operating Agency	Government-Chartered Corporation	Library Adminis-tration	Strengthen the Present System
One reproducible copy	5	5	5	5	3
Complete coverage	5	5	5	5	2
Locatable copy	4	5	5	5	2
Efficient management techniques	5	5	5	4	3
Decentralized local access points	5	4	4	4	4
Long-term preservation and retention	5	5	5	5	4
Minimize unnecessary redundancy	4	5	5	4	3
Standards and compatibility of products	4	5	5	4	3
Processing and servicing of requests	5	5	5	5	3
Minimize redundant keyboarding	3	3	3	3	2

Table 11-4   Requirements Regarding the Production and Representation of Documents

Requirement	Alternative Concepts				
	Bureau/ Responsible Agent	New Operating Agency	Government-Chartered Corporation	Library Adminis-tration	Strengthen the Present System
Increase in volume of documents	5	5	5	5	3
Critical review	4	3	3	3	2
Time lag from research to publication	4	2	2	2	2
Federal support for professional societies	5	4	3	4	3

Table 11-5   Requirements Regarding Dissemination and Special Services

Requirement	Alternative Concepts				
	Bureau/ Responsible Agent	New Operating Agency	Government-Chartered Corporation	Library Adminis-tration	Strengthen the Present System
Efficient and economic dissemination	5	4	4	4	3
Minimize constraints on dissemination	5	4	3	4	3
Minimize cost to users	5	4	4	4	4
Foreign source materials	5	5	5	5	3
Oral and informal communications	3	3	2	3	2
Information analysis centers	5	4	4	4	3

Table 11-6   Requirements for System Evolution

Requirement	Alternative Concepts				
	Bureau/ Responsible Agent	New Operating Agency	Government-Chartered Corporation	Library Adminis-tration	Strengthen the Present System
Minimize disruption	4	2	1	1	5
Quality assurance program	5	4	4	4	3
Review of operation	4	4	5	4	3
Efficient and timely modification	5	4	5	4	3
Responsive to changes from user needs, new techniques, and research	5	4	4	4	3

Table 11-7   Requirements for Education, Training, Research, and Development Requirements

Requirement	Alternative Concepts				
	Bureau/ Responsible Agent	New Operating Agency	Government-Chartered Corporation	Library Adminis-tration	Strengthen the Present System
Education and training of users	5	3	2	3	2
Sufficient operational personnel	4	3	4	3	3
Minimal training for system operation	4	2	2	3	3
Coordination of research and development programs	5	4	3	4	3

GENERAL SUMMARY

All the system concepts, with the exception of the one that was based on strengthening the present system, adequately satisfy most of the system requirements. The distribution of the values of the five-point scale, for each of the alternative concepts, is shown in Table 11-8. Since the different concepts are not clearly differentiable on solely technical grounds, the problem of choosing which concept to recommend involves political, technical, and implementation considerations. A separate cost summary is presented after this discussion.

The new operating agency and the library administration concepts both involved a radical change in operations and administration which are not consonant with our conception of the requirement for evolutionary development. The bases from which we could arrive at detailed specifications for a centralized operating system are as yet inadequate. Additionally, the library administration concept requires the transfer of the Library of Congress to the executive branch, which would probably be politically difficult. Both concepts involve extensive transfers of responsibilities and central control of document-handling services.

The corporation concept is an attractive alternative because of its interfaces with the nonfederal sector, but it has the overriding weakness of infringing strongly on solely federal activities.

The option of strengthening the present system was rejected on the grounds that it fails to satisfy the majority of the system requirements adequately and does not show a satisfactory prospect of adequately satisfying them in the future.

The recommended design is the bureau/responsible agent concept. This concept is evolutionary in nature and represents the optimal solution in meeting the requirements. Furthermore, of all the designs considered, it provides the greatest degree of flexibility in being capable of adapting to changing requirements. Finally, since it requires the least change to existing operations, it would be the solution most acceptable to the current responsible S&T document and information handling organizations.

COST SUMMARY

A comparison of costs for each of the alternative system concepts in meaningful only in a qualitative sense. Quantitative comparison would be virtually impossible since we are dealing with gross estimates. Indeed, the capital investment and the annual cost of operations of the present system are not completely known. A consideration of relative trends is the most significant feature of any cost comparison discussion. This cost summary will focus on the period from 1965 to 1970.

The bureau would require from direct appropriation only those funds necessary for the administration and management of the system for S&T document and information handling. The responsible agents would require additional appropriations of funds in those instances where subject coverage responsibilities were to be expanded beyond their present scope. These additional costs would tend to be offset, however, by the economies in operations inherent in the responsible agent concept. Funds for the operations of the S&T document and information services and centers would be directly appropriated to these services and centers. Such funding would be subject to the review and approval of the bureau.

Table 11-8   *Distribution of Values in the Five-Point Scale*
(*derived from Tables 11.1 to 11.7*)

Number of Occurrences	Bureau/ Responsible Agent	New Operating Agency	Government- Chartered Corporation	Library Administration	Strengthen the Present System
5 = Highly responsive	25	19	21	14	1
4 = Fairly responsive	15	14	10	19	6
3 = Somewhat deficient	3	7	7	8	28
2 = Very deficient	0	3	4	1	8
1 = Not responsive at all	0	0	1	1	0

The new operating agency would require that funds be directly appropriated for full administrative and operational capability. Efficiencies would be realized in such a way that its eventual cost would tend to decline while, at the same time, the system would become more responsive and have an increased capability for providing services. These efficiencies would result primarily from centralized management, the elimination of duplicative services and collections, and an overall reduction in personnel requirements attributable, in part, to the system's use of a substantial amount of high-speed automatic equipment.

Funding arrangements for the corporation would be the most complex of all the concepts. Initial financial support for the corporation would come primarily from the federal government. As it becomes operational, the corporation would be supported by a combination of receipts for services (both from federal and nonfederal users) and government subsidies. Gradual reduction in the costs of services may come about as the result of close federal scrutiny of subsidy arrangements. The corporation concept also requires the funding of a federal S&T information commission.

In contrast to the agency and the corporation, the library administration concept would require significantly lower capital investment, but its costs for services would be higher. Lower capital investment would result from not having to invest heavily in new plant and equipment. Higher service costs would be attributable to the concept's broader range of services (i.e., gradual expansion of activities to include all other non-S&T library and document-handling functions of the federal government). Funding would be directly appropriated to the library administration for administration and operations.

It would appear that strengthening the present system would require the least additional expenditure of funds. Minimal funds would be necessary to support the additional staffs for OST, COSATI, and NSF. This concept, however, does not adequately provide for overall fiscal planning, thus perpetuating uncoordinated spending. In the long run, the continuance of overlapping collections and duplicative services, combined with an increasing number of users and S&T documents, will result in costly inefficiencies and perhaps the highest ultimate cost.

Although the bureau/responsible agent concept is apparently no less costly in the long run than the agency, the corporation, or the library administration, it provides the best cost/effectiveness. Minimal additional annual investment would result in the realization of significant efficiencies in coordination and operations in a short period of time. Also, in contrast to large centralized systems, automation would be introduced on a more gradual basis and would be better suited to possible changes in requirements. Thus, from the cost viewpoint as well as others, the bureau/responsible agent concept appears to be the best.

Chapter Twelve

Present Status and Future Programs

INTRODUCTION

The document-handling and information retrieval field is developing very rapidly and many actions have taken place since the Fall of 1965 when the report on which this book is based was written. The purpose of this chapter is to review several recent developments within the organizations related to the federal government and also to report on some recent activities in the nonfederal sector. While this chapter will be devoted to domestic developments, it should also be noted that there is worldwide awakening to the importance and problems of document handling. In addition to the formation of professional organizations in many of the nations of the world there is the International Federation for Documentation, with national membership. In the United States representation is by the United States National Committee for the International Federation for Documentation.

DEVELOPMENTS WITHIN THE FEDERAL SECTOR

The report on which this book is based was submitted to COSATI and is largely based on it. The COSATI Task Force on National Systems developed their own report which was transmitted to the full COSATI Committee [1]. The major conclusions and recommendations of the COSATI report tend to follow those contained in this book, although there are some modifications. Among the conclusions are:

1. The following functions should be undertaken by a central federal mechanism, working in concert with federal agencies and nongovernmental groups, to develop the integrated national network:

(a) Define the subject areas, in addition to medicine and agriculture, for which individual federal departments and agencies may accept responsibility for ensuring effective national information and document-handling systems.

(b) Develop federal policies for
—support of and cooperation with nongovernmental libraries
—support and sponsorship of specialized information centers in science and technology
—operation and support of government depository libraries
—support of nongovernment publications
—support of communications by means of nondocumentary mechanisms (e.g., meetings)
—education and training of librarians and information technologists
—acquisition and translation of foreign documents
—copyrights and patents in information "software" and the new information transfer technologies.

(c) Review, in relation to the needs of the integrated national network, agency information budgets and programs.

(d) Propose legislation necessary for the integrated national network.

(e) Review, in view of the needs of the integrated national network, agency legislative proposals.

(f) Develop minimal technical and performance standards for federal information and document activities.

(g) Develop guidelines for costs and other statistical information about federal information and document activities.

(h) Coordinate agency programs for federal support of prototype information systems of advanced design leading toward the integrated national network.

(i) Develop and maintain long-range plans for the integrated national network, modifying these plans in the light of changing needs, costs, technologies, manpower, and facilities.

2. The Office of Science and Technology, with the advice and assistance of the Committee on Scientific and Technical Information, should begin the exercise of these functions in selected areas of science and technology, to test the practicality of the centralized-mechanism-plus-responsible-agent concept. The task group concludes that at present no organization other than the Office of Science and Technology can successfully undertake this assignment, and that a successful trial would provide a sound basis for further steps requiring new executive or legislative action.

3. Responsibilities for ensuring, either internally or through other mechanisms, the effective operation of the document-handling subsystems in fields of science and technology should be discharged through existing federal departments and agencies as an integral part of their research and development program. This includes the establishment, if necessary, of new organizational entities, such as switching centers and libraries for fields in science and technology.

Important parts of the recommendations are the following:

1. The Office of Science and Technology should accelerate its efforts on the overall planning, policy formulation, organization, coordination, and evaluation of the integrated *national* network of information and document-handling systems in science and technology. The Office of Science and Technology should take appropriate steps to clarify areas of responsibility among the federal agencies in this area.

2. The Office of Science and Technology, in collaboration with the Bureau of the Budget, federal departments, agencies, and other organizations involved in science and technology, should undertake the following tasks at once:

(a) Develop a comprehensive, coordinated program for ensuring the acquiring, cataloging, and announcing of the significant worldwide scientific and technical literature. The establishment of one or more national libraries in fields of science and technology in addition to medicine and agriculture, under the aegis of appropriate federal departments and agencies should be considered as elements of the integrated national network.

(b) Develop policies concerning the legislative bases for document and information services in or sponsored by the departments and agencies.

(c) Propose or endorse legislation necessary to enable departments and agencies to assume responsibility for ensuring effective information and document-handling services in agreed-upon areas of science and technology.

3. The Office of Science and Technology, in collaboration with appropriate federal agencies, should encourage the private sector to formulate document-handling plans and programs for its consideration (and for review by appropriate agencies) in the development of the integrated national network.

4. The Committee on Scientific and Technical Information should recommend actions in the following areas:

(a) A new task to be undertaken is the development of a coordinated plan and criteria for federal support of experiments in the technology of information science, including prototype information systems designed to provide design data for the integrated national network.

(b) Development of standard procedures for processing documents so that interagency exchange can be more efficient and comprehensive.

(c) Development of guidelines for cost and budgetary analyses and control by agencies of their document and information services.

(d) Development of education and training curricula for the operators and users of the document and information systems.

(e) Development of policies for acquisition, dissemination, and translation of unclassified foreign documents in science and technology, and the dissemination of federally produced information and data to foreign countries and organizations.

The content of the report and the COSATI recommendations have been briefed to both the Federal Council for Science and Technology and the President's Science Advisory Committee. As a result of these briefings the President's science advisor, Dr. Donald Hornig, is pressing forward for the implementation of the system recommended in the COSATI report. Although definitive action cannot be detailed at this time, it is understood that Dr. Hornig's Office of Science and Technology is investigating means for undertaking a pilot demonstration of the capping agency/responsible agency concept. It seems probable that this pilot project will take place

within the National Science Foundation and perhaps one of the other major departments of government. The purpose of the demonstration will be to test out the feasibility of the full-scale implementation of the program recommended by COSATI and outlined in this book.

The recommendations contained in the COSATI report were largely concerned with problems of document handling. It is clear that the total problem of information handling, document handling, and information retrieval goes beyond the scope of the present study. COSATI recognizes the need for additional studies in this area and has undertaken two different actions to better cover the total field. On the one hand, various panels consisting of COSATI members and other experts from the federal departments have been formed to study a number of specialized areas. For example, there are panels dealing with problems of training, with the many aspects of procedural standardization, with the application of automation techniques and systems, and with international cooperative problems. These panels are studying these problems in detail and will make reports to COSATI for guidance of the federal government. In addition, COSATI has felt it wise to commission some additional studies through outside contractors. Currently three studies, in addition to the present document-handling study, are contemplated. As has been emphasized, there is a major element of scientific and technical communication which takes place through informal means. COSATI hopes to undertake an extensive study of the nature of the informal means of communication to understand the extent of information transfer through these techniques as well as to evaluate their effectiveness.

Another study is in the area of abstracting and indexing. Here the effort will be to describe the total abstracting and indexing activities as they relate to scientific and technical documents and to make recommendations regarding government policy in the support of abstracting and indexing services. The final area is concerned with data and data handling. Here there a number of different problems ranging from the data contained in scientific handbooks to large collections of information which is in numerical form and can be exploited for many scientific and technical uses. The study in this area would attempt to describe present methods of data handling and the extracting of information from such data as well as to assess advances that can be made through more systematic and automated techniques.

Another development in the federal area has been the formation by the National Academy of Science and the National Academy of Engineering of a joint Committee on Scientific and Technical Communication. This committee is being funded by the National Science Foundation, and represents a concern on the part of COSATI and NSF that the various professional and technical societies be involved and consulted with regard to federal actions in the document-handling area. The "Newsletter" of the American Documentation Institute [2] describes the function of the committee as follows:

"The Committee will provide a focus for participation by scientists and engineers through their societies in the consideration of plans for a national network of information systems in science and technology, as proposed by the Committee on Scientific and Technical Information (COSATI) of the Federal Council for Science and Technology.

"In its study of the present status of future requirements of the national scientific and engineering communities with respect to the flow and transfer of scientific and technical information, the Committee expects to work closely with COSATI, the Office of Science Information Service of the National Science Foundation, and the Office of Science and Technology of the executive office of the President. The Committee will maintain at all times close contact with the professional groups that perform information services.

"The Committee will give special attention to information activities and policies of private groups and non-profit organizations, both at home and abroad. Of special interest will be the interactions and inter-relations of the Federal Government and the private organizations, especially Federal actions or operations that affect them.

"Of particular concern will be: (1) methods for promoting more effective relationships between information systems and the principal producers and users of scientific and technical information: (2) techniques and systems for improving information transfer; (3) new means of providing greater selectivity and consolidation in information transfer.

"The Committee will make recommendations both to private organizations and to Federal agencies on courses of action it feels are required to maintain effective communication within and among fields of science and technology."

One of the most significant developments in recent months has been the decision of the Library of Congress to proceed with the automation of the bibliographic function of the Library of Congress. In 1963 the "King Committee" [3] issued a report describing the steps that needed to be taken in the automation of many of the Library of Congress activities. Now the Librarian of Congress has decided to proceed with the various studies and system design efforts required for the ultimate automation of the Library's bibliographic processes. In the Library of Congress's Request for Proposal, seven phases of study were outlined as follows:

Phase 1. Survey of the Present Manual System

PURPOSE. To describe and analyze the present operation.

Phase 2. System Requirements Analysis

PURPOSE. To identify the objectives of the library's bibliographic functions and to identify specific operational requirements.

Phase 3. Functional Description of Recommended System

PURPOSE. To recommend a system which will, in an efficient manner, accomplish the objectives and meet the requirements identified in Phase 2.

Phase 4. System Specifications

PURPOSE. To state the types and capabilities of the hardware needed to fulfill the functional requirements of the new system as described in Phase 3.

Phase 5. System Design

PURPOSE. To state the specific hardware and software configurations which satisfy the system specifications.

Phase 6. Implementation of New System

PURPOSE. To bring the "paper" system to reality.

Phase 7. Operation of New System

PURPOSE. To operate the new library system.

Although a contractor has only recently been selected to undertake the work, the importance of this new development should be emphasized. As has been pointed out, the Library of Congress plays a key role in the nation's library system. To some extent the cautious approach to automation represented in the nation's libraries is a reflection of the caution exercised by the Library of Congress in entering this new area. In the Request for Proposal it is indicated that the full implementation of the system design is not contemplated until 1972, which gives a good indication of the speed with which automation of the rest of the nation's libraries will progress. Although some will be disturbed at the length of time involved, it should not be forgotten that it is important that the Library of Congress program be successful and that a cautious and deliberate approach probably gives a higher probability of successful implementation than would a more rapid and bold approach to the problem.

GENERAL DEVELOPMENTS IN THE DOCUMENT-HANDLING AND INFORMATION RETRIEVAL FIELD

There are many activities being vigorously pursued throughout the information retrieval and library world. It would be presumptious to attempt to review them all in this concluding chapter, so only a few which seem particularly interesting will be mentioned although many others of equal importance can be discovered by the interested reader.

In recent years the development of time-sharing concepts in the application of advanced computers have made it both economically and technically feasible to envisage the sophisticated application of computer technology to information retrieval and document-handling problems. It is perhaps not surprising that much document-related work has progressed at the Massachusetts Institute of Technology in conjunction with the facilities of Project MAC and at the System Development Corporation in conjunction with their time-sharing system on a large military computer. The work of Myer M. Kessler in automating the bibliographic aspects of the physics literature is well known [4]. Recently Harold Borko and Howard Burnaugh of the System Development Corporation have developed a bibliographic on-line display system. In a

paper presented at the Third Annual National Colloquium on Information Retrieval, Burnaugh [5] describes the BOLD system, emphasizing its usefulness both in a browse mode and a search mode. The BOLD system is a general-purpose vehicle for real-time bibliographic and document retrieval, operating in a time-sharing environment and available to multiple simultaneous users. While this system, as well as Kessler's, is concerned primarily with the development of a vehicle for research and demonstration, it seems apparent that as time-sharing systems become widely adopted there will be many applications of library functions to remote stations throughout an organization.

It is interesting to consider the recent developments in student education. For example, it is reported that at Dartmouth some 80 per cent of all the students will be taking at least an elementary course in computer programming and that there will be some 200 remote input-output stations located throughout the campus. Through these stations any student or faculty member can gain assess to a time-shared computer. As the system progresses it seems probable that, in addition to computational and data-handling capabilities, computers such as the one at Dartmouth will have added to their repertoire the bibliographic functions of the school library. Dartmouth is only one example of the many colleges where student involvement in the use of computer technology is growing very rapidly. We can only speculate at the demands of these students as they become members of the larger civilian community, but it may be inferred that as the computer becomes a part of their regular skills they will demand the facilities to exercise these skills on their jobs and in their everyday life.

Another important development is known as Project Intrex. The purpose of Project Intrex is to undertake research and development leading toward the technical library of the future. The program is directed by Dr. Carl Overhage of M.I.T. Dr. Overhage is actively investigating the information transfer system that hopefully will exist at M.I.T. in 1975. During the summer of 1965 a number of experts participated in an extensive planning conference which has led to the initiation of activities toward the goal mentioned above. This conference is reported at length in a book titled "Intrex" [6]. In the project's Semiannual Activity Report (March 15,

1966) it is reported that research and development activities can be classified in three areas. First there is an investigation of text access. The purpose of studies in this area is to investigate methods by which the content of text can be stored. Various off-line storage media such as microform, magnetic media, and photo optical devices are being investigated. A comparative study is being made to determine the relative suitability of these media when used in a technical library. In addition, the possibility of storing the content of documents within computer memory is also being considered but is felt initially to be outside the capability available to the Intrex staff. In addition to methods of storing text, the problems of input and display are particularly important. The text access project of Intrex is exploring various optimum parameters for display equipment, such as the number of scan lines, brightness and contrast, and techniques for obtaining hard copy inexpensively at the user's location. The second major area of interest is the development of an augmented catalog. The plan is to store augmented catalog information in memory disk files and to make it available to library users at time-shared computer terminals through specially designed interaction languages. It is felt that not only is the content of such augmented catalogs important but the structuring of the language to be used as a means for searching the catalog and allowing maximal use of the stored information needs to be explored. Finally, Intrex is studying the use of wide-band communication links in document handling and information transfer. Problems in the use of coaxial cable and microlink transmission are being explored. It should be added, incidentally, that many experts believe that the provision of adequate communication channels will become one of the major bottlenecks in adequately exploiting modern technology for data handling and information retrieval purposes. In view of the highly sophisticated technology available at M.I.T. and the extremely able staff being assembled by Dr. Overhage it can be confidently expected that Project Intrex will make many of the major contributions to document-handling and information retrieval in the next decade.

Another important national development is the establishment of the Interuniversity Communications Council known by the acronym EDUCOM. EDUCOM is an affiliation of a num-

ber of universities throughout the country for the purpose of utilizing modern computer and communications technology for the benefit of the cooperating universities. As of this writing, membership in EDUCOM consists of some 32 different institutions representing more than 100 campuses throughout the United States. The principal organizer of EDUCOM is Dr. James G. Miller of the University of Michigan. Among EDUCOM's interests are networks of automated library services, information networks, and programmed instruction. It is also possible that a nationwide television network will be developed under EDUCOM's sponsorship. A planning grant has been obtained from the Kellogg Foundation and a number of conferences and symposia have been held and additional ones are being planned. It seems possible that this nationwide development heralds a significant development in cooperation and interdependence between the universities throughout the country.

It was mentioned at the beginning of this chapter that only a few of the many significant developments could be mentioned here. This is emphasized by the last item to be described, namely, the appearance of *Documentation Abstracts* [7]. This new journal is being published quarterly by the American Documentation Institute and the Division of Chemical Literature of the American Chemical Society. Volume 1, Number 1, appeared in March 1966 and contained 479 abstracts of articles in the documentation literature. It includes articles falling in a number of areas, such as library automation, personnel education and training, research in information, equipment and machine application, indexing and abstracting, etc. Perhaps the

appearance of this abstract of material in the documentation field underlines better than any other single action the growing literature and extensive involvement in this field. All the signs seem to indicate that the field of documentation and information retrieval will undergo a rapid expansion and sophistication. The technology is now available. A high level of federal concern assures that funds and support will be forthcoming. The challenge rests with those of us who believe that the development of this field will lead to a richer and more effective exploitation of the creative and insightful work reported in the scientific and technical literature.

REFERENCES

1. Recommendations for National Document Handling Systems in Science and Technology. Committee on Science and Technical Information, Federal Council for Science and Technology. November 1965, PB 168 267.

2. *Newsletter of the American Documentation Institute.* March–April 1966, **5**, 2.

3. King, G. W. *Automation and the Library of Congress.* A study sponsored by the Council on Library Resources, Washington, D. C. Library of Congress, 1963.

4. Kessler, M. M. The M.I.T. Technical Information Project. Cambridge, Massachusetts Institute of Technology. 1964, AD 608 502.

5. Burnaugh, Howard P. The BOLD (Bibliographic On-Line Display) System. SP-2338/000/01. System Development Corporation, Santa Monica, Calif. April 6, 1966.

6. Overhage, C. F. L., and Harman, R. J. Intrex, Report of a Planning Conference on Information Transfer Experiments. The M.I.T. Press, Cambridge, Mass., 1965.

7. *Documentation Abstracts.* 1966, **1**, 1. American Documentation Institute and the Division of Chemical Literature of the American Chemical Society. Washington, D. C.

Advanced Information Systems, Equipment, and Software

This appendix analyzes the state of the art and the future of document- and information-handling systems from two viewpoints. The first portion contains a discussion of three advanced systems that have been under development or in operation and the varying philosophies of system automation that they represent. The second portion contains descriptions of components that can be seen as necessary or potentially applicable in document- and information-handling systems in the relatively near future—the next five to ten years. Beyond that span, predictions about systems and their components inevitably become speculative, though they can be extremely interesting and encouraging (as are, for example, the reports by Licklider and by Kemeny cited in the Selected Bibliography), since new components and techniques could conceivably make possible entirely new concepts and capabilities for systems.

RESEARCH, TECHNOLOGY, AND ADVANCED INFORMATION SYSTEMS

A look at some of today's information-handling systems that are describable as "advanced" reveals great diversity and betrays the absence of a core of information-retrieval theory. We must keep this point in mind, not only in appreciating recent developments, but also in understanding what progress in the next few years is likely to consist of. A unified formulation—a theory—of information-handling would be valuable, if it already existed. But people responsible for document- and information-handling systems cannot afford to wait for such a theory.

The lack of theory makes it difficult to find a criterion by which to say that a system is "advanced." A system could be built around the most capacious computer, the most versatile photoelectric print reader, the most powerful cathode-ray display system, and the largest available memory. Each component in its turn could be arguable as "most advanced" by reference to well-understood criteria, and yet the system as a whole could be unsatisfactory and seldom used. Such a system would be "advanced" in name only, and would be a good illustration of the fact that a system is more than merely the sum of its parts.

The involvement of advanced components is a necessity, but is not a unique condition for attainment of an "advanced system." At least one other necessary condition must be satisfied before we can legitimately claim that a system is advanced: the system must provide a *needed facility* for its users through which they can attain objectives that otherwise are attainable less economically, or with greater difficulty, or not at all.

In this appendix we examine several advanced information systems which could provide, by virtue of advanced components or concepts, a needed facility. We consider three systems, chosen to reflect the breadth of the frontier of applications and the diversity of approaches:

1. The automated library of Florida Atlantic University (FAU).
2. The scientific and technical information system of the National Aeronautics and Space Administration (NASA).
3. The system for storage and retrieval of crime information, in the form of natural language text, of the Los Angeles Police Department (LAPD).

It is helpful to think of these systems as reflecting three divergent approaches. The FAU

system reflects the approach of primarily automating clerical aspects of library operation, rather than introducing radical innovations in concepts of operation. This approach is well suited to a university situation, where the collection is broad and contains relatively old documents and where access is for the student and the scholar—people who have an abundance of reference-finding tools outside the library. The NASA system reflects an approach tailored to handling documents that are primarily new and relatively specialized, with large emphasis on current awareness and timeliness. Finally, in the LAPD system, information is so informal and of such unpredictable value that "documentation" in the usual sense (or such concomitants as editing, distribution, and classification) would not be worthwhile. Here the approach is one of expending a bare minimum of time and effort on the *average* information item (which will probably never be used) and a maximum of investment in dealing with the contingency that some unknown small percentage of the items might turn out to be very important.

Library Automation and the Florida Atlantic University

Description of the FAU Library System. Florida Atlantic University, in Boca Raton, was founded in 1961. The Library, being a new installation, was in a position to use machines without the burden of data conversion that an established library would have to bear, and is perhaps the first in the United States to introduce data processing into its operations from the very beginning. Many of the methods and ideas of this undertaking grew out of the University Library Information Systems Project of the University of Illinois [1].

In its outward appearance to a user the FAU Library is much like a conventional university library. This reflects the fact that most of the clerical processes in library operation go on behind the scenes. Some hint of modern technology might be perceived at the circulation desk where an IBM 357 Data Collection system for circulation control records each transaction, and at the catalog where a computer-produced book catalog is found in place of the familiar rows of card trays. The IBM 1460 computer, which does much of the data processing, is not in evidence.

The end products of the FAU Library's data processing consist almost entirely of "computer printouts," yielding 23 basic kinds of library information in four basic categories:

1. Catalogs and authority lists.
2. Circulation data.
3. Serials records.
4. Acquisition data.

Some of the information can be printed out in several different arrangements. Circulation lists, for example, can be ordered by call number; by the borrower's identification number; and, by either of these numbers, for overdues or for hold requests. The number of different kinds of printouts reflects the large variety of information-processing tasks necessary in running a typical university library.

Philosophies of Information-System Automation. The FAU effort, along with a number of other more or less similiar projects around the country, represents an approach that has come to be called "library automation." It is a rallying point for librarians who recognize the need for improvement and the opportunities for advancement opened by modern technology, but have been skeptical of some of the ideas suggested under the heading of "information retrieval." In the words of Phyllis Richmond, of the University of Rochester Library: "I would be disinclined to argue with a computer over computation, which is its field of competence. In other fields, what it produces depends on what its programmers thought the problem was. Up to the present, their assessment of needs of libraries has been grossly inadequate. Things are improving, however, as people with sound experience begin to look for ways of applying the computer. Our clerical jobs will be pretty well mechanized in 5 to 10 years. . . ." Library automation in this sense may be overdue, as was once the case with the application of punched-card machines. Keppel [2] forthrightly admits: "I blush to think for how many years we watched . . . business machines juggle payrolls and bankbooks before it occurred to us that they might be adapted to dealing with library cards with equal dexterity. . . ."

It is important to realize that the library-automation approach regards the computer as primarily an aid to the librarian, and only indirectly as an aid to the user. The user-librarian interaction is expected to remain basically unaffected,

and the user will rarely, if ever, deal with the computer himself. Only the librarian is found at the man-machine interface. In deciding how to use automation, the approach is to enable the librarian to serve the user more effectively.

This attitude, in a time of much interest in user-oriented systems, is based upon a premise that the search systems that librarians must use are so complicated that few users would have the patience to learn how to use them directly. As Koller et al. [3] expressed it: "If the user must master a complex coding system before he can make use of the system, he is less likely to accept it and use it to best advantage. An educational program to acquaint users with the facilities provided by the system is required. A practical method of operation permits the user to state his question in common language, and a technically trained person, who is intimately familiar with the system, translates the question into the system language. . . ." More emphatic versions of this sentiment have the user so far out of the picture that the idea of letting user studies affect system design is intolerable, as with Taube [4]: "The design of such systems remains a matter of professional competence. . . . The inevitable conclusion of this paper is that use studies have no value as direct guides to the design of information systems, any more than consumer acceptance or rejection is a guide to the value of Salk vaccine. . . ."

The FAU Library, consequently, embodies an approach that is "prescriptive" within a range of views of system improvement, whose limits are, as pointed out by Katter [5] as: "(a) 'prescriptive' attempts to promote increased standardization of the . . . system personnel's understandings of the system, and (b) 'adaptive' attempts to make the representative . . . features of the system commensurate with the language habits of the user." In addition, another statement of the adaptive approach to information-system automation is that of Isaacs and Herrmann [6]:

"1. Avoid perpetuating shortcomings of an existing system by merely automating present procedures.

"2. Develop a system that operational personnel can communicate with and utilize for their operational needs.

"3. Search for and incorporate the most advanced concepts and techniques that are available within development time constraints.

"4. Recognize the impact of new technology on operations, organization, and procedures.

"5. Create an appropriate climate for modifying the operational approaches in order to maximize the benefits to be obtained from new technology."

Because the "prescriptive" philosophy is likely to govern the majority of automation efforts in document handling during the next few years, not only in the university environment but in science and technology generally, the progress of the FAU effort will deserve close watching as a prototype. We discuss below some implications of the prescriptive philosophy in choices of technologies to be utilized and of researches to be undertaken:

The technologies to be employed are not likely to diverge very soon from those used generally in business data-processing. Conventional general-purpose digital computer systems will probably predominate, with little or no exotic input/output equipment (e.g., display consoles and print readers) or sophisticated software, such as that involved in real-time processing. This will be due not merely to the record-keeping nature of the operations, but also to cost factors. The total experience in business data processing has been huge, and provides a wealth of data on what equipments are cheapest for a specified complex of operations.

Under the prescriptive approach, some librarians will study programming to help ensure their continued control of their profession. Because they will probably be successful in making this transition, research activities in library automation can be expected to continue to reflect the fact that the librarian is in charge. Interest in user studies may continue to be modest, for reasons cited above, and there may be even less interest in man-machine studies.

Because most computer report outputs will be periodic (daily, monthly, etc.) in library automation, there is apt to be little need for flexible, immediate-access systems such as on-line teletypes. Exceptions such as IBM's Los Gatos automation project will probably remain exceptions.

The greatest changes in the technology can be expected in output media. FAU Library experiences indicate that existing standard computer line-printers are not desirable for the production of book catalogs of the quality desirable in a library. Improvement in this situation might

well come in the form of photocomposing machines such as those used by the National Library of Medicine and the Government Printing Office. Eventually it may be found that randomly accessible computer-stored catalogs are a more convenient proposition than book catalogs. This could well lead to the introduction of user consoles.

Automation will tend to be directed at making traditional search methods more efficient, not at implementing basically new approaches to information access. This tendency will be bolstered by statistics from some libraries that indicate topical search requests are relatively infrequent and that the bulk of requests made by patrons can be answered through straightforward numerical or alphabetical file searching. In a university environment in particular, the variety of reference pathways outside the library is so great that the pressure for topical search methods within the library may continue to be too small to inspire basic change.

The mechanization of interlibrary exchanges will probably be slow. Unless someone with unusual foresight and influence establishes workable standardization, the history of library coordination as a mechanizable system complex may be as turbulent as the history of higher-order computer languages has been. Unfortunately, the rush of library automation efforts could be so rapid that each installation, preoccupied with attaining its own internal efficiency, might not notice the incompatibilities of its formats, codes, etc., with those of other libraries unless strong efforts are made to coordinate these aspects of library automation.

The NASA S&T Information System and the Middle-of-the-Road Approach

Description of the NASA System. The S&T information system of the National Aeronautics and Space Administration serves a complex of regional centers, NASA contractors, universities, and—to a lesser extent—users and centers outside the aerospace industry. Through filling the role of an information center, the NASA Facility nonetheless has major functions in common with a library. Like a library, it must acquire information items. It must analyze the items and reference data (index terms, etc.). It must provide for storage and retrospective search. But because an information center's task is so different from that of a library, these functions are apt to be carried out in a markedly different

way. Moreover, some functions which are usually minor in a library, such as announcement of new acquisitions, become major in a NASA-type system. In some cases they may overshadow other major library functions in the amount of effort expended (on the part of users as well as by system personnel).

Because the NASA system is undergoing change, it is difficult to be accurate in describing its present operational components. This problem can best be resolved by not distinguishing, herein, between actual and soon to be implemented components.

The NASA facility is designed to encourage decentralization, but this does not mean that centralized repositories and access thereto are to be excluded. Present planning aims toward three levels of centralization, and in practice there may turn out to be four or more, depending on the user. The highest level, representing the most centralization, is the central system at Washington. The next highest level resides in NASA's regional centers; plans call for shifting of retrospective search, dissemination, and hard-copy delivery functions from Washington to the regional centers in the interest of faster service. Washington will act more and more like a wholesaler to serve these centers. The third level is the user himself, who may achieve access to the literature via subject indexes and announcement bulletins, published and distributed at the highest level. If the user is a NASA contractor with its own library, four or more levels of access can exist.

The bulk of NASA's acquisitions are unpublished technical reports generated within the NASA complex. When an organization supported by NASA generates a report, a copy is sent to NASA for review and appraisal of its applicability to aerospace technology. Appropriate documents are then sent to Documentation Incorporated, Bethesda, Maryland, which is under contract to process the input and operate much of NASA's system at Washington. The documents are analyzed there by professional indexers and assigned two sets of indexing terms:

1. An average of about five terms per document to be used as index entries in the announcement publication *Scientific and Technical Aerospace Reports* (STAR) and in cumulative indexes of STARs.

2. From 15 to 20 indexing terms for access by (coordinate) computer-searching. Books,

journals, and other items of published aerospace literature are also indexed in a similar fashion, but the announcement publication is separate from STAR and is denoted as *International Aerospace Abstracts* (IAA). The separateness of IAA and STAR is due to the fact that the procurement, indexing, and abstracting of items cited in IAA is done by the American Institute of Aeronautics and Astronautics, the publisher of IAA. The abstracts and indexing worksheets for IAA, however, are sent on to NASA, so that thereafter all technical processing for STAR and IAA are essentially identical and are accomplished by the same facilities and equipment.

A high degree of mechanization is evident in the processes for publishing STAR and IAA. These publications both have a section of abstracts, plus subject, author, and other indexes. The indexes are generated by Documentation Incorporated's IBM 1410-1401 computer system from keypunched input derived from the indexing worksheets. The initial form of the abstract is keypunched into paper tape which is used to drive a Photon photocompositor to produce mats for printing the abstract portion of STAR. The other indexes included in STAR are printed from another photocompositor output.

A new technique employed in STAR and IAA is the use of an expanded (annotated) title, called a "Notation of Content," consisting of two or three dozen words consistent with the system's indexing vocabulary. The Notation of Content can be used to feed computer indexing process, known as SWIFT (Selected Word in Full Title), which should give more dependable access than an index derived from the uncontrolled original title [7].

Machine searches, using the 1410-1401 system, can be performed not only by index term or combination of terms, but also by a complex of bibliographic classifications and search restrictions. Machine-search requests are implemented by search analysts. (This mode of access is one of the prescriptive features of the NASA system, tempered, however, by heavy emphasis on feedback-derived improvement.) Analysts are encouraged to interact with users when requests are inherently vague or difficult to implement; decentralization, of course, will greatly facilitate this kind of interaction. Improvement of the searching system and methods of using it is promoted through use of the NSA Search System Analysis Sheet [8]. Data on search inaccuracy

(e.g., relevant items missed, irrelevant items retrieved) are noted and fed back from the search analyst to the indexers, who thereupon upgrade vocabulary, re-index reports, correct keypunch errors, and so on.

The NASA system incorporates some advanced software packages as well as advanced equipment. One of the foremost of these is the current operational version of SDI, IBM's computer-based selective dissemination system. It differs from the previous SDI system in providing greater capability for the user's control of the type and quantity of information he receives. This is done in part through more sensitive processes for revising the user's profile, whose terms are the basis for matching against the index terms of incoming documents and consequent selection. The profile updating is effected both by users actions and by system vocabulary changes, which in SDI can be, in large part, automatically implemented. SDI also introduces numerous analytical reports for monitoring user and system performance.

For storage in the NASA system, documents are photoreduced in a microfiche process that accommodates up to 58 pages per 4 x 6 in. film. The camera facilities, duplicating and enlargement devices, and ancillary equipment comprise an up-to-date and flexible microcopying system. Regional centers and users can order "shoeboxes" of microfiched documents according to technical subject specialty. Through this means, many of NASA's decentralization aims can be accomplished.

The Middle-of-the-Road Approach. NASA, like FAU, is a relatively new organization and, therefore, is in a good position to apply new ideas and technology. The NASA system for information handling represents a "middle of the road" approach, a blend of generally used and recently developed methods. NASA's approach partakes strongly of the "adaptive" philosophy, as previously defined. It is consequently ready to experiment with new search methods, usually user-oriented, made possible by computers. Though the adaptive philosophy may not today be standard in the automation of information-handling systems, it appears to be gaining ground steadily. Thus it may be helpful to look at some of the features of the NASA system, to see which of them tend to give it an adaptive orientation.

The multilevel access structure of the NASA

system has important consequences for the evolution of the entire system. It provides a family of use options and opportunities for specialization that are certain to facilitate changes. That such changes will occur has been anticipated by the system planners, who are setting up elements of the system in such a way that operations need not stop during transitions. They are also providing for means to assure equipment and format compatibility throughout the information-handling complex. The effect of providing options to the user and planning for evolution is a large part of the adaptive approach in the NASA system.

The manual indexing procedures in the NASA system are not basically different from those used by other information centers during the last 15 years. In particular, full-text computer storage and computer indexing methods are not involved in the NASA system. The indexing and terminology-control features are among the more prominent prescriptive elements that make the NASA approach "middle-of-the-road" rather than strongly adaptive. There is still much mistrust, by nearly all those responsible for systems for access to S&T information, of the nonstandardized vocabulary inherent in computer-prepared indexes derived from natural-language textual material. Indeed, in order to consider a strongly adaptive system, as we do later in this appendix, we have to go outside the area of S&T information processing.

The steps that take place in the NASA system after indexing and abstracting, however, are very much on the forefront of application of new technology, and furthermore (unlike the FAU Library system) involve numerous innovations in concepts and methods of information handling. The high degree of mechanization in the processes for publishing STAR and IAA, the use of the Notation of Content and SWIFT modified-title techniques, the 1410-1401 machine searching methods, and the microfiche storage techniques are all evidences of an orientation in the NASA system toward the adaptive philosophy of automation.

The emphasis in the NASA system's selective dissemination program on system responsiveness to the user is, of course, an adaptive line of development. It is also a good example of a general principle that we can observe in the information-handling field, namely, that adaptive approaches seem to occur most frequently and most massively in forms of information-handling that have not yet had extensive or lengthy usage. In observing this, however, we must be careful to realize that cause-and-effect relations in the history of information-handling systems are difficult to understand. Adaptiveness may be a result of newness, so that longer experience could lead to a corps of specialists with a more prescriptive view. Or adaptiveness may be a permanent value that could not have been realized in pre-computer information-handling institutions without undue effort and expense.

It is not possible to say that either the prescriptive philosophy, as exemplified by the FAU Library, or the adaptive philosophy is the more significant guide to advancement. Because libraries are sometimes viewed as tending toward the prescriptive approach, and information centers as tending toward the adaptive approach, it may be helpful to consider some of the differences. In a discussion contrasting libraries and information centers, Rees [9] has stressed: "The truth is that there is no basis for comparison. The information center and the library are laboring to perform two distinct tasks. The center is the essence of visible incarnation of the invisible college. It represents the attempt to formalize the informal exchange of information amongst a closed or semi-closed set of users. . . ."

Some of the host of characteristics and requirements that distinguish information centers from libraries may be stated here. First, information centers are a twentieth-century phenomenon brought into being by the growth and specialization of knowledge and by requirements for more rapid information transfer. Their specialized nature leads to these consequences:

1. Diversity of function from one center to another, corresponding to intrinsic variations in user requirements.
2. Participation of scientists and technologists as information specialists.
3. Geographical dispersion of users.
4. The necessity to pioneer in the organization of the knowledge in the field served by a center.

In the last decade of intensive efforts in defense and in space, still other factors have become more prominent:

1. The increased need for current awareness and flexible dissemination of new material.

2. The requirements for state-of-the-art reports and other summarizations, which information centers are in the best position to produce.

3. Greater pressure for across-the-board updating of indexes, files, and other reference systems.

4. Because of the large volume and rapid obsolescence of S&T information, enhanced interest in mechanisms for data file purging. These differences which set information centers apart from libraries partly account for the variations between adaptive and descriptive in philosophies of information-handling automation.

These differences may also lead to divergent paths in research and technology utilization.

In a system that tends toward the adaptive philosophy, such as that of NASA, it is much more difficult to make forecasts about utilization of research and technology than it is for a system such as the FAU Library, where the definition of change tends to be expressed in the question: Which of my manual procedures is it worthwhile to automate next? The prescriptive-oriented automation movement is consistent with a spirit of computer applications common in the 1950–1960 decade, where the possibilities (i.e., the set of concepts viewed as being possible of implementation) were limited in scope to pre-computer practices. Perhaps it is appropriate that NASA, which characteristically sponsors aerospace projects that could not have been accomplished before 1960, serves as an example of applications to information problems in areas with a much larger range of possibilities, whose limits are somewhere in between the class of existing processes we can speed up, and the vastly greater class of processes that modern technology makes possible.

Natural-Language Processing at the Los Angeles Police Department

The Need for Computer Searching of Natural-Language Materials. In prescriptive approaches to the automation of information- and document-handling systems, the costs associated with such activities as cataloging and control of terminology are high, but are justifiable because the cost (and by implication, the value) of each information item is commensurately high. There exists in modern civilization, however, a vast amount of information that is worth recording in written form but whose value is so marginal that only the crudest of filing procedures can be justified. Newspapers have morgues filled with old clippings, photographs, and back issues that may be worth saving but not worth dusting off. Items such as automobile accident reports and medical case histories accumulate in great volume. Such data, in fact, are part of a vast literature about the lives of people and could be the basis of highly revealing studies. Unfortunately, though the aggregate value of this information may be potentially very large, the actual value per individual item is so small that detailed or refined processing of each item is not usually carried out.

This sort of information could gain additional value through the possibility of increased accessibility. Indeed, information that we might think not even worth writing down (such as tape-recorded meetings) might acquire substantial value if a large amount of it were accumulated, and if the sheer accumulation did not impede the rapidity and variety of access. The increase in value might, for example, justify the cost of automated processing of some or all of the information.

This potentiality applies especially where any one of a large number of items might suddenly and unpredictably increase in value. A doctor, for example, might remember that a set of symptoms was "exactly like" that of another case he had treated five years before. Unfortunately, he might not remember the treatment of the case, and could not have justified filing the record under any of the symptom descriptors because there would have been no way to predict that a case like it would ever arise again. And so an important bit of S&T information would be lost.

Metropolitan police departments build up large files of the sort of information whose value is highly contingent on something that may happen months or years in the unpredictable future: reports of crime by unknown assailants, descriptions of stolen property, intelligence data on organized crime, etc. The largest cities, such as Los Angeles, often realize that their crime problem is getting out of hand partly because the crime-information collection is too large to be managed. This realization becomes especially painful when we note the contrast between the ease of access to certain highly formattable kinds of information and the near-unfeasibility of

access to necessarily informal types of information such as victims' accounts of the behavior and description of an assailant. Information about automobiles is a good example of intrinsically formattable information that can be retrieved with high speed and accuracy. A member of the California Highway Patrol can radio a central office and generally find out all he needs to know about a suspicious automobile in less time than it takes to write a traffic ticket.

The problem of computer searching of difficult-to-format information is considerably more complicated. Yet this is the problem confronting police departments that need to be able to store, at low expense (i.e., with little or no formatting), such natural-language* materials as victims' and policemen's accounts of crimes, for possible use at some later time. The sheer volume of such materials makes it highly attractive to consider the possibility of computer processing, especially if it could be accomplished in a relatively short time (a search time of only a few minutes would be desired in many situations). From the standpoint of computerized processing, the difficulties here consist in the need for searching unformatted natural-language text, and the need for doing that very rapidly. But grounds for hope are offered by recent developments in the time-shared use of computers and in techniques for computer searching of natural-language texts, such as the development of Project MAC at the Massachusetts Institute of Technology and the system being discussed in this section.

The central idea of time-sharing a computer is to allow many users to have on-line access to the computer simultaneously, with each user being in a position to behave as if the computer were exclusively under his control. This state of affairs is achievable whenever computer program operating speed is faster than the actions taken by the user at his station in deciding on and implementing a response to the output of his program. An example of such a response would be the user's reading the answer to his previous question, as outputted on a typewriter driven by the computer, and his deciding to ask another question. Even so short a human reading time as one or two seconds is much

* The term "natural language" has come into use to refer to ordinary spoken and written language, as contrasted with the structured data input formats used in computer processing.

slower than associated computer time requirements.

Time-sharing systems are uniquely fitted for situations where computer users are geographically dispersed, and very rapid processing is a system requirement. In time-shared computer usage, where on-line transactions between remote users and the central computer occur via commercial cable, mere distance should have little effect except on cable costs. In the NASA system, machine-search requests addressed to the Central System at Washington may take as long as five days (including mailing and internal response times) to be answered. Clearly, under these conditions we would prefer decentralized facilities. Time-shared access, when it becomes sufficiently inexpensive, could change this picture drastically. However, time-shared access is a more expensive way of using computers than, for example, in the generation, publication, and distribution of indexes—assuming, of course, that users are numerous and require moderately frequent access.

Description of the LAPD Crime Information System. The Los Angeles Police Department has been developing a system in which difficult-to-format descriptions of robberies and other serious crimes can be stored and retrieved in natural-language form. The system, built around a teletype-accessed, time-shared IBM computer, has been developed in a joint experimental project by the LAPD and the System Development Corporation (SDC). The retrieval method in which text items can be accessed by the words, terms, or phrases contained in the text, is an adaptation of an earlier research vehicle, the Synthex question-answering system [10], wherein "answers" furnished by the system are sentences chosen from a large corpus of text because they contain key content words present in the input question.

Isaacs and Herrmann [6] describe the system's principles of operation as follows: "Current reports of robberies in the City of Los Angeles are now converted word-for-word into machine-readable paper tape at the LAPD and stored on magnetic tape at SDC. The Synthex program automatically indexes the reports essentially by making a concordance of the actual content words exactly as they appear in the text. . . . Each word, such as 'newspaper' or 'revolver' . . . is maintained alphabetically on

the index tape, along with a numerical listing of each volume, report, paragraph, and sentence in which the word appeared. If one is looking for a certain type of crime report, a 'question' is asked in English. For example, suppose we are looking for all reports of liquor store robberies where the bandit asked for a pack of cigarettes. The question would be: '*Liquor store, asked for pack of cigarettes.*' The computer would search its alphabetic index, find all question words and the reports in which they appeared, sort these to choose those reports in which some number of question-words appeared together in sentences, and print out for the user a list of the most relevant reports, in order of their relevance, plus automatically-produced abstracts of each report. The entire report can also be printed out, if desired. . . ."

Synthesis

We have examined the interface at which the most advanced products of research and technology, in hardware and software, become integrated into working systems for access to information. In doing so, we noted that the interface is truly panoramic. The words "automation" and "automatic" are used over the entire breadth of information processing activity, from information-handling environments that are old in their history as well as in their content, to environments that are brand new because they have just become technically possible.

The three systems described herein were chosen not so much because they are at the forefront of advancement, but because they are prototypical. We can, therefore, expect to see numerous similar systems spring up in the next few years. We must appreciate that no one of these prototype systems is more or less appropriate than another as a means of handling S&T information, because of the scope and diversity of scientific information requirements.

In the prescriptive environment we find monographs, textbooks, histories, comprehensive treatises, classics, critiques, and other highly processed information typical of the academic world. The task of a librarian is not very far removed from that of a teacher or a professor, and a prescriptive approach is not out of tune with the aims of education. In the center we find the more tentative S&T documents, technical reports, journal articles, conference papers, and review articles; because this is information

sought by working scientists and technicians, whose numbers are increasing much faster than the general population, S&T information- and document-handling systems today receive the most attention. A more adaptive approach may be needed, because document-handling systems do compete with scientists talking to each other—at conferences and by the ever-handier long-distance telephone—and because a corps of competent prescriptionists is difficult to find in a rapidly changing field.

Continuing along the spectrum to the adaptive environment, we find information of highly tentative character. Here is the world of progress reports, lab notebooks, tape-recorded seminars and think sessions, memoranda and correspondence, proposals and specifications, equipment and instrumentation brochures, program documentation, technical news, and—in general—anything informative that is worth putting on paper. Assimilation of such information is vital in the pursuit of S&T goals, and even more so in the management of this pursuit. Such information ought to be worth retrieving, but there is too much of it, and each item is too cheap and too tentative; it has little value—except under certain unforeseeable circumstances. In this realm, we are close to the informal, everyday process wherein no coding or cataloging system could possibly be managed, even if it were worthwhile. But means will be developed whereby such information will come cheaply into ever larger and more rapid computer memories, in natural-language form. People are today accessing such information on-line, and they will learn rapidly how to access it better.

FROM SYSTEMS TO COMPONENTS

In the preceding portions of this appendix we have been concerned with advanced current information- and document-handling systems, and with varying approaches to the automation of such systems. Our focus now shifts to the equipment components available for use in current and future systems.

Some limited use of advanced automated equipment and associated software has been made in recent years in the processing of S&T information and documents. These components offer a strong current capability in the processing, transmission, storage, retrieval, dissemination, and reproduction of S&T information. The

following discussion treats these components under five headings: (a) digital computers and associated equipment; (b) software involved in their operation; (c) telecommunication equipment; (d) reproduction devices; and (e) microform devices. For each of these types of components, we present a summary of the current state of the art, an assessment of the maximum current potential, a five-year prognostication, and illustrative cost data.

Our discussions of components are intended to serve three purposes. The first is to provide statements of equipment potential in document-handling applications, as an aid in establishing a contexual framework for equipment elements included in proposed systems. The second purpose is to provide a basis for further data gathering, analysis, and planning in the equipment-related aspects of document-handling systems. The third is to provide a picture of the state of the art in document-handling equipment.

The systems we have looked at in the preceding portions of this appendix were, necessarily, developed within organizational, fiscal, personnel, and policy restraints. From now on, however, our considerations will involve no restraints other than those of technical capability, economic feasibility, and geographical coverage. The material outlined here has been used in estimating investment costs for equipment to be used in the systems discussed in Chapter 9. But it must be realized that the costs of any operational document-handling system depend heavily on such factors as input volumes, number of producer and user centers included, types of communication media used, and volumes of output produced.

It should be noted that equipment and software are treated here in terms of their applicability in the handling of textual and graphic information, although they may have been developed for other purposes. Equipment and software used solely in classified applications are not analyzed here unless their characteristics have been publicly described in an unclassified context.

Digital Computers and Associated Equipment

The State of the Art. The digital computer is a strong tool for the processing of textual and graphic information. The major domestic computer manufacturing corporations recently have

brought forth "families," or groups, of highly compatible computers with unprecedented speed, storage capacity, and versatility. The Control Data Corporation "6000 Series" of computers is an example of such a "family," as are the general purpose RCA "Spectra 70 Series," Sperry Rand Univac "9000 Series," IBM "360 Series," Honeywell "200 Series," and the General Electric "600 Series." These "families" represent unprecedented compatibility of characteristics within and across manufacturers' lines, and the most powerful models of each series generally can perform logical, clerical, and arithmetical instructions at a rate of 5 to 10 million operations per second. For convenience, they will be referred to here as the "new computer generation."

New technological developments (e.g., silicon transistor circuitry) have made it possible to contain as many as 4 million characters of data in central computer memories, and as many as 16 million characters in high-speed auxiliary memories. (By high-speed we mean here the capability of transferring a single character within 8 μsec, i.e., millionths of a second). Because the average length of an English word is approximately five characters, these memories can contain 0.8 million and 3.2 million words, respectively. Slower, random-access auxiliary computer storage subsystems are in operation with a capacity on the order of billions of characters.

In addition to the storage devices described, the central portion of a computer contains arithmetic and logical processing units whose tasks comprise overall operation of internal storage and processing activities, and transmission of data to and from the central element. Computer input and output devices include telecommunication equipment and such computer-oriented media as punched card, magnetic tape, and printing equipment. The current state of the art will allow hundreds of magnetic tape units to be attached to a central computer. A reel of the tape most commonly used on these new computers contains as many as 20 million characters of information.

Another class of computer input and output devices includes punched card readers, punched paper tape readers associated with typewriters, and similar equipment used in converting documents into forms acceptable for computer processing. A typical punched card contains 80 characters of data, while a punched paper tape

record may represent thousands of characters. Current computers can receive as many as 150,000 characters per minute from each such card reader. Many of these devices may be attached simultaneously to a computer.

Electro-mechanical printers can be attached to a computer for direct printing of information in a formatted form. Large computer systems include one or more smaller satellite computers to drive such printers. A printing rate of 1100 lines per minute, each of 132 characters of formatted data, is within today's state of the art, and is equivalent to 20,000 English words per minute. Since a large computer configuration may have several such printers in simultaneous operation, it is apparent that large-scale computer-generated printing is an accomplished fact. This printing is usually in the nature of a "computer printout"; as such, it is to be distinguished in form and quality from computer-controlled printing composition, which is discussed in the section on reproduction devices. High-speed printers which independently print computer-generated output are also discussed in the section on reproduction devices.

Current Maximum Potential of Digital Computers and Associated Equipment. There is no known planned application of the new computer generation to the processing of documentary data. Some of these computer configurations have been designed basically for scientific computation, but they are all usable for document storage, manipulation, retrieval, and transmission. Since the new equipment represents a ten-fold increase in storage and calculation power over the most powerful computer configurations currently used in document-handling applications, the use of these new large computers would greatly enhance document-handling and transmission capabilities. The greatly increased random-access storage capability is particularly important for computer-based information retrieval and dissemination activities, since it would allow more rapid processing of documents than current systems that use magnetic tape storage media. If one of the new generation computer configurations were utilized at the center of a document system, with computers being linked to it from decentralized information centers, a large increase in the rate of automatic processing of textural and graphic information could occur.

Rapid transmission of information to the system user is possible with computer input and output devices that allow man-machine intercommunication. These new devices include such items as the RAND Graphic Tablet, light pens, and sophisticated display consoles with manual keyboard input and output. Use of these advanced man-machine devices on a comprehensive scale, in association with computer storage of large document files and bibliographic tools, would represent extension of a basic capability in existence at MIT and elsewhere. Utilization of new computer generation equipment and advanced telecommunication equipment in such applications would depend on development of adequate computer programs and associated software, which are discussed later in this appendix.

It should be emphasized that computer equipment selected for a document-handling application should feature storage elements and instructions repertoires best suited to document processing. That is, such equipment should be capable of rapid, direct storage, retrieval, and processing of textual data on a character-by-character basis. This capability allows optimal sorting, transfer, and comparison of data, which are the key computer processing operations used in manipulating documentation files.

Voluntary manufacturer action is increasing in standardization of data codes, input and output device characteristics, and computer instruction repertoires. This is evidenced by current examples such as the resemblances between the IBM 360 Series and the RCA Spectra Series, and the compatibilities of the Honeywell 200 Series and the IBM 1400 Series. Magnetic tape and wire transmission device compatibilities have become much more common in recent years. Standardization of computer operation codes, of data representations on magnetic tape and in computer memories, and of transmission devices would strongly enhance computer capability through enhanced ability of installations to exchange computer programs and data without conversion.

Expected Digital Computer Capabilities in the Near Future. A capability of storing large volumes of documentary material within the storage units of a computer may be expected within the next few years. More extensive use of television tape and advanced microform storage devices will enable both textual and nontextual

material to be stored in great volume, and retrieved with extreme rapidity. They will also afford more rapid mechanized retrieval of textual and nontextual documentary data than is possibly by using current random-access disk and drum storage devices. These storage media are also discussed later in this appendix. Another future capability for enhanced storage, processing, and retrieval is that of greatly expanded central computer memories. Computer memories under development can be expected to afford memory storage and high-speed processing of billions of characters of information.

A reasonable capability for simultaneous retrieval of information from large holdings by regional information centers should also be within the state of the art in the next several years. This development is contingent upon adoption of compatible input and output transmission devices in all information centers concerned, as well as compatible types of central and regional computer configurations. Also required are methods of simultaneously processing a large number of information requests at an information network center. This capability depends heavily on developments in computer software and reproduction devices, which are discussed later in this appendix.

Character-reading devices offer a very important potential for computer input. Current devices may accept as many as 18 different type fonts. Although the current maximum accurate reading rate is a few hundred characters of data per second, or several hundred typewritten double-spaced pages per hour, there are problems at present with the clarity of type and paper quality, with false recognition of characters, and with the recognition of mathematical and scientific notation. This state of affairs applies to computer-attached document readers manufactured by such firms as Farrington, and to print readers produced by Philco, Rabinow, and other firms. Within five years it is expected that these devices will be capable of accurately reading multiple-font *text* material at rates in the range of several thousand pages per hour. Complete recognition of specialized scientific and technical notation may take more than 5 years to achieve.

Voice input devices offer a strong future input capability, but are currently in the research phase. Existing equipment of this type may be connected to new generation computers. They are currently used to prepare voice messages for voice-media transmission. This is made possible through selection of constituent elements of voice *output* messages by computer program analysis of narrowly defined nonvoice inputs. The current capability for dealing with voice *input* is quite limited, for example, recognizing the spoken digits "zero" through "nine."

Costs of Digital Computers and Associated Equipment. The cost of a new generation computer and its associated equipment would fall into the range of $5 million to $8 million. A configuration could be rented for approximately $150,000 to $250,000 per month. The associated equipment would include the auxiliary high-speed memory, mass random access storage, and satellite computer mentioned above. Approximately twenty magnetic tape units and a character-reading machine would also be in such a configuration, in addition to transmission terminals and multiplexors used in remote data transmissions.

Random access mass storage devices fall within a broad range of purchase prices and rental rates, which vary across and within magnetic drum, disk, magnetic card, and magnetic tape equipment classes. Representative purchase prices for medium-speed (i.e., approximately 90 msec access time for data) devices with 100 million characters of storage capacity would fall within the $300,000 to $400,000 range, while monthly rental charges would be in the $4000 to $7000 range. Higher-speed devices, allowing access to data in very few milliseconds, may require a five- to tenfold increase in outlay for equivalent storage capacity.

Print readers fall within the $150,000 to $500,000 cost range and may be rented monthly for $3000 to $15,000. Magnetic tape units may be rented for $300 to $800 per month, while computer-associated punched card and paper tape readers may be rented for $100 to $200 per month.

Software for Digital Computer Operation

The State of the Art. Our discussion of software is restricted to computer programs, although the term "software" can also include equipment manuals, written compilations of equipment characteristics, and instructions for personnel who operate or maintain the equipment. Though these other kinds of software are not treated

here, they are required for successful operation of a computer-based system.

Computer programs are as indispensable for the utilization of computers and computer-based systems as is the equipment discussed elsewhere in this appendix. Yet it is sometimes not fully recognized that the writing of computer programs is often a very difficult, costly, and time-consuming process. Such recognition is important in planning for future systems.

No comprehensive software has yet been developed for large-scale computer-based document-handling systems. The most extensive operational software package is probably that of NASA, which is approached in scope by only two known comparable computer-based systems. It should be emphasized that these three large-scale systems do not have compatible software or equipment.

The plethora of computer programming languages—more than 1000 in use at present—prevents effective interchange of programs among computer users. Even in the case of the most widely used languages, COBOL for business and document applications and FORTRAN for scientific computation, more than twenty versions of each are currently used. However, new computer generation software trends emphasize the use of COBOL, FORTRAN, and a new language combining features of both. This definitely is an encouraging trend.

Computer software for such activities as direct interrogation of stored document files, using display consoles and similar devices, is still in the research and development phase. Significant examples of such software systems are to be found in Project MAC at MIT, the JOSS System at RAND Corporation, the Time Sharing System at SDC, and several other comparable activities. The general technique in use here is parallel execution in a computer of programs initiated from remote locations through telecommunication devices. A current limitation in this area is that programming languages are not compatible between many of the installations that are developing time-sharing software.

The user-oriented computer technique known as "selective dissemination," used in the NASA S&T System (see *Description of the NASA System*) employs key words, which represent individual users' interests and which are compared with words that have been assigned to documents to indicate their contents. A computer program matches the user's key words with doc-

ument key words, applies weighting and qualification factors, and notifies the users that documents of potential interest to them are available. Software packages for such activities currently exist but are not in wide general use.

Software for automatic indexing and abstracting of input document material is in the research and development phase. A functionally related technique is that of permuted titles, also known as the "key word in context" technique. This is currently used in several applications, such as *Chemical Titles,* and in a modified version in the NASA system.

A strong feature of the current software state of the art is the existence of comprehensive monitoring programs used on the new generation computers. These software packages manage varied forms of input and output, including those transmitted by telecommunications devices, with minimal attention being required on the part of the programmer or computer operator. The packages have also made concurrent execution of several individual computer programs a truly operational feature.

Current Maximum Potential of Computer Software. Current software potential would be greatly enhanced if certain standardizations were encouraged. The use of a very limited number of higher-order computer languages would be a major factor in raising the state of the art above its current level of effectiveness, particularly through reduction of redundant programming. General use of retrieval and dissemination software would be possible if the programs were written in one computer language for execution on compatible computers. Today's software packages are written for different computers with different characteristics, and are therefore not interchangeable or usable across the computing community. There is a need for a central comprehensive index of computer software packages, existing and under development, as well as a comprehensive index of all computer types and their characteristics. Such indexes would be strong aids in realizing the maximum current potential of computers and their software.

Software for document processing, editing, retrieval, dissemination, and transmission is within the state of the art. Its development for the new computer generation would take advantage of their great speed and storage capabilities. Existing document-handling software packages

operate on computers with much less capacity than that of the new computer generation. Such existing software features as natural-language formulation of retrieval requests, bibliographic reference list interrogation, selective dissemination of document citations, and weighed document search and retrieval should be developed for the new generation of computers.

Expected Computer Software Capabilities in the Near Future. It can be expected that firms producing computer software will increasingly standardize on the COBOL and FORTRAN computer languages, or on a new language incorporating their major features, such as the new PL-1 business-scientific language.

It also can be expected that comprehensive document-handling software packages will be developed for the new generation of computers. These computers appear to have such versatile and powerful operating capabilities that major software changes will not be caused in the next few years by changes in technical computer characteristics. Foreseeable developments should include comprehensive program packages for all aspects of computer-based information storage, retrieval, dissemination, and transmission. The increased storage and processing-speed capabilities of computer hardware will allow this new software to direct the processing by computer of heretofore impracticably large amounts of documentary data.

Costs of Digital Computer Software. It has been estimated that $2 billion was spent in 1964 on development and maintenance of computer programs in the United States, an estimate that surely indicates a large expense involved in computer software activity. It may be compared with the GSA estimate that the current expenditure for all government-operated computer *equipment* is also $2 billion.

Telecommunication Equipment

The State of the Art. Telecommunication equipment is discussed here in terms of transmission speeds and geographic coverage of significant national S&T centers. This approach leads to division of the analysis into two groups: first, low-speed textual and nontextual transmission devices using narrow-band wire transmission; and second, high-speed devices using broadband wire, microwave, and cable telecommunication media.

By slow-speed equipment, we mean here narrow-band telephone, telegraph, and teletype wire transmission circuitry in the 2- to 4-kc range. Such equipment comprises the majority of current telecommunication coverage in the United States. Telephonic devices, e.g., Dataphone, allow transmission of data signals over voice telephone circuits. The maximum rate of such transmission is approximately 4000 English text words per minute, and a sustained transmission rate is approximately 2000 words per minute. Teletype circuitry is effectively limited to typewriter speed, with transmission of 100 words of data per minute being a standard rate. U. S. Army Strategic Communications Command teletype equipment is rated at 200 text words per minute, and the fastest known commercially available teletype speed is 400 words per minute.

This class of wire equipment is a major element in many current systems. It affords a relatively cheap and accurate vehicle for bulk data transmission, and is the most widespread and widely compatible telecommunication medium. It also allows relatively economical transmission of nontextual graphic information to remote locations through use of facsimile devices, which are discussed later in this section.

"Intermediate-speed" broad-band circuits are also used for textual data transmission. In 48-kc circuitry, as many as 90,000 words can be transmitted per minute of operation. This class of telecommunication circuitry is used for computer-to-computer communication. The IBM 7702, the General Electric Datanet 30, and similar units link computer input devices with the telecommunication circuitry. These computer telecommunication linkage units coordinate data flow and perform all necessary speed and data transformations. Equipment in the 3- to 4-kc range (as well as intermediate-capacity media) are also used to service such computer input media as punched card receivers, punched paper tape devices, magnetic tape terminals, random access storage units, and central computer memory buffers. These 4-kc and 48-kc media (e.g., "Telpak A") generally are available between locations in the United States.

Microwave and cable telecommunication media are discussed separately here because they afford very high-speed transmission capabilities, and are not as widespread geographically as the wire transmission media discussed above.

Microwave equipment forms a significant element in the telephone systems of the United States, and is also used extensively by such enterprises as railroads and pipeline companies. The AT&T system has microwave connections between 600 cities. The Western Union Microwave System connects Boston, Philadelphia, Buffalo, New York, Washington, Atlanta, Chicago, Kansas City, Houston, St. Louis, San Francisco, Los Angeles, and Seattle.

The AT&T microwave elements form part of a telephone system. The Western Union elements constitute a microwave network which connects with Canadian and Mexican communications networks. Both are linked with the Automatic Digital Network (AUTODIN) and Federal Telecommunications Network (FTS) systems discussed later.

High-speed telecommunication media are discussed here in terms of AT&T "Telpak" equipment. "Telpak B," with a 96-kc capacity, is equivalent in capacity to 24 4-kc "standard land lines" and is limited to voice and teletype transmission. "Telpak C," at 240 kc, and "Telpak D," at 960 kc, are used for general data transmission. The upper range of data transmission of these (and comparable) systems is a million textual words per minute. It should be kept in mind that this value relates to media capable of multiple simultaneous two-way (duplex) transmissions.

Special-purpose television circuits can transmit alphabetical and numerical data. The National Aeronautics and Space Administration maintains such a network between the Goddard Space Flight Center at Greenbelt, Maryland, the Manned Spacecraft Center at Houston, Texas, and the NASA installation at Cape Kennedy, Florida. The other major example of television transmission is the coaxial cable circuitry used by the major commercial television networks, which allows transmission of television images between affiliated network stations. There are roughly 50,000 miles of circuitry leased for this purpose at present. These circuits would offer good coverage for a document-handling network application, but they are "dedicated" (reserved) for other federal government and commercial use.

The types of devices that can be connected with the data-transmission media described above include: computer-connected consoles and display devices; microfilm transmission and reproduction devices; photographic transmission and reproduction devices; magnetic tape, punched card and paper tape units; photographic and hand-writing facsimile devices; electrostatic high-speed printers; and analog computers, whose physical representations of scientific and technical data may be converted by various special-purpose devices to numerical form suitable for transmission over all the media specified above. It should be noted that facsimile devices linked to high-speed telecommunication media are currently capable of handling data at relatively slow transmission rates. However, many slow-speed messages can simultaneously be transmitted by high-speed telecommunication media.

Current telecommunication networks contain the circuitry and devices outlined above and afford wide national coverage. The low-speed, narrow-band telegraph (2 kc) and voice-grade telephone (3 to 4 kc) networks may be considered as covering all U. S. localities. Most significant localities are covered by 48-kc broadband media. Major cities are connected by television coaxial cable circuitry, and there is extensive high-speed microwave linkage between major U. S. regional centers. The military AUTODIN and the civil FTS afford broad U. S. coverage.

These networks are not currently integrated. The National Communications System organization, established in 1963, is directed toward coordinated planning and optimized use of federal telecommunications resources. AUTODIN and FTS nets are now capable of data interchange, but no truly integrated, compatible federal telecommunications network exists today. In addition, the existing commitments and responsibilities of these networks currently require use of a major portion of their overall capacity.

The IBM "Global Teleprocessing System" used transatlantic cables for its Armonk, New York, to Ensomme, France, linkage. The European and United States portions of this network use high-speed land lines, and the network is monitored by computer and data transmission devices. This network, and comparable examples effected by major carriers, illustrate advanced computer-centered telecommunication networks operated in the private sector.

Current Maximum Potential of Telecommunication Equipment. The capability of transmitting

data between information centers in the country exists today through telephone and teletype devices. Although for economic and geographic reasons, television, microwave, and other intermediate- and high-speed transmission (and associated reproduction) media do not fill the information-transfer needs of the U. S. information network, they have the technical potential for doing so.

It should be noted here that facsimile transmission, reception, and reproduction equipment is much less developed than computer and other telecommunication equipment. Such items as handwriting facsimile transmission and reproduction devices and graphic cathode-ray image pointers (as the RAND Graphic Tablet) are in the advanced development phase; their use in computer-based applications depends on computer software which is still being developed, although the devices are operational.

The current maximum potential for use of telecommunications equipment in document-handling applications would be coaxial cable and microwave transmission of data and user requests between computer-centered document facilities and a widespread group of user facilities. The centers would use advanced communications linkage equipment and new generation computer equipment configurations.

A network of this scope and transmission power would exceed current average speed capacities of the AUTODIN and FTS networks. Dedication of sufficient circuitry for system requirements would be essential for such a level of performance. Use of new reproduction equipment described in the next section would enhance the capability of such a system. This combination of the best available communication, manipulation, and reproduction equipment would represent a significant increase over existing major systems. Establishment of this capability, which would be extremely expensive at this time, would require a centrally-planned, integrated telecommunication network to be effective.

Expected Telecommunication Equipment Capabilities in the Near Future. It is reasonable to expect an increase in the data-transmission rates of telecommunication equipment. Extension of the capabilities of such devices will enable the foundation of a national system employing automated document-handling. Increases also can be expected in the speed and accuracy of transmitting data of a nontextual nature by using facsimile equipment.

Extensive use of television media in a national document-handling system would be possible. However, television would probably be too expensive for use in extensive networks, unless technological and manufacturing developments significantly reduce the cost.

Such optical data transmission devices as lasers are in the "field test phase" of development for governmental and private application. While these devices may provide strong future capability, it is not expected that they will be used extensively as elements in national-scale communications media within the immediate future.

Communications satellites, currently in the testing and development phase, could be a strong future element in the international exchange of information. They also have a potential for eventually serving in a domestic documentary data-transfer system. Current Communications Satellite Corporation and U. S. Army Strategic Communications Command satellite communication activities indicate the technical feasibility of using satellites in the near future for high-speed data transmission.

The current use of troposcatter and wave propagation techniques, illustrated in the Florida-Bahamas linkage and military systems, is an indication of new and growing capability to use advanced non-line-of-sight transmission techniques as part of a telecommunications net. Increased commercial use of these high-speed media may be expected in future years.

Cost of Telecommunication Equipment. These cost data relate to purchase and rental charges applicable to individual items of current telecommunications equipment. Estimates of total network costs may best be obtained from national telecommunications system information and from Department of Defense, NASA, and private telecommunications network cost data.

The first group of costs relates to low-speed telephonic and teletype circuitry and devices, which represent the major portion of existing U. S. communications networks. Transcontinental Wide Area Telephone Service (WATS) full-time wire charges are roughly $1 per mile of circuitry per month. Private line charges for low-speed wire circuits are higher than for

shared circuits. Representative monthly rental charges in this transmission range include $15 for a telephone terminal; $100 to $125 for teletype terminals; $100 to $150 for low-speed punched paper tape devices, and $150 to $225 per month for low-speed magnetic tape keyboarding and transmission units.

There is a wide range of rental and purchase rates for modems* and terminals used in intermediate- and high-speed transmission activity. Monthly rental charges for these devices range from about $400 to $1500 per terminal for high-speed magnetic tape, punched card, punched tape, document facsimile, and direct computer-to-computer data transmissions. There is a wide range of rates within each class of equipment, in addition to variations in manufacturer pricing policies.

The most significant factor in high-speed data transmission costs is the charge made for the broad-band circuitry between terminals, which overshadows terminal costs. Rental rates for circuitry (using AT&T "Telpak" as a base) are illustrated in the accompanying table.

or approximately $80 per month per mile for the circuitry in use. These costs illustrate one of the reasons for limited use of exclusive, or "dedicated," high-speed telecommunication media. There are no known volume discount pricing policies in effect today.

The cost for exclusive rental of a Telpak "C" circuit between New York and San Francisco would approximate $800,000 per year. Since a high-speed document-handling network would require many miles of similar (or faster) circuitry, costs would be very high. A comparison of cost for such a network with overall network costs in the lower capacity AUTODIN and FTS networks would illustrate the expensiveness of high-speed telecommunications.

Increasing use of high-speed media may be expected, but a document-handling application would use a combination of low-speed and high-speed media in the foreseeable future. Extensive use of high-speed media in document-handling applications would require a federal determination that such applications were of a high order of priority.

Representative Rental Charges for High-Rate Telecommunication Circuitry

Medium	Monthly Charge Per Mile of Transmission Circuits	Remarks
Telpak "A" (48 kc, 12-line) (equivalent to 12 telephone lines)	$15 plus $15 or more per terminal modem	Used in low- and intermediate-speed card, tape, and facsimile transmission.
Telpak "B" (96 kc, 24-line)	$20 plus $100 to $300 (or more) per terminal	Multiplexed voice and teletype only; not broadband
Telpak "C" (240 kc, 60-line)	$25 plus $400 (or more) per terminal modem	Used for highest-speed facsimile transmission.
Telpak "D" (960 kc, 240-line)	$45 plus $400 to $1500 per terminal modem	Used for highest-speed magnetic tape transmission.
Television-Range Transmission Circuitry	$80 and more, with very high (and variable) modem rates.	Generally reserved or dedicated, usage.

Domestic commercial television networks lease over 50,000 miles of video bandwidth circuitry for program transmission. The cost exceeds $1000 per mile per year for this service,

* Modems are devices for conversion between digital (alphabetical and numerical) data entering and leaving terminals, and electrical (analog) signals comprising data during transmission (through telecommunication media) between terminals.

Reproduction Devices and Equipment

The State of the Art. Reproduction devices are divided here into the following major classes: printers associated with digital computers, facsimile devices primarily associated with telecommunication networks, and printing composition equipment driven by computers. Microform-related equipment is treated separately later.

HIGH-SPEED PRINTERS. In discussing computers earlier, we mentioned a printing capability of approximately 1100 132-character lines per minute as a normal rate. These printers usually employ a drum, or rotating chain, containing alphabetical, numerical, and punctuation symbols, against which the advancing paper is pressed by hammers. More rapid types of computer printers are available that use a nonimpact electrostatic printing process and attain rates as high as 5000 lines per minute. However, they usually do not print a standard page image. In addition, these printers are subject to problems in the area of font quality. Because of these factors, sustained high-volume, high-quality computer-directed printed at these speeds is not yet really practical.

The most rapid known computer-associated printer is a Radiation, Incorporated, product producing as much as 30,000 lines of copy per minute. Computer-generated magnetic tape is the input medium. The paper is similar to the "glossy" facsimile paper or "flimsy" used with telecommunication facsimile devices. The printing representation is "wire-dot" characters, such as those found on interpreted punched cards. The paper is fed from rolls, and is automatically folded after printing. Although this device does not use high-quality paper for printing and features an unusual printing representation, it illustrates a very powerful tool for use in document-handling applications.

The use of current computer prints for preparation of finished copy, suitable for publication, is not yet an economical process. This is due in part to technical problems of providing ribbons and paper of suitable quality at a reasonable cost, and also to computer-printer design factors that currently prevent optimal use of space on the paper.

FACSIMILE DEVICES. There are many types of facsimile and reproduction devices that may be connected with telecommunication equipment to transmit and reproduce alphabetical, numerical, graphic, and handwritten data into hardcopy media and other representations.

One class of facsimile device is electrostatic printers. Two such devices represent the most advanced remote facsimile devices in operation. The first is the Xerox Corporation High-Speed LDX C135 Printer, which is used with a 240-kc Telpak "C" circuit. This printer can print up to sixteen standard (i.e., $8\frac{1}{2} \times 11$ in.) pages in a minute of operation. The second device is the A. B. Dick Videograph 921, which is used with equivalent telecommunication linkage. It produces ten or more pages per minute of operation. Similar printers with slower rates may be used in conjunction with lesser bandwidths. An example is the Xerox LDX A135, which is used with Telpak "A" circuitry.

Another class of facsimile equipment is the analog image device which will reproduce graphic (as well as textual material into hardcopy form. Alden Electronics, Litton Industries/Westrex, Telautograph Corporation, and Western Union are the principal manufacturers of these devices which fall into two groups. The more rapid, which use Telpak "A" high-speed circuits, can reproduce two to four standard pages of data per minute. The second group, which uses 3-kc narrow-band circuits, has a rate of four to eight minutes per page of copy. The low-speed facsimile devices are those most commonly used. Major current facsimile applications are weather data transmission, military logistical information transmission, and industrial and commercial message services.

Alphabetical, numerical, and graphic information may also be transmitted by photographic transmission devices. These devices can reproduce such transmissions at the rate of approximately two pages in nine minutes of operation, using telephone circuits. Special-purpose facsimile scanners and recorders for handwritten information operate over telephone circuits at a rate of approximately two pages per minute. Another type of facsimile transmission and reproduction equipment is a device that transmits normal handwriting from one installation to another, with ballpoint pens being available on both terminals. These telephone-circuit devices are able to reproduce messages at normal handwriting speed, and the product is hard copy produced by the receiver.

COMPUTER-MANAGED PRINTING COMPOSITION. Composition of mats and other media for use in conventional printing is now within the state of the art in computer installations. An example is the GRACE photographic compositor in use at the National Library of Medicine MEDIARS Project. The Honeywell computer at MEDLARS produces magnetic tape which is used to guide the GRACE in composing pages for *Index Medi-*

cus. The GRACE, a Photon Corporation product, has a capacity for 226 different characters, and composes 300 characters per second on a line-by-line basis. Another Photon Corporation photographic compositor (in the "900 Series") is driven by computer-generated magnetic tape. This is a line-by-line device that has a 286-character capacity, and can compose approximately 500 characters per second.

Slower computer-driven compositors are available, composing characters on a line-by-line basis. These include devices manufactured by Harris Intertype and other firms.

A new development scheduled for operation early in 1967 at the Government Printing Office promises a strong capability in computer-managed composition. This is the Linotron, a CBS Laboratories-Mergenthaler development. It has a 1024-character capacity, operates on a page-by-page basis, and can compose up to 600 pages per hour of operation. It is driven by magnetic tapes produced by IBM 1400- and 360-Series computers. The 1024 characters and symbols may be represented in eight point sizes. These point sizes, ranging from 6-point to 18-point, effectively govern the speed of the Linotron; 6-point characters are composed at a rate of 1000 characters per second and larger point sizes are composed at slower proportionate speeds. The 1024-character capacity of the Linotron is effectively divided into four character sets of 256 symbols, each of which includes a complete font of type (with related graphic arts characters) in roman, italic, small capital, and boldface representations. Mathematical notation also is provided for. This photocomposition device, currently undergoing advanced application testing, represents a major advance in automated printing composition.

Current Maximum Potential of Reproduction Devices and Equipment. Computer-associated printers are used by some installations in the printing of copy which is photographed and used as a basis for printing published materials. For example, the NASA Scientific and Technical Information Facility uses such a technique to produce a portion of its announcement journals (see *Description of NASA System*). This example demonstrates that the use of computer print-outs as the basis of published materials is within the state of the art. So also is the use of computer printers as a high-speed, high-

volume reproduction device for documentary data.

Hard-copy and photographic facsimile devices are in operational use today. Facsimile devices for the transmission and reproduction of handwritten material are less common. Also uncommon in documentation use is the lightpen, a cathode-ray tube graphic stylus that transmits signals to a digital computer. It has been developed to the point where it is used operationally today in a number of applications, and could be used for such document-handling applications as browsing in a computer-stored document file.

Consoles and display devices have a significant potential use, within the state of the art, as a means of interrogating computer-stored bibliographic tools and document files. Large-scale use of consoles and display devices has been confined to command and control applications, and to experimental uses in time-sharing research applications. The new generation computer configurations can include inquiry consoles with cathode-ray tube displays and manual keyboard input units.

General Electric, Sanders, CDC, IBM, RCA, and other firms recently have produced devices which serve as new computer generation console-display units. Such devices have a cathode-ray tube that can display simultaneously 1024 or more alphabetical, numerical, and punctuation characters. A keyboard with 64 or more characters is included for communication with the central computer. Two hundred or more characters of data per second can be received by these units, which may be linked by standard (3 kc) telephone circuits. Each of the new generation computers may have 50 or more such consoles connected with it.

Console and display devices provide a strong aid in direct human search and analysis of computer-stored documentary resources. The major limitation on their use is the requirement to provide appropriate, operational software for the new computer generation. If both the necessary software and the necessary dedicated telecommunication media were available, these devices could be utilized in a document-handling network.

Computer-managed photocomposition already is operational. Full-page, multiple-font print composition managed by computers is imminent though still in the developmental phase.

Reproduction Equipment in the Foreseeable Future. It is reasonable to expect improvement in the quality of printing available from computer printers. Computer systems in the foreseeable future will be able to process information from input data through to output of documents suitable for publication.

The quality of facsimile reproduction equipment will undoubtedly reach higher levels of speed and accuracy of reproduction. One expectable development is improvement in the speed of reproduction of graphic material by facsimile equipment. Developments in computer-managed printing composition can be expeted to add significantly to the speed of high-quality printing of large volumes of material. This capability would directly benefit an automated information system.

Cost of Reproduction Equipment. Rental charges and purchase price of illustrative reproduction devices are summarized here. Data represent single items of equipment.

HIGH-SPEED PRINTERS. Computer-driven high-speed impact printers are normally attached to an auxiliary small computer associated with the central computer. Since the auxiliary computer edits and formats data for printing, its rental charge is included with that of one such printer. Hence, one printer must be considered to be in the $2500 to $4000 monthly rental class. The price of the auxiliary computer and single printer falls within a range of $150,000 to $250,000.

Very high-speed nonimpact computer printers may be obtained for varying rates. The ultra-high-speed, dot-printing Radiation, Inc. printer, may be purchased for approximately $250,000. Other slower nonimpact devices may be rented for $400 to $1000 per month.

FACSIMILE ELECTROSTATIC PRINTERS. Such equipment as the A. B. Dick Videograph 921 may be purchased for $50,000; the Xerox LDX 135C rents for $800 per month. This charge normally includes several thousand page-copying operations. Additional charges are made for use of the printer beyond this basic page allowance. The cost of transmission circuitry should be considered in conjunction with the cost of this range of printing facsimile devices.

FACSIMILE ANALOG DEVICES. This equipment includes other facsimile transmission and reception devices which process textual and nontextual material. This class includes photographic and handwritten message facsimile apparatus. The monthly rental charge for such equipment generally is between $50 and $150. Speed of transmission and bandwidth capabilities generally determine the charge for a device.

COMPUTER-MANAGED PRINTING COMPOSITION DEVICES. Line-by-line compositors with a 10- to 15-character per second composition speed are priced between $20,000 and $60,000.

Line-by-line photo compositors with a 300- to 500-character per second rate of composition may be purchased for $200,000 to $300,000.

CONSOLES AND DISPLAY UNITS. The IBM 2260 and comparable "new computer generation" console display units may be rented monthly for $75 to $125. "Keyboard-only" consoles may be rented for $30 to $50 per month. Large display units and large console units rent at considerably higher monthly rates.

Microform Equipment

Definitions of Media

MICROFICHE. Microfiche is essentially a special format of microfilm. A page image is reduced to a 16-mm microfilm image to form a microfiche chip. Many of these chips are then mounted in a transparent plastic microfiche. The standard microfiche format of the National Microfilm Association contains 58 page-image chips in a 4 x 6 in. microfiche. This standard has been recommended for the federal government by COSATI.

APERTURE CARD. The aperture card is a microfiche chip inserted into a punched card. An aperture-card microfiche chip may hold one to four page images. When the required documentary identification is punched into the card, the microfiche page image can be retrieved or manipulated by computer equipment.

OPAQUE MICROCARD. Opaque microcard devices generally use media other than transparent microfilm as a document-storage vehicle. This group of devices includes highly reduced printing of document pages on special forms of paper, as well as other special techniques.

VIDEO FILM. Video film is a tape-recording medium, prepared by scanning and transcribing

a television camera image. Six to eight 8½ x 11 in. page images may be stored on a linear inch of video tape. Reels of video tape are made in 3600- and 7200-ft lengths. The maximum announced storage capacity for 3600-ft reels is 360,000 page images; a more commonly used value is 500,000 images per 7200-ft reel.

Microform Uses and Techniques. Microform devices are widely used as document storage and retrieval vehicles. Two primary uses may be distinguished: first, that of reduction of volume; and second, permanent retention of documents that otherwise would be lost because of the deterioration of the paper on which they are printed. Such deterioration is a serious problem with respect to commercial paper produced since about 1870s.

Microfilm images are normally formed in serial film reels. Two basic means of retrieval of microfilm information are in use today. The more widely used is based on the following type of operation. A requester asks for a document which is stored in a microfilm file. An index is consulted which gives the beginning reel, and the beginning frame on the reel, where the document's page images start. Successive serial microfilm page images may then be viewed and reproduced in hard-copy form. The alternative microfilm-search technique is based on recording of document identification and content data on part of the microfilm image. This leads to a capability for automatically searching a microfilm file for all document images that meet the requester's criteria.

Use of microfilm reels for transmission of information is normally restricted to those cases where a large volume of information is desired by the recipient. In the case of microfiche, current experimental efforts are being made to transmit microfiche reproductions of documents to a requester in place of documents. There is evidence that the cost of transmitting information stored on microfiche is much less than the cost of document transmission. An essential element in effective operational use of this technique is the availability of economical and truly effective microform readers.

Another important factor is the preference of many users for printed material rather than film image representations. This factor will be significant in planning for expanded use of microform images.

Microform printing and transmission devices are operational. A currently available 35-mm microfilm scanner is capable of scanning aperture cards and reproducing their images at a rate of approximately 2 page images in 9 minutes. This is a companion device to the photographic transmission device mentioned earlier.

In addition, there have been dramatic advances in the computer processing of microfilm images. An example is a General Dynamics Corporation microfilm device that can accept, from magnetic tape, computer-generated data defining graphic images in numerical form, and including alphabetical and other information. The device, in essence a special-purpose computer, interprets the numerical information and reproduces a graphic image on microfilm, along with any associated alphabetical information. It is capable also of taking a photograph of the microfilm image and printing this image on paper. This powerful tool has had application in areas where graphs, charts, maps, and other representations may be derived by computers or other means, and then microfilmed and printed without significant human intervention.

Maximum Current Potential of Microform Media. Four major federal agencies have adopted a standard form of microfiche representation: the Atomic Energy Commission, the National Aeronautics and Space Administration, the Clearinghouse for Federal Scientific and Technical Information, and the Defense Documentation Center. This microfiche standardization was accomplished under the auspices of COSATI.

Transmission of microform images by telecommunication equipment is practicable. Use of this capability can be expanded in order to transmit images of documents to requesters at remote locations, following which the image can be put into hard copy form if desired. Though this is a slow and expensive process, it is available today.

There are current experiments in dissemination of microfiche images in place of user-requested documents they represent. Currently available microfiche readers cost $150 or more, and render a fair visual image. Although there is room for considerable improvement in such devices, their use in this and other applications could be expanded.

The computer-related microfilm-image photo-

graphic and printing device is a powerful resource for processing graphic information into a microfilm image, with simultaneous printed visual output. Consideration should be given to extending the use of such devices. They are expensive at present, but they represent a significant enhancement of the traditional role of microfilm for secondary document and data storage.

The (Ampex) video-file concept allows computer-controlled search of video-tape reels in a manner analogous to search of microfilm reels. Currently available devices allow 7200 feet of video tape to be searched in approximately 120 seconds for randomly ordered document page images. This is currently a serial, document-number search process. Display consoles and television communication circuits may be linked to the video-file system. Total costs of the video devices, file updating, and image transmission are extremely high, but this equipment offers a powerful medium for document storage and transmission. Current regional or national potential is limited by the restricted availability of telecommunication circuits, but local use of this medium offers immediate potential. There is also potential for use of this system with slow-speed facsimile devices using telephone-circuit linkage, which could be exploited.

Microform Developments in the Foreseeable Future. The cost of microfiche-image reproduction is approximately 10 cents per page copied, and is expected to become even less because of manufacturing and technological advances taking place today. This may well lead to widespread dissemination of documentation in microform representation rather than in traditional document media.

Advances in the remote transmission and reproduction of microform media can be expected, as can a reduction in the cost of such equipment. This may well lead to maintenance of documentary resources in microform representation, from which they may be automatically retrieved and transmitted without appreciable delay.

Improvements can be expected in the (NCR) photochromic photo-reduction process. Document page images may be stored on special film through an ultraviolet exposure process. This device is limited at present by severe deterioration of the medium during use, and by stringent storage-environment requirements. Its display facil-

ity and life expectancy are being improved. Since a single microfiche-sized frame of this material may contain as many as 2000 page images, this device has great potential in document storage and handling.

More use may be made of slow-speed (telephone circuit) transmission of video-file document images. The images could be stored in a central document facility. Retrieval of video document images on the basis of internal contents may well be initiated. Reduction of video-file input preparation costs and transmission expenses would be required for its widespread national use in any document-handling network.

Costs of Microform-Related Equipment. Illustrative purchase and rental cost data for selected microform-related devices are summarized here. Special-purpose and sophisticated equipment models are differentiated, where cost or functional considerations so indicate. Equipment costs are emphasized rather than microform costs per se.

CAMERAS. These devices fall into two general groups. The first group requires hand input feeding, produces a minimal image, and cannot insert identification data on film images. Purchase prices vary from a minimum of $700 to about $1500.

The second group of cameras have capability to produce good film images. This group may be purchased for $1500 to $9000. Equipment in the $3000 to $5000 price range has automatic document feeding, very good image generation capability, and the capability of inserting document identification data on film images. The highest range, $5000 to $9000, includes cameras of excellent image generation quality. This group features the capability of inserting sophisticated indicators of document and content identification into the microfilm image.

FILM PROCESSORS AND MOUNTERS. Processing equipment costs range widely, as do the costs of other microform-related equipment. An illustrative price for a good film processor would be $3000 to $4000; additional quality and performance options result in higher prices.

Equipment specifically designed for mounting microfilm clips into other media is illustrated by the aperture card mounter, which inserts the processed microform image into a Hollerith or

edge-punched card. This class of device may be obtained for roughly $500.

MICROFORM DUPLICATORS. The cost of microfilm preparation promotes the use of duplicating devices. Aperture-card to microfilm-roll duplicators fall within the $5000 to $8000 price range, as does roll-to-roll duplication equipment.

MICROFILM READER-PRINTERS. This equipment allows a user to examine serial microfilm images, and to convert images into hard copy form. Such items may be rented for $150 to $200 monthly and purchased for $3000 to $5000.

MICROFILM SEARCH EQUIPMENT. These devices have a capability to examine microform files on the basis of document identification and content. The simpler type of device accepts microfilm rolls and locates desired images by their serial position on a given microfilm roll. This type of device may be rented for $2000 to $3000 per month, and purchased for about $120,000.

More sophisticated microfilm search equipment has a capability of searching stored document files by using Boolean logic on document identification and content items. These equipments may be purchased for $150,000 and more.

MICROFILM READERS. These vary in price and range from low-power hand readers to desktop-size microfilm readers. Readers providing acceptable resolution and clarity are available within the $150 to $300 price range. Prices of such readers have been declining within the recent past.

APERTURE-CARD EQUIPMENT COSTS. The cost of aperture-card processing varies with the type of equipment used. Punched card, computer, and "peek-a-boo" devices are used to sort, search, and otherwise manipulate these cards.

Aside from image and card preparation, the operation will generally be more expensive than microfilm activities. An advantage gained from this additional expense is the ability to manipulate and search the card file with computer and punched-card equipment.

COMPUTER-ASSOCIATED MICROFILM EQUIPMENT COSTS. The automated preparation of aperture cards may be illustrated through the new IBM "Cypress" system which stores, retrieves, processes, and mounts aperture card images. The use of high-pressure ammonia in the (diazo) development process is monitored by a computer, as is retrieval from a large, variable-size store containing cells of aperture card images. This unit may operate independently, or be associated with a larger computer configuration, and rents for $4000 and more per month.

Another type of computer-associated microform equipment is represented by such devices as the General Dynamics-Stromberg Carlson 4000 Series equipment. The basic capability to convert computer-generated alphabetical and numerical data to graphic forms on microfilm is available for $4000 to $5000 per month. Varying additional charges depend upon additional options available.

VIDEO FILE SYSTEMS COSTS. This class of storage and retrieval system is very expensive. A local installation with tape generation and display console features may cost as much as $1 million. A factor in this cost is short-distance transmission charges and equipment installation fees.

REFERENCES

Research Technology and Advanced Systems

Cited References

1. Schultheiss, L. A., Culbertson, D. S., and Heiliger, E. M. *Advanced Data Processing in the University Library*. New York, The Scarecrow Press, Inc., 1962.

2. Keppel, F. P. "Looking Forward, a Fantasy," in Danton, E. M., Ed., *The Library of Tomorrow*, 1939, pp. 1–11.

3. Koller, H. R., Marden, E., and Pfeffer, H. "The HAYSTAQ System: Past, Present, and Future," in *Preprints of the International Conference on Scientific Information*, **2**, 1958, p. 1143.

4. Taube, M. "An Evaluation of Use Studies of Scientific Information." Bethesda, Maryland, Documentation Inc., December 1958, AD 206 987.

5. Katter, R. V. "Research Bases of Language Data Processing System Design." TM-1199. Santa Monica, System Development Corporation, 1963.

6. Isaacs, H. H., and Hermann, W. W. "Advanced Computer Technology and Crime Information Retrieval." SP-1927. Santa Monica, System Development Corporation, 1965.

7. Newbaker, H. R., and Savage, T. R. "Selected Words in Full Title (SWIFT): A New Program for Computer Indexing," in *Automation and Scientific Communication* (Short Papers, Part 1, ADI Annual Meeting, 1963) pp. 87–88.

8. Brandhorst, W. T., and Eckert, P. F. "NASA Search System Analysis Sheet," *American Documentation*, Vol. 16, No. 2 (1965), pp. 124–126.

9. Rees, A. M. "Why Are Information Centers Successful?" in *Proceedings of the American Documentation Institute*, **1**, 1964, pp. 173–176.

10. Simmons, R. F., and McConlogue, K. "Maximum-Depth Indexing for Computer Retrieval of English Language Data," *American Documentation*, Vol. 14, No. 1 (1963), pp. 68–73.

General References

Adams, Scott. "The Scientific Revolution and the Research Library," in *Library Resources and Technical Services*, Vol. 9, No. 2, 1965, pp. 138–139.

Becker, Joseph. "System Analysis—Prelude to Library Data Processing." in *ALA Bulletin*, April 1965.

Becker, Joseph. "Demonstrating Remote Retrieval by Computer at Library/USA," in *ALA Bulletin*, October 1964.

Becker, Joseph, and Hayes, R. M. *Information Storage and Retrieval: Tools, Elements, Theories.* New York, John Wiley and Sons, 1963.

Borko, Harold, Ed. *Automated Language Processing.* New York, John Wiley and Sons, 1966.

Farell, Jules. "Textir: A Natural Language Information Retrieval System." TM-2392. Santa Monica, System Development Corporation, May 5, 1965.

Garvin, Paul L., Ed. *Natural Language and the Computer.* New York, McGraw-Hill Book Co., Inc., 1963.

Howerton, Paul W., and Weeks, David C., Eds. *Vistas in Information Handling*, Vol. 1, Washington, D. C., Spartan Books, 1963.

Isaacs, Herbert H., "Crime Pattern Recognition in Natural Language." SP-2077. Santa Monica, System Development Corporation, May 1965.

Shaw, C. J. "A Bibliography For Generalized Information System Designers." TM-2289. Santa Monica, System Development Corporation, March 26, 1965.

Simmons, R.F. "Natural Language Processing and the Time-Shared Computer." SP-1974/001/00. Santa Monica, System Development Corporation, April 23, 1965.

Vickery, B. C. *On Retrieval System Theory.* London, Butterworths, 1961.

From Systems to Components

Computer, High-Speed Memories, and Bulk Storage Devices

Auerbach Corporation "Special Report Random Access Storage: A State-of-the-Art Report," *Standard EDP Report.*

Hobbs, L. C. "Comparison: Major Types of Mass Memories," *Data Systems Design*, January 1964, pp. 16–21.

Kohn, G. "Future of Magnetic Memories," *Proceedings of the IFIP Congress*, 1965, pp. 131–136.

"Magnetic Tape Systems," in *Computers and Data Processing Management*, November 1964, pp. 21–23.

Weik, Martin H. Jr. "Digital Developments," *Proceedings of the 1964 Systems Engineering Conference*, Vol. 1, Clapp & Poliak, Inc., pp. 254–264.

Winsor, Paul, III. "The Future of Magnetic Tape Units," in *Business Automation*, November 1964, pp. 34–37.

Input and Output Equipment

Auerbach Corporation, "Special Report Data Collection Systems: A State-of-the Art Report," in *Standard EDP Reports.*

Hughes, Robert W. "Developments in the Data Print-Out Equipment," *Proceedings of the 1964 Systems Engineering Conference*, Vol. 1, Clapp and Poliak, Inc., pp. 292–298.

Statland, Norman. "A Look at High-Speed Printers," *Computers and Automation*, November 1964, pp. 14–18.

Statland, Norman, and Hillegass, John. "A Survey of Input-Output Equipment," *Computers and Automation*, July 1964, pp. 16–28.

Entry and Display Equipment

Bagg, T. C., and Stevens, M. E. "Information Selection Systems Retrieving Replica Copies: A State-of-the-Art Report, *Technical Note 157*, Washington, D. C., National Bureau of Standards, December 31, 1961.

Data System Design, September 1964 issue.

Davis, Ruth M. "The Information Display Field as It Exists Today," *Information Display*, September/October 1964, pp. 28–30.

"Display System Pictorial Report," *Computers and Automation*, May 1964, pp. 19–21.

Erickson, W. L., and Soller, T. M. "Computer-Driven Display Systems," *IEEE International Convention Record*, Part 3, 1965, pp. 72–84.

Johnson, Robert W. "Digital Data Display Systems: An Assessment," *Computers and Automation*, May 1964, pp. 12–17.

Levine, S. "Input/Output Equipment for Information-Handling Systems," *IEEE International Convention Record*, Part 3, 1965, pp. 86–89.

Oscar, Irving S. "Developments in Data Display Equipment, in *Proceedings of the 1964 Systems Engineering Conference*, Vol. 1, Clapp and Poliak, Inc., pp. 286–291.

"The RAND Tablet: A Man-Machine Communication Device," in *Computer Design*, April 1965, pp. 36–38.

Digital Data Transmission Equipment

Lessler, S., and Sperling, I. "Survey of Data Phone Communications Systems," N-(L)-19560/225/00A, System Development Corporation, April 5, 1963.

Pigott, William H. "Data Transmission Equipment and Techniques," *Proceedings of the 1964 Systems Engineering Conference*, Vol. 1, Clapp and Poliak, Inc., pp. 238–242.

Facsimile Transmission Equipment

Alden, William L. "Cutting Communications Costs With Facsimile," in *Data Processing*, September 1964, pp. 11–14.

Bliss, Warren H. "Advancements in the Facsimile Art During 1963," 1964.

Microfilm and Microfiche Equipment

Barrow, W. J., and Sproull, R. C. "Permanence in Book Papers," in *Science*, Vol. 129, No. 3356, 24 April 1959, pp. 1075–1084.

Kiriyama, Iwao and Teplitz, Arthur. "Introduction to Microfilm Systems," TM-1987/000/01, System Development Corporation, November 15, 1964.

Ullmann, Hans C. "Microfiche: An Introduction," N-WD-985, System Development Corporation, February 1965.

Print Reading Equipment

Schwartz, Jay W., Turner, Robert D. and Vlahos, Petro. "Application of Print Readers to the Needs of Intelligence Agencies," *A Preliminary Survey of Present Machine Capability*, Institute for Defense Analyses, March 1964.

Stein, Edward S. and Associates. "Factors Influencing the Design of Original-Document Scanners for Input to Computers," Techincal Note 245, National Bureau of Standards, August 19, 1964.

Print Composing Equipment

Bozman, William R. "Phototypsetting of Computer Output, An Example Using Tabular Data," in Technical Note 170, Washington, D. C., National Bureau of Standards, June 25, 1963.

"Computers and the Newspaper Publishing Industry, *Automatic Data Processing Newsletter*, Vol. IX, No. 23, April 12, 1965.

"Review of Computer Typesetting Conference—Proceedings 1964," in *Automation Reports*, No. 43, 1965.

Document Reproduction and Handling Equipment

Becker, Joseph, and Hayes, R. M. "Printed Data and the Creation of a Machine Language," *Information Storage and Retrieval: Tools, Elements, Theories*, Chapter 5, New York, John Wiley and Sons, 1963.

Brooks, Frederick, P., Jr., and Iverson, Kenneth E. "Manual Data Processing Equipment," *Automatic Data Processing*, Chapter 2, John Wiley and Sons, 1963.

Speech Processing Systems

Edwards, Paul G., and Clapper, John, Jr., "Better Vocoders are Coming," *IEEE Spectrum*, September 1964, pp. 119–129.

Olson, Harry F. "Speech Processing Systems, in *IEEE Spectrum*, February 1964, pp. 90–102.

Data Organization, Storage, and Retrieval

Bobrow, Daniel G. and Raphael, Bertram. "A Comparison of List-Processing Computer Languages," *Communications of the ACM*, Vol. 7, No. 4, April 1964, pp. 231–240.

Buchholz, Werner. "File Organization and Addressing," in *IBM Systems Journal*, June 1963, pp. 86–111.

Stevens, M. E. *Automatic Indexing: A State-of-the-Art Report*, Monograph 91, Washington, D. C., National Bureau of Standards, March 30, 1965.

On-Line, Multi-Access Systems

Computer Research Corporation. "Time-Sharing System Scorecard: A Survey of On-Line Multiple User Computer Systems." Belmont, Massachusetts, Computer Research Corp., 1965.

Samuel, Arthur L. "Time-Sharing on a Multiconsole Computer," *Project MAC*, MAC-TR-17, Massachusetts Institute of Technology, March 1965.

Systems and Concepts

"Advanced Programming Developments: A Survey," ESD, Hanscom Field, Bedford, Massachusetts, September 1964.

Borko, H. "The Conceptual Foundations of Information Systems." SP-2057. System Development Corporation, May 6, 1965.

Kochen, Manfred. *Some Problems in Information Science With Emphasis on Adaptation to Use Through Man Machine Interaction*, Vol. II of 11, (Contract AF 19(628)-2752), New York, IBM Corporation, April 2, 1964.

Simmons, R. F. "Answering English Questions by Computer: A Survey." SP-1556. System Development Corporation, April 2, 1964.

Appendix Two

Statistical Review

The statistical data presented in this section highlight several features of national scientific and technical document- and information-handling activities and are categorized according to manpower data, document-related data, cost data, and institutional data.

The reader is cautioned against literal interpretation and extrapolation of the data into general conclusions. Some data, for example, come from surveys based on a limited and nonrepresentative sample; other data are of questionable validity because they are out of date. Moreover, it was difficult to acquire all data as of a particular calendar year, due to delays in publication, the variety of data sources, the variances in data compilations, etc. In most cases, however, data included herein refer to the calendar years 1962 through 1964.

The lack of adequate, accurate, and reliable data illustrates one of the most noticeable drawbacks of the present method of compiling information. At best, these data can only supply

Table A2-1   Historical Perspective of Scientific Manpower (Source 1:7)

	1940	*1950*	*1960*	*1963 Estimate*	*1970 Estimate*
	In Millions				
USA population	132.0	152.3	180.7	190	209
Labor force	56.2	64.7	73.1	76	86
Manpower in science and technology	0.86	1.47	2.37	2.7	4.0
Percentage of labor force	1.5%	2.2%	3.2%	3.6%	4.7%
	In Thousands				
Scientists	145	245	435	500	740
Engineers	300	545	840	935	1400
Technicians	300	550	875	1000	1600
Teachers of science and mathematics in Secondary Schools	110	130	220	250	300
Physical scientists, mathematicians	65	120	225	225	390
Life scientists including psychologists	50	80	140	160	235
Social scientists	30	45	70	85	115
Civil engineers	80	135	160	170	240
Electrical engineers	50	110	180	220	325
Mechanical, aeronautical and astronautical engineers	75	130	210	240	370
Industrial, chemical, and other engineers	95	170	290	305	465
All scientists and engineers	445	790	1275	1435	2140
Doctoral scientists and engineers	28	45	89.2	106	170
Doctoral scientists	27.5	43.5	81.7	96	153
Doctoral engineers	0.5	1.5	7.5	10	17

Table A2-2 Scientists and Engineers by Work Activity (1960) (Source 3:192)

Activity	All (thousands)	Percentage*
All activities	1275	100
scientists	435	100
engineers	840	100
Research	135	10.5
scientists	100	23.0
engineers	35	4.1
Development	290	22.7
scientists	75	17.2
engineers	215	25.6
Production and operations	395	30.9
scientists	105	24.1
engineers	290	34.5
Administration and manage-ment	125	9.8
scientists	40	9.2
engineers	85	10.1
Teaching (college)	80	6.3
scientists	70	16.0
engineers	10	1.2
Other	250	19.6
scientists	45	10.3
engineers	205	24.4

* Percentages refer to totals for all activities.

Table A2-3 Scientists and Engineers by Field, 1960 and 1963 (Source 3:193)

Field	1960 (thousands)	1963 (thousands)
All scientists and engineers	1275	1435
Engineers	840	935
aeronautical and astro-nautical	50	
mechanical	160	240
civil	160	170
electrical	180	220
chemical	45	
industrial	95	305
other	150	
Scientists	435	500
Physical scientists and mathematicians	225	255
chemists	110	
earth scientists	25	
mathematicians	30	
metallurgists	15	
physicists	32	
other physical scientists	13	
Life scientists, including psychologists	140	160
agricultural scientists	40	
biological scientists	40	
medical scientists	30	
psychologists	30	
Social scientists	70	85
anthropologists	2	
economists	20	
sociologists	10	
other social scientists	38	

information in terms of the problem's order of magnitude—and in some instances even this leaves much to be desired.

MANPOWER DATA

By 1970 the number of scientists and engineers will be approximately 2.14 million as compared to the 1960 total of 1.28 million. Of the 1.44 million in 1963, over 66 per cent worked in private industry and about 10 per cent worked for the federal government. Approximately one-third of all scientists and engineers presently devote their primary efforts to research and development activities. The average predicted increase in manpower for all scientific and engineering disciplines 1960–1970 is 69 per cent. The range of increase runs from 25 per cent for geologists and geophysicists to 107 per cent for mathematicians. The germane feature of these data is that the increase in scientists and engineers also represents an increase in users and producers of scientific and technical documents.

By contrast, predictions indicate that the ratio of librarians to scientists and engineers is declining. Such data tend to highlight an unfortunate trend which has long-term ramifications. This growing shortage of trained librarians (most of whom are not trained in the science and/or technology of information handling) can be broadened to include all types of information science personnel. One survey [15:iii]* has indicated that federal government managers perceived

* This and similar references are found at the back of this Appendix. Each reference is to the number of a source item and the cited page; for example, 15:iii refers to item 15, page iii.

Table A2-4   Scientists, Engineers, and Technicians, by Occupation, and Projected Increase by 1970 (Source 14:8)

Occupation	Percentage Increase 1960–1970
Scientists and Engineers	69
engineers	67
scientists	73
chemists	64
physicists	98
metallurgists	68
geologists and geophysicists	25
mathematicians	107
medical scientists	90
agricultural scientists	67
biological scientists	88
other scientists	42
Technicians	67

Table A2-5   Scientists and Engineers by Type of Employer (1960) (Source 3:193)

Employer	Total (thousands)	Percentage
All scientists and engineers	1275	100
Industry	865	67.8
scientists	185	42.5
engineers	680	80.9
Federal, state, and local government	185	14.5
scientists	75	17.2
engineers	110	13.1
College and university	155	12.1
scientists	130	29.8
engineers	24	2.9
Other	70	5.5
scientists	45	10.3
engineers	25	2.9

shortages of information sciences personnel and difficulty in recruiting such individuals. (The data from this study are not included due to a lack of clarity; however, as an indication of a general trend the study may have some merit.)

Manpower data concerning the total Federal employment in scientific and technical document-handling activities are, at best, very superficial. Table A2-8 indicates that one problem facing the Federal Government is in devising a more attractive salary schedule for information personnel. Similar employment data for the private sector are not available except for a limited group of isolated activities. Tables A2-9 and A2-10 are examples of the type of personnel data available from the private sector.

DOCUMENT-RELATED DATA

It is estimated that about 10,000,000 scientific papers have been published since science began [4:35]. Estimates concerning the number of scientific and technical serials in existence or that have existed vary from 35,000 to 100,000. Gottschalk [17] claims that 35,000 is a realistic estimate. The National Federation of Science Abstracting and Indexing Services, NFSAIS [16], Bourne [8], and the National Science Foundation Office of Science Information Sciences [18] all appear to "agree" with this estimate. The United Kingdom Lending Library has been unable to locate more than 27,000 current serials. We find little substantial evidence for estimates that there are over 50,000 serials. Most estimates agree in principle, that the increase in scientific

Table A2-6   Scientists and Engineers by Work Activity and Type of Employer, 1960 (Source 1:22)

Work Activity	Total	Employer			
		Industry	Government	College and University	Other
Total (thousands)	1275	865	185	155	70
Research	135	55	15	50	15
Development	290	240	40	5	5
Production and operations	395	340	35	...	20
Administration and management	125	75	30	10	10
Teaching	80	...	...	80	...
Other	250	155	65	10	20

papers is about 5 or 6 per cent a year [19 and 4]. De Solla Price [19:8] points out that these rates imply a doubling of volume every 15 years. The National Science Foundation, NSF [18], estimates the current annual number of scientific articles to be 1,700,000, and NFSAIS's estimate is 1,985,000 (Table A2-18). Others claim that a saturation point has been reached or will be reached soon. Regardless of which estimate we favor, there seems to be little doubt that the

Table A2-7 Percentage Distribution of Degrees, by Field and Level: United States and Outlying Areas, 1953–54 to 1973–74 (Source 2:13ff)

Year	Total Number of Degrees	Natural Sciences	Social Sciences and Humanities	Library Sciences
			Percentage of Total Degrees	
Bachelor's or First-Professional				
1953–1954	291,503	27.8	72.2	.5
1963–1964	488,000	26.8	73.2	.5
1973–1974	788,000	28.3	72.4	.4
Master's or Second-Professional				
1953–1954	56,823	20.8	79.2	.2
1963–1964	95,100	26.4	73.6	.7
1973–1974	158,600	28.5	71.5	.9
Doctor's				
1953–1954	8,996	48.2	51.8	.1
1963–1964	13,200	49.6	50.4	.1
1973–1974	24,300	50.2	49.8	.1

Table A2-8 Number of Federal Information Personnel by Category (1962) (Source 4:18)

	Median GS level	Number
Translators	9	330
Technical writers and editors	11	1157
Archivists	9	337
Librarians	9	3311
Total		5135

It is important to note that these figures represent *only* those individuals with these specific job classifications. It is clear that this number should *not* be interpreted as the total of professional information personnel working in the federal government. Personnel from allied fields, such as data processing, are obviously not accounted for. The important feature of the table is the distribution of the job categories referenced and the median GS levels.

Table A2-9 Personnel Distribution in Academic Research Libraries 1963–1964 (Source 6:2)

	Professional Staff	Nonprofessional Staff	Total Staff
		Personnel	
Total	3811	5596	9410
Median 1963–1964	51	70	117
Median 1962–1963	45	65	110

This study, by the Association of Research Libraries, used the 64 largest academic libraries in the United States as the data base.

Table A2-10 Composition of the Staffs of Special Libraries and Information Centers by Type of Organization (Source 5:34ff)

	College and University	Company	Government Agency	Public	Other	Total
Number of libraries reporting	1588	1477	831	290	1325	5,511
Total professional staff	3353	2461	3390	1187	1821	12,212
Total nonprofessional staff	4844	3813	4980	995	2278	16,910
Total staff	8197	6274	8370	2182	4099	29,122
Percentage professional	40.9	39.2	40.5	54.4	44.4	41.9
Average professional staff	2.1	1.6	4.1	4.1	1.4	2.2
Average nonprofessional	3.1	2.6	6.0	3.4	1.7	3.1
Average total staff	5.2	4.2	10.1	7.5	3.1	5.3

Kruzas states that the study "does not presume to include all specialized library facilities in the United States. However, sufficient data in all categories was available to provide reliable evidence of distributions and trends." The total sample used in the study was 8533. Also, note that the data are for special libraries and information centers *only*.

Table A2-11   Documents Generated in the World's Technical Literature (Source 7:435)

Subject	Number of Significant Documents, Estimated Annual Volume			
	1961		1965	1970
Aero/space	10,000	(5,000)	30,000	50,000
Astronomy	6,000	(5,000)	8,000	10,000
Biological chemistry	30,000	(20,000)	40,000	50,000
Biology	150,000	(60,000)	200,000	250,000
Chemistry	150,000	(100,000)	225,000	300,000
Engineering	150,000	(10,000)	175,000	200,000
(aeronautical, civil, electrical, marine, mechanical, military)				
Geodesy	5,000	(3,000)	6,500	8,000
Geography	30,000		40,000	50,000
Geology	20,000	(5,000)	25,000	30,000
Geophysics	10,000	(5,000)	15,000	20,000
Mathematics	10,000	(5,000)	12,500	15,000
Mechanics	5,000	(4,000)	7,500	10,000
Metallurgy	30,000	(30,000)	40,000	50,000
Nuclear science	10,000	(5,000)	20,000	30,000
Physics	30,000	(10,000)	40,000	50,000
Psychology	12,000	(10,000)	16,000	20,000
Totals	658,000	(277,000)	900,500	1,143,000

All figures are estimates and involve subjective judgment as to subject categories in which particular documents belong. Figures in parentheses are estimates of the number of abstracts in each subject being prepared for reprocessing for storage into a machine record.

problem of acquiring, processing, and disseminating scientific and technical documentation is a monumental one. Evidence of the strain this the rapid growth of abstracting and indexing burgeoning documentation puts on our existing "information system" can be seen, for example, in services and the minimal coverage that such services are able to supply overall.

Gottschalk [17] estimates that some 18 per cent, 6200, of the world's scientific and technical serials are published in the United States and that 60 per cent are published in English. Interesting differences in the mission orientation of the five leading countries publishing scientific and technical journals may be seen in Tables A2–14 and A2–15.

Publication lags seem to be well substantiated by the data (Tables A2-21 and A2-26). These delays, coupled with the controlled distribution practices of the federal government are two serious roadblocks to any solution of the national document-handling problem.

Table A2-12   Total Number* of Current Scientific and Technical Serials Published as of 1961 (Source 17:190)

Africa (continent)	650	Latin America	2650
Australia	450	(Caribbean area, Central and South	
Austria	500	America, Mexico)	
Belgium	1250	Netherlands	650
Bulgaria	150	New Zealand	150
Canada	550	Norway	250
China (People's Republic)	650	Pakistan	100
China (Republic)	200	Philippines	100
Czechoslovakia	400	Poland	750
Denmark	400	Portugal	250
Finland	300	Rumania	150
France	2800	Spain	300
Germany (East and West)	3050	Sweden	700
Greece	50	Switzerland	800
Hungary	250	Thailand	50
India	650	Turkey	100
Indonesia	100	U.S.S.R.	2200
Ireland	50	United Kingdom	2200
Italy	1500	United States	6200
Japan	2800	Yugoslavia	400
Korea (Democratic People's Republic)	50	Other Countries	400
Korea (Republic)	100		
		Total	35,300†

* Figures have been rounded off to the nearest 50. Those countries which published fewer than 50 journals have been grouped together under "Other Countries."

† The error has been estimated as ±10% due to selection based on titles rather than serials, the incompleteness of listings checked, and the undetermined mortality rate.

"Science and technology" is defined as comprising the natural, physical and engineering sciences, and psychology. Social sciences are excluded. Omitted are promotional literature, house organs, technical reports, proceedings of international organizations, and translations.

Table A2-13 World Serials (Science and Technology) for the Five Principal Producers (Source 17:191)

United States	6,200
East and West Germany	3.000
Japan	2,800
France	2,700
U.S.S.R.	2,200

Estimated total = 35,000 serials
± 10%, therefore: 16,900
                         (or 48% of total)

The qualification applying to table A2-12 also applies to the data in this table.

Although general agreement does not exist (and probably never will) concerning the problems of acquisition, coverage, abstracting, indexing, and dissemination of all forms of scientific and technical literature, it may be concluded from a cursory look at the available data

that the problem with us today will be with us tomorrow.

COST DATA

The estimated R&D cost to the federal government for 1964 is $15.1 billion. For the same year an estimated $200 million will be spent for scientific and technical information. Two-thirds of this total will be attributed to the activities of the Department of Defense (31%), the Department of Commerce (17%), and the Department of Health, Education, and Welfare (18%). Our judgment, based on long experience and on the impressions gained from interviews during the course of the present study, is that there are many unreported costs, such as overhead and other indirect costs, that should be attributed to information activities. These costs together with those that are overlooked or deliberately not reported (e.g., classified costs) approximate the costs that *are* reported. Hence, we feel that

Table A2-14   The Five Principal Journal Producers, by Selected Mission* (Source 17:191)

Country	Percentage of Total Serial Output in			
	Technology	Agriculture	Medicine	Natural and Physical Sciences
USA (6200)	56% (3470)	23% (1430)	13% (800)	8% (500)
Germany (3000)	44% (1320)	16% (480)	21% (630)	19% (570)
Japan (2800)	45% (1260)	23% (650)	18% (490)	14% (390)
France (2700)	49% (1320)	18% (490)	21% (570)	12% (330)
U.S.S.R. (2200)	49% (1078)	16% (350)	12% (270)	23% (510)
Average (16,900)	49% (8280)	19% (3210)	17% (2880)	15% (2540)

* Again, the qualification for table A2-12 applies here.

Table A2-15 *Total Volume of Production of Technical Journals by Language (Source 8:164)*

Language	Per Cent of Total
English	60
Russian	11
German	11
French	9
Japanese	3
Spanish	2
All other	4

These figures are only approximate.

Table A2-16 *Medical and Chemical Literature by Language of Publication (Source 8:164ff)*

Medical Literature

Language	Per Cent of Total
English	37.3
German	13.0
French	12.9
Japanese	7.8
Italian	7.5
Spanish	6.2
(polylingual)	3.3
Russian	3.1
All other	8.9

Chemical Literature

English	50.5
Russian	16.8
German	9.7
Japanese	6.1
French	5.5
Italian	3.6
All other	7.8

Table A2-17 *United States Journals/Manpower Ratios (Source 18:6)*

	No. of Serials (1959) (Source 17:190)	Manpower (1960) (Source: NSF)	Ratio Journals/ Manpower
Technology	3470	1,715,000*	1:490
Agriculture	1430	40,000	1:28
Medicine	800	30,000†	1:37
Physical and natural sciences	500	365,000	1:730
Total	6200	2,150,000‡	1:350

* Includes engineers and technicians.
† Does not include M.D.'s in practice or those not primarily conducting research.
‡ Does not include secondary school teachers of science and mathematics.

Table A2-18 *1970 Forecast of World Output of Scientific and Technical Articles by Discipline (Annual) (Source 16:74)*

Discipline	1958–60 (Thousands)	1970 (Thousands)
Agriculture	150	260
Biology	150	260
Chemistry	150	290
Engineering:		
aero space	35	75
civil	15	15
electrical and electronic	80	150
industrial	15	15
mechanical	10	20
metallurgical	35	50
Geoscience	71	118
Mathematics	15	30
Medical	220	390
Meteorology	20	40
Nuclear science	35	75
Physics	40	80
Psychology	15	30
All other	929	1882
Total	1985	3795

Table A2-19   Abstract and Citation Coverage Provided by Members of The National Federation of Science Abstracting and Indexing Services (Source 10:20)

Abstract Services	1963	Estimate for 1964	% Increase Over 1957
Applied mechanics reviews	7,400	7,600	79%
ASTM bibliography and abstracts*	1,500†	1,500	. . .
Bibliography of chemical reviews (CA)*[1]	8,600†	. . .	. . .
Biological abstracts (BA)	100,862	107,000	167%
Chemical abstracts (CA)	170,000	190,000	68%
Corrosion abstracts*	3,600	3,600	. . .
Engineering index	45,000	50,000	90%
Fire research abstracts and review*	150†	150	. . .
GeoScience abstracts*	5,000	6,000	. . .
International aerospace abstracts	16,113	20,000	195%
Mathematical reviews	11,700†	11,700	27%
Meteorological and geoastrophysical abstracts	24,000	19,000	280%
Nuclear science abstracts	42,427	50,000	256%
Prevention of deterioration abstracts*[2]	3,607	. . .	. . .
Psychological abstracts	8,381	9,500	5%
Review of metal literature	27,388	36,000	338%
Scientific and technical aerospace reports (NASA)*	13,523	20,000	. . .
Technical abstract bulletin (DDC)	36,600	50,000	1069%
Technical translations (OTS)*	17,000	17,000	. . .
Tobacco abstracts*	2,695	3,000	. . .
U.S. government research reports (OTS)	25,000	25,000	198%
Wheat abstracts*	6,275	6,275	. . .
Subtotal	576,821	633,325	168%
Title Listing Services			
Bibliography of agriculture	103,765	104,000	8%
Biochemical title index (BA)*[3]	30,015	. . .	. . .
Chemical titles (CA)*	79,600	79,600	. . .
Index Medicus	136,968	145,000	39%
Meteorological and geoastrophysical titles*	7,000	7,000	. . .
Subtotal	357,348	335,600	67%
GRAND TOTAL	934,169	968,925	122%

* New service or new member since 1957.
† Estimate for 1963.
[1,2,3] Service discontinued.

Table A2-20   American Book Title Output 1963–1964 (Source 11:58)

Field	1963			1964			Per Cent Net Change
	New Books	New Editions	Totals	New Books	New Editions	Totals	
Agriculture	219	67	286	209	76	285	− 0.5
Medicine	752	302	1054	876	335	1211	+15
Philosophy and psychology	505	214	719	528	238	766	+ 6
Science	1648	563	2211	1923	815	2738	+24
Sociology and economics	1932	555	2487	2445	827	3272	+32
Technology	960	197	1157	939	186	1125	− 3
Total	6016	1898	7914	6920	2477	9397	

Titles represent commercial publications in the U. S. only. Field classifications are gross and are derived from the Dewey classification system.

Table A2-21 Per cent of Technical Reports Appearing in Scientific or Technical Journals and the Time Required for Publication (Source 4:37)

Department or Agency	Total Per Cent	0–12 Months after Completion of Research	13–24 Months after Completion of Research	More Than 24 Months after Completion of Research
Agriculture	48	15	18	15
Commerce:				
National Bureau of Standards	80	80	. . .	. . .
Coast and Geodetic Survey	80	70	10	. . .
Patent Office	50	25	25	. . .
Weather Bureau	60	30	25	5
Public Roads	90	60	25	5
Defense:				
Office of Secretary of Defense	15	4	7	4
Army	40	33	5	2
Air Force	30	10	10	10
Navy	NA	NA	NA	NA
Health, Education, and Welfare:				
Food and Drug Administration	100	75	20	5
Office of Education	11	10	1	. . .
St. Elizabeth's Hospital	75	75	. . .	. . .
National Center for Health Statistics	10	5	5	. . .
National Institutes of Health	98	40	52	6
Bureau of Medical Services	75	75	. . .	. . .
Bureau of State Services				
(environmental health)	86	40	40	6
Division of Accident Prevention	90	80	10	. . .
Communicable Disease Center	75	. . .	75	. . .
Division of Dental Public Health and				
Resources	80	50	20	10
Division of Hospital and Medical Facilities	95	40	40	15
Division of Nursing	90	. . .	. . .	90
Social Security Administration	95	75	. . .	20
Division of Vocational Rehabilitation	55	46	6	3
Interior	50–90	10–75	25–90	50–90
Labor	80–90	80–90	. . .	. . .
State:				
Agency for International Development	80	80	. . .	. . .
Treasury:				
Coast Guard	100	100	. . .	. . .
Post Office	*	*	. . .	. . .
Arms Control and Disarmament Agency	†	. . .	. . .	. . .
Federal Aviation Agency	5	5	. . .	. . .
Federal Communications Commission	100	25	25	50
Federal Housing Administration	90	50	25	15
National Aeronautics and Space Administration	25	6	12	7
National Science Foundation	95	65	20	10
Office of Emergency Planning	10	10	. . .	. . .
Smithsonian Institution	100	10	80	10
Tennessee Valley Authority	50	28	12	10
Veterans' Administration	45	41	4	. . .

* Under 10

† Less than 5

NA = Not available

Technical reports are also known as "technical notes" or "technical memorandums" and are informal in nature.

Table A2-22 Number of Technical Reports
Completed in Fiscal Year 1963 by Agency and
Percentage Controlled (Source 4:45)

Department or Agency	Number of Technical Reports Reports	Percentage Controlled for Any Reason
Agriculture	957	2
Commerce	1,109	40
Defense:		
OSD	764	83
Army	11,416	30
Navy	15,000	57
Air Force	11,700	80
Total	38,880	62
Health, Education, and Welfare (excluding NIH)	1,963	0
Interior	2,446	3
Labor	200	0
Post Office	180	100
State, AID	24	10
Treasury, Coast Guard	51	95
Arms Control and Disarmament Agency	21	67
Atomic Energy Commission	9,000	13
Civil Service Commission	4	0
Federal Aviation Agency	194	44
Federal Communications Commission	6	0
Federal Housing Authority	8	0
National Aeronautics and Space Administration	4,232	6
National Science Foundation	*	†
Smithsonian Institution	100	0
Tennessee Valley Authority	153	0
Veterans' Administration	908	0
Total	60,436	. . .

* 5000 administrative reports completed by NSF grantees.
† Not applicable.

A "controlled" technical report is one not available for unrestricted dissemination because, for example, of security or proprietary reasons.

Table A2-23 Age of Scientific Journals°
(Source 9:5)

Discipline	Average Age in Years	Age of Oldest Journal	Median Age	Number Established Since 1959
Biology (88)†	38.6	142	39.5	5
Chemistry (12)	19.9	57	15.5	3
Earth sciences (8)	59.3	144	51.5	0
Engineering (17)	19.0	82	9.0	1
Mathematics (18)	26.9	83	19.0	4
Miscellaneous (10)	41.2	113	49.0	1
Physics (13)	28.6	69	29.0	1
Social sciences (39)	37.5	76	35.0	0
Society (140)	34.8	113	31.0	5
Commercial (42)	28.5	142	17.5	10
University press (23)	45.8	144	37.0	0
All journals (205)	34.8	144	29.0	15

* Note: Tables A2-23–A2-27 concern general trends. The survey used (Source 9) "211 hard core" scientific journals as the sample. We feel that the sample is biased (e.g., biological journals comprise almost 43% of the sample). Only trends of a very broad and general nature may be interpreted from these data.
† The number of journals included in an analysis is shown in parentheses. This convention is used throughout this report.

Table A2-24 Average Annual Circulation°
(Source 9:9)

Discipline	U.S. Circulation Average‡	Foreign Circulation Average	Total Circulation Average	Total Circulation Median
Society journals (117)†	3810	1200	5020	3450
biology (51)	3130	1170	4300	2450
chemistry (7)	4700	2580	7280	2550
earth sciences (4)	3790	1660	5450	3790
engineering (12)	6860	1100	7960	7520
mathematics (11)	3910	800	4700	3630
miscellaneous (5)	1380	740	2120	1950
physics (10)	5850	1990	7830	7970
social sciences (17)	2700	710	3410	2940
Commercial (17)	1950	680	2630	2190
University press (18)	1350	620	1970	1550
All journals (152)	3310	1080	4400	. . .

* See note * following Table A2-23.
† See note † following Table A2-23.
‡ The circulation averages were calculated by summing the reported journal circulations and dividing this sum by the number of journals.

Table A2-25 *Average Total Circulation**
(*Source 9:10*)

	Journal Category			
Discipline	Society	Commercial	University Press	Total
Biology	4100 (55)†	1,870 (11)	1760 (5)	3620 (71)
Chemistry	7280 (7)	...	...	7280 (7)
Earth sciences	4480 (6)	...	2710 (2)	4040 (8)
Engineering	8100 (14)	15,000 (1)	...	8560 (15)
Mathematics	4640 (12)	...	1050 (4)	3740 (16)
Miscellaneous	2120 (5)	350 (1)	1250 (2)	1680 (8)
Physics	7830 (10)	...	2530 (1)	7350 (11)
Social sciences	3390 (17)	1,990 (4)	2710 (5)	3000 (26)
Total	4910 (126)	2,590 (17)	1950 (19)	4320 (162)

* See note (*) following table A2-23.
† See note (**) following table A2-23.

Table A2-26 *Average Number of Papers Published, in Review, and in Backlog**
(*Source 9:15*)

Discipline	Average Number of Papers:			Backlog‡ as a % of Total Number of Research Papers Published
	Published	Under Review	In Backlog‡	
Society journals (131)†	161	67	50	30.9
biology (56)	146	58	46	31.2
chemistry (8)	324	116	87	26.9
earth sciences (4)	230	77	40	17.2
engineering (14)	99	73	30	30.3
mathematics (9)	88	91	61	69.6
miscellaneous (7)	68	26	23	33.8
physics (10)	514	127	115	22.3
social sciences (23)	69	45	36	51.9
Commercial journals (23)	84	26	36	42.9
University press (20)	53	19	24	45.8
All journals (174)	138	56	45	32.6

* See note * for Table A2-23.
† See note † following Table A2-23.
‡ Backlog includes papers accepted and awaiting publication.

Table A2-27 *Index and Abstract Publication Practices** (*Source 9:24*)

Discipline	Per Cent of Journals Publishing Abstracts or Synopses with			Per Cent† Journals Whose Abstracts or Synopses Are Prepared by			% Journals that:				
	All	Some Papers	No	Authors	Editorial Staff	Others	Editor Is Responsible for Adequacy of Abstracts	Send Abstracts Automatically to Secondary Service	Publish Annual Author Index	Publish Annual Subject Index	Publish Cumulative Indexes
Society journals	50	21	29	97	8	1	50	70	93	78	46
biology	45	21	34	97	11	3	49	80	94	93	42
chemistry	63	25	12	100	29	0	29	63	100	100	50
earth sciences	83	17	0	100	0	0	17	67	100	83	83
engineering	63	31	6	87	13	0	50	47	75	75	40
mathematics	31	31	38	100	0	0	29	50	100	75	54
miscellaneous	29	29	42	100	0	0	67	25	100	100	50
physics	70	20	10	100	0	0	75	89	100	100	50
social sciences	52	8	40	100	0	0	33	75	90	70	67
Commercial	60	5	35	100	3	3	67	75	96	33	38
University press	39	22	39	92	8	0	43	67	82	65	44

* See Note (*) for Table A2-23.
† Percentages for one discipline may equal more than 100% because some journals reported that abstracts were prepared by more than one group.

$400 million is a more accurate figure. It is difficult to substantiate a figure of $400 million, but we feel it is closer to the *actual* costs for scientific and technical information than the $200 million figure which is the total of *reported* costs for such activities in the federal government. For indicating trends, the distribution of this reported $200 million is significant. For example:

	Per Cent
Publication and distribution	40.0
Bibliographic and reference services	40.0
Scientific symposia and technical meetings	12.5
R&D in scientific communication and documentation	7.5

Another distribution shows that the federal government performed 65 per cent of this work in-house (intramurally) and obligated 35 per cent of these funds to nongovernment organizations (extramurally). Approximately $3 million was spent by the federal government (outside the intelligence community, for which figures are not available) in 1963 for translations of foreign scientific and technical literature.

The National Science Foundation, NSF (18), states that for 1961 the estimated cost per abstract was $30 and the estimate for an index or citation entry was $10. Therefore, a total of $2 million for abstracting and $9 million for all

Table A2-28 Expenditures for Research and Development and Basic Research by Character of Work, Research, and Field of Science (1964 Estimated) (Source 12:130)

Basic research	$1,782,000,000
Applied research	4,003,000,000
Development	9,296,000,000
Total	$15,081,000,000

Table A2-29 Federal Obligations for Scientific and Technical Information, by Agency* (Source 12:61)

	Fiscal Year 1962 (Actual)	Fiscal Year 1963 (Estimated)	Fiscal Year 1964 (Estimated)
Defense	$37.6	$53.7	$61.0
Commerce	28.1	31.6	37.4
Health, Education, and Welfare	24.0	28.9	36.2
National Aeronautics and Space Administration	7.5	14.2	18.4
National Science Foundation	9.9	11.6	15.4
All other agencies	21.5	26.9†	32.8
Total (millions)	$128.5	$166.9	$201.2

* These costs are *reported* ones only.
† All other agencies, Fiscal Year 1963:

Total (millions)	$26.9
Library of Congress	7.4
Interior	6.2
Atomic Energy Commission	4.4
Agriculture	4.3
Other agencies	4.6

Table A2-30 Percentage Distribution of Obligations for Scientific and Technical Information by Selected Agency and Activity, Fiscal Year 1963 (Source 12:69)

Agency	Total Obligations	Percentage Distribution				
		Total	Publication and Distribution	Bibliographic and Reference Source	Scientific Symposia and Technical Meetings	R&D in Scientific Communication and Documentation
Total, all agencies	$166.9	100	40	40	13	8
Agriculture	4.3	100	36	33	31	...
Commerce	31.6	100	60	35	2	3
Defense	53.7	100	40	44	8	8
Health, Education, and Welfare	28.9	100	22	27	38	12
Interior	6.2	100	72	19	4	5
Atomic Energy Commission	4.4	100	55	36	6	4
Library of Congress	7.4	100	...	99	*	*
National Aeronautics and Space Administration	14.2	100	40	47	11	1
National Science Foundation	11.6	100	26	41	8	26
All other agencies	4.5	100	55	13	27	5

* Less than 0.5 per cent.

Table A2-31   Federal Obligations for Scientific and Technical Information by Performer *
(Source 12:68)*

	Millions of Dollars		
	Extramural	Intramural	Total
Fiscal Year 1962 (Actual)	46.4	82.1	128.5
Fiscal Year 1963 (Estimated)	59.1	107.9	166.9
Fiscal Year 1964 (Estimated)	72.7	128.5	201.2

* Intramural refers to those obligations performed by Federal employees. Extramural refers to those obligations performed by organizations and individuals under contract to the Federal Government.

index and citation entires gives an estimated cost of $30 million in 1961 for secondary publications.* NSF also estimates that, at $30 per page for both scientific and technological journals (500 scientific journals with 1050 pages per journal per year and 5700 technological journals with 1200 pages per journal per year), the total annual cost for all U. S. journals in science and technology is approximately $250,000,000.

The problem of the *real* cost of scientific and technical information remains a very muddy one. Only *estimates* seem to be available. A question such as how much the Federal Government

* The term "total cost" is given no definition by NSF/OSIS for these estimates.

Table A2-32   Intramural and Extramural Obligations for Scientific and Technical Information by Agency, Fiscal Years 1962–64 * (Source 12:68)*

Agency	Intramural			Extramural		
	Actual	Estimates		Actual	Estimates	
	1962	1963	1964	1962	1963	1964
Total, all agencies (thousands of dollars)	82,087	107,866	128,479	46,419	59,065	72,746
	Percentage Distribution					
Defense	28	34	33	31	29	26
Commerce	34	29	29	†	1	†
Health, Education, and Welfare	9	10	10	35	31	32
Library of Congress	8	7	7	†	...	...
Interior	6	6	6	†	†	†
National Aeronautics and Space Administration	4	5	6	9	15	15
Agriculture	5	4	4	...	...	...
Atomic Energy Commission	3	3	3	2	3	4
National Science Foundation	1	1	1	20	18	20
All other agencies	2	2	2	2	4	2

* See note following Table A2-31.
† Less than 0.5 per cent.

Table A2-33   Comparative Costs of Eight Nonfederal A&I Services (Source 13:1)

Nonfederal Abstracting and Indexing Services	Percentage of Federal Support	Total Prod. Costs (1964)	Total No. Abstract/References (1964)	Unit Cost Per Abstract/References
Applied mechanics reviews	36.6%	$ 131,000	7,600	$17.2
Biological abstracts	0	929,000	107,000	8.7
Chemical abstracts	0	4,904,850	188,000	26.0
Engineering index	15.8	450,000	45,000	10.0
GeoScience abstracts	57.0	81,000	6,000	13.5
Mathematical reviews	27.3	405,598	13,000	31.2
Meteorological and geoastrophysical abstracts	84.0	300,000	9,000	33.3
Psychological abstracts	0	100,000	10,500	9.5
		$7,301,448	386,100	Ca. $18.60

Table A2-34 Costs of Translations Performed by Non-Governmental Organizations for Federal Agencies* (Source 4:69)

	Fiscal Year 1963	Estimated 1964
Agriculture (Agricultural Research Service) $	5,511 $	6,000
Commerce	33,347	46,798
Defense:		
Army	164,350	181,500
Navy	11,076	9,030
Air Force	717,000	930,000
Health, Ed., and Welfare:		
National Institutes of Health (including grants)	30,189	66,227
Bureau of State Services	15,000	15,000
Bureau of Medical Services	271,685	441,350
Coast Guard	2,231	900
Federal Aviation Agency	903	126
National Aeronautics and Space Administration	130,000	180,000
National Science Foundation (NSF) (grants and contracts)†	1,584,035	1,707,301
Total	$2,965,327	$3,584,232

* These costs do not include classified translations or research on machine translations.
† NSF also spends $1,000,000 under P.L. 480.

Table A2-35 Average Annual Journal Cost* (Source 9:53)

Discipline		Average Cost Per Year
Society (126)	$60,900	
biology (50)		$ 41,500
chemistry (5)		97,000
earth sciences (5)		87,500
engineering (15)		71,500
mathematics (11)		36,900
miscellaneous (6)		30,100
physics (10)		219,300
social sciences (24)		30,200
Commercial (21)	$47,200	
University press (20)	$23,800	
All journals (167)	$54,700	

* See cautionary note * following Table A2-23.

should invest in capital equipment must remain unanswered for the present.

INSTITUTIONAL DATA

This section is admittedly being used for the collection of miscellaneous data; to summarize these data would serve no useful purpose. One point should be made in order to re-emphasize

the inherent problems in present-day data concerning scientific and technical document handling. Tables A2-38, A2-39, and A2-40 indicate the number of scientific and technical information facilities (centers) in the federal government. Table A2-38 shows 259 of these facilities, and Table A2-40 indicates that there are 858 (and this is only a sample of a larger population). Admittedly, Table A2-40 has duplications (e.g., branches of the same facility are included in the totals), but even when this fact is taken into account there is still a great disparity. Also, different authors have varying definitions as to what is an "information center," "information facility," or "special information center or library." These problems only add to the existing statistical confusion.

Additional statistical data for the current system may be found in Chapters 2 and 3.

Table A2-36 Scientific and Technical Information Studies Underway (1964) (Source 4:79)

	In-House	Contract or Grant	Total
National Science Foundation	0	60	60
Health, Education, and Welfare	18	28	46
Army	9	19	28
Navy	3	20	23
Air Force	0	19	19
Office of the Secretary of Defense	8	2	10
Commerce	5	5	10
Interior	6	2	8
Atomic Energy Commission	1	3	4
National Aeronautics and Space Administration	0	2	2
Others	8	4	12
Total	58	164	222

Table A2-37 Purposes of Federal Agency Studies (Source 4:79)

Information storage and retrieval	123
User needs	36
Machine translations	26
Publication problems	17
Library services	12
Clearinghouses	8
Total	222

Table A2-38   Federal Scientific and Technical Information Facilities Reported to Select Committee on Government Research* (Source 4:22)

Departments and Agencies	Number of Facilities	In-House	Nonprofit	Profitmaking
Agriculture	17	17	. . .	. . .
Commerce	17	15	2	. . .
Defense†	142	109	24	9
Office of Secretary of Defense	(31)	(10)	(18)	(3)
Army	(42)	(40)	(0)	(2)
Navy	(48)	(42)	(4)	(2)
Air Force	(21)	(17)	(2)	(2)
Health, Education, and Welfare	40	18	21	1
National Institutes of Health	(26)	(6)	(19)	(1)
Interior	7	7	. . .	. . .
Post Office	1	1	. . .	. . .
State	1	1	. . .	. . .
Atomic Energy Commission	10	1	3	6
Arms Control and Disarmament Agency	1	1	. . .	. . .
Civil Service Commission	1	1	. . .	. . .
Federal Aviation Agency	3	3	. . .	. . .
Federal Communications Commission	1	1	. . .	. . .
National Aeronautics and Space Administration	12	8	2	2
National Science Foundation	3	1	2	. . .
Smithsonian Institution	1	1	. . .	. . .
Library of Congress	2	2	. . .	. . .
Total	259	187	54	18

* *Reported* facilities only (see summary comments in paragraph on "Institutional Data.")
† Includes centers which are considered solely Department of Defense facilities, supported by the military departments and, in some cases, jointly with other federal agencies.

Note: Figures enclosed in parentheses are subtotals.

Table A2-39   Number and Percentage of Special Libraries and Information Centers by Subject and Type of Organization* (Source 5:13ff)

Main Subject	College & University No.	%	Company No.	%	Gov't. Agency No.	%	Public No.	%	Other Organizations No.	%	Total Number
Agriculture	54	2.4	6	0.3	11	0.9	0	0.0	19	0.7	90
Medicine	196	8.7	22	1.0	265	21.4	4	0.9	552	21.4	1039
Science technology	590	26.1	1275	57.4	308	24.9	76	16.4	251	9.7	2500
Social sciences	130	5.8	7	0.3	72	5.8	37	8.0	140	5.4	386
Total	970		1310		656		117		962		4015
Libraries represented	2202		2163		1221		387		2560		8533

* Sample size is 8533. Kruzas states that the survey "does not presume to include all specialized library facilities in the United States. However, sufficient data in all categories were available to provide reliable evidence of distributions and trends."

Table A2-40 Distribution of Special Libraries and Information Centers by Government Level* (Source 5:13ff)

Government Unit	Number	Percentage
County	5	0.4
Federal	848	69.5
Foreign	25	2.0
International	8	0.7
Municipal	36	2.9
Regional	7	0.6
State	291	23.8
Territory	1	0.1
Total	1221	100.0

* See note following Table A2-39.

Table A2-41 Number of Facilities Engaged in Publication of Various Types of Periodicals and Compilations of Information, and Manner of Distribution* (Source 4:27)

	Abstracts	Bibliographies	Journals	Other[b]
Originating agencies	80	121	36	135
Distributed as follows to:				
Other federal agencies	55	73	31	80
contractors	35	50	18	48
grantees	17	22	14	23
industry	33	45	22	45
academic institutions	40	52	25	60
public	25	33	16	33
others	26	38	15	37

* This table reflects reports given to the Elliott Committee from the 259 reported federal scientific and technical information facilities (see Table A2-38). It attempts to get at the kinds of services offered to users.

SOURCES OF STATISTICAL DATA

1. National Science Foundation. "Profiles of Manpower in Science and Technology." (NSF 63-23), Washington, D. C., 1963.

2. U. S. Department of Health, Education, and Welfare, Office of Education. "Projections of Educational Statistics to 1973–74." Washington, D. C., 1964.

3. U. S. Congress. House Select Committee on Government Research. "Statistical Review of Research and Development," Study No. IX. 88th Congress, 2d Session, Washington, D. C., Government Printing Office, 1964.

4. U. S. Congress. House Select Committee on Government Research. "Documentation and Dissemination of Research and Development Results," Study No. IV. 88th Congress, 2d Session, Washington, D. C., Government Printing Office, 1964.

5. Kruzas, Anthony T. "Special Libraries and Information Centers: A Statistical Report on Special Library Resources in the United States." Detroit, Gale Research Company, 1963.

6. "Academic Library Statistical 1963–1964," Association of Research Libraries, 1964.

7. U. S. Congress. "Hearings before the Ad Hoc Subcommittee on a National Research Data Processing and Information Retrieval Center of the Committee on Education and Labor on

Table A2-42 Number and Percentage of A&I Services by Category of Service (U. S. only*) (Source 20:14)

Category of Service	Number (1959)	Percentage
Technology, including engineering	145	29
Medicine	188	38
Agriculture	25	5
Biology	27	5
Earth sciences	15	3
Chemistry	14	3
Physics	11	2
Mathematics	4	1
Psychology, Anthropology	14	3
General science and technology	49	10
Broad-coverage services	15	
Documentation	20	
Patents and standards	9	
Foreign literature	5	
Total	492	

* A later NFSAIS survey (1961) shows 365 A&I services with 115 new additions to the list and 242 dropped from this 1959 list.

Table A2-43 Serial Holdings of Major Libraries, etc. (Source 18:15)

Library of Congress (Science and Technology Division)	20,000 (1960)
National Library of Medicine	9,000 (1960)
National Agricultural Library	20,000 (1963)
Titles listed by NFSAIS members	17,000 (1960)

312   *Appendix Two*

H. R. 1946, A Bill to Amend Title X of the National Defense Education Act of 1958 to Provide for a Science Information Data Processing Center to be located at one place in Chicago, Illinois." Appendix to Vol. I, Parts 1, 2, and 3. 88th Congress, 1st Session, Washington, D. C., Government Printing Office, 1963.

8. Bourne, Charles P. "The World's Technical Journal Literature: An Estimate of Volume, Origin, Language, Field, Indexing, and Abstracting," *American Documentation,* Vol. 13, No. 2, April 1962, 159–168.

9. Campbell, David T. H., and Jane Edmisten. "Characteristics of Professional Scientific Journals: A Report to the Office of Science Information Service, National Science Foundation." Washington, D. C., Herner and Company, 30 April 1964.

10. *Biological Abstracts,* Vol. 45, No. 15, 1964.

11. *Bowker Annual of Library and Book Trade,* 1965.

12. National Science Foundation. "Federal Funds for Research, Development, and Other Scientific Activities, Fiscal years 1962, 1963, and 1964." Surveys of Science Resources Series, Vol. XII (NSF 64-11), 1964.

13. Informal data supplied by the Office of Scientific Information Services (OSIS).

14. National Science Foundation. "Scientists, Engineers, and Technicians in the 1960's: Requirements and Supply." A report prepared by the U. S. Department of Labor, Bureau of Labor Statistics for the National Science Foundation. (NSF 63-64), Washington, D. C., Government Printing Office, 1964.

15. Craven, Leonard and Craven, Kenneth. "Science Information Personnel," Modern Language Association of America, 1961.

16. "Reference Notes to a National Plan for Science Abstracting and Indexing Services," Robert Heller and Associates, 1963.

17. Gottschalk, Charles M. and Desmond, Winifred F. "Worldwide Census of Scientific and Technical Serials," *American Documentation,* Vol. 14, No. 3, July 1963, 188–194.

18. "Science Information Fact Sheet," Informal OSIS document, September 1964.

19. De Solla Price, Derek J. *Little Science, Big Science,* 1963.

20. "A Guide to U. S. Indexing and Abstracting Services in Science and Technology," NFSAIS, 1960.

Review of Federal Legislation and Executive Orders

This appendix reviews significant Federal legislation and executive orders pertaining to scientific and technical information, libraries, and document handling. The presentation is divided into two parts. The first covers current statutes that affect principally the nonfederal sector, or that are not dealt with in the following section. The second part consists of a revised reprint of the COSATI report, "Executive Agency Responsibilities for Scientific and Technical Information."

This survey indicates that there is a need for on-going review of current orders and statutes and coordination of proposed legislation in this area. For example, several laws require matching funds and/or operating support from nonfederal entities, particularly the states, as a condition of participation in the programs. Such legislation includes P.L. 480, P.L. 87-579, P.L. 88-269, P.L. 89-329, and P.L. 89-182. There does not appear to have been coordination between the agencies promulgating this legislation, or any systematic effort to gauge the effects of interaction of the several programs upon the institutions concerned. Often the intent of federal programs is emasculated because the states or other cognizant bodies will not provide funding adequate to take advantage of federal grants. The other fact that must be remembered is that although many statutes authorize large sums, the amounts appropriated are often much less. This, too, has a baleful effect on both planning and implementation of these programs.

CURRENT STATUTES

P.L. 89-291, *Medical Library Assistance Act of 1965, October 22, 1965*

This Act amends Title III of the Public Health Service Act. Its basic features are:

"(1) assist in the construction of new, and the renovation, expansion, or rehabilitation, of existing medical library facilities (grants not to exceed 75% of approved cost);

"(2) assist in the training of medical librarians and other information specialists in the health sciences (total not to exceed $1,000,000 in any fiscal year);

"(3) assist, through the awarding of special fellowships to physicians and scientists, in the compilation of existing, and the creation of additional, written matter which will facilitate the distribution and utilization of knowledge and information relating to scientific, social and cultural advancements in sciences related to health (total not to exceed $500,000 in any fiscal year);

"(4) assist in the conduct of research and investigations in the field of medical library science and related activities, and in the development of new techniques, systems and equipment for processing, storing, retrieving, and distributing information in the sciences related to health (total not to exceed $3,000,000 in any fiscal year);

"(5) assist in improving and expanding the basic resources of medical libraries and related facilities (total not to exceed $3,000,000 in any fiscal year);

"(6) assist in the development of a national system of regional medical libraries each of which would have facilities of sufficient depth and scope of supplement the services of other medical libraries within the region served by it (total not to exceed $2,500,000 in any fiscal year); and

"(7) provide financial support to biomedical scientific publications (total not to exceed $1,500,000 in any fiscal year)."

P.L. 89-182, State Technical Services Act of 1965, September 15, 1965

In order to provide for the "wider diffusion and more effective application of science and technology, this act provides incentives and support to the States individually and in cooperation with each other for the establishment and maintenance of state and/or regional technical information services." This law authorizes $60 million in matching grants over a three-year period. A state may designate a focal point within that state (public or private) to administrate and coordinate such services. To qualify for the program, each governor must appoint an agency in the state to prepare a five-year plan outlining technological and economic conditions, identifying problems, and setting forth the state's approach to implementation of the act's provisions.

P.L. 89-329, Higher Education Act of 1965, November 8, 1965

The purpose of this law is "to strengthen the educational resources of our colleges and universities and to provide financial assistance for students in postsecondary and higher education."

Among other provisions, $50 million is authorized annually for 3 years for grants to institutions of higher education for acquisition and binding of library materials. In addition, $15 million is authorized for grants in library training and research for the same period. Five million is authorized to be transferred to the Library of Congress for fiscal '66, with $6,315,000 and $7,770,000 allotted for the following two years to acquire "All library materials currently published throughout the world which are of value to scholarship; and provide catalog information for such materials promptly after receipt, and using for exchange and other purposes such of these materials as are not needed for the Library of Congress collection."

P.L. 88-665, National Defense Education Act and Amendments 1964 (October 16, 1964)

The law extends the original Act for 3 additional years until 1968 and extends Public Laws 815 and 874. Among other provisions, the law extends the loan program for students and increases the amounts available for a longer period. It authorizes some $32,750,000 each for fiscal years 1965 to 1968 for institutes for teachers or supervisors, student teachers, school library personnel, teachers of modern foreign languages, history, geography, English, or educational media specialists.

P.L. 87-579, Depository Library Act of 1962 (August 9, 1962)

"Government publications, except those determined by their issuing components to be required for official use only or those required for strictly administrative or operational purposes which have no public interest or educational value and publications classified for reasons of national security, shall be made available to depository libraries through the facilities of the Superintendent of Documents for public information. Each component of the Government shall furnish the Superintendent of Documents a list of publications (with the above exceptions) which it issued during the previous month that were obtained from sources other than the Government Printing Office.

"The Government publications, which may be selected from lists prepared by the Superintendent of Documents and when requested from him, shall be distributed to depository libraries specifically designated by law and to such libraries as have or shall be designated by (senators, representatives and commissioners) with certain restrictions. The Superintendent of Documents shall currently issue a classified list of Government publications in suitable form, containing annotations of contents and listed by item identification numbers in such manner as to facilitate the selection of only those publications which may be needed by designated depository libraries. The selected publications shall be distributed to depository libraries in accordance with regulations issued by the Superintendent of Documents, so long as they fulfill the conditions provided by law.

"The Superintendent of Documents shall currently inform the components of the Government which order the printing of publications as to the number of copies of their publications required for distribution to depository libraries. The cost of printing and binding those publications which are distributed to depository libraries, when obtained elsewhere than from the Government Printing Office, shall be borne by components of the Government responsible for their issuance; those requisitioned from the Gov-

ernment Printing Office shall be charged to appropriations provided the Superintendent of Documents for that purpose.

"All land-grant colleges shall be constituted as depositories to receive Government publications subject to the provisions and limitations of the depository law.

"The Superintendent of Documents shall receive reports from designated depository libraries at least every two years concerning the condition of each and shall make first-hand investigation of conditions for which need is indicated; the results of such investigations shall be included in his annual report."

P.L. 83-480, Agricultural Trade Development and Assistance Act of 1954 and Amendments

This law provides for the use of foreign currencies accruing to the United States through the sale of surplus agricultural commodities. The amendments relating to scientific and technical information not covered in the COSATI report are as follows:

P.L. 85-931, September 6, 1958 amended section 104, "(n) for financing under the direction of the Librarian of Congress, in consultation with the National Science Foundation and other interested agencies, in such amounts as may be specified from time to time in appropriation acts, (1) programs outside the United States for the analysis and evaluation of foreign books, periodicals, and other materials to determine whether they would provide information of technical or scientific significance in the United States and whether such books, periodicals, and other materials are of cultural or educational significance; (2) the registry, indexing, binding, reproduction, cataloging, abstracting, translating, and dissemination of books, periodicals, and related materials determined to have such significance; and (3) the acquisition of such books, periodicals, and other materials and the deposit thereof in libraries and research centers in the United States specializing in the areas to which they relate; "(o) For providing assistance, in such amounts as may be specified from time to time in appropriation acts, by grant or otherwise, in the expansion or operation in foreign countries of established schools, colleges, or universities founded or sponsored by citizens of the United States, for the purpose of enabling

such educational institutions to carry on programs of vocational, professional, scientific, technological, or general education; and in the supporting of workshops in American studies or American educational techniques, and supporting chairs in American studies."

EXECUTIVE AGENCY RESPONSIBILITIES FOR SCIENTIFIC AND TECHNICAL INFORMATION

This part of the review presents an amended reprint of the COSATI report bearing the above title, which was a supplement to the summary report of the Committee to the Federal Council on Science and Technology. The material is organized by agency in alphabetical order and consists largely of a selection of detailed quotations from the pertinent legislative and executive actions. No attempt is made to evaluate or interpret the quotations.

Agriculture

The actions considered most pertinent to technical information activities are embodied in the following items:

Organic Act of May 15, 1862 (5USC511)

Bankhead-Jones Act of June 29, 1935 (P.L. 182)

McSweeney-McNary Forest Research Act of May 22, 1928 (45 Stat. 699), as amended and supplemented (16USC581a-581i, 581i-1)

Federal Reports Act of December 24, 1942 (P.L. 831)

Agricultural Marketing Act of August 14, 1946 (60 Stat. 1087), as amended (7USC1621, 1622(b), 1624)

Cooperative Marketing Act of 1926 (P.L. 450)

Soil Conservation Act of April 27, 1935 (P.L. 46)

Department of Agriculture and Related Agencies Appropriation Act for 1963 (76 Stat. 1211)

Hatch Act of 1955 (7USC 361)

Executive Order 9069, "Consolidating Certain Agencies Within the Department of Agriculture," February 23, 1942

Department of Agriculture Organic Act of 1944 (5USC552a)

Memorandum No. 1496, "The National Agricultural Library" March 23, 1962

Administrative Regulations of the U. S. Department of Agriculture, 1964. 1AR Chapters 2 & 13, 2AR, 3AR pp. 33–34.

There are some 180 additional provisions of law applicable to the work of the Department of Agriculture in disseminating information, publishing on various subjects, and making regulations. These have not been separated into those referring only to dissemination or handling of scientific information.

From Organic Act of May 15, 1862:

"Section 1: . . . the general designs and duties of which shall be to acquire and to diffuse among the people of the United States useful information on subjects connected with agriculture in the most general and comprehensive sense of that word."

"Section 3: . . . it shall be the duty of the Commissioner of Agriculture to acquire and preserve in his Department all information concerning agriculture which he can obtain by means of books and correspondence."

From Executive Order 9069, February 23, 1942:

"To further the successful prosecution of the war through the better utilization of agricultural resources and industries, it is hereby ordered as follows: . . . 4. All libraries administered by agencies of the Department of Agriculture and all units of the Department providing library and bibliographical service and their functions, personnel, property, and records are consolidated and shall be administered through such facilities of the Department as the Secretary of Agriculture shall designate."

From Secretary of Agriculture Memorandum No. 1496, March 23, 1962:

"From the date of its inception the Library of the Department of Agriculture has served as a national library, and is generally considered today as the national agricultural library. It is appropriate and fitting, therefore, as we observe the centennial of the founding of the Department, that the national scope of its collection and services be recognized in its name.

"Accordingly, the Library of the Department of Agriculture is hereby designated, and shall be known as, the National Agricultural Library."

From USDA1AR, Chapter 2, November 27, 1964:

"The following assignment of functions is hereby made to the National Agricultural Library:

"a. Acquisition and preservation of all information concerning agriculture.

"b. Formulation of immediate and long-range library policies, procedures, practices and technical standards necessary for acquisition, cataloging, loan, bibliographic, and reference service to meet the needs of scientific, technical, research and administrative staffs of the Department, both in Washington and the field.

"c. Evaluating special library programs developed for agencies of the Department; exercising such controls as are needed to coordinate library services in the Department and to avoid duplication of effort.

"d. Provision of consultative service in library science and documentation, including systems for information storage and retrieval, to Department officials.

"e. Coordination of scientific and technical information activities of the Department.

"f. Coordination of the collection policy and program of the National Agricultural Library with the Library of Congress and the National Library of Medicine.

"g. Representation of the Department on library matters before Congressional Committees, in international library activities, in professional societies, and in science information and documentation activities; and cooperation with other Government agencies, and educational institutions on all matters relating to library services."

Atomic Energy Commission

The following sections of the Atomic Energy Act of 1954, as amended, relate to the responsibilities of the Commission for scientific and technical information:

"Sec. 3. PURPOSE. It is the purpose of this Act to effectuate the policies set forth above by providing for:

"a. a program of conducting, assisting, and fostering research and development in order to encourage maximum scientific and industrial progress;

"b. a program for the dissemination of unclassified scientific and technical information and for the control, dissemination, and declassification of Restricted Data, subject to appropriate safeguards, so as to encourage scientific and industrial progress;

. . .

"d. a program to encourage widespread participation in the development and utilization of atomic energy for peaceful purposes to the maxi-

mum extent consistent with the common defense and security and with the health and safety of the public;

"e. a program of international cooperation to promote the common defense and security and to make available to cooperating nations the benefits of peaceful applications of atomic energy as widely as expanding technology and considerations of the common defense and security will permit; and

"f. a program of administration which will be consistent with the foregoing policies and programs, with international arrangements, and with agreements for cooperation, which will enable the Congress to be currently informed so as to take further legislative action as may be appropriate."

"Sec. 141. POLICY. It shall be the policy of the Commission to control the dissemination and declassification of Restricted Data in such a manner as to assure the common defense and security. Consistent with such policy, the Commission shall be guided by the following principles:

"a. Until effective and enforceable international safeguards against the use of atomic energy for destructive purposes have been established by an international arrangement, there shall be no exchange of Restricted Data with other nations except as authorized by Section 144; and

"b. The dissemination of scientific and technical information relating to atomic energy should be permitted and encouraged so as to provide that free interchange of ideas and criticism which is essential to scientific and industrial progress and public understanding and to enlarge the fund of technical information."

"Sec. 144. INTERNATIONAL COOPERATION.

"a. The President may authorize the Commission to cooperate with another nation and to communicate to that nation Restricted Data on:

"(1) refining, purification, and subsequent treatment of source material;

"(2) reactor development;

"(3) production of special nuclear material;

"(4) health and safety;

"(5) industrial and other applications of atomic energy for peaceful purposes, and

"(6) research and development relating to the foregoing:

"Provided, however, that no such cooperation shall involve the communication of Restricted Data relating to the design or fabrication of atomic weapons: And provided further, that the cooperation is undertaken pursuant to an agreement for cooperation entered into in accordance with section 123, or is undertaken pursuant to an agreement existing on the effective date of this Act."

"Sec. 146. GENERAL PROVISIONS. Control of Information:

"a. Sections 141 to 145, inclusive, shall not exclude the applicable provisions of any other laws, except that no Government agency shall take any action under such other laws inconsistent with the provisions of those sections.

"b. The Commission shall have no power to control or restrict the dissemination of information other than as granted by this or any other law."

Sec. 161. GENERAL PROVISIONS. General Authority—In the performance of its functions the Commission is authorized to:

"i. Prescribe such regulations or orders as it may deem necessary (1) to protect Restricted Data received by any person in connection with any activity authorized pursuant to this Act, (2) to guard against the loss of diversion of any special nuclear material acquired by any person pursuant to section 53 or produced by any person in connection with any activity authorized pursuant to this Act, and to prevent any use or disposition thereof which the Commission may determine to be inimical to the common defense and security, and (3) to govern any activity authorized pursuant to this Act, including standards and restrictions governing the design, location, and operation of facilities used in the conduct of such activity, in order to protect health and to minimize danger to life or property;

Sec. 251. REPORT TO CONGRESS. The Commission shall submit to the Congress, in January and July of each year, a report concerning the activities of the Commission. The Commission shall include in such report, and shall at such other times as it deems desirable submit to the Congress, such recommendations for additional legislation as the Commission deems necessary or desirable."

Commerce

The actions considered most pertinent to technical information activities are embodied in the following items, which relate to specific elements of the Department of Commerce:

Coast and Geodetic Survey	PL 373, 80th Congress, Chapter 504, 1st Session (61 Stat 787) Approved August 6, 1947
	PL 86-409, 86th Congress, 2nd Session (74 Stat 16) Approved April 5, 1960
Bureau of Standards	Organic Act of March 3, 1901 (31 Stat 1449)
	Department Order No. 90, Sections 6.02 18 and 7.04, June 11, 1958
Patent Office	Title 35, USC
Census Bureau	Title 13, USC8b
Weather Bureau	Title 5, USC 458a Title 15, USC 313 and 320 Title 49, USC 603 (Item 7) PL 657, 80th Congress PL 85-726, 85th Congress

In addition, broad powers are given the Department of Commerce and its Office of Technical Services in the following legislative actions:

"Powers and duties of Department. (United States Code 596)

"It shall be the province and duty of said Department to foster, promote, and develop the foreign and domestic commerce, the mining, manufacturing, shipping, and fishery industries, and the transportation facilities of the United States; and to this end it shall be vested with jurisdiction and control of the departments, bureaus, offices, and branches of the public service, hereinafter specified, and with such other powers and duties as may be prescribed by law. (Feb. 14, 1903, ch. 552, 3, 32 Stat. 826.)"

In addition to this general authority, the Department of Commerce was allocated specific responsibility by the Congress in September, 1951, when Public Law 776 was enacted by the 2nd Session, 81st Congress:

"Be it enacted that the purpose of this Act is to make the results of technological research and development more readily available to industry and business, and to the general public, by clarifying and defining the functions and responsibilities of the Department of Commerce as a central clearinghouse for technical information which is useful to American industry and business.

"Clearinghouse for Technical Information

"Sec. 2. The Secretary of Commerce . . . is hereby directed to establish and maintain within the Department of Commerce a clearinghouse for the collection and dissemination of scientific, technical, and engineering information, and to this end to take such steps as he may deem necessary and desirable:

"a. To search for, collect, classify, coordinate, integrate, record, and catalog such information from whatever sources, foreign and domestic, that may be available;

"b. To make such information available to industry and business, to State and local governments, to other agencies of the Federal Government, and to the general public, through the preparation of abstracts, digests, translations, bibliographies, indexes, and microfilm and other reproductions, for distribution either directly or by utilization of business, trade, technical, and scientific publications and services;

"c. To effect, within the limits of his authority as now or hereafter defined by law, and with the consent of competent authority, the removal of restrictions on the dissemination of scientific and technical data in cases where consideration of national security permit the release of such data for the benefit of industry and business."

Federal Aviation Agency

The actions considered most pertinent to technical information activities are the following excerpts from the Federal Aviation Act of 1958, Public Law 85-726:

Collection and Dissemination of Information

"Sec. 311. The Administrator is empowered and directed to collect and disseminate information relative to civil aeronautics (other than information collected and disseminated by the [Civil Aeronautics] Board under titles IV and VII of this Act); to study the possibilities of the development of air commerce and the aero-

nautical industry; and to exchange with foreign governments, through appropriate governmental channels, information pertaining to civil aeronautics."

Note: Title IV concerns economic regulation of air carriers; title VII concerns aircraft accidents.

The Federal Aviation Act also provides for cooperative exchange of information with the Department of Defense and the National Aeronautics and Space Administration.

Exchange of Information

"Sec. 302. (d) In order to assist the Administrator further in the discharge of responsibilities under this Act, the Administrator and the Secretary of Defense, and the Administrator and the Administrator of the National Aeronautics and Space Administration, are directed to establish by cooperative agreement suitable arrangements for the timely exchange of information pertaining to their programs, policies, and requirements directly relating to such responsibilities."

Health, Education, and Welfare

The following excerpts concern technical information activities of the Public Health Service, including the National Library of Medicine and the National Institutes of Health; other agencies of HEW such as the Food and Drug Administration are not included:

The Public Health Service Act, 42 USC, ch. 6A:

TITLE II—Administration

"Sec. 217 . . . (c) The National Advisory Mental Health Council . . . is authorized . . . (2) to collect information as to studies being carried on in the field of mental health, and with the approval of the Surgeon General, make available such information through the appropriate publications for the benefit of health and welfare agencies or organizations (public and private), physicians, or any other scientists, and for the information of the general public. . . ."

TITLE III—General Powers and Duties of Public Health Service

Part A—Research and Investigations:

"Sec. 301. The Surgeon General shall conduct in the Service, and encourage, cooperate with, and render assistance to other appropriate pub-

lic authorities, scientific institutions, and scientists in the conduct of, and promote the coordination of, research, investigations, experiments, demonstrations, and studies relating to the causes, diagnosis, treatment, control and prevention of physical and mental diseases and impairments of man, including water purification, sewage treatment, and pollution of lakes and streams. In carrying out the foregoing the Surgeon General is authorized to—

"(a) Collect and make available through publications and other appropriate means, information as to, and the practical application of, such research and other activities."

Part B—Federal-State Cooperation:

"Sec. 213. To secure uniformity in the registration of mortality, morbidity and vital statistics the Surgeon General shall prepare and distribute necessary forms for the collection and compilation of such statistics which shall be published as a part of the health reports published by the Surgeon General."

"Sec. 315. From time to time the Surgeon General shall issue information related to public health, in the form of publications or otherwise, for the use of the public, and shall publish weekly reports of health conditions in the United States and other countries and other pertinent information for the use of persons and institutions engaged in work related to the functions of the Service."

Part H—National Library of Medicine (added by PL 941 (58 Stat 681) 84th Congress; August 3, 1956):

Purpose and Establishment of Library

"Sec. 371. In order to assist the advancement of medical and related sciences, and to aid the dissemination and exchange of scientific and other information important to the progress of medicine and to the public health, there is hereby established in the PHS a National Library of Medicine.

"Sec. 372. (a) The Surgeon General, through the Library and subject to the provisions of subsection (a), shall:

"(1) acquire and preserve books, periodicals, prints, films, recordings and other library materials pertinent to medicine;

"(2) organize the materials specified in clause (1) by appropriate cataloging, indexing, and bibliographical listings;

"(3) publish and make available the catalogs, indexes, and bibliographies referred to in clause (2);

"(4) make available, through loans, photographic or other copying procedures or otherwise such material in the Library as he deems appropriate;

"(5) provide reference and research assistance; and

"(6) engage in such other activities in furtherance of the purpose of this part as he deems appropriate and the Library's resources permit.

"(b) The Surgeon General may exchange, destroy, or otherwise dispose of any books, periodicals, films or other library materials not needed for the permanent use of the Library.

"(c) The Surgeon General is authorized, after obtaining the advice and recommendations of the Board . . . , to prescribe rules under which the Library will provide copies of its publications or materials . . . Such rules may provide for making available such publications, materials, facilities, or services (1) without charge as a public service, or (2) upon a loan, exchange, or charge basis, or (3) in appropriate circumstances, under contract arrangements made with a public or other non-profit agency, organization, or institution."

TITLE IV—National Research Institutes

Part A—National Cancer Institute:

"Sec. 404. [The National Cancer Advisory] council is authorized . . .

"(b) to collect information as to studies which are being carried on in the United States or any other country as to the cause, prevention, and methods of diagnosis and treatment of cancer, by correspondence or by personal investigation of such studies, and with the approval of the Surgeon General make available such information through the appropriate publications for the benefit of health agencies and organizations (public or private), physicians, dentists, or any other scientists, and for the information of the general public."

Part B—National Heart Institute:

"Sec. 412. In carrying out the purposes of section 301 with respect to heart diseases the Surgeon General, through the Institute and in cooperation with the National Advisory Heart Council, . . . shall— . . . "(e) establish an information center on research, prevention, diagnosis, and treatment of heart diseases, and col-

lect and make available through publications and other appropriate means, information as to, and the practical application of, research and other activities carried on pursuant to this part."

"Sec. 414. The [National Advisory Heart] council is authorized to— . . . (d) collect information as to studies which are being carried on in the United States or any other country as to the cause, prevention, or methods of diagnosis or treatment of heart diseases, by correspondence or by personal investigation of such studies, and with the approval of the Surgeon General make available such information through appropriate publications for the benefit of health and welfare agencies and organizations (public or private), physicians, or any other scientists, and for the information of the general public."

"Sec. 424. The [National Advisory Dental Research] council is authorized . . . (b) to collect information as to studies which are being carried on in the United States or any other country as to the cause, prevention, or methods of diagnosis or treatment of dental diseases and conditions, by correspondence or by personal investigation of such studies, and with the approval of the Surgeon General make available such information through appropriate publications for the benefit of health agencies and organizations (public or private), physicians, dentists, or any other scientists, and for the information of the general public."

The Federal Water Pollution Control Act, Public Law 660, 84th Congress, authorizes the Secretary to:

"collect and make available, through publications and other appropriate means, the results of and other information as to research, investigations, and demonstrations, relating to the prevention and control of water pollution, including appropriate recommendations in connection therewith. . . ." [Sec. 4 (a) (1).]

It also provides that:

"The Secretary shall, in cooperation with other Federal, State, and local agencies having related responsibilities, collect and disseminate basic data on chemical, physical, and biological water quality and other information insofar as such data or other information relate to water pollution and the prevention and control thereof." [Sec. 4 (c).]

The National Health Survey Act, Public Law 652, 84th Congress, adds section 305 to the Public Health Service Act. Section 305 provides as follows:

"(a) The Surgeon General is authorized (1) to make, by sampling or other appropriate means, surveys and special studies of the population of the United States to determine the extent of illness & disability and related information such as: (A) the number, age, sex, ability to work or engage in other activities, and occupation or activities of persons afflicted with chronic or other disease or injury or handicapping condition; (B) the type of disease or injury or handicapping conditions of each person so afflicted; (C) the length of time that each such person has been prevented from carrying on his occupation or activities; (D) the amounts and types of services received for or because of such conditions; and (E) the economic and other impacts of such conditions; and (2) in connection therewith, to develop and test new or improved methods for obtaining current data on illness and disability and related information.

"(b) The Surgeon General is authorized, at appropriate intervals, to make available, through publications and otherwise, to any interested governmental or other public or private agencies, organizations, or groups, or to the public, the results of surveys or studies made pursuant to subsection (a)."

Public Law 159, 84th Congress, as amended: . . .

"(b) The Surgeon General may . . . (2) collect and disseminate information relating to air pollution and the prevention and abatement thereof: . . ."

Public Law 87-582, the DHEW Appropriation Act for FY 1963, states:

PREAMBLE

"For necessary expenses in carrying out the Public Health Service Act, as amended (42 U.S.C., ch. 6A) (hereinafter referred to as the Act), and other Acts, including . . . expenses incident to the dissemination of health information in foreign countries through exhibits and other appropriate means; . . ."

Interior

The following U. S. Code citations are the legislative authority for specific elements within the Department of the Interior. Provisions for collecting technical information, and often for making it public, are found throughout these sections. One such section, concerning the Bureau of Mines, is quoted below as an example:

U. S. Fish and Wildlife Service

16 U. S. C.	631i	742a
	661	742c(a)
	662(b) & (f)	742d
	663(c)	742d-1
	665	742f-h
	701	744–778a
	715b	921
		1008

U. S. Geological Survey

43 U. S. C.	31	38
	36	41–44
	36a	49
	36b	50

U. S. Bureau of Mines

30 U. S. C.	1	401	553
	3	411	556
	4	451	641
	5–8	452	645
	13–16	456	

U. S. Bureau of Land Management

43 U. S. C.	2	17
	6	18
	13	

U. S. Bureau of Reclamation

43 U. S. C.	379	422g
	412	435g(f)
	422(c)	435(a)

U. S. National Park Service

16 U. S. C.	14a	455a
	17k	462
	18a	469a
	18f	

U. S. Office of Coal Research

30 U. S. C.	662
	666
	667

U. S. Office of Saline Water

42 U. S. C.	1952
	1953
	1956
	1958a
	1958b

U. S. Department of the Interior
The Secretary
5 U. S. C.   488
              489
              495
              501

43 U. S. C.   52–56
              87
              361
              364
              364b–364e
              751

Public Law 386 February 25, 1913, amending the original Bureau of Mines Act of 1910, requires the Bureau to disseminate information concerning its investigations "in such manner as will best carry out the purpose of this Act" (i.e., with a view to increasing the safety, efficiency, and economic development of the U. S. mining and mineral industries).

National Aeronautics and Space Administration (NASA)

NASA responsibilities for technical information were established by the following excerpts from the National Aeronautics and Space Act of 1958, Public Law 85-568, 85th Congress; July 29, 1958:

"Sec. 203(a)(3). The Administration in order to carry out the purpose of this Act, shall . . . provide for the widest practicable and appropriate dissemination of information concerning its activities and the results thereof."

"Sec. 102(c)(1). The aeronautics and space activities of the United States shall be conducted so as to contribute materially to one or more of the following activities: . . . The expansion of human knowledge of phenomena in the atmosphere and space."

National Science Foundation (NSF)

The following is a list of all known legislative and executive authorities affecting the responsibilities of NSF for technical information services:

National Science Foundation Act of 1950, Public Law 507, 81st Congress, 2nd Session.
National Defense Education Act of 1958, Title IX, Public Law 85-864, 85th Congress; September 2, 1958 (H.R. 13247).

Executive Order 10807, "Federal Council for Science and Technology," March 17, 1959; which also amended Executive Order 10521, "Administration of Scientific Research by Agencies of the Federal Government," March 19, 1954.

Presidential Letter to Director, National Science Foundation (Dr. Waterman), dated January 22, 1959.

Agricultural Trade Development and Assistance Act of 1954, Public Law 83-480 as amended by the Mutual Security Act of 1958, Public Law 85-477 (approved June 30, 1958) and as interpreted by Executive Order 10900, "Administration of the Agricultural Trade Development and Assistance Act of 1954, as Amended," January 6, 1961.

From Public Law 507:

"Functions of the Foundation
"Sec. 3(a) The Foundation is authorized and directed . . .
"(1) . . .
"(5) to foster the interchange of scientific information among scientists in the United States and foreign countries; . . .

"General Authority of Foundation
"Sec. 11. The Foundation shall have the authority, within the limits of available appropriations, to do all things necessary to carry out the provisions of this Act, including, but without being limited thereto, the authority—
"(a) . . .
"(g) to publish or arrange for the publication of scientific and technical information so as to further the full dissemination of information of scientific value consistent with the national interest, ..."

Under the terms of Title IX (Sections 901 and 902) of the National Defense Education Act of 1958, the Foundation was directed to establish a Science Information Service which would "(1) provide, or arrange for the provisions of indexing, abstracting, translating and other services leading to a more effective dissemination of scientific information and (2) undertake programs to develop improved methods, including mechanized systems, for making scientific information available." The Act also provided for the establishment of a Science Information Council to advise and make recommendations to the Science Information Service.

The passage of this law was followed by the

President's approval on December 7, 1958, of a plan (Baker report) proposed by his Science Advisory Committee for the effective coordination of scientific information activities within the federal government, and for the review, coordination, and stimulation, on a nation-wide basis, of activities in all areas of scientific information. By a letter of January 22, 1959, the President asked the Foundation to carry responsibility for implementing this plan. This letter was followed by Executive Order 10807, dated March 13, 1959, which created the Federal Council for Science and Technology and directed the Foundation to provide "leadership in the effective coordination of the scientific information activities of the Federal Government with a view to improving the availability and dissemination of scientific information." Federal agencies were directed to cooperate with and assist the Foundation in performance of this function.

In accordance with the provisions of the National Defense Education Act, the Science Information Service was established by the Foundation on December 11, 1958. The Office of Science Information Service assumed the responsibilities of its predecessor, the Office of Scientific Information, and undertook the expanded and increased functions stipulated in the law. Appointment of the Science Information Council was completed on December 30, 1958. Its membership, specified in the Act, consists of the Librarian of Congress, the Director of the National Library of Medicine, the Director of the National Agricultural Library, the Head of the Foundation's Science Information Service, and 15 additional members drawn from various fields of science, librarianship, scientific documentation, and the lay public.

NSF activities in the field of translations, etc. are covered in part by the following excerpts:

"Sec. 502 (1) Sec. 104 of the Agricultural Trade Development and Assistance Act of 1954 (Public Law 480, Eighty-third Congress; 7 U. S. C. 1704), as amended, is further amended by adding after paragraph (j) the following new paragraph:

"(k) To collect, collate, translate, abstract, and disseminate scientific and technological information and to conduct research and support scientific activities overseas including programs and projects of scientific cooperation between the United States and other countries such as coordinated research against diseases common to all of mankind or unique to individual regions of the globe, and to promote and support programs of medical and scientific research, cultural and educational development, health, nutrition, and sanitation: Provided, that foreign currencies shall be available for the purposes of this subsection (in addition to funds otherwise made available for such purposes) only in such amounts as may be specified from time to time in appropriation Acts."

Public Law 86-108, (H.R. 7500), 73 Stat. 246, approved July 24, 1959, amended this subsection by adding the word "research" after the word "conduct" and by rephrasing the provision relating to the appropriation procedure. Public Law 86-341, (H.R. 8609), 73 Stat. 606, approved September 21, 1959, added the following after the word "globe," "and to promote and support programs of medical and scientific research, cultural and educational development, health, nutrition, and sanitation."

Responsibilities were delegated in Executive Order 10900 as follows:

"Sec. 4. *Foreign Currencies.* . . .

(d) the purposes described in the lettered paragraphs of sec. 104 of the Act (7 U. S. C. 1704) shall be carried out, with foreign currencies made available in consonance with law and the provisions of this order, as follows: . . .

(11) Those under sec. 104 (k) of the Act as follows: (i) Those with respect to collecting, collating, translating, abstracting, and disseminating scientific and technological information by the Director of the National Science Foundation and such other agency or agencies as the Director of the Bureau of the Budget, after appropriate consultation, may designate. (ii) Those with respect to programs of cultural and education development, health nutrition, and sanitation by the Department of State. (iii) All others by such agency or agencies as the Director of the Bureau of the Budget, after appropriate consultation may designate. As used in this paragraph the term "appropriate consultation" shall include consultation with the Secretary of State, the Director of the National Science Foundation, and any other appropriate Federal agency. . . ."

Office of Science and Technology

Reorganization Plan No. 2 of 1962 creates the Office of Science and Technology. In his

transmittal of the Plan to Congress on March 27, 1962, the President included the following comments:

"Considering the rapid growth and far-reaching scope of Federal activities in science and technology, it is imperative that the President have adequate staff support in developing policies and evaluating programs in order to assure that science and technology are used most effectively in the interests of national security and general welfare.

"To this end it is contemplated that the Director [of OST] will assist the President in discharging the responsibility of the President for the proper coordination of Federal science and technology functions. More particularly, it is expected that he will advise and assist the President as the President may request with respect to:

"(1) Major policies, plans and programs of science and technology of the various agencies of the Federal Government, giving appropriate emphasis to the relationship of science and technology to national security and foreign policy, and measures for furthering science and technology in the Nation.

"(2) Assessment of selected scientific and technical developments and programs in relation to their impact on national policies.

"(3) Review, integration, and coordination of major Federal activities in science and technology, giving due consideration to the effects of such activities on non-Federal resources and institutions.

"(4) Assuring that good and close relations exist with the Nation's scientific and engineering communities so as to further in every appropriate way their participation in strengthening science and technology in the United States and the Free World.

"(5) Such other matters consonant with law as may be assigned by the President to the Office.

"The National Science Foundation has proved to be an effective instrument for administering sizable programs in support of basic research and education in the sciences and has set an example for other agencies through the administration of its own programs. However, the Foundation, being at the same organizational level as other agencies, cannot satisfactorily coordinate Federal science policies or evaluate programs of other agencies. Science policies, transcending agency lines, need to be coordinated and shaped at the level of the Executive Office of the President drawing upon many resources both within and outside of Government. Similarly, staff efforts at that higher level are required for the evaluation of Government programs in science and technology.

"Thus the further steps contained in the reorganization plan are now needed in order to meet most effectively new and expanding requirements brought about by the rapid and far-reaching growth of the Government's research and development programs. These requirements call for the further strengthening of science organization at the Presidential level and for the adjustment of the Foundation's role to reflect changed conditions. The Foundation will continue to originate policy proposals and recommendations concerning the support of basic research and education in the sciences, and the new Office will look to the Foundation to provide studies and information on which sound national policies in science and technology can be based."

By appointment of the President, the Director of the Office of Science and Technology also serves as Chairman of the Federal Council for Science and Technology, which was established by Executive Order 10807, March 17, 1959:

"Sec. 2. Functions of Council. (a) The Council shall consider problems and developments in the fields of science and technology and related activities affecting more than one Federal agency or concerning the over-all advancement of the Nation's science and technology, and shall recommend policies and other measures (1) to provide more effective planning and administration of Federal scientific and technological programs, (2) to identify research needs including areas of research requiring additional emphasis, (3) to achieve more effective utilization of the scientific and technological resources and facilities of Federal agencies, including the elimination of unnecessary duplication, and (4) to further international cooperation in science and technology. In developing such policies and measures the Council, after consulting, when considered appropriate by the Chairman, the National Academy of Sciences the President's Science Advisory Committee, and other organizations, shall consider (i) the effects of Federal research and development policies and pro-

grams on non-Federal programs and institutions, (ii) long-range program plans designed to meet the scientific and technological needs of the Federal Government, including manpower and capital requirements and (iii) the effects of non-Federal programs in science and technology upon Federal research and development policies and programs.

"(b) The Council shall consider and recommend measures for the effective implementation of Federal policies concerning the administration and conduct of Federal programs in science and technology."

"Sec. 3. Agency assistance to Council.

"(a) For the purpose of effectuating this order, each Federal agency represented on the Council shall furnish necessary assistance to the Council in consonance with section 214 of the act of May 3, 1945, 59 Stat. 134 (31 U. S. C. 691). Such assistance may include (1) detailing employees to the Council to perform such functions, consistent with the purposes of this order, as the Chairman may assign to them, and (2) undertaking, upon request of the Chairman, such special studies for the Council as come within the functions herein assigned to the Council.

"(b) Upon request of the Chairman, the heads of Federal agencies shall, so far as prac-

ticable, provide the Council with information and reports relating to the scientific and technological activities of the respective agencies.

"Sec. 4. Standing Committees and Panels. For the purpose of conducting studies and making reports as directed by the Chairman, standing committees and panels of the Council may be established in consonance with the provisions of section 214 of the act of May 3, 1945, 59 Stat. 134 (31 U. S. C. 691). At least one such standing committee shall be composed of scientist-administrators representing Federal agencies, shall provide a forum for consideration of common administrative policies and procedures relating to Federal research and development activities and for formulation of recommendations thereon, and shall perform such other related functions as may be assigned to it by the Chairman of the Council."

In accordance with provisions of Section 4 of Executive Order 10807 and as a result of recommendations of a Task Group on Scientific and Technological Communication in the Government, the Federal Council established a "Committee on Information" at its May 22, 1962 meeting. The Committee later adopted the name, Committee on Scientific and Technical Information (COSATI).

Glossary

This group of operational definitions is intended as a guide to the novice and is limited to remarks pertinent to use of each term in this book. However, any term whose "definition" proved excessively controversial was omitted as a potential source of more confusion than guidance. For such terms the experienced reader will have formed his own usage and needs no guidance; the new recruit to the field is better served by extensive interaction with experienced associates and scholarly sources.

Abstract	Textual summary of source document (see *Descriptive abstract, Informative abstract,* and *Extract*).
Acquisitioning	Process of identifying desired item, verifying need, selecting source, and ordering. May include order follow-up, receiving, and paying.
Active dissemination	Notification of accession and sometimes distribution of a document to a user, based on his probable interest as evidenced by a match between a list of descriptors for the document and one for the user. Matching may be manual or automated.
Administrative terminal system (ATS)	IBM on-line document preparation system; uses Selectric typewriter or IBM 1050 terminals communicating with disk-memory computer.
ADP	Automatic data processing.
Aperture card	Card stock, usually tab card size, in which a hole is die-cut, to accommodate mounting a film chip —also called a unitized card.
Aspect file	Inverted index, which see.
ATS	Administrative terminal system, which see.
Blow-back	Reenlargement of microform image.
Capping agency	Overall executive or management agency.
Case	All characters (originally, stored in the same case) of capital letters—i.e., upper case—or of small letters, characterized by ascenders and descenders —i.e., lower case—of a size of type style.
Cataloging	Process of providing systematic bibliographic and subject description of documents, to record and display the resources of a collection, library, or group of libraries.
Cathode-ray tube (CRT)	Vacuum tube in which a controlled electron beam creates a visible image on the phosphorescent face of the tube—e.g., a television tube.
Clearinghouse	An exchange organization —in documentation, a supplier or distributor of report literature originating in more than one source organization.
COBOL	Acronym for COmmon Business Oriented Language, a language used for writing computer programs for business applications.
Compos-O-Line	Sequential card camera manufactured by Fridèn.
Control file	File describing some other

file—e.g., an order file (describes potential addition to collection), catalog and index (describe collection), circulation file (describes subset of collection and borrowers), authority file (prescribes vocabulary of other files).

Coordinate index   Index in which more than one index file entry identifies each document or aspect of each document. (See also *Inverted index.*)

CRT   Cathode-ray tube, which see.

Data center   Organization handling numeric data—ostensibly without evaluation. (See also *Information evaluation center.*)

Data-phone   Telephone line terminal equipment providing for dialing and completing connection between digital equipment and transmission lines.

Depository   Organization designated to receive, maintain, and make available to requestors all documents distributed by a particular source—e.g., AEC, NASA, or GPO.

Descriptive abstract   Textual notation about document contents, sometimes using words from a controlled vocabulary that is also used for indexing —does not summarize contents. (See also *Informative abstract.*)

Diazo   Photosensitive, organic dye, set by ammonia fumes, nonreversible— e.g., bluelines or blueprint reproductions.

Digest   See *Informative abstract.*

Digitize   Originally, to convert non-discrete data (e.g., a continuously varying electrical signal) into a discrete form (e.g., a string of binary numbers). By extension, to convert alphabetic, numeric, or graphic data into a form acceptable for processing by a digital computer.

Documentation   Creation, management, and exploitation of documents.

Documentation center   Organization acquiring, announcing, abstracting, indexing, distributing, and selectively disseminating documents; handles requests stated in terms of content desired.

Document center   Organization distributing documents in response to requests for identified items.

EAM   Electronic accounting machine, for handling punched (tab) cards and the data they bear.

Electrostatic reprography   Replication of a document image as a pattern of electric charge on a metal plate. Carbon particles attracted to the charge pattern are transferred to and bonded on an accepting surface—e.g., paper, multilith mats.

Electrotype plate   Master printing press plate created by electrolytic deposit of metal on wax mold.

Extract   Excerpts from a document, used to represent the whole. (See also *Abstract.*)

Face   Style of type—e.g., sans serif (block characters), roman, italic, script.

Fan-fold   Continuous form, used in high-volume machine operations to avoid excessive paper-loading time.

Feedback   Reaction by a destination (individual, equipment, or system) to a transfer of information, and trans-

fer of (part of) reaction to information source. Required for source-system evaluation and adaptation.

Fiche Short form for Microfiche, which see.

Flatbed press Press in which the form containing type or the plate is mounted flat—a letterpress.

Flexowriter Tape-perforating typewriter manufactured by Fridèn.

Font See *Typefont*.

FORTRAN Short form for FORmula TRANslation, a language used for writing computer programs for computation.

Fotolist Sequential card camera manufactured by Varityper.

Galley Tray in which type slugs are arranged for pulling proof copy; also, the proof copy.

Graphic tablet Electromechanical input-output device used in computer-based system. Images traced by a special stylus on the tablet are written on the tablet and in computer memory.

Hard copy Document or replica legible to ordinary sight without special equipment.

Hardware Equipment components of a man-machine system.

Head, Header Line of text or tabular data considered the topic or class encompassing subordinate entries—a headline.

Indexing Process of selecting or assigning identifiers of document subject contents (e.g., terms, sometimes from controlled vocabulary) and, in computer systems, of selecting, assigning, and compiling document identifiers (e.g., author and source names, title).

Indicative abstract See *Descriptive abstract*.

Information center Organization purveying informational or substantive responses to inquiries, as distinct from document centers, which see.

Information evaluation center Organization analyzing, synthesizing, and repackaging the contents of documents.

Information science Science that studies creation, management, and exploitation of recordable knowledge — theoretical basis for the field of documentation.

Information specialist Specialist in exploitation of document contents, with strong competence in the subject matter being analyzed.

Information technologist One who processes and manages documents—including librarians, system designers and operators, microform and data processing specialists, indexers, abstracters, etc.

Informative abstract Textual summary of document contents, echoing the viewpoint of the document author but sometimes including commentary by the abstractor.

Interest profile List of terms that collectively characterize the technical or scientific interests of an individual or organization (see *Active dissemination*).

Interface Information or control transfer point shared by two or more systems or components.

Inverted index Index consisting of terms against each of which are posted identifications of all documents to which the term applies; fragments a document unit

Justowriter — record into its identifying aspects.
Tape-perforating typewriter manufactured by Fridèn, equipped to insert additional space between words to lengthen a given string of words to fit a specified line width, for composing text with a justified (even) right margin.

Keyboard — (Verb) To operate a keyboard; to introduce symbols or codes by operating a keyboard.

Keyword-in-context (KWIC) index — Originally a permuted title index. Now generic for indexes generated automatically and consisting of context either permuted or listed under headers; latter are sometimes called KWOC.

KWIC — Keyword in context (an index), which see.

KWOC — Keyword out of context —see *Keyword-in-context (KWIC) index.*

Laser — Device amplifying a concentrated light beam for long-range and/or extremely precise transmission. Output may be modulated for voice or digital information transmission or storage.

Letterpress — Press in which paper and typebed (or plate) are flat and paper contacts type flatly.

Light pen — Stylus such that its contact with the face of a cathode-ray tube (in a system responsive to the pen) activates the system to record, flag, augment, or alter the portion contacted.

Linotron — High-speed computer-based photocomposer manufactured by CBS Laboratories and Mergenthaler.

Listomatic — Sequential card camera manufactured by Recordak.

Literature researcher — See *Information specialist.*

Machine translation — Conversion by a programmed automatic data processing system of vocabulary and explicitly formulatable syntax of one language to those of another.

Magnetic core — Toroid of iron oxide particles bonded in ceramic, magnetic polarization of which constitutes "recording" into memory. (See also *Random access storage.*)

Magnetic tape — See *Serial storage.*

Matrix — Master type character die in typesetter; master character set grid in photocomposer.

Memory (of a computer) — Aggregation of circuits, each capable of being set in one of two "states." Combinations of states are interpreted as numeric or alphabetic symbols; hence, as information. Circuits may center around magnetic cores. Loosely used to refer to internal storage circuits.

Microfiche — Sheet microform, ordinarily a negative transparency, accommodating about 60 page images.

Microform — Miniature facsimile of a document—e.g., microfilm reels and cartridges, microfiche, microcards, aperture cards, film strips.

Modulate — To vary, by means of discontinuity or around a modulus or standard measure. In communications, to impose a message by variations of a carrier signal.

MTST — Magnetic Tape Selectric Typewriter system, manufactured by IBM.

Multiplexor — Device acting as time or impedance buffer between a computer central processor and several input-output terminal devices.

"Natural habitat effect" — Hypothesis that information services most closely satisfy and are responsive to changes in user needs when geographically or organizationally close to the user.

On-line — In computer usage, in direct communication (through a buffer) with a central processor.

Page charge — Charge imposed by primary publisher on author to defray part of publication cost.

Perforated tape — See *Tape-perforating typewriter*.

Periodical — Document title issued at a specified frequency—e.g., monthly journal. (See also *Serial*.)

Permuted index — Index generated, usually automatically, from terms in a string—such as a title—by cycling the string to successively position each term in a fixed "indexing" position on a line, then alphabetizing all resulting entries on that position. (See also *Keyboard-in-context (KWIC) index*.)

Photocomposition — Generation of type characters, lines, or pages on photographic negatives from perforated or magnetic tape or keyboard input.

Point — Unit of measurement of type: 72 points = 1 inch

Preprint — Document distributed prior to its presentation or publication.

Primary distribution — Transmittal of copies of a document to a distribution list by source organization or individual.

Primary publication — Publication (as opposed to copying) of a source document.

Proceedings — Published aggregation of presentations and contributions to a conference or meeting.

Proprietary information — Information owned by virtue of discovery or purchase.

Purge — (Verb) To remove a document from a collection. May involve destruction or relocation, as to a collection to which access is made less frequently than that from which the document was purged.

Quadrant — Aperture card image printer, designed for cards containing 4 page images, manufactured by Minnesota Mining and Manufacturing.

Random access storage — Computer storage, retrieval from which takes the same amount of time regardless of the physical location of the desired data. Central memories, such as magnetic core memories, are fully random access. Disk and magnetic card memories are random access with respect to records. (See also *Serial storage*.)

RA system — Responsible agent (which see) system.

Referee — (Verb) To evaluate the content of a document to determine acceptability for publication.

Referral center — Organization directing inquirers to most probable source of appropriate response to the inquiry.

Reprint — Duplicate of a paper published in a journal or special publication. Usu-

	ally supplied or sold to the author or other requestor by the publisher. A press overrun distributed independently of the aggregation in which the original appeared.
Repro	Short for "reproducible copy." A graphic unit which may consist wholly of text, for publication production.
Reprography	Document image replication.
Responsible agent concept	View of relationships between agencies. Responsibility for services in each subject or mission in science and technology to be undetaken by a particular agency on the basis of compatibility, interest, and capability.
SDI	See *Selective dissemination of information.*
Secondary distribution	Supplying or selling copies of documents by other than the source publisher. Primary function of a document center or clearinghouse.
Secondary publication	Document announcing primary publications, by means of condensations and indexes. Tool for retrieving primary publications responsive to inquiries phrased in the index vocabulary.
Secondary service	Service retrieving citations and condensations.
Selective dissemination of information (SDI)	IBM's name for its system of computer-based active dissemination.
Sequential card camera	Equipment accepting and automatically photographing text or graphics in a specified (image) area on cards keyed for automatic feed through the camera.
Serial	Publication issued in successive parts, usually at regular intervals and in-

	tended to be continued indefinitely—e.g., periodicals, annuals, journals, proceedings.
Serial storage	Storage organization method. Access depends on the physical location of the desired data relative to that available at a read position at a given moment. Magnetic tape memory is a computer form of serial storage.
Sidehead	Head (which see) in text. Distinct from a running head, which occurs on each unit (page) of a document.
Slug	Lead casting bearing type characters.
Software	All nonhardware elements of a computer-based system—e.g., computer programs, procedures for training and operating, support documentation, (sometimes) design and test documentation, including films and magnetic tape records.
Stereotype plate	Master printing press plate created by pressure forming a cork or felt base.
Switching center	Organization equipped to accept, through electronic networks, inputs from many sources and quasi-automatically route each to appropriate destinations. Inputs may be data or inquiries. (See also *Referral center.*)
Synchrotape	Tape-perforating typewriter manufactured by Univac.
Tape-perforating typewriter	Equipment, actuation of whose keyboard results in both a print action and a punch action. A unique combination of holes is punched in a row across

the width of a paper tape to represent each type character and typographic control (e.g., case shift, space).

Technical information — Information concerning the study, practices, methodology, and tools of any art, science, trade, or profession.

Thesaurus — Guide to conceptual relationships assumed or assigned among words and/or terms. Need not reflect linquistic usage.

Time-phased downgrading — Technique for systematically removing restrictions on distribution of information originally protected for purposes of national security.

Typefont — Set of characters constituting one size of a given type style or face.

Typesetter — Equipment, actuation of whose keyboard results in selection of type characters and in production of a lead casting (slug) of each line of type. Type is reused after the slug is ejected.

Union list — List of document entries or titles (usually serials) indicating location of each in one or more collections.

Unitized card — See *Aperture card.*

"Wholesaler-retailer" concept — View of relationship between document center (wholesaler), maintaining a supply of items, and local library or information center (retailer), interfacing with the center on behalf of a user (consumer).

Xerography — Xerox Corporation's electrostatic reproduction method. Also used generically.

Selected Bibliography

This bibliography lists references that provide general guidance or background information in areas related to this report. Some of these references may also be found in individual section listings. They are repeated here because of their general applicability to the overall content of the report.

American Documentation Institute. *Proceedings of the 1964 Annual Meeting: Parameter of Information Science.* Vols. I and II. Washington, D. C., Spartan Press, and London, Cleaver-Hume Press, 1964. (See also the *Proceedings* of other annual meetings of ADI, especially that of 1962.)

American Library Association. *The Library and Information Networks of the Future.* Chicago, American Library Association, 1963. AD 401 347.

Baker Report; see President's Science Advisory Committee listings.

Bershadskiy, R. Y. *Uchenyy Kotoryy Znaet Vse.* (Soviet Developments in Information Storage and Retrieval), Moscow, 1962 (translation by U. S. Dept. of Commerce, 1963). AD 400 597.

Borko, H. *The Conceptual Foundations of Information Systems.* SP-2057. Santa Monica, Calif., System Development Corp., May 1965. AD 615 718.

Borko, H., Ed., *Automated Language Processing.* New York, John Wiley and Sons, in preparation.

Bourne, Charles P., et al. *Requirements, Criteria, and Measurements of Performance of Information Storage and Retrieval Systems.* Menlo Park, Calif., Stanford Research Institute, December 1961. AD 270 942.

Bourne, Charles P. *Methods of Information Handling.* New York, John Wiley and Sons, 1963.

Brooks Report; see U. S. Congress listings.

Clapp, Verner W. *The Future of the Research Library.* Urbana, Ill., University of Illinois Press, 1964.

Crawford Report; see U. S. Dept. of Commerce listing.

Cuadra, Carlos A., Ed. *Annual Review of Information Science and Technology.* Vol. 1. New York, John Wiley and Sons, 1966. (See especially Chapter 13, "National Information Issues and Trends," by John Sherrod.)

Danton, E. M., Ed. *The Library of Tomorrow.* Chicago, American Library Association, 1939.

Elliott Report; see U. S. Congress listings.

Evans, L. H., et al. *Federal Departmental Libraries.* Washington, D. C., Brookings Institution, 1963.

Fussler, H. H., and J. L. Simon. *Patterns in the Use of Books in Large Research Libraries.* Chicago, University of Chicago Press, 1961.

Hanson, C. W., and Marian Janes. "Coverage by Abstracting Journals of Conference Papers," *Journal of Documentation,* Vol. 17, No. 3 (September 1961), pp. 143–149.

Hearle, E. *System Considerations in Regional Information Exchange.* P-2662. Santa Monica, Calif., RAND Corp., 1962.

Henderson, Madeline M., et al. *Cooperation, Convertibility, and Compatibility Among Information Systems: A Literature Review.* National Bureau of Standards Miscellaneous Publication 276. Washington, D. C., GPO, 1966.

Herbert, E. "Information Transfer," *International Science and Technology,* No. 51 (March 1966), pp. 26–37, 104, 106.

Hoshovsky, A. G., and H. H. Album. "Toward a National Technical Information System," *American Documentation,* Vol. 16, No. 4 (October 1965), pp. 313–322.

Humphrey Report; see U. S. Congress listings.

Isaacs, H. H. *User-Oriented Information Systems for State and Local Government.* SP-1988. Santa Monica, Calif., System Development Corp., March 1965.

Kemeny, John G. "A Library for 2000 A.D." in Greenberger, M., Ed., *Management and the Computer of the Future.* New York, John Wiley and Sons, 1963.

Kessler, M. M. *The MIT Technical Information Project.* Cambridge, Massachusetts Institute of Technology, 1964. AD 608 502.

King, G. W., et al. *Automation and the Library of Congress.* Washington, D. C., GPO, 1963.

Knox, W. T. "The Government Makes Plans," *Physics Today,* Vol. 19, No. 1 (January 1966), pp. 39–44.

Librarian of Congress, *Annual Report of the Librarian of Congress for FY 64.* Washington, D. C., GPO, 1965.

Licklider, J. C. R. *Libraries of the Future.* Cambridge, Massachusetts Institute of Technology Press, 1965.

Little, Arthur D., Inc. *Centralization and Documentation.* (2nd ed.). C-64409. Cambridge, Mass., A. D. Little, Inc., June 1964.

Malov, V. S. "Results of Check of Fulfillment of Resolution of Council of Ministers of USSR 'About Measures for Improvement of Organization of Scientific and Technical Information in this Country'," *Scientific and Technical Information (Selected Articles),* No. 6, 1964. Foreign Technology Division, Air Force Systems Command, Wright-Patterson Air Force Base, Ohio. (Report No. FTD-MT-65-07.)

Markuson, Barbara E., Ed. *Libraries and Automation.* Proceedings of the Conference on Libraries and Automation held at Airlie Foundation, Warrenton, Virginia, May 26–30, 1963. Washington, D. C., Library of Congress, 1964.

Menzel, Herbert. "The Flow of Information Among Scientists—Problems, Opportunities, and Research Questions." (Mimeo.) New York, Columbia University, Bureau of Applied Social Research, 1958.

Menzel, Herbert. "The Information Needs of Current Scientific Research," *Library Quarterly*, Vol. 34, No. 1 (January 1964), pp. 4–19.

MITRE Corp. *Information System Sciences.* Preprints for the Second Congress on the Information Sciences. Washington, D. C., Spartan Books, 1965.

Mohrhardt, F. E. "National Systems," *Library Trends*, Vol. 2, No. 1 (July 1953), pp. 44–62.

National Academy of Sciences. "Communication Problems and Bio-Medical Research: Report of a Study," *Federation Proceedings*, Vol. 23, No. 5 (September–October 1964).

National Science Foundation. *Current Research and Development in Scientific Documentation, No. 12: Bibliography of References Cited in Issues No. 1-11.* Washington, D. C., 1965.

National Science Foundation. *Current Research and Development in Scientific Documentation.* No. 13. Washington, D. C., November 1964. (Latest of a series.)

National Science Foundation. *Scientific Information Activities of Federal Agencies.* Washington, D. C., Government Printing Office. (A series of reports published aperiodically under this title.)

Overhage, Carl F. J., and R. Joyce Harman, Eds. *Intrex.* Cambridge, Massachusetts Institute of Technology Press, 1965.

President's Science Advisory Committee. *Improving the Availability of Scientific and Technical Information in the United States.* Washington, D. C., The White House, December 1958. (The Baker Report.)

President's Science Advisory Committee. *Science, Government, and Information: The Responsibilities of the Technical Community and the Government in the Transfer of Information.* Washington, D. C., The White House, January 1963. (The Weinberg Report.)

Price, Derek J. de Solla. *Little Science, Big Science.* New York, Columbia University Press, 1963.

Pucinski Hearings; see U. S. Congress listings.

Rubinoff, M., Ed. *Toward a National Information System.* Second Annual National Colloquium on Information Retrieval, April 23–24, 1965, Philadelphia, Pennsylvania. Washington, D. C., Spartan Books, and London, Macmillan and Co., Ltd., 1965.

Schultheiss, Louis A., Don S. Culbertson, and Edward M. Heiliger. *Advanced Data Processing in the University Library.* New York, The Scarecrow Press, 1962.

Swanson, D. R. "Library Goals and the Role of Automation," *Special Libraries*, Vol. 53, No. 8 (October 1962), pp. 466–471.

"Toward National Information Networks," special section of *Physics Today*, Vol. 19, No. 1 (January 1966), pp. 38–53.

U. S. Air Force Office of Scientific Research, and System Development Corp. *Proceedings of the Workshop on Working with Semi-Automatic Documentation Systems at Airlie Foundation—Warrenton, Virginia, May 2–5, 1965.* Springfield, Va., Defense Documentation Center, 1965.

U. S. Congress, House of Representatives, Committee on Education and Labor. *Hearings before the Ad Hoc Subcommittee on a National Research Data Processing and Information Retrieval Center on H. R. 1946.* 88th Congress, 1st Session. Washington, D. C., GPO, 1963. (The Pucinski Hearings.)

U. S. Congress, House of Representatives, Committee on Government Operations, Select Committee on Government Research. *Documentation and Dissemination of Research and Development Results.* 88th Congress, 2nd Session. Washington, D. C., GPO, November 1964. (The Elliott Report.)

U. S. Congress, Senate, Committee on Government Operations. *Report to the President on the Management of Automatic Data Processing in the Federal Government.* 89th Congress, 1st Session, Senate Doc. No. 15. Washington, D. C., GPO, March 1965.

U. S. Congress, House of Representatives, Committee on Government Operations. *Automatic Data Processing Equipment.* 89th Congress, 1st Session. Washington, D. C., GPO, March 1965. (The Brooks Report.)

U. S. Congress, Senate, Committee on Government Operations. *Summary of Activities Toward Interagency Coordination.* Report No. 369, 89th Congress, 1st Session. Washington, D. C., GPO, June 1965. (The Humphrey Report.)

U. S. Department of Agriculture. *Report of Task Force ABLE: Agricultural Biological Literature Exploitation.* Washington, D. C., GPO, March 1965.

U. S. Department of Commerce. *Scientific and Technological Communication in the Government.* Washington, D. C., GPO, 1962. AD 295 545. (The Crawford Report.)

Weinberg Report; see President's Science Advisory Committee listings.

Weinberg, Alvin M. "Second Thoughts on Scientific Information," *College and Research Libraries*, Vol. 25, No. 6 (November 1964), pp. 463–471.

Wiesner, J. B. *Where Science and Politics Meet.* New York, McGraw-Hill Book Co., 1965. (See especially Part II, Chapter 6, "What to do about Scientific Information.")

Williams, V. Z., E. Hutchisson, and H. C. Wolfe. "Consideration of a Physics Information System," *Physics Today*, Vol. 19, No. 1 (January 1966), pp. 45–49.

Index